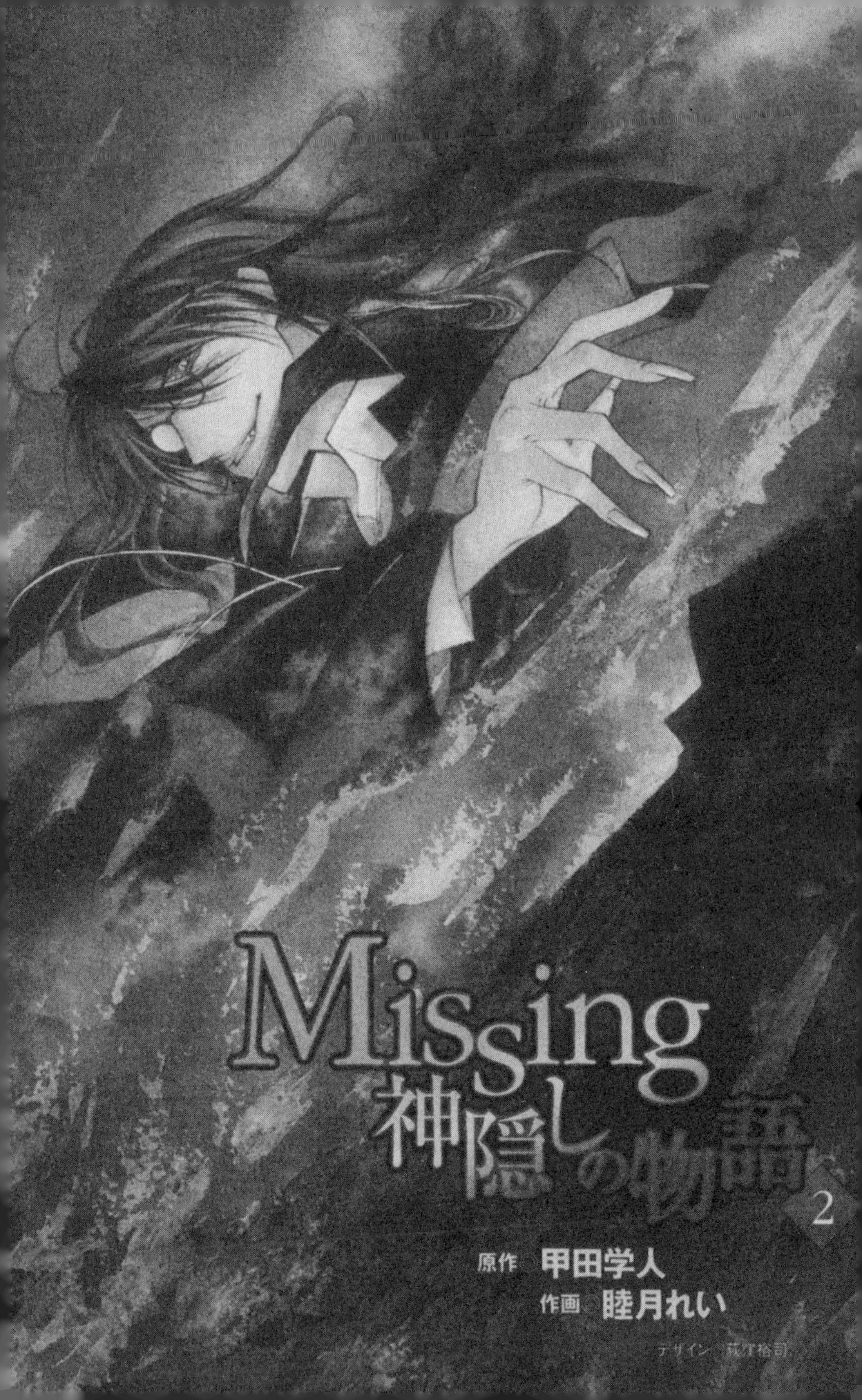
Missing
神隠しの物語
2
原作 甲田学人
作画 睦月れい
デザイン 荻窪裕司

Missing -Kamikakushi no Monogatari- Volume 2
Story By Gakuto Coda
Art By Rei Mutsuki

Translation - Nan Rymer
English Adaptation - Jason Deitrich
Copy Editor - Stephanie Duchin
Retouch and Lettering - Star Print Brokers
Production Artist - Michael Paolilli
Graphic Designer - Louis Csontos

Editor - Hope Donovan
Digital Imaging Manager - Chris Buford
Pre-Production Supervisor - Erika Terriquez
Production Manager - Elisabeth Brizzi
Managing Editor - Vy Nguyen
Creative Director - Anne Marie Horne
Editor-in-Chief - Rob Tokar
Publisher - Mike Kiley
President and C.O.O. - John Parker
C.E.O. and Chief Creative Officer - Stuart Levy

A 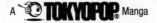 Manga

TOKYOPOP Inc.
5900 Wilshire Blvd. Suite 2000
Los Angeles, CA 90036

E-mail: info@TOKYOPOP.com
Come visit us online at www.TOKYOPOP.com

ISBN: 978-1-4278-0067-1
First TOKYOPOP printing: December 2007
10 9 8 7 6 5 4 3 2 1
Printed in the USA

MISSING
KAMIKAKUSHI NO MONOGATARI

Story by Gakuto Coda
Art by Rei Mutsuki

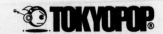

HAMBURG // LONDON // LOS ANGELES // TOKYO

Kyoichi Utsume, a.k.a. "His Majesty, Lord of Darkness," is a dark and compelling mystery—so much so that his fellow Literature Club members would rather discuss him than books!

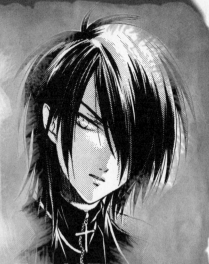

Kyoichi Utsume

yoko Kusakabe

The other members—bubbly Takemi, sunshine-y Ryoko, sardonic Aki and brooding Toshiya—all worship Kyo in their own way, and each holds a key to understanding his personality, as well as shares his fascination with the paranormal.

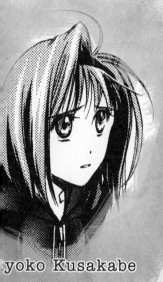

When "His Majesty" vanishes in front of their very eyes, his friends are left with several unanswered questions: What is the source of Kyoichi's long-standing obsession with the "other side"?

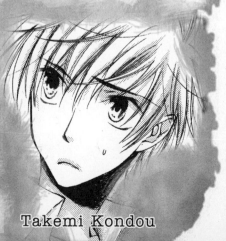

Takemi Kondou

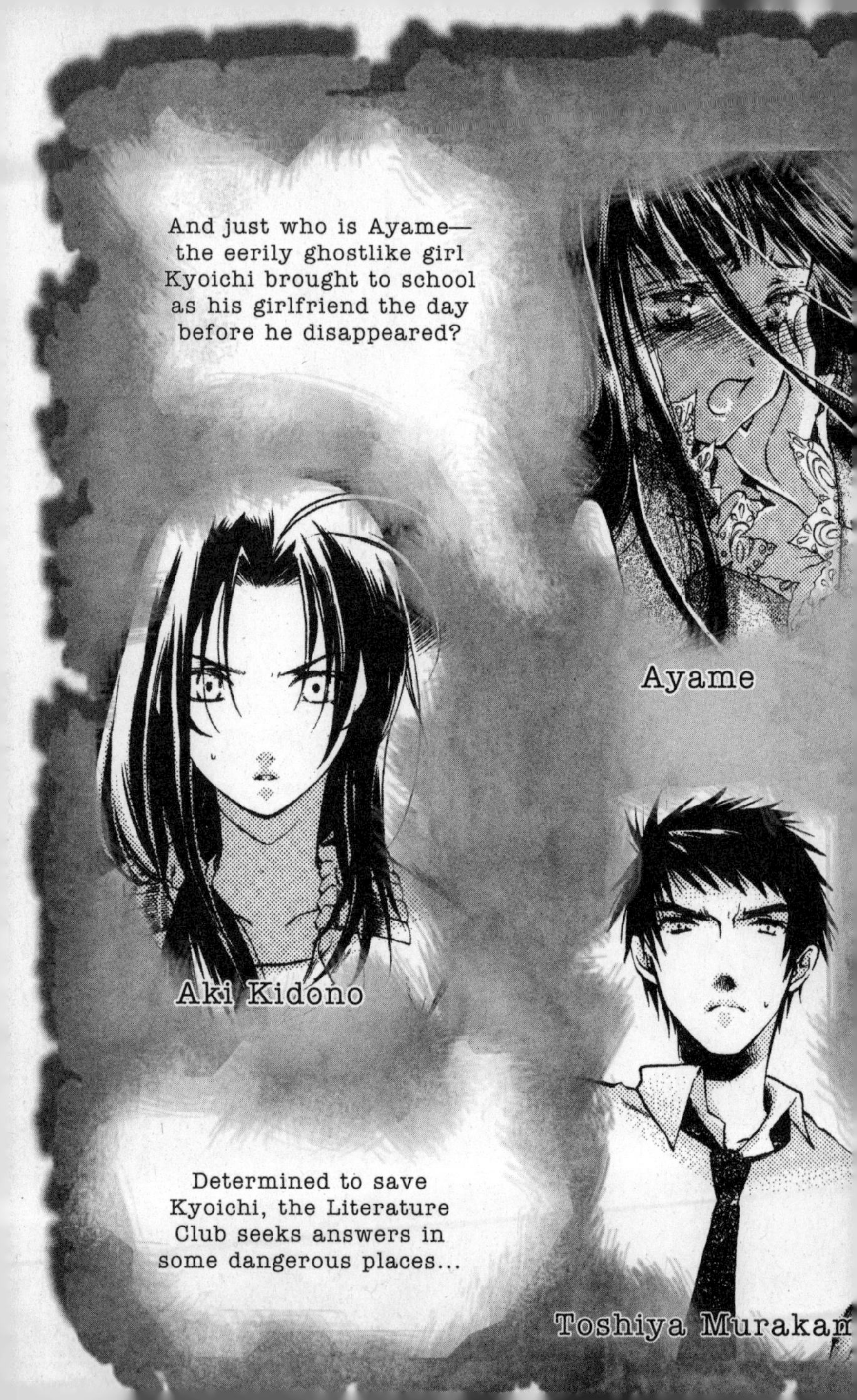
And just who is Ayame—
the eerily ghostlike girl
Kyoichi brought to school
as his girlfriend the day
before he disappeared?
Ayame
Aki Kidono
Determined to save
Kyoichi, the Literature
Club seeks answers in
some dangerous places...
Toshiya Muraka

Table of Contents

Missing
神隠し物語

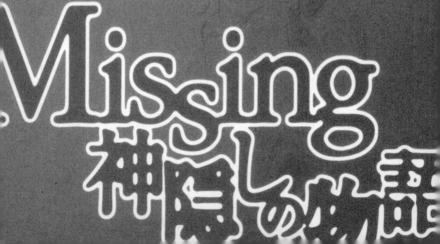

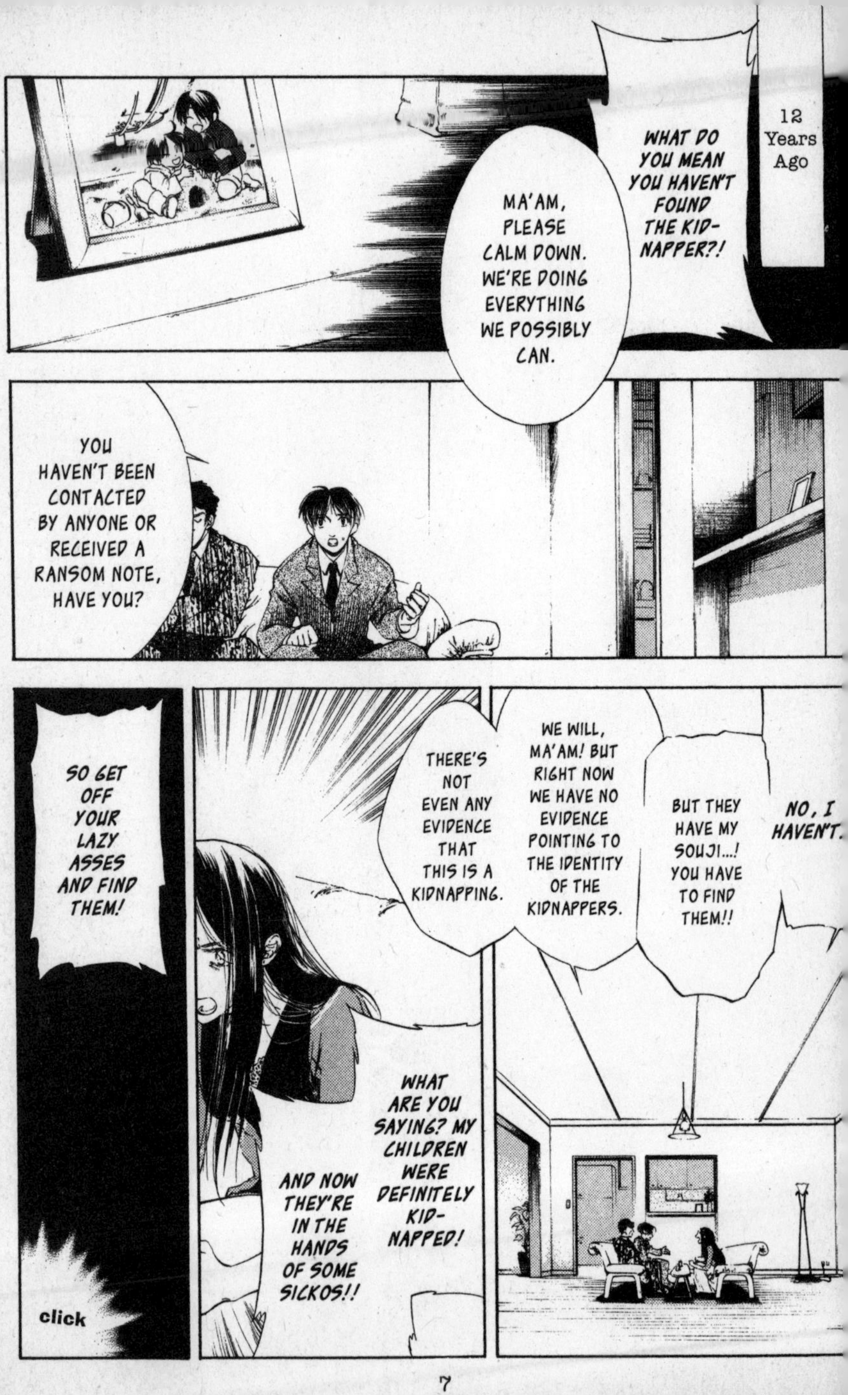
12 Years Ago
WHAT DO YOU MEAN YOU HAVEN'T FOUND THE KID-NAPPER?!
MA'AM, PLEASE CALM DOWN. WE'RE DOING EVERYTHING WE POSSIBLY CAN.
YOU HAVEN'T BEEN CONTACTED BY ANYONE OR RECEIVED A RANSOM NOTE, HAVE YOU?
NO, I HAVEN'T.
BUT THEY HAVE MY SOUJI...! YOU HAVE TO FIND THEM!!
WE WILL, MA'AM! BUT RIGHT NOW WE HAVE NO EVIDENCE POINTING TO THE IDENTITY OF THE KIDNAPPERS.
THERE'S NOT EVEN ANY EVIDENCE THAT THIS IS A KIDNAPPING.
WHAT ARE YOU SAYING? MY CHILDREN WERE DEFINITELY KID-NAPPED!
AND NOW THEY'RE IN THE HANDS OF SOME SICKOS!!
SO GET OFF YOUR LAZY ASSES AND FIND THEM!
click

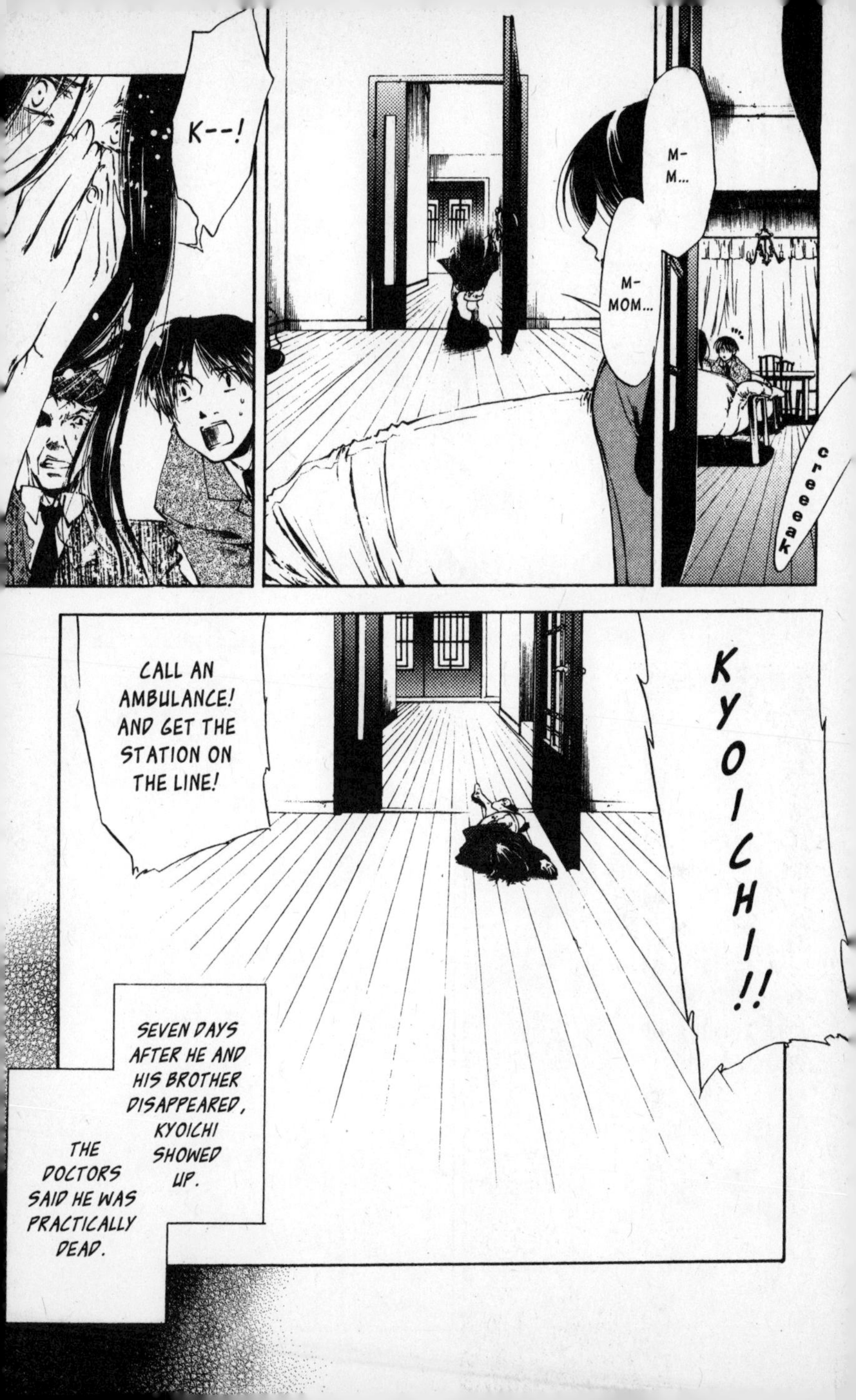
M-
M...
M-
MOM...
creeeak
K--!
KYOICHI!!
CALL AN AMBULANCE! AND GET THE STATION ON THE LINE!
SEVEN DAYS AFTER HE AND HIS BROTHER DISAPPEARED, KYOICHI SHOWED UP.
THE DOCTORS SAID HE WAS PRACTICALLY DEAD.

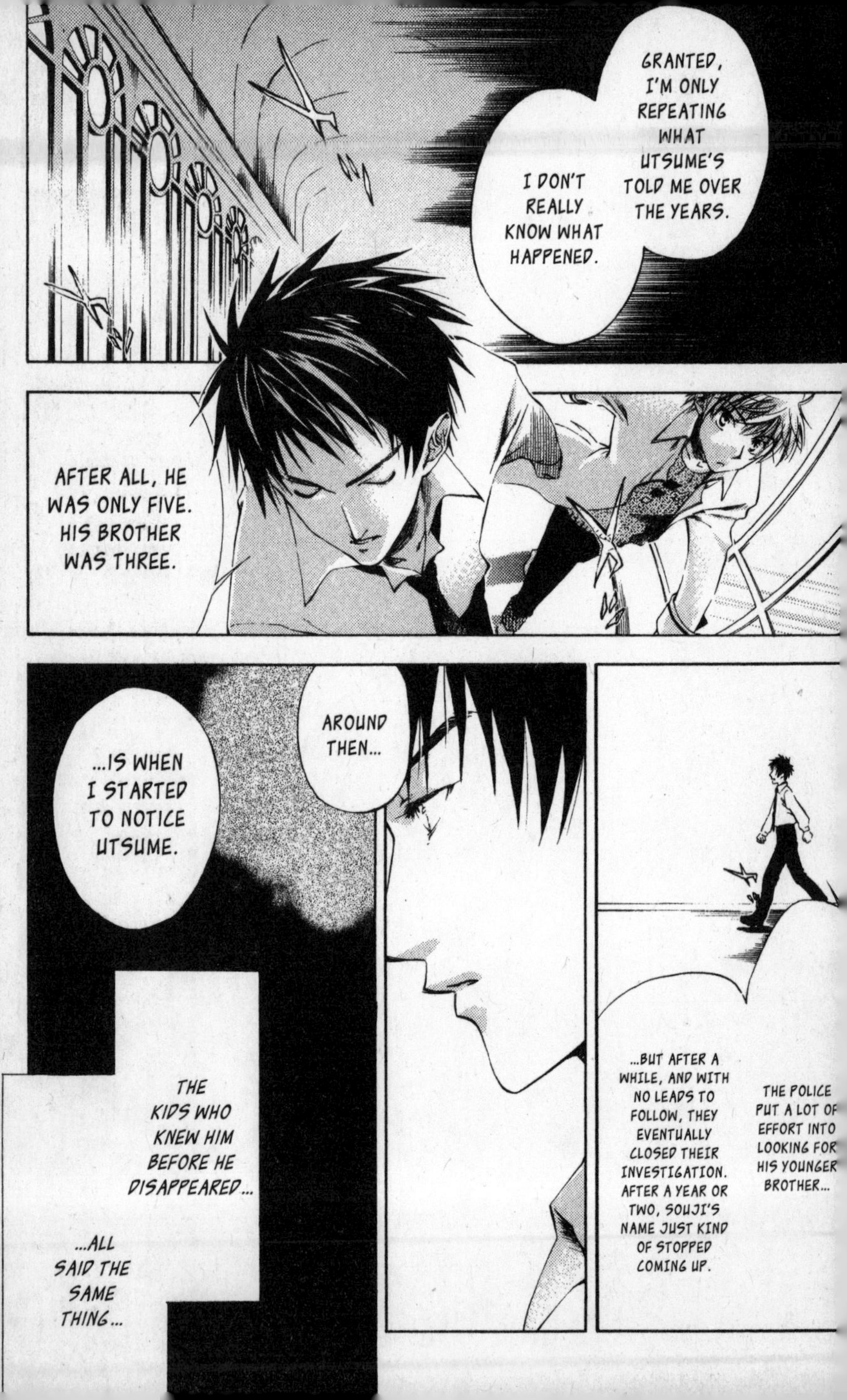
GRANTED, I'M ONLY REPEATING WHAT UTSUME'S TOLD ME OVER THE YEARS.
I DON'T REALLY KNOW WHAT HAPPENED.
AFTER ALL, HE WAS ONLY FIVE. HIS BROTHER WAS THREE.
THE POLICE PUT A LOT OF EFFORT INTO LOOKING FOR HIS YOUNGER BROTHER...
...BUT AFTER A WHILE, AND WITH NO LEADS TO FOLLOW, THEY EVENTUALLY CLOSED THEIR INVESTIGATION. AFTER A YEAR OR TWO, SOUJI'S NAME JUST KIND OF STOPPED COMING UP.
AROUND THEN...
...IS WHEN I STARTED TO NOTICE UTSUME.
THE KIDS WHO KNEW HIM BEFORE HE DISAPPEARED...
...ALL SAID THE SAME THING...

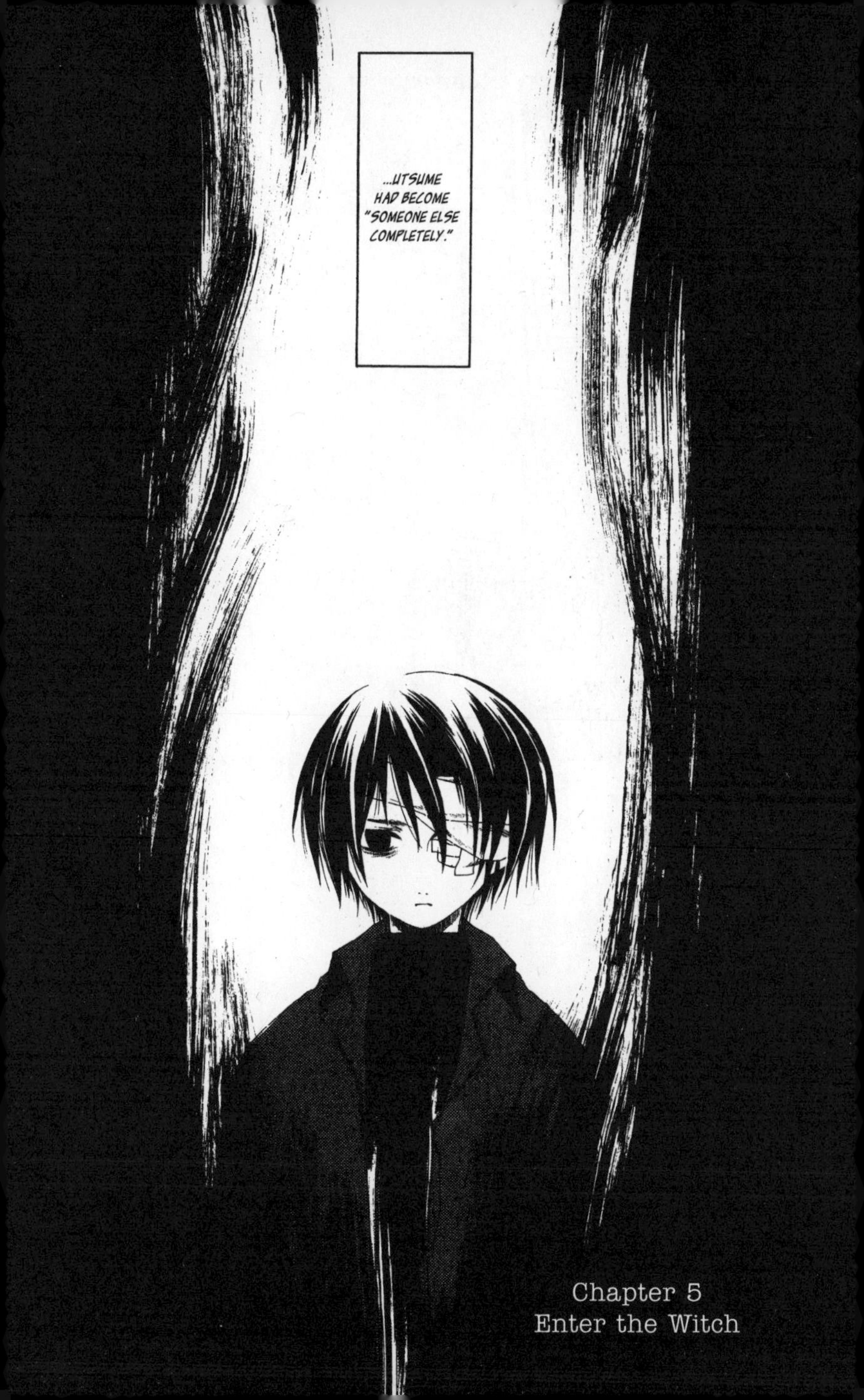
...UTSUME HAD BECOME "SOMEONE ELSE COMPLETELY."
Chapter 5
Enter the Witch

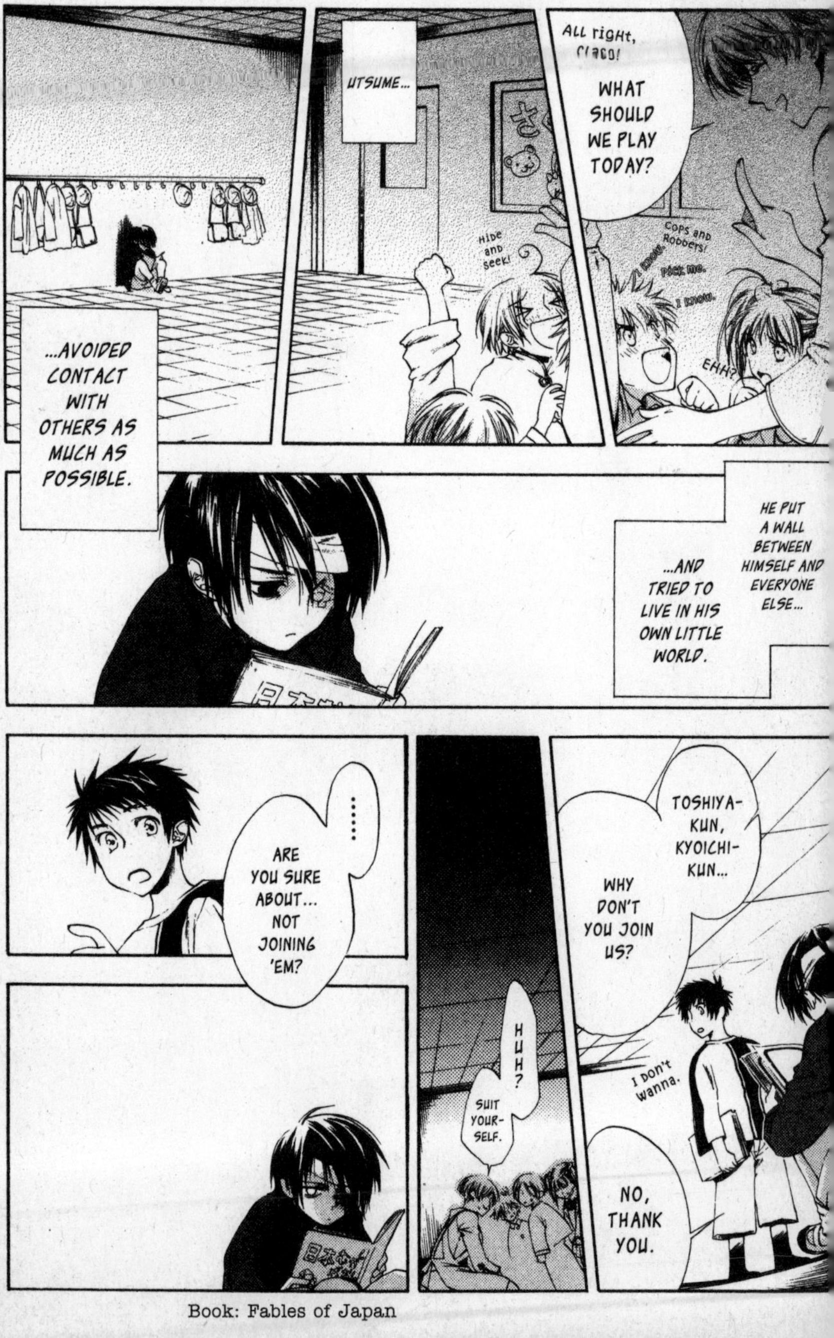
All right, class!
WHAT SHOULD WE PLAY TODAY?
Cops and Robbers!
I know.
Pick me.
I know.
EHH?
Hide and Seek!
UTSUME...
...AVOIDED CONTACT WITH OTHERS AS MUCH AS POSSIBLE.
HE PUT A WALL BETWEEN HIMSELF AND EVERYONE ELSE...
...AND TRIED TO LIVE IN HIS OWN LITTLE WORLD.
TOSHIYA-KUN, KYOICHI-KUN...
WHY DON'T YOU JOIN US?
I don't wanna.
NO, THANK YOU.
HUH?
SUIT YOURSELF.
......
ARE YOU SURE ABOUT... NOT JOINING 'EM?

Book: Fables of Japan

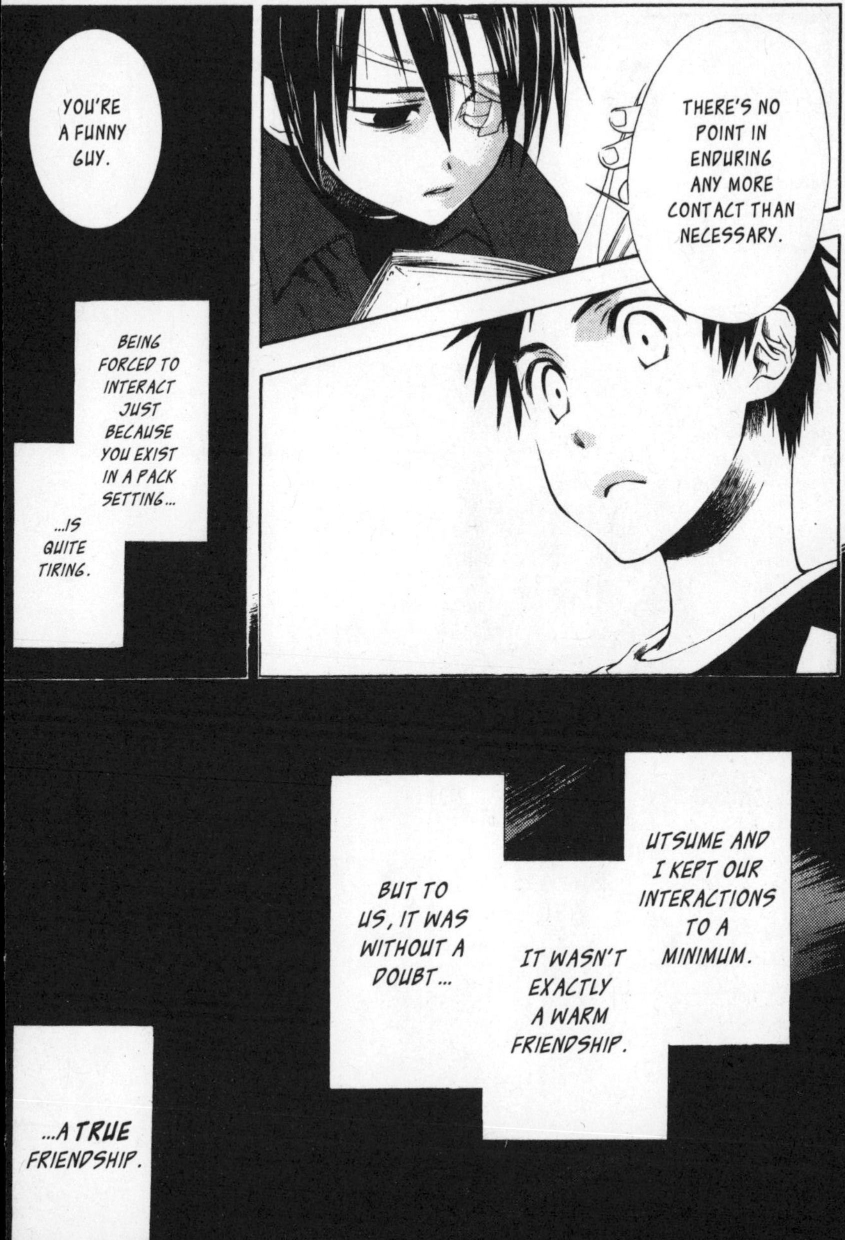
THERE'S NO POINT IN ENDURING ANY MORE CONTACT THAN NECESSARY.
YOU'RE A FUNNY GUY.
BEING FORCED TO INTERACT JUST BECAUSE YOU EXIST IN A PACK SETTING...
...IS QUITE TIRING.
UTSUME AND I KEPT OUR INTERACTIONS TO A MINIMUM.
IT WASN'T EXACTLY A WARM FRIENDSHIP.
BUT TO US, IT WAS WITHOUT A DOUBT...
...A TRUE FRIENDSHIP.

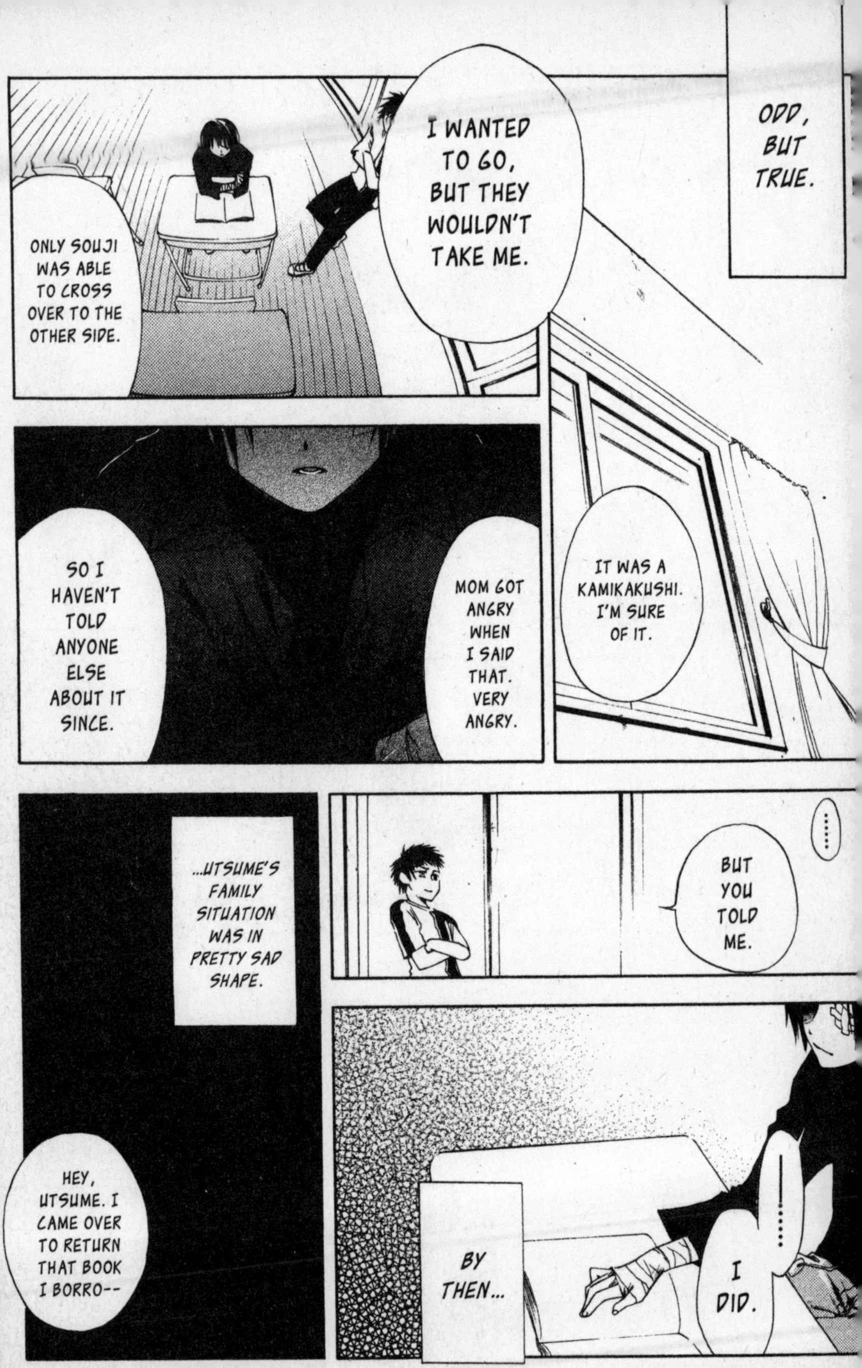
ODD, BUT TRUE.
I WANTED TO GO, BUT THEY WOULDN'T TAKE ME.
ONLY SOUJI WAS ABLE TO CROSS OVER TO THE OTHER SIDE.
IT WAS A KAMIKAKUSHI. I'M SURE OF IT.
MOM GOT ANGRY WHEN I SAID THAT. VERY ANGRY.
SO I HAVEN'T TOLD ANYONE ELSE ABOUT IT SINCE.
......
BUT YOU TOLD ME.
......
I DID.
BY THEN...
...UTSUME'S FAMILY SITUATION WAS IN PRETTY SAD SHAPE.
HEY, UTSUME. I CAME OVER TO RETURN THAT BOOK I BORRO--

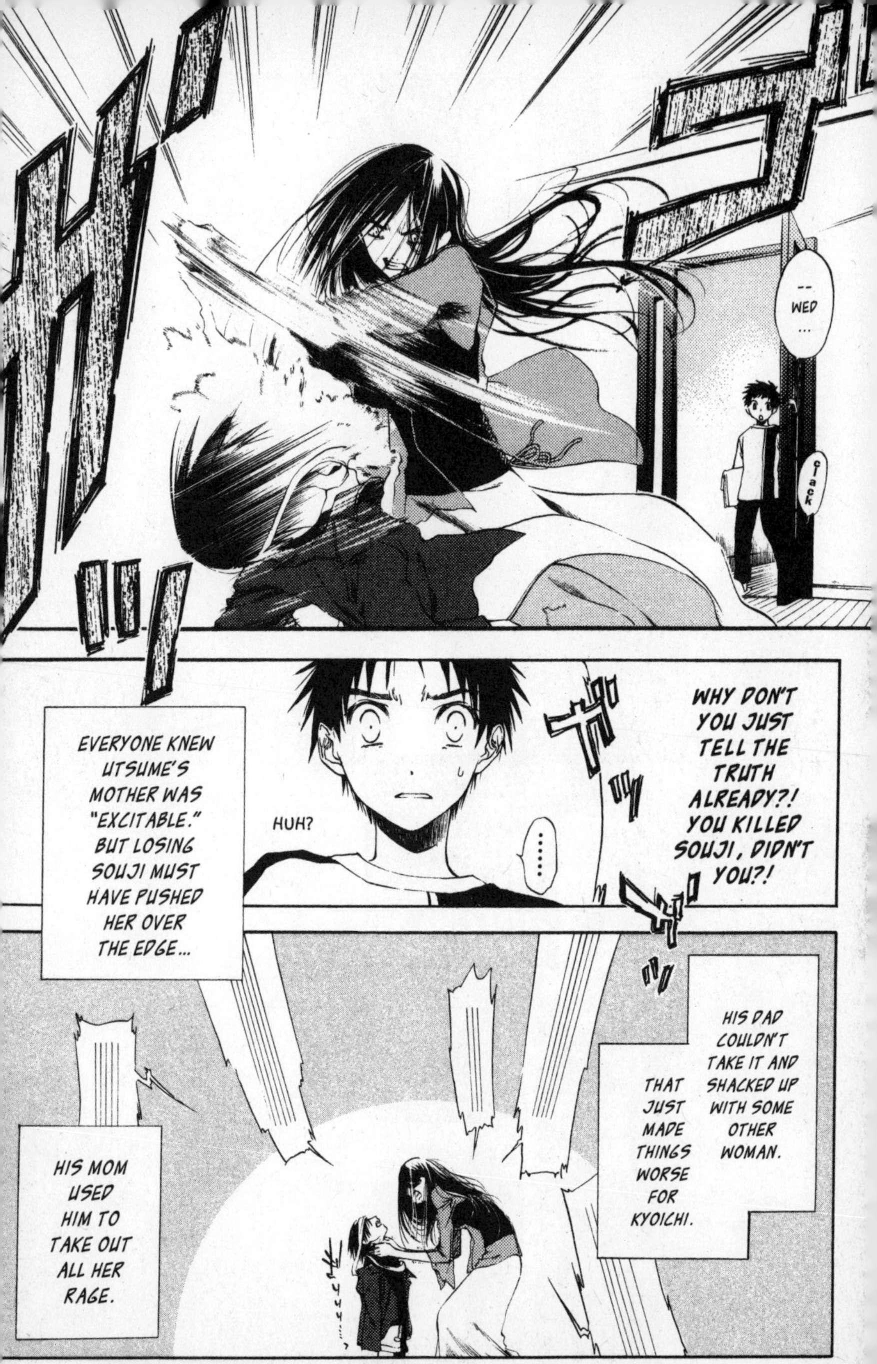

--WED...
clack
WHY DON'T YOU JUST TELL THE TRUTH ALREADY?! YOU KILLED SOUJI, DIDN'T YOU?!
......
HUH?
EVERYONE KNEW UTSUME'S MOTHER WAS "EXCITABLE." BUT LOSING SOUJI MUST HAVE PUSHED HER OVER THE EDGE...
HIS DAD COULDN'T TAKE IT AND SHACKED UP WITH SOME OTHER WOMAN.
THAT JUST MADE THINGS WORSE FOR KYOICHI.
HIS MOM USED HIM TO TAKE OUT ALL HER RAGE.

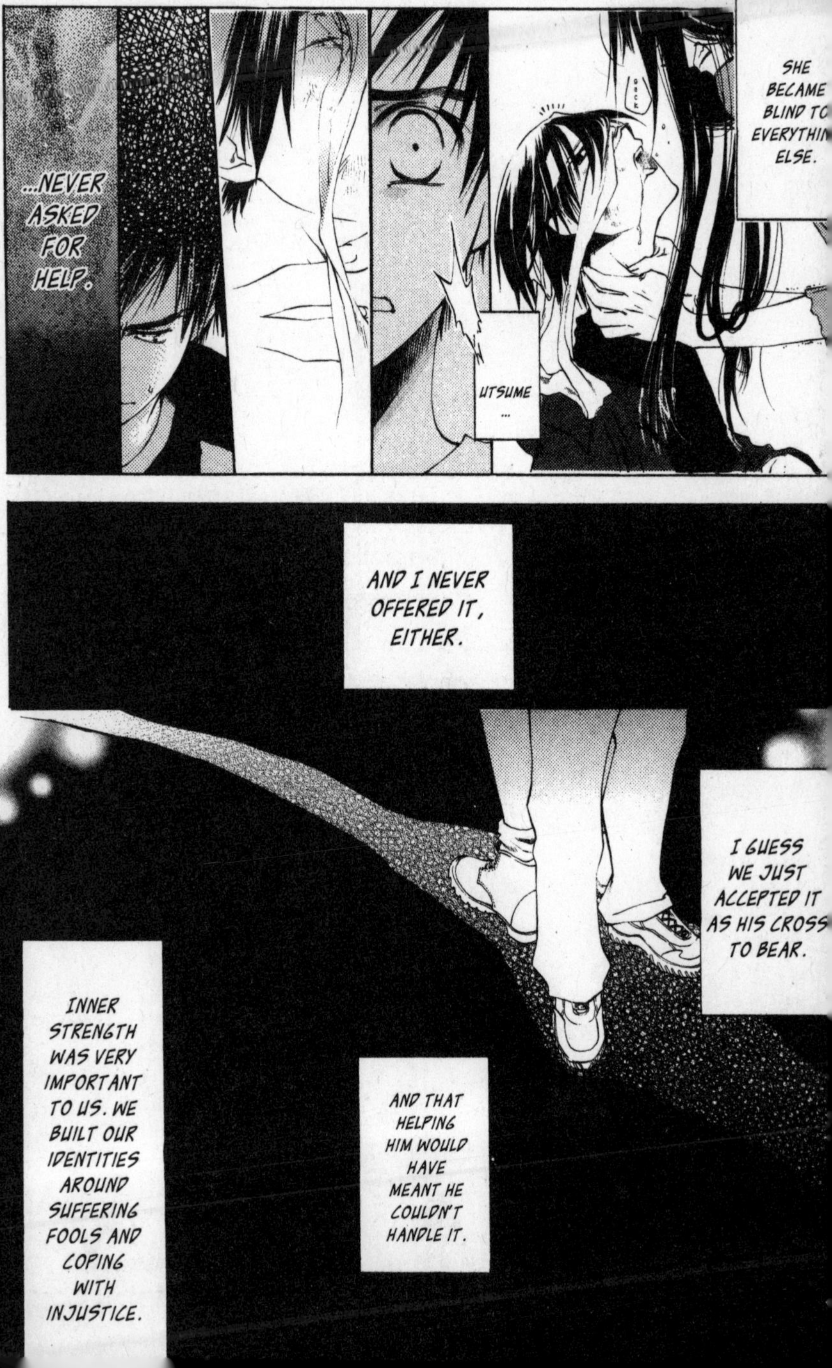
SHE BECAME BLIND TO EVERYTHIN ELSE.
UTSUME ...
...NEVER ASKED FOR HELP.
AND I NEVER OFFERED IT, EITHER.
I GUESS WE JUST ACCEPTED IT AS HIS CROSS TO BEAR.
AND THAT HELPING HIM WOULD HAVE MEANT HE COULDN'T HANDLE IT.
INNER STRENGTH WAS VERY IMPORTANT TO US. WE BUILT OUR IDENTITIES AROUND SUFFERING FOOLS AND COPING WITH INJUSTICE.

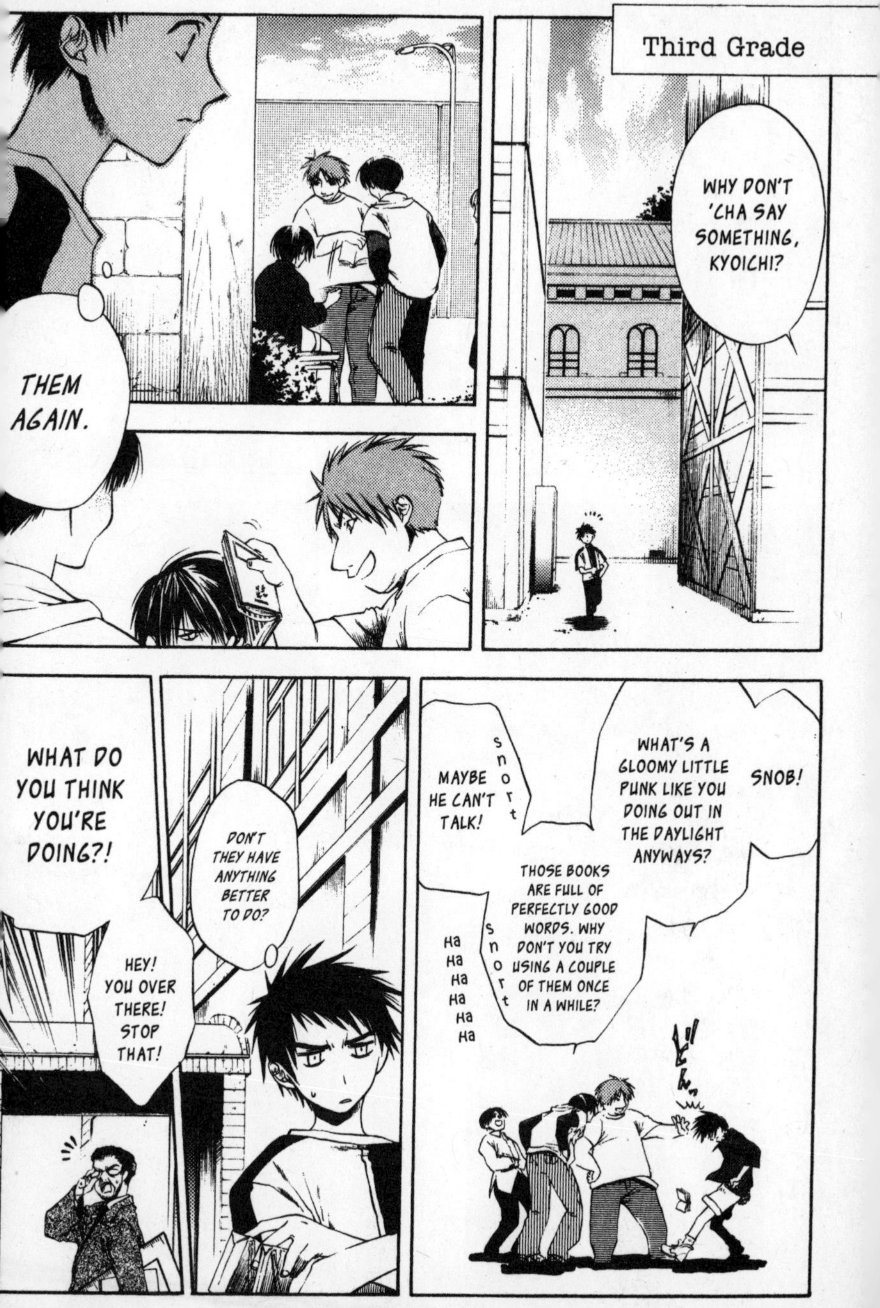
Third Grade
WHY DON'T 'CHA SAY SOMETHING, KYOICHI?
THEM AGAIN.
SNOB!
WHAT'S A GLOOMY LITTLE PUNK LIKE YOU DOING OUT IN THE DAYLIGHT ANYWAYS?
snort
MAYBE HE CAN'T TALK!
THOSE BOOKS ARE FULL OF PERFECTLY GOOD WORDS. WHY DON'T YOU TRY USING A COUPLE OF THEM ONCE IN A WHILE?
snort
Ha Ha Ha Ha Ha Ha
DON'T THEY HAVE ANYTHING BETTER TO DO?
WHAT DO YOU THINK YOU'RE DOING?!
HEY! YOU OVER THERE! STOP THAT!

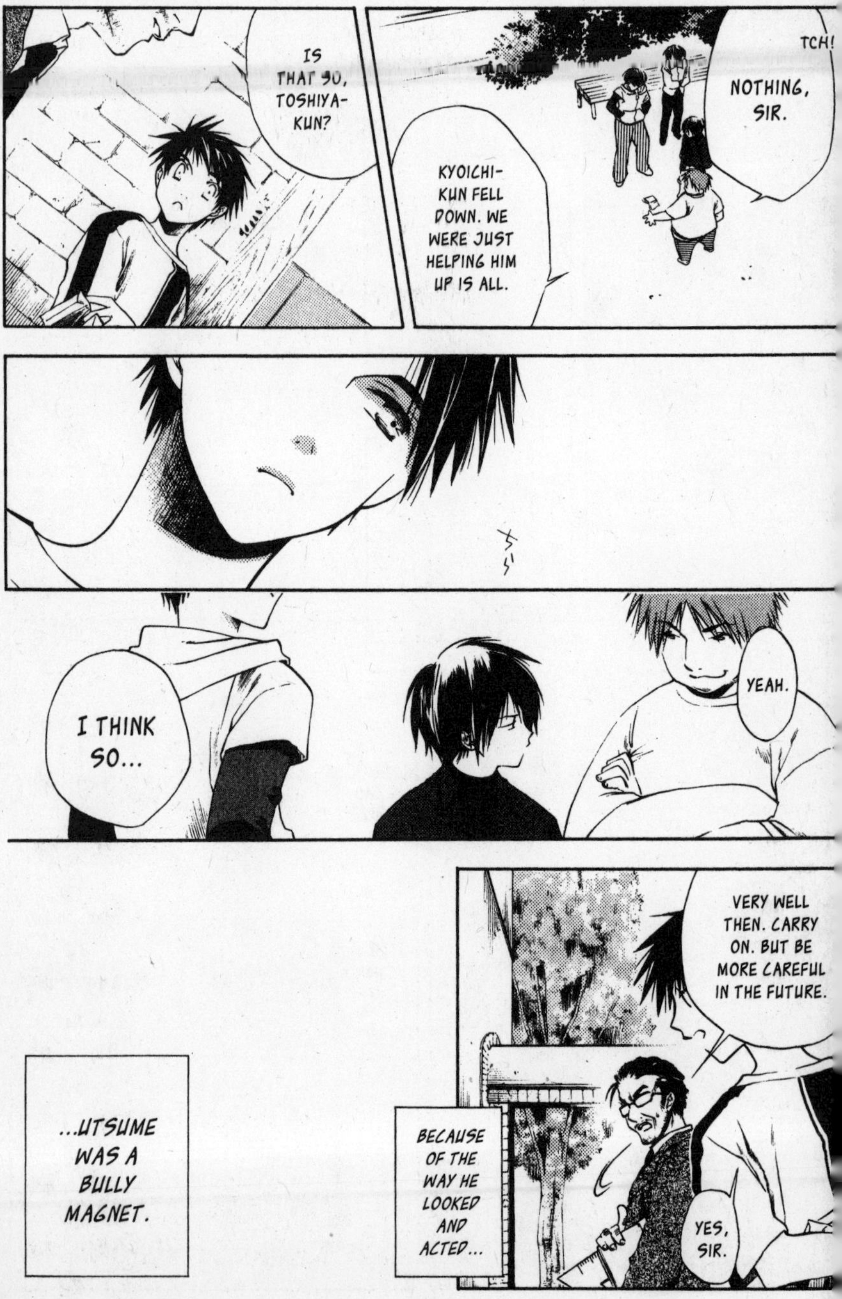
TCH!
NOTHING, SIR.
KYOICHI-KUN FELL DOWN. WE WERE JUST HELPING HIM UP IS ALL.
IS THAT SO, TOSHIYA-KUN?
YEAH.
I THINK SO...
VERY WELL THEN. CARRY ON. BUT BE MORE CAREFUL IN THE FUTURE.
YES, SIR.
BECAUSE OF THE WAY HE LOOKED AND ACTED...
...UTSUME WAS A BULLY MAGNET.

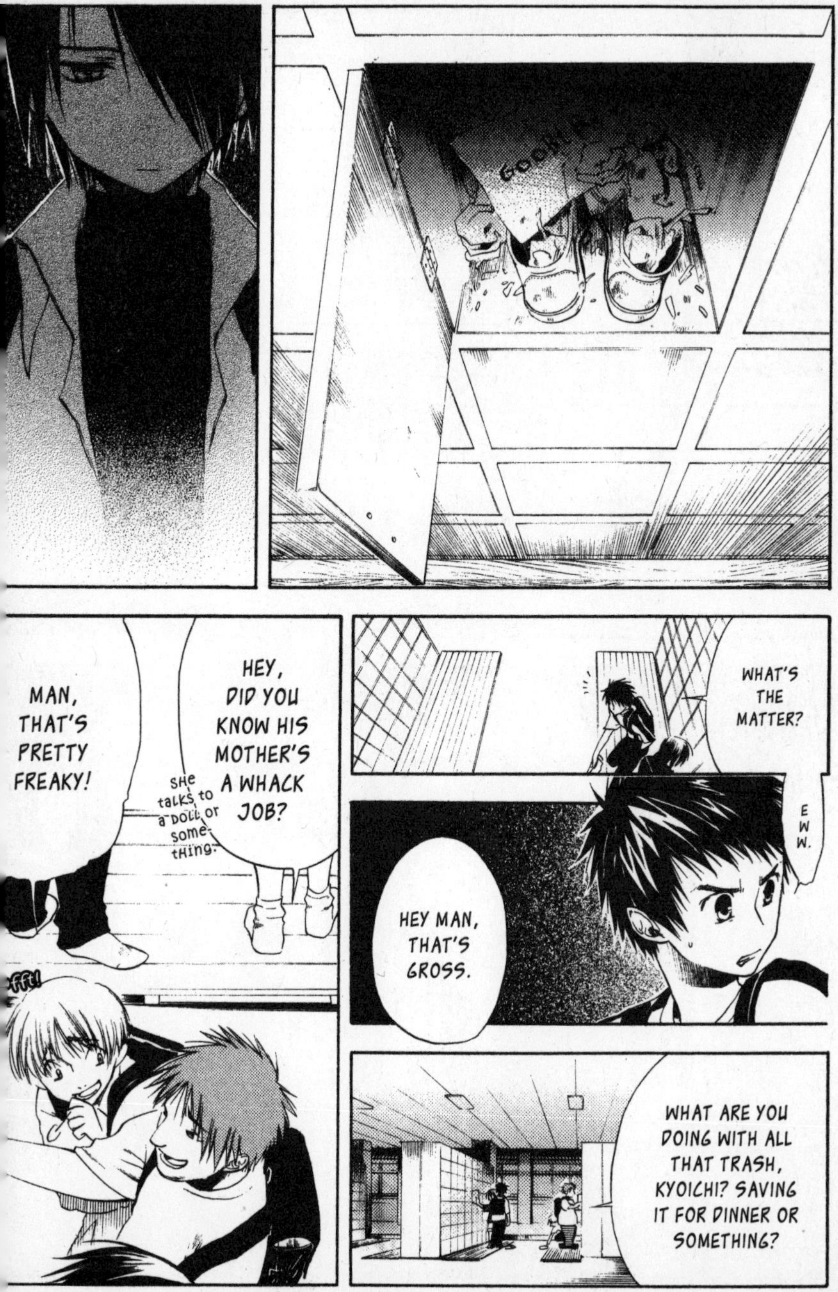
WHAT'S THE MATTER?
EWW.
HEY MAN, THAT'S GROSS.
HEY, DID YOU KNOW HIS MOTHER'S A WHACK JOB?
She talks to a doll or something.
MAN, THAT'S PRETTY FREAKY!
WHAT ARE YOU DOING WITH ALL THAT TRASH, KYOICHI? SAVING IT FOR DINNER OR SOMETHING?

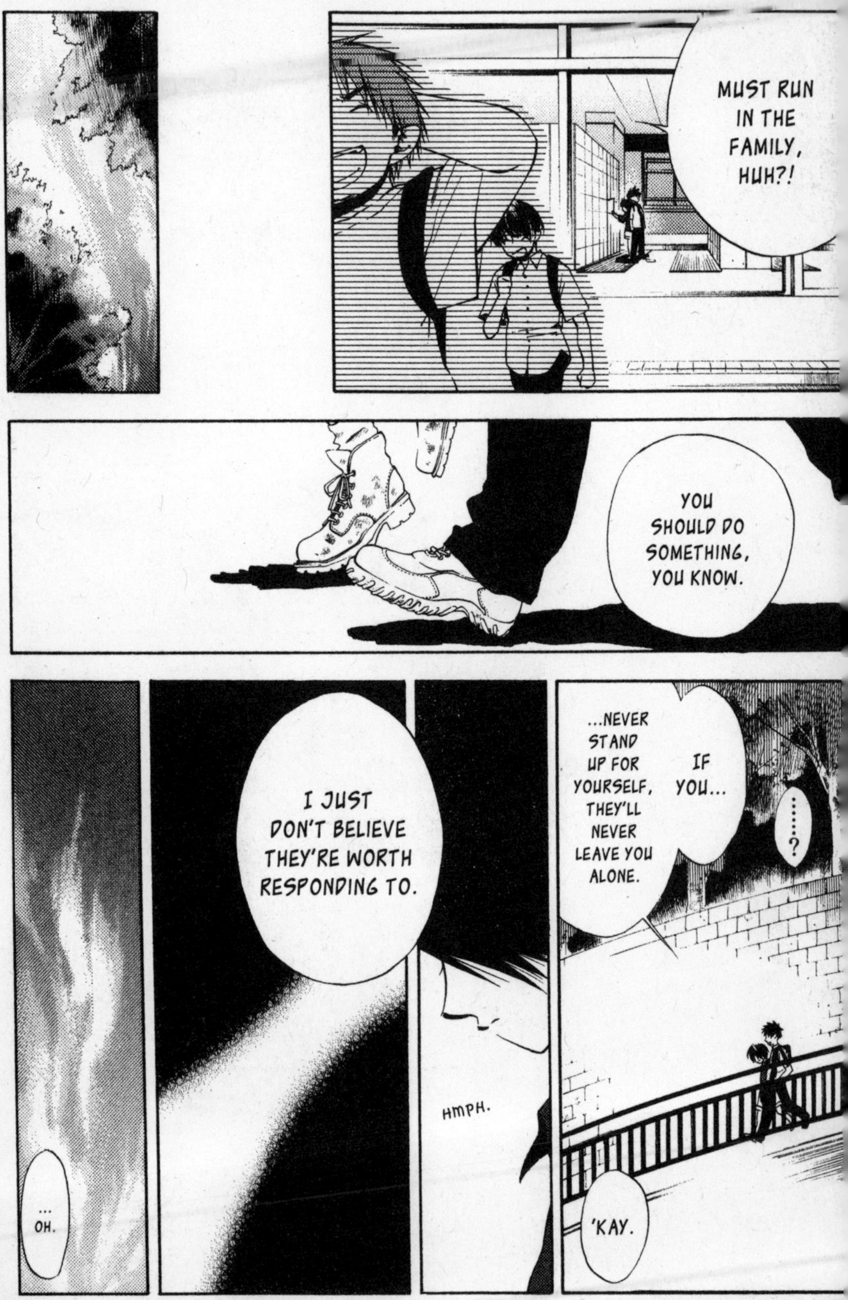
MUST RUN IN THE FAMILY, HUH?!
YOU SHOULD DO SOMETHING, YOU KNOW.
IF YOU...
...NEVER STAND UP FOR YOURSELF, THEY'LL NEVER LEAVE YOU ALONE.
......?
'KAY.
HMPH.
I JUST DON'T BELIEVE THEY'RE WORTH RESPONDING TO.
... OH.

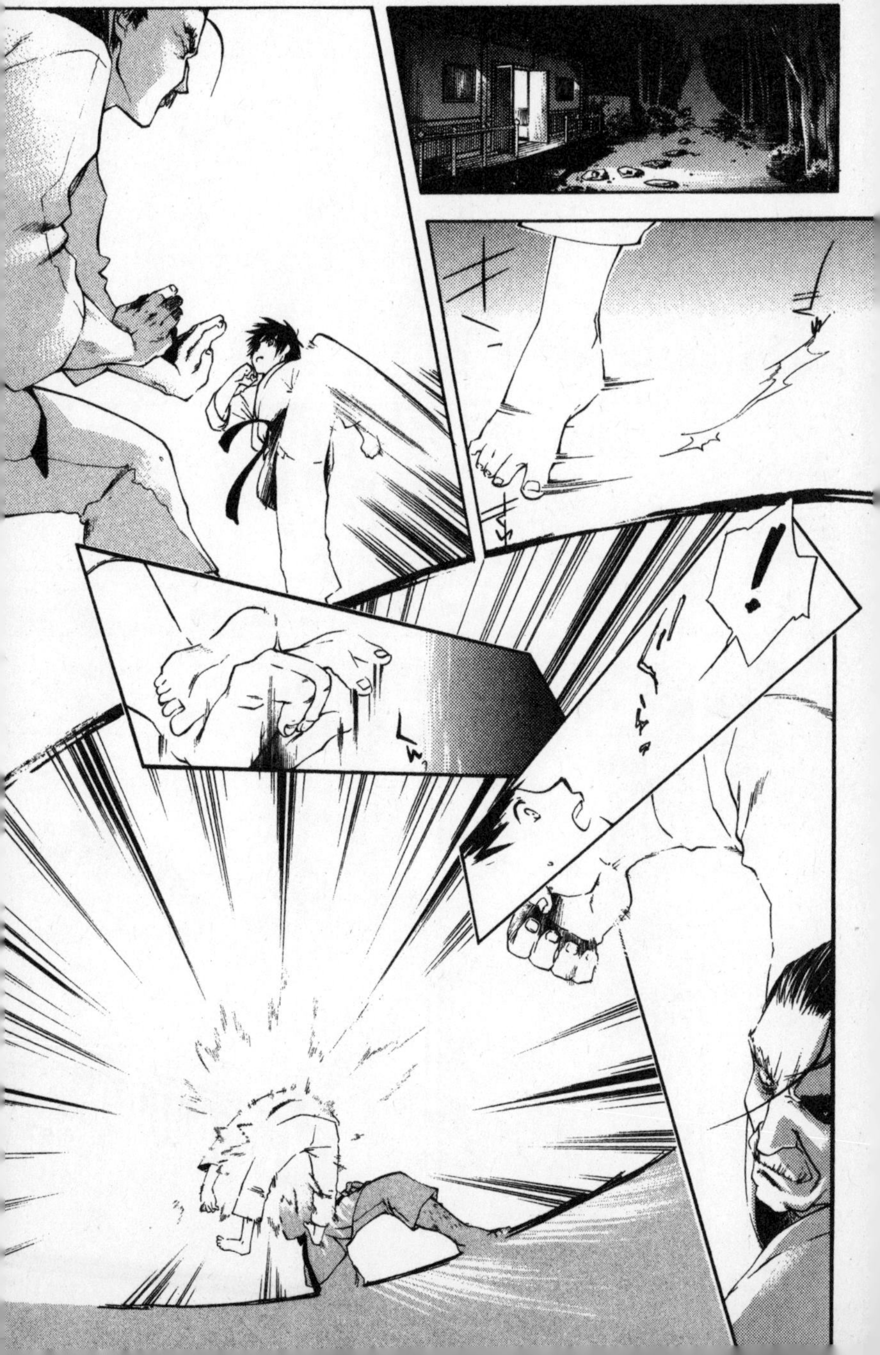
!

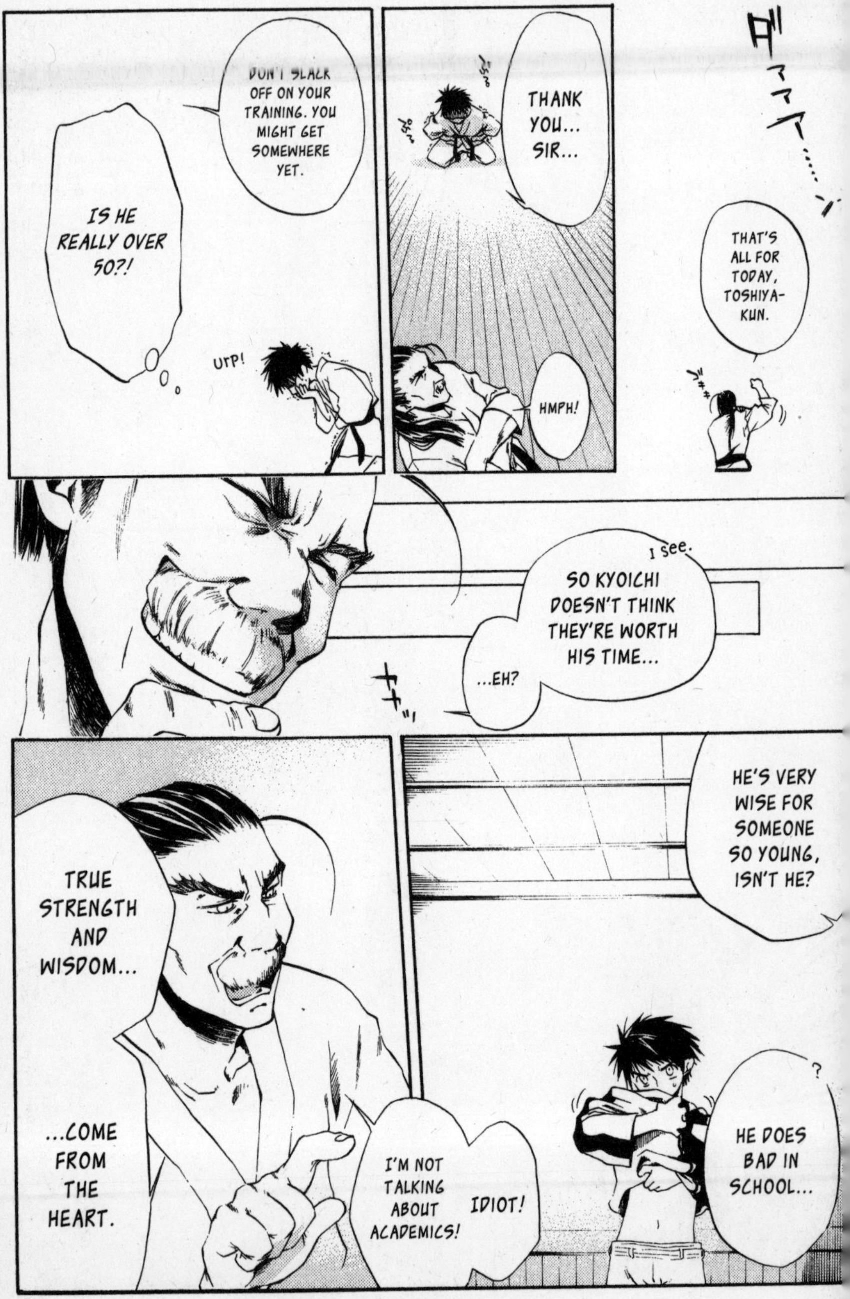
THAT'S ALL FOR TODAY, TOSHIYA-KUN.
THANK YOU... SIR...
HMPH!
DON'T SLACK OFF ON YOUR TRAINING. YOU MIGHT GET SOMEWHERE YET.
URP!
IS HE REALLY OVER 50?!
I see.
SO KYOICHI DOESN'T THINK THEY'RE WORTH HIS TIME...
...EH?
HE'S VERY WISE FOR SOMEONE SO YOUNG, ISN'T HE?
?
HE DOES BAD IN SCHOOL...
I'M NOT TALKING ABOUT ACADEMICS!
IDIOT!
TRUE STRENGTH AND WISDOM...
...COME FROM THE HEART.

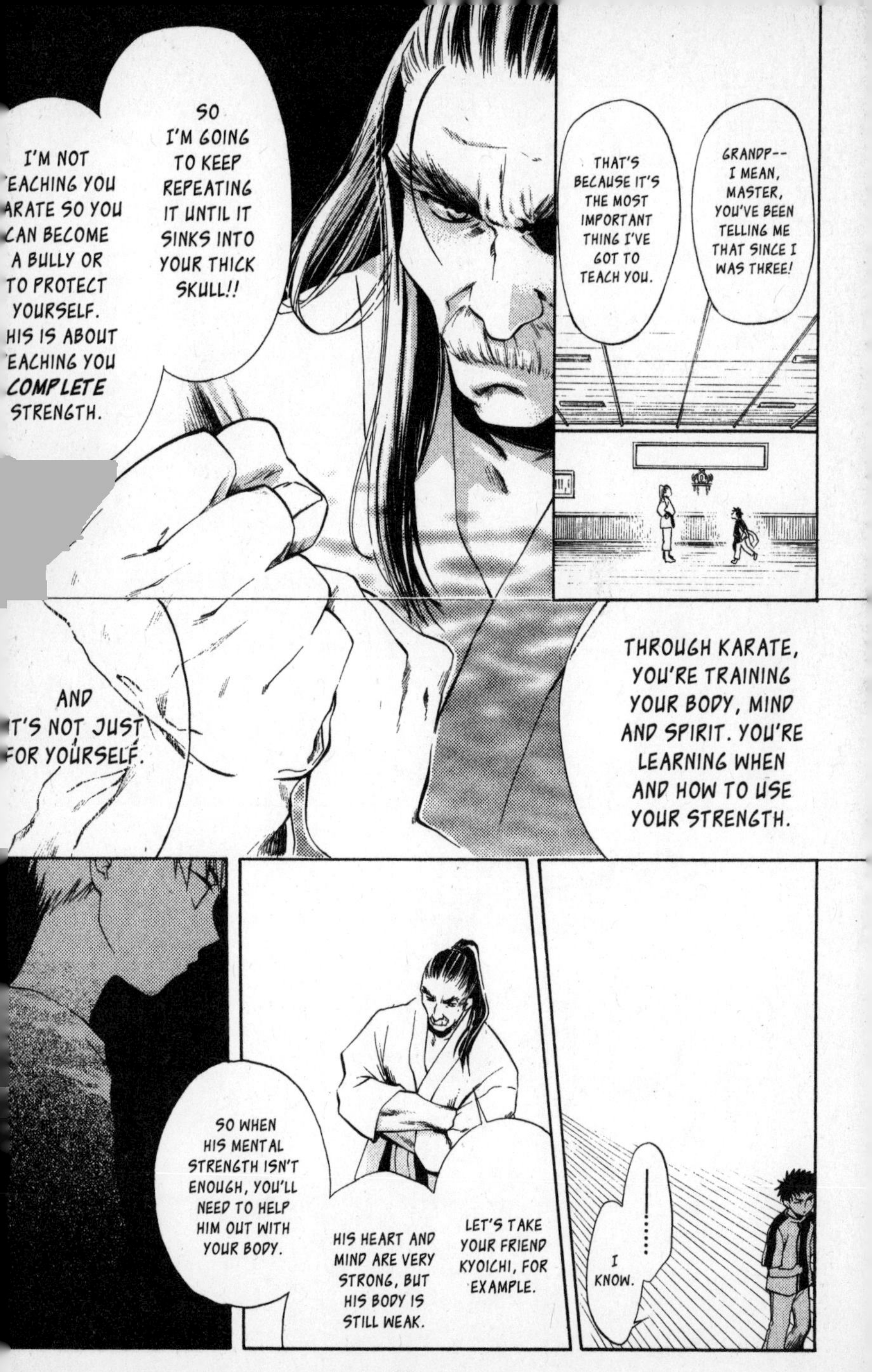
GRANDP-- I MEAN, MASTER, YOU'VE BEEN TELLING ME THAT SINCE I WAS THREE!
THAT'S BECAUSE IT'S THE MOST IMPORTANT THING I'VE GOT TO TEACH YOU.
SO I'M GOING TO KEEP REPEATING IT UNTIL IT SINKS INTO YOUR THICK SKULL!!
I'M NOT EACHING YOU ARATE SO YOU CAN BECOME A BULLY OR TO PROTECT YOURSELF. HIS IS ABOUT EACHING YOU *COMPLETE* STRENGTH.
THROUGH KARATE, YOU'RE TRAINING YOUR BODY, MIND AND SPIRIT. YOU'RE LEARNING WHEN AND HOW TO USE YOUR STRENGTH.
AND IT'S NOT JUST FOR YOURSELF.
......! I KNOW.
LET'S TAKE YOUR FRIEND KYOICHI, FOR EXAMPLE.
HIS HEART AND MIND ARE VERY STRONG, BUT HIS BODY IS STILL WEAK.
SO WHEN HIS MENTAL STRENGTH ISN'T ENOUGH, YOU'LL NEED TO HELP HIM OUT WITH YOUR BODY.

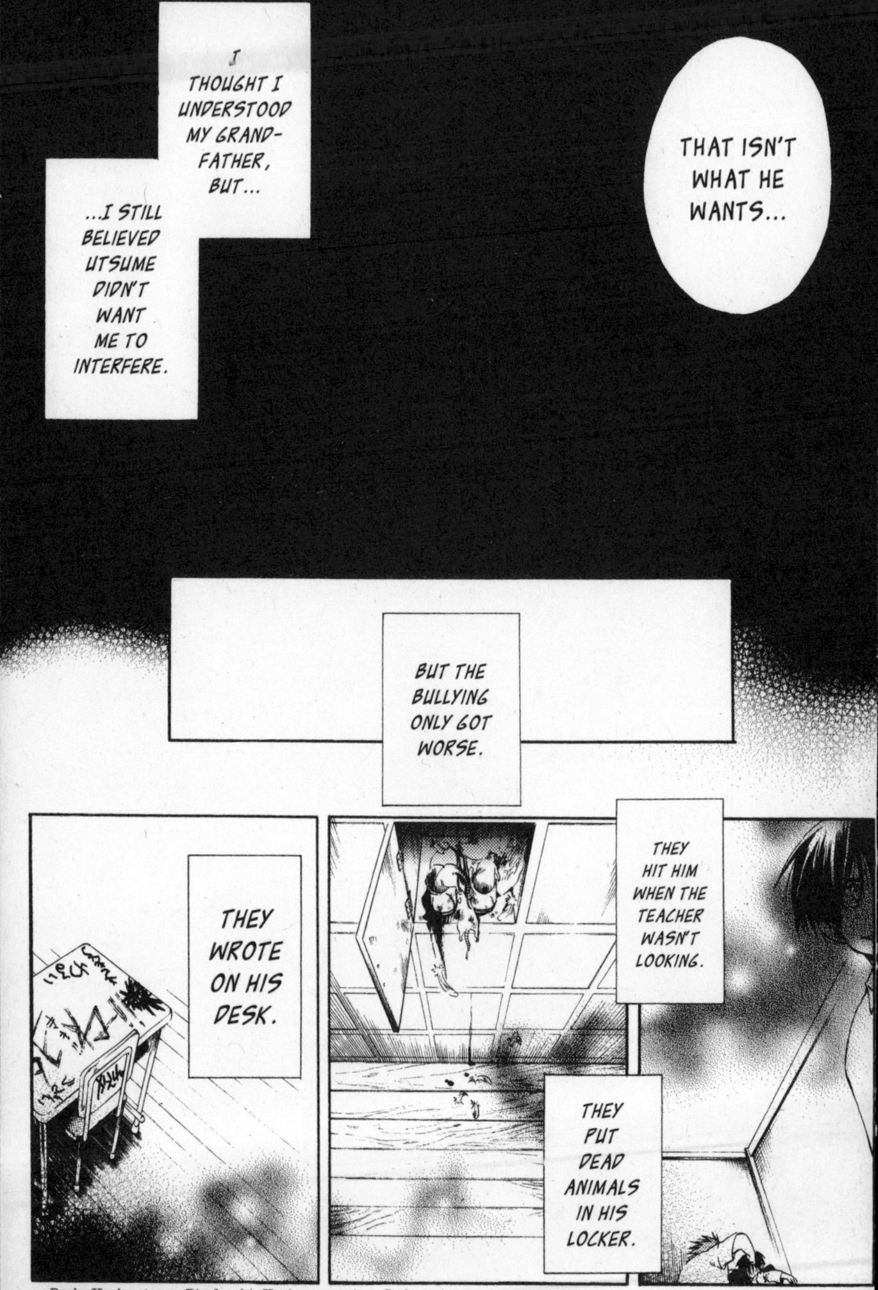

THAT ISN'T WHAT HE WANTS...
I THOUGHT I UNDERSTOOD MY GRAND-FATHER, BUT...
...I STILL BELIEVED UTSUME DIDN'T WANT ME TO INTERFERE.
BUT THE BULLYING ONLY GOT WORSE.
THEY HIT HIM WHEN THE TEACHER WASN'T LOOKING.
THEY PUT DEAD ANIMALS IN HIS LOCKER.
THEY WROTE ON HIS DESK.

Desk: You're gross; Die freak!; You're annoying; Go home!

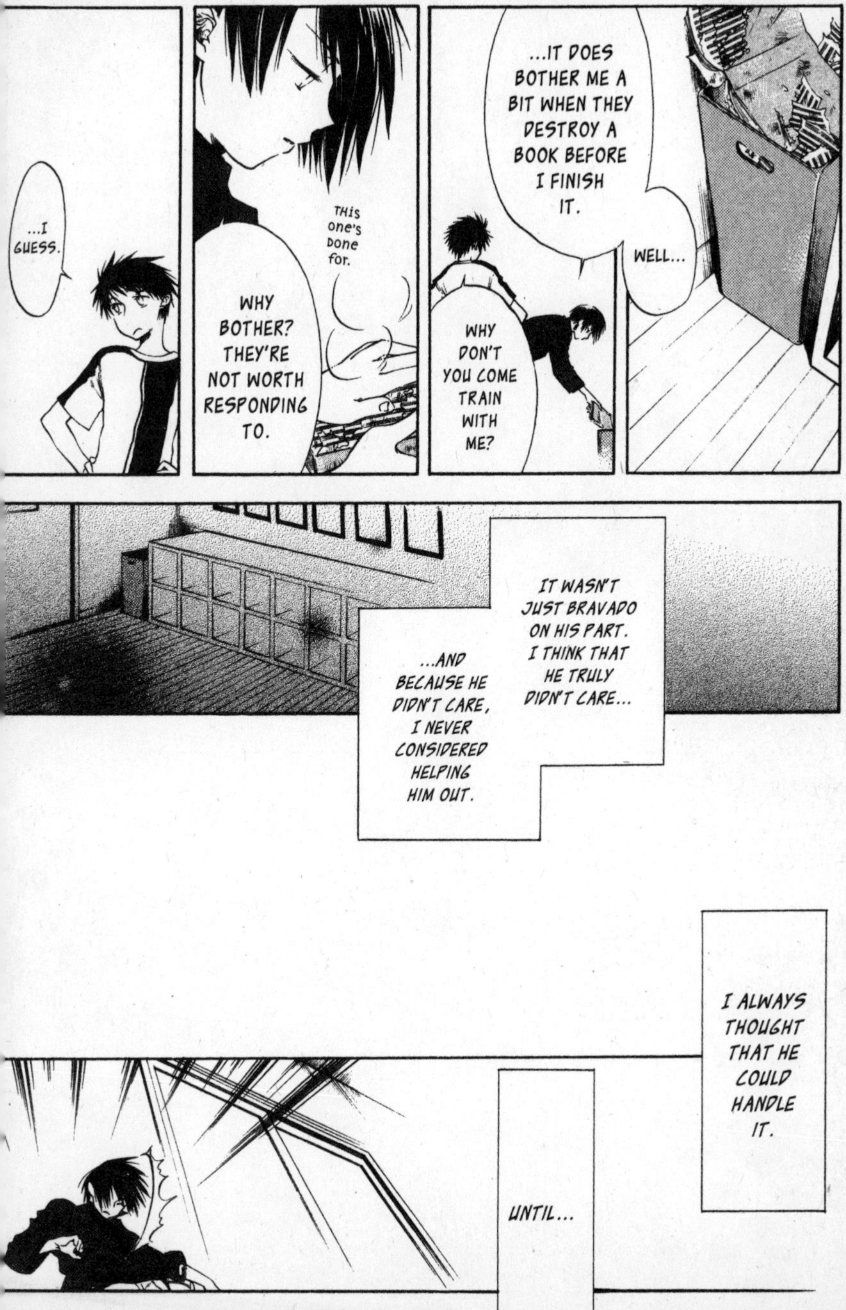
WELL...
...IT DOES BOTHER ME A BIT WHEN THEY DESTROY A BOOK BEFORE I FINISH IT.
WHY DON'T YOU COME TRAIN WITH ME?
This one's Done for.
WHY BOTHER? THEY'RE NOT WORTH RESPONDING TO.
...I GUESS.
IT WASN'T JUST BRAVADO ON HIS PART. I THINK THAT HE TRULY DIDN'T CARE...
...AND BECAUSE HE DIDN'T CARE, I NEVER CONSIDERED HELPING HIM OUT.
I ALWAYS THOUGHT THAT HE COULD HANDLE IT.
UNTIL...

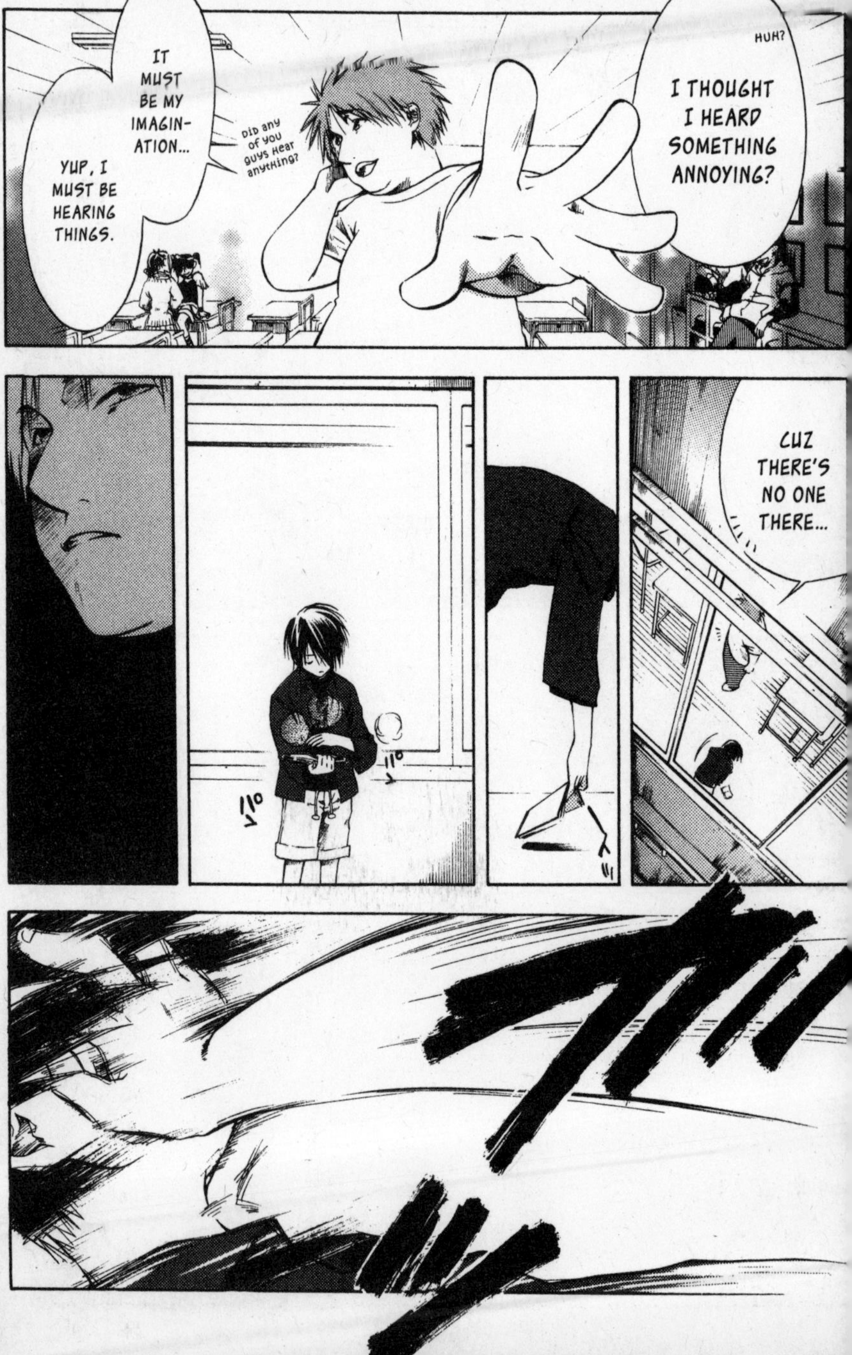
HUH?
I THOUGHT I HEARD SOMETHING ANNOYING?
Did any of you guys Hear anything?
IT MUST BE MY IMAGINATION...
YUP, I MUST BE HEARING THINGS.
CUZ THERE'S NO ONE THERE...

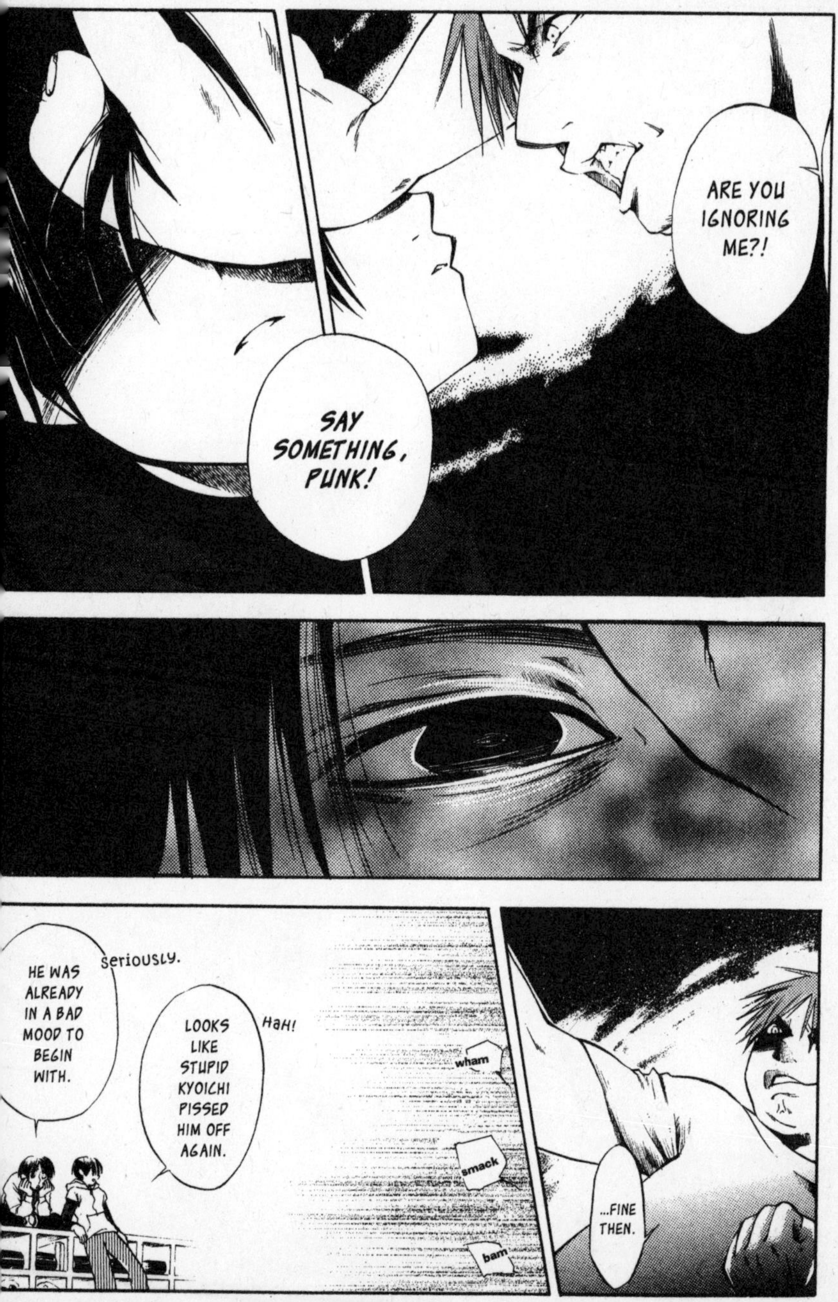
ARE YOU IGNORING ME?!
SAY SOMETHING, PUNK!
...FINE THEN.
wham
Hah!
seriously.
LOOKS LIKE STUPID KYOICHI PISSED HIM OFF AGAIN.
HE WAS ALREADY IN A BAD MOOD TO BEGIN WITH.
smack
bam

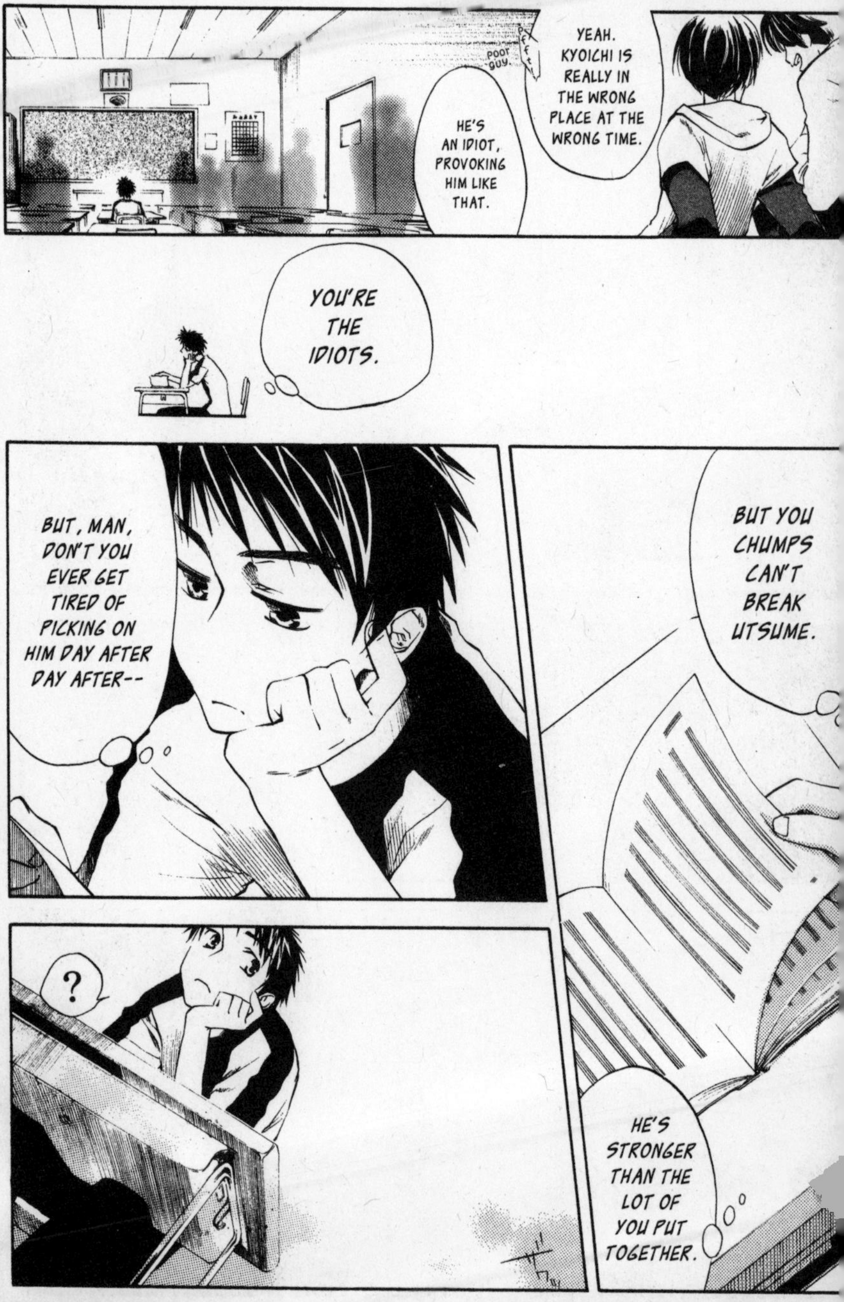
YEAH. KYOICHI IS REALLY IN THE WRONG PLACE AT THE WRONG TIME.
poor guy.
HE'S AN IDIOT, PROVOKING HIM LIKE THAT.
YOU'RE THE IDIOTS.
BUT YOU CHUMPS CAN'T BREAK UTSUME.
HE'S STRONGER THAN THE LOT OF YOU PUT TOGETHER.
BUT, MAN, DON'T YOU EVER GET TIRED OF PICKING ON HIM DAY AFTER DAY AFTER--
?

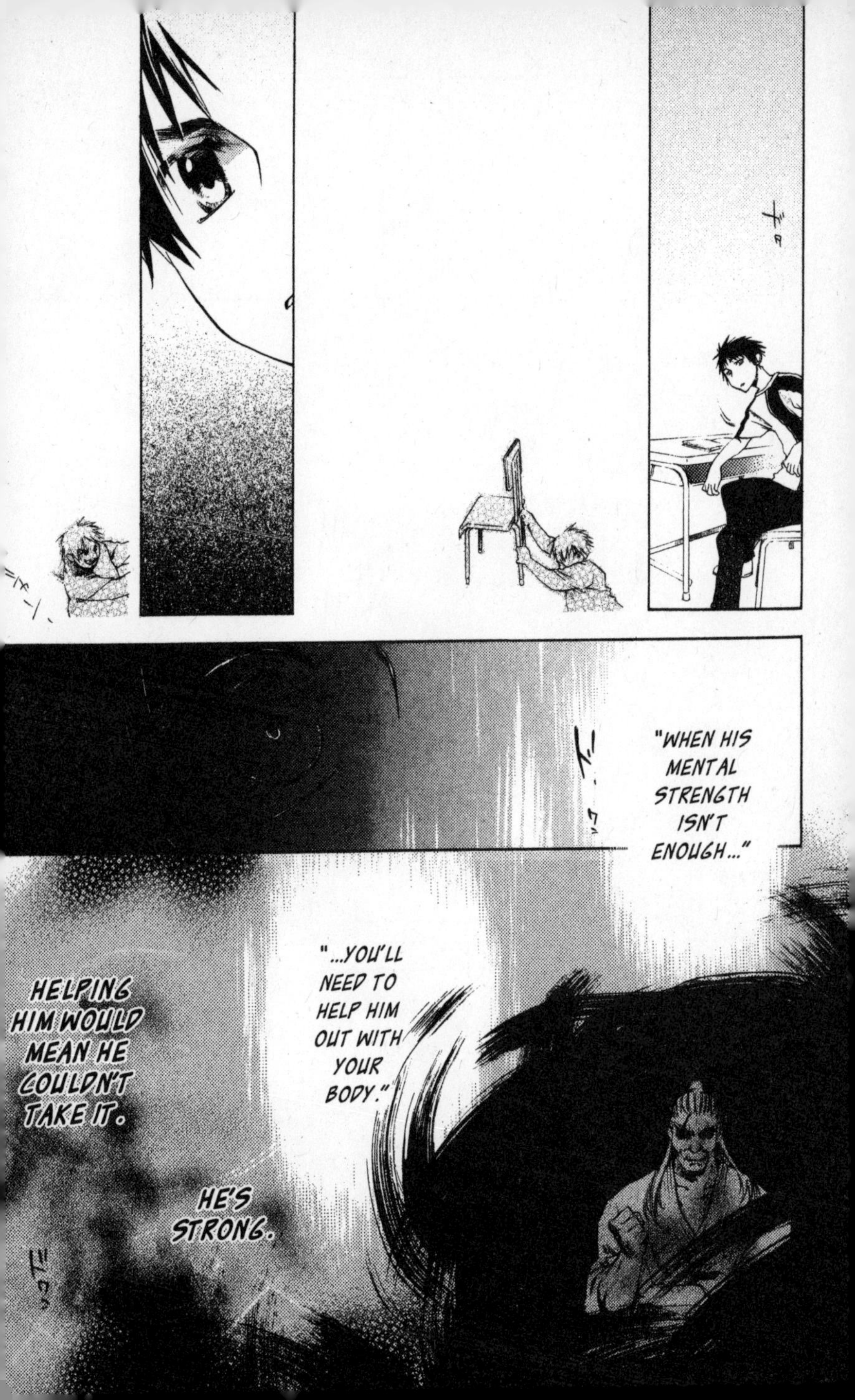
"WHEN HIS MENTAL STRENGTH ISN'T ENOUGH..."
"...YOU'LL NEED TO HELP HIM OUT WITH YOUR BODY."
HELPING HIM WOULD MEAN HE COULDN'T TAKE IT.
HE'S STRONG.

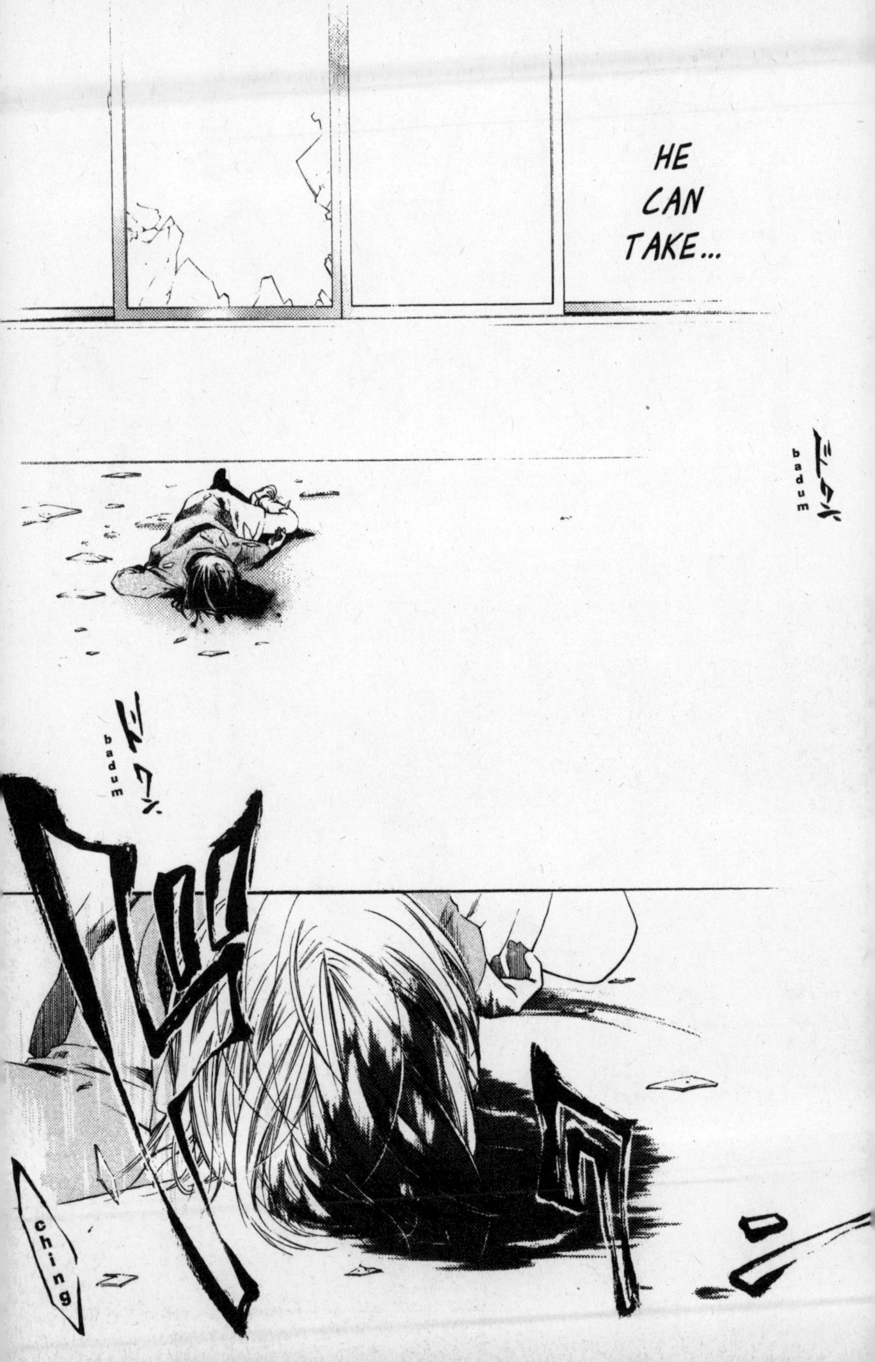
HE CAN TAKE...
badum
badum
ching

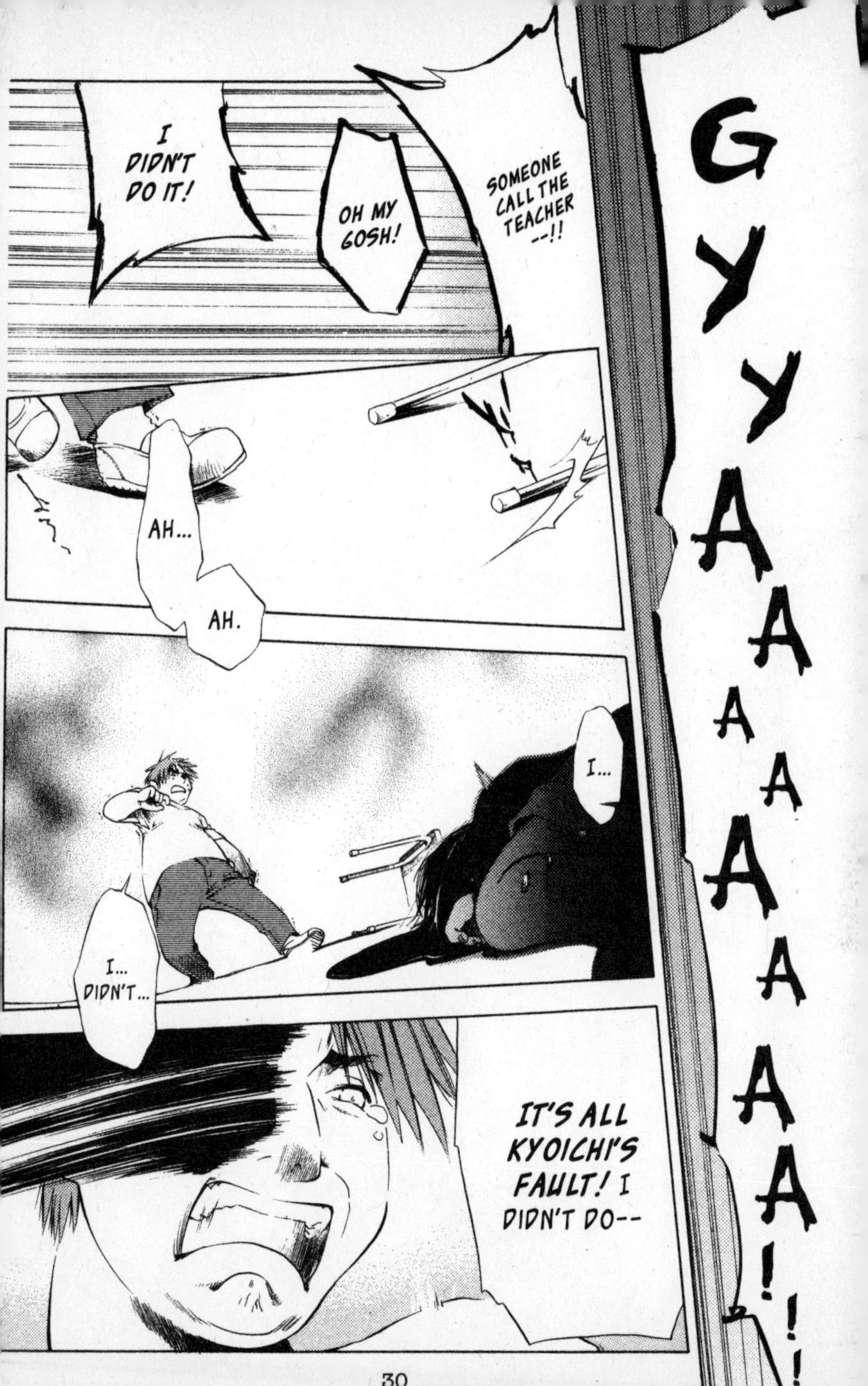
GYYAAAAAAAAA!!!
SOMEONE CALL THE TEACHER--!!
OH MY GOSH!
I DIDN'T DO IT!
AH...
AH.
I...
I... DIDN'T...
IT'S ALL KYOICHI'S FAULT! I DIDN'T DO--

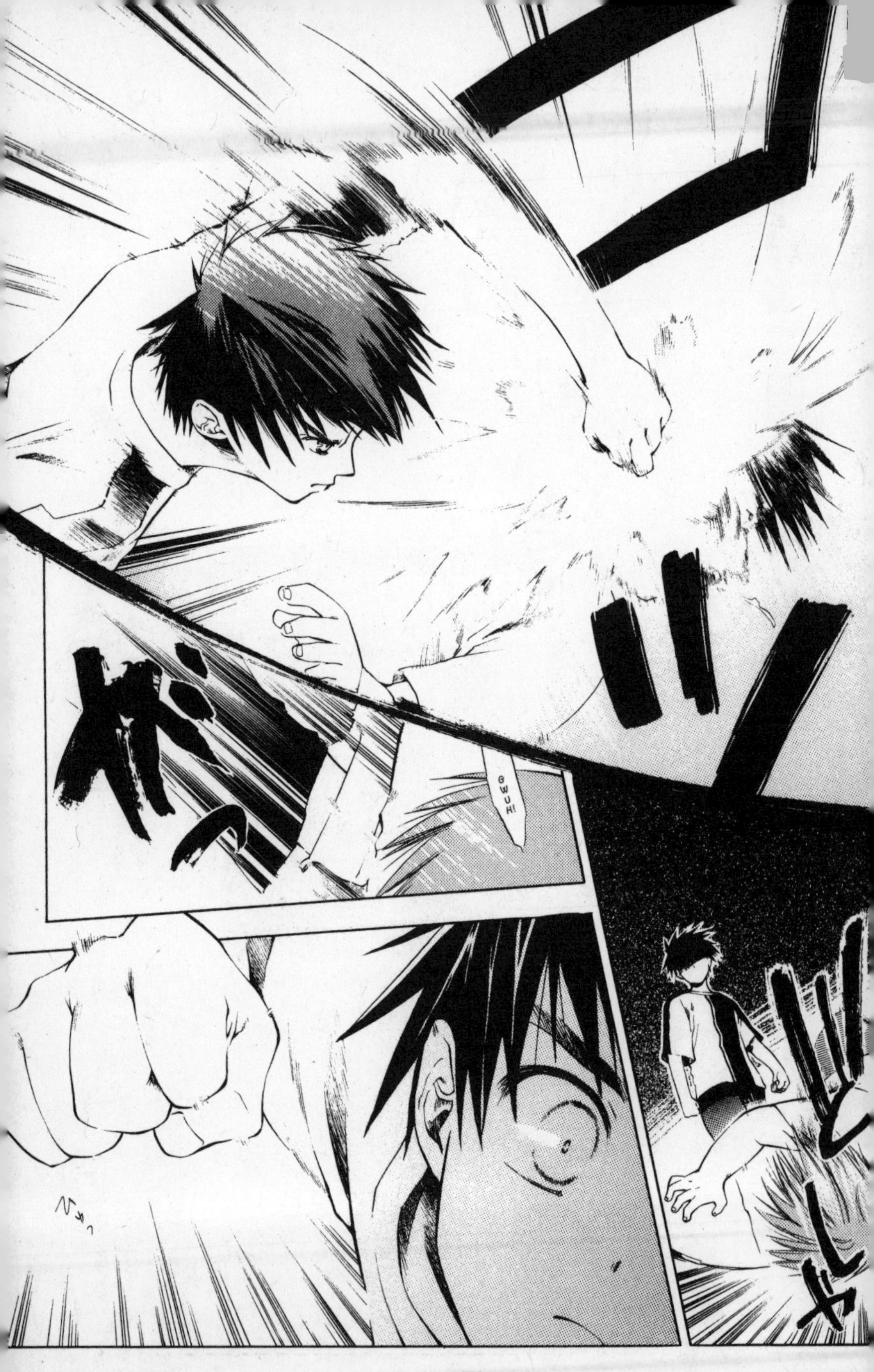
GWUH!

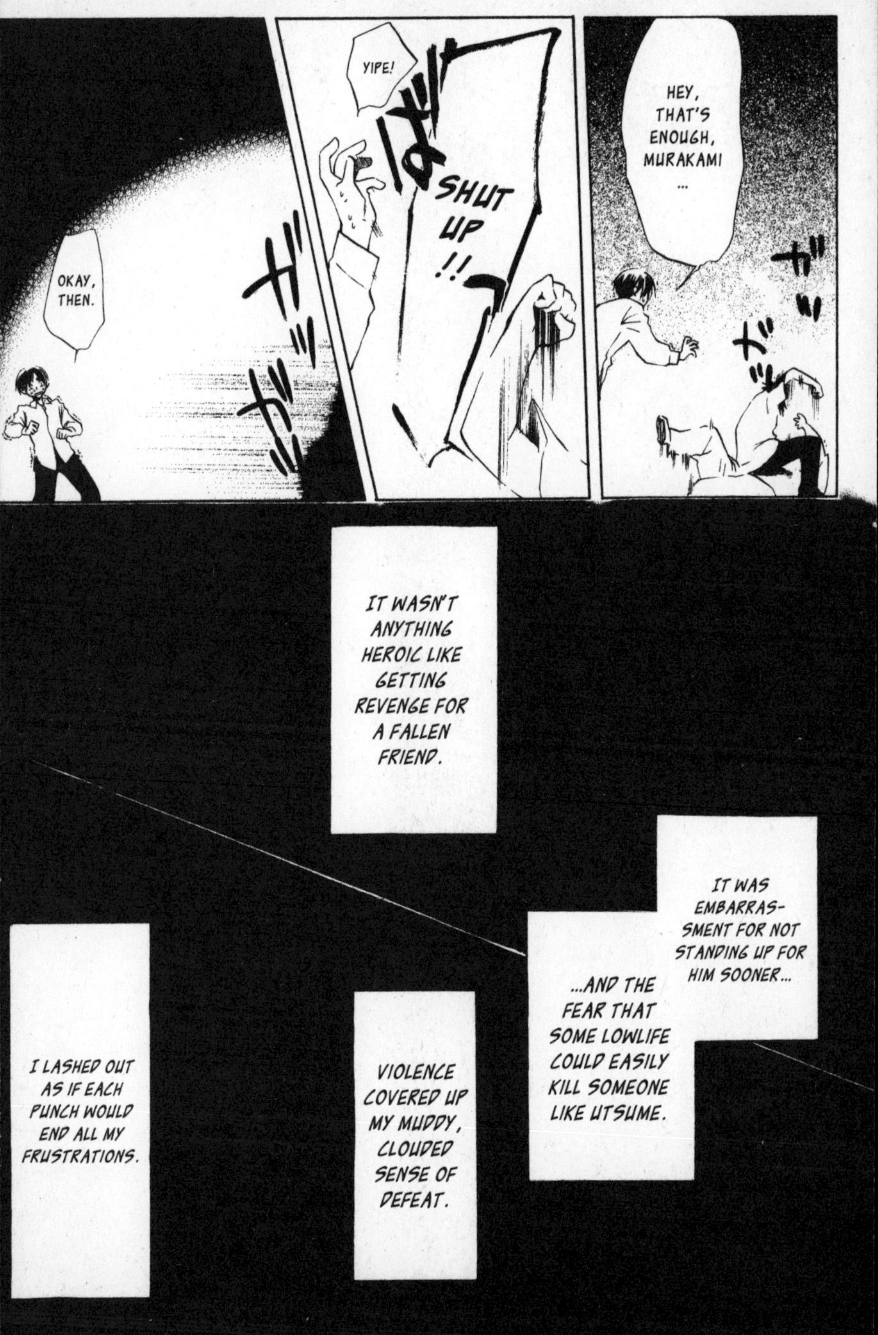
HEY, THAT'S ENOUGH, MURAKAMI ...
YIPE!
SHUT UP !!
OKAY, THEN.
IT WASN'T ANYTHING HEROIC LIKE GETTING REVENGE FOR A FALLEN FRIEND.
IT WAS EMBARRAS-SMENT FOR NOT STANDING UP FOR HIM SOONER...
...AND THE FEAR THAT SOME LOWLIFE COULD EASILY KILL SOMEONE LIKE UTSUME.
VIOLENCE COVERED UP MY MUDDY, CLOUDED SENSE OF DEFEAT.
I LASHED OUT AS IF EACH PUNCH WOULD END ALL MY FRUSTRATIONS.

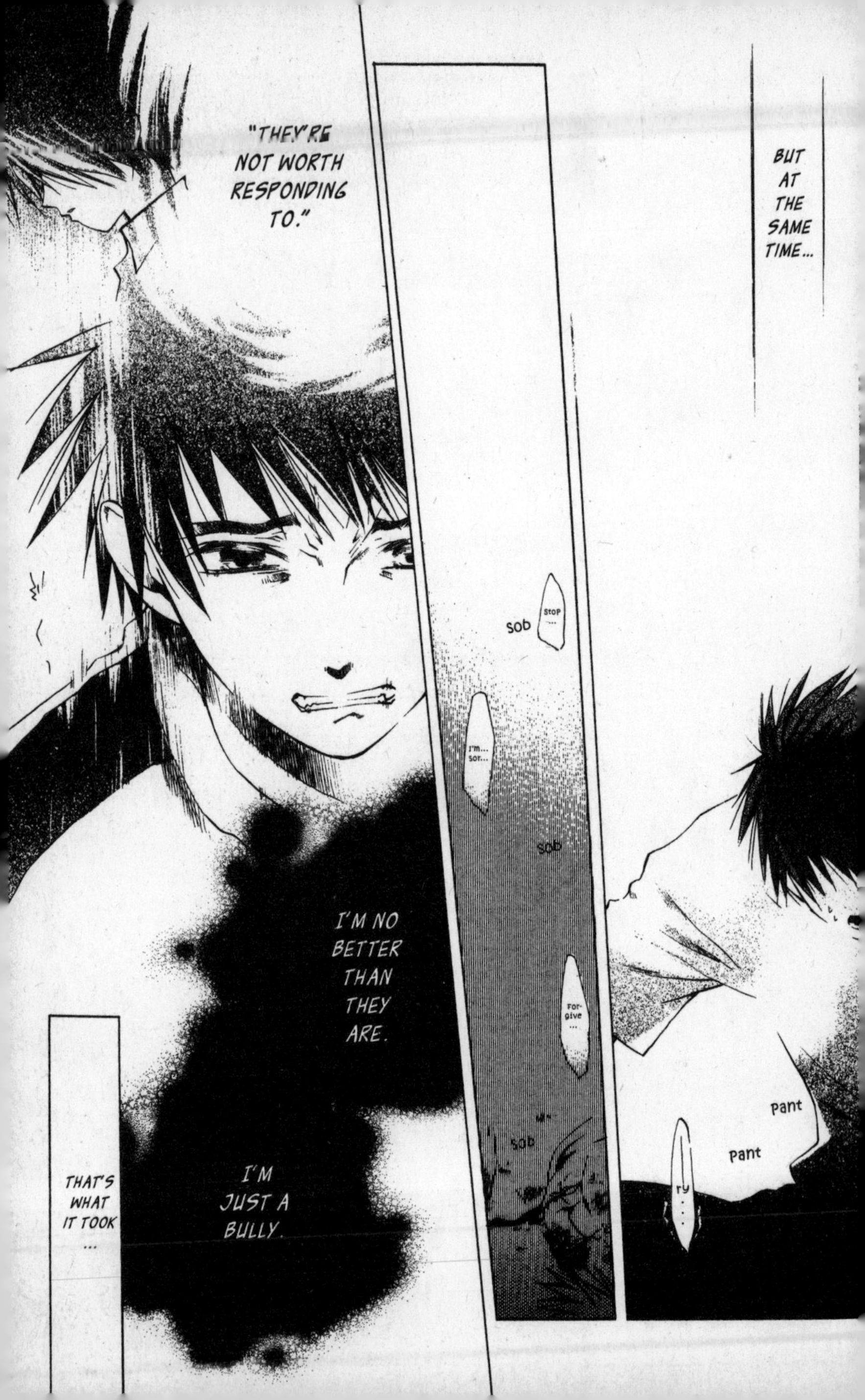
BUT AT THE SAME TIME...
Pant
Pant
ry...
sob
Stop...
I'm... sor...
sob
For-give...
sob
"THEY'RE NOT WORTH RESPONDING TO."
I'M NO BETTER THAN THEY ARE.
I'M JUST A BULLY.
THAT'S WHAT IT TOOK...

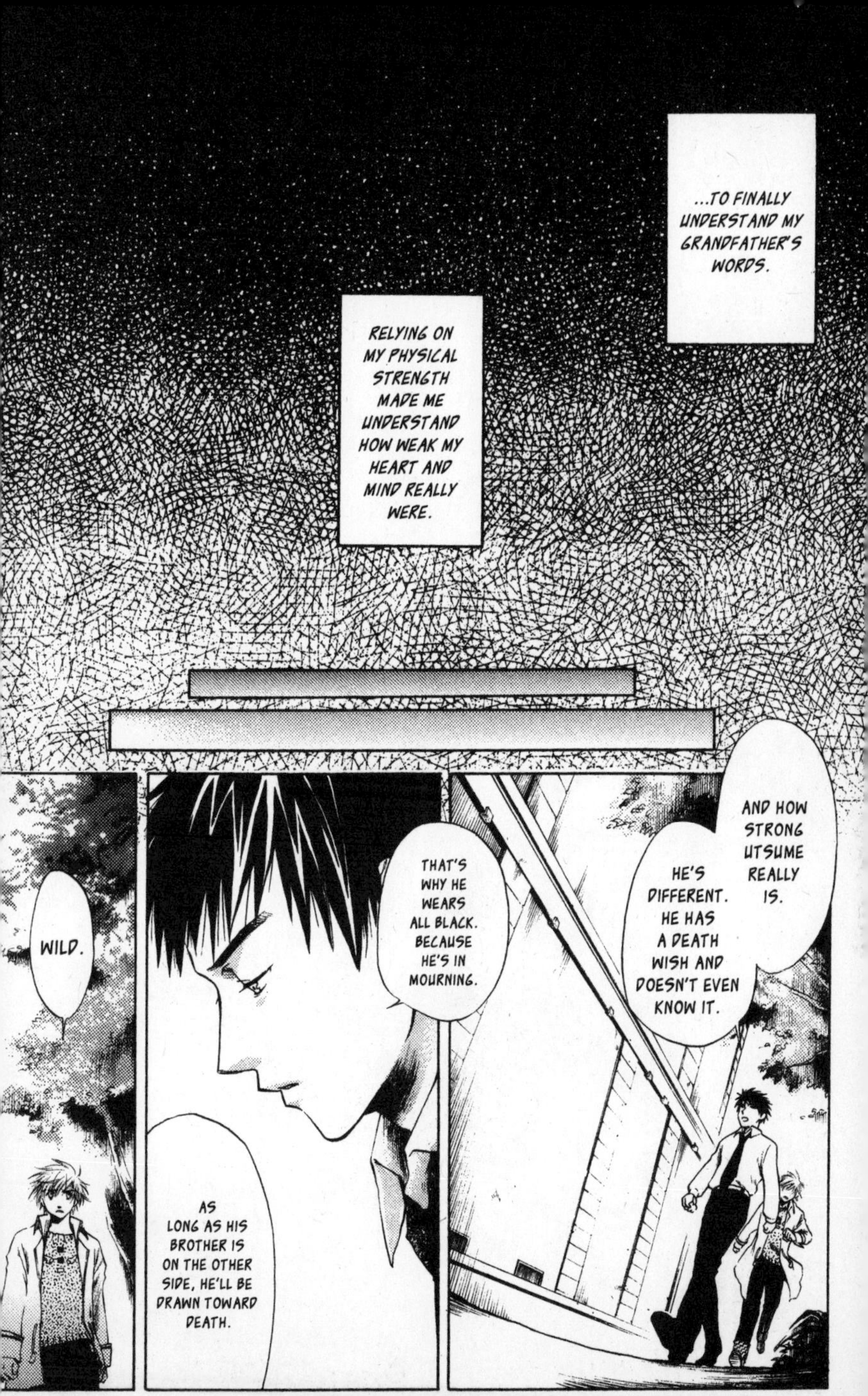
...TO FINALLY UNDERSTAND MY GRANDFATHER'S WORDS.
RELYING ON MY PHYSICAL STRENGTH MADE ME UNDERSTAND HOW WEAK MY HEART AND MIND REALLY WERE.
AND HOW STRONG UTSUME REALLY IS.
HE'S DIFFERENT. HE HAS A DEATH WISH AND DOESN'T EVEN KNOW IT.
THAT'S WHY HE WEARS ALL BLACK. BECAUSE HE'S IN MOURNING.
AS LONG AS HIS BROTHER IS ON THE OTHER SIDE, HE'LL BE DRAWN TOWARD DEATH.
WILD.

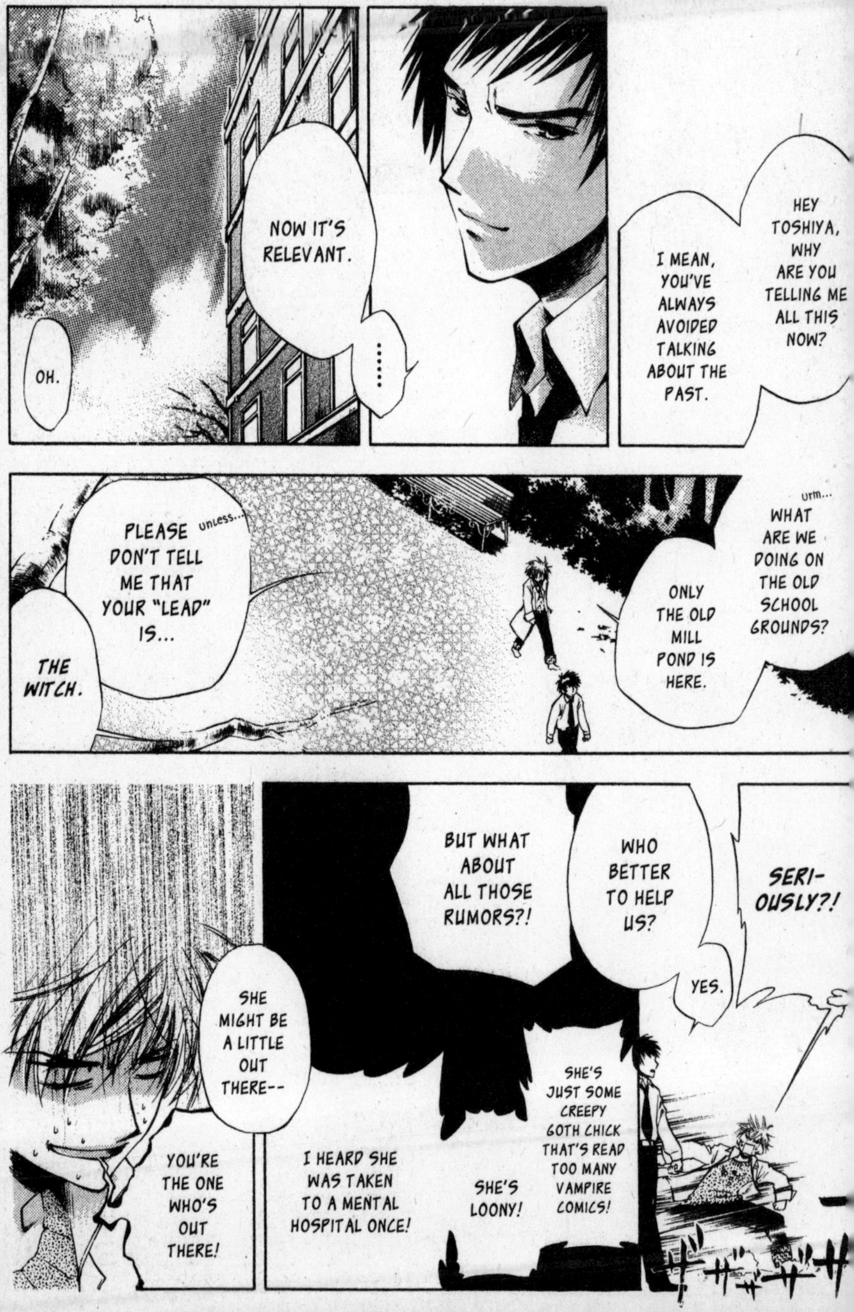
HEY TOSHIYA, WHY ARE YOU TELLING ME ALL THIS NOW?
I MEAN, YOU'VE ALWAYS AVOIDED TALKING ABOUT THE PAST.
NOW IT'S RELEVANT.
......
OH.
urm...
WHAT ARE WE DOING ON THE OLD SCHOOL GROUNDS?
ONLY THE OLD MILL POND IS HERE.
unless...
PLEASE DON'T TELL ME THAT YOUR "LEAD" IS...
THE WITCH.
SERI-OUSLY?!
YES.
WHO BETTER TO HELP US?
BUT WHAT ABOUT ALL THOSE RUMORS?!
SHE'S JUST SOME CREEPY GOTH CHICK THAT'S READ TOO MANY VAMPIRE COMICS!
SHE'S LOONY!
I HEARD SHE WAS TAKEN TO A MENTAL HOSPITAL ONCE!
SHE MIGHT BE A LITTLE OUT THERE--
YOU'RE THE ONE WHO'S OUT THERE!

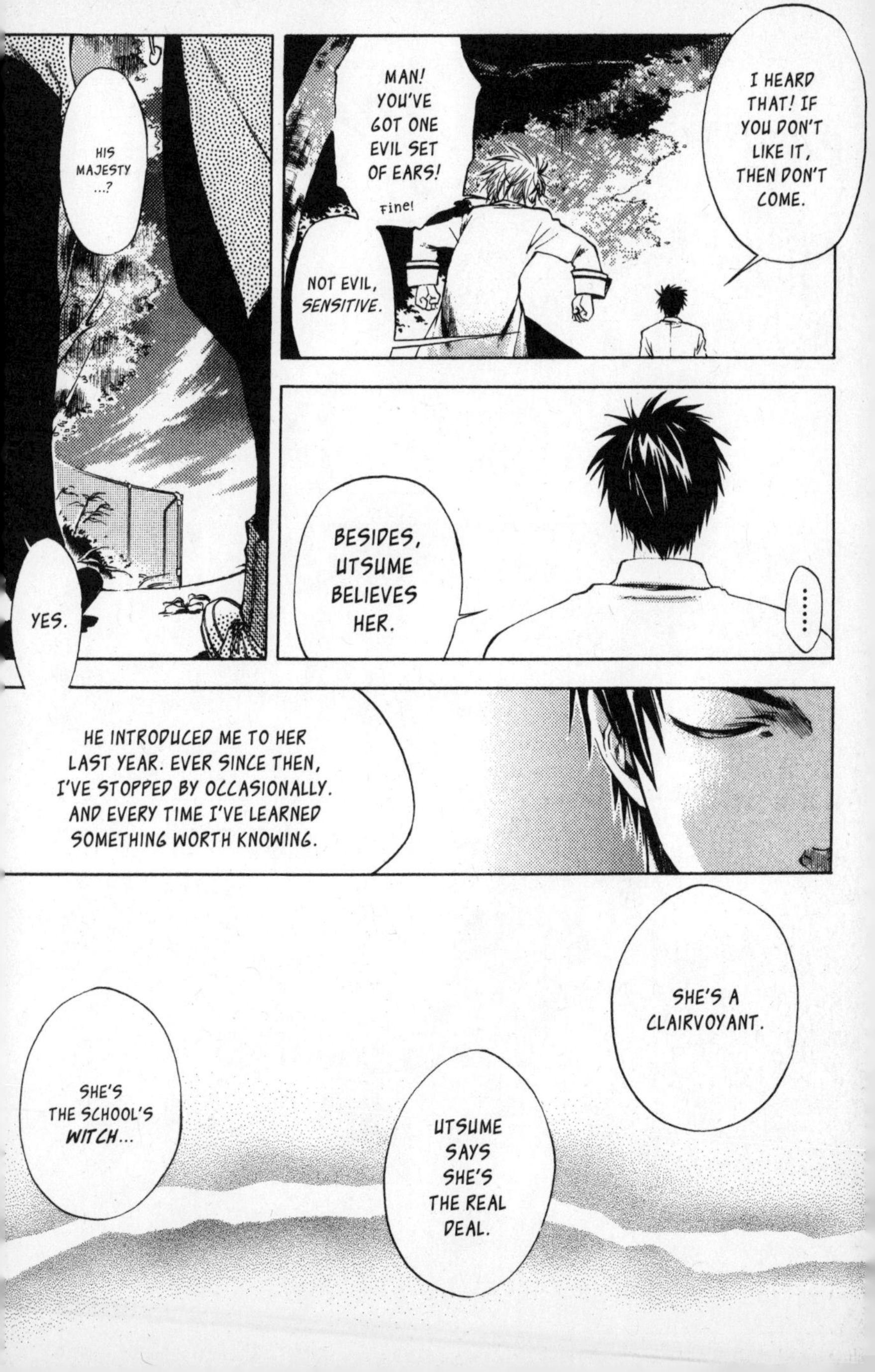
I HEARD THAT! IF YOU DON'T LIKE IT, THEN DON'T COME.
MAN! YOU'VE GOT ONE EVIL SET OF EARS!
Fine!
NOT EVIL, SENSITIVE.
......
BESIDES, UTSUME BELIEVES HER.
HIS MAJESTY ...?
YES.
HE INTRODUCED ME TO HER LAST YEAR. EVER SINCE THEN, I'VE STOPPED BY OCCASIONALLY. AND EVERY TIME I'VE LEARNED SOMETHING WORTH KNOWING.
SHE'S A CLAIRVOYANT.
UTSUME SAYS SHE'S THE REAL DEAL.
SHE'S THE SCHOOL'S *WITCH*...

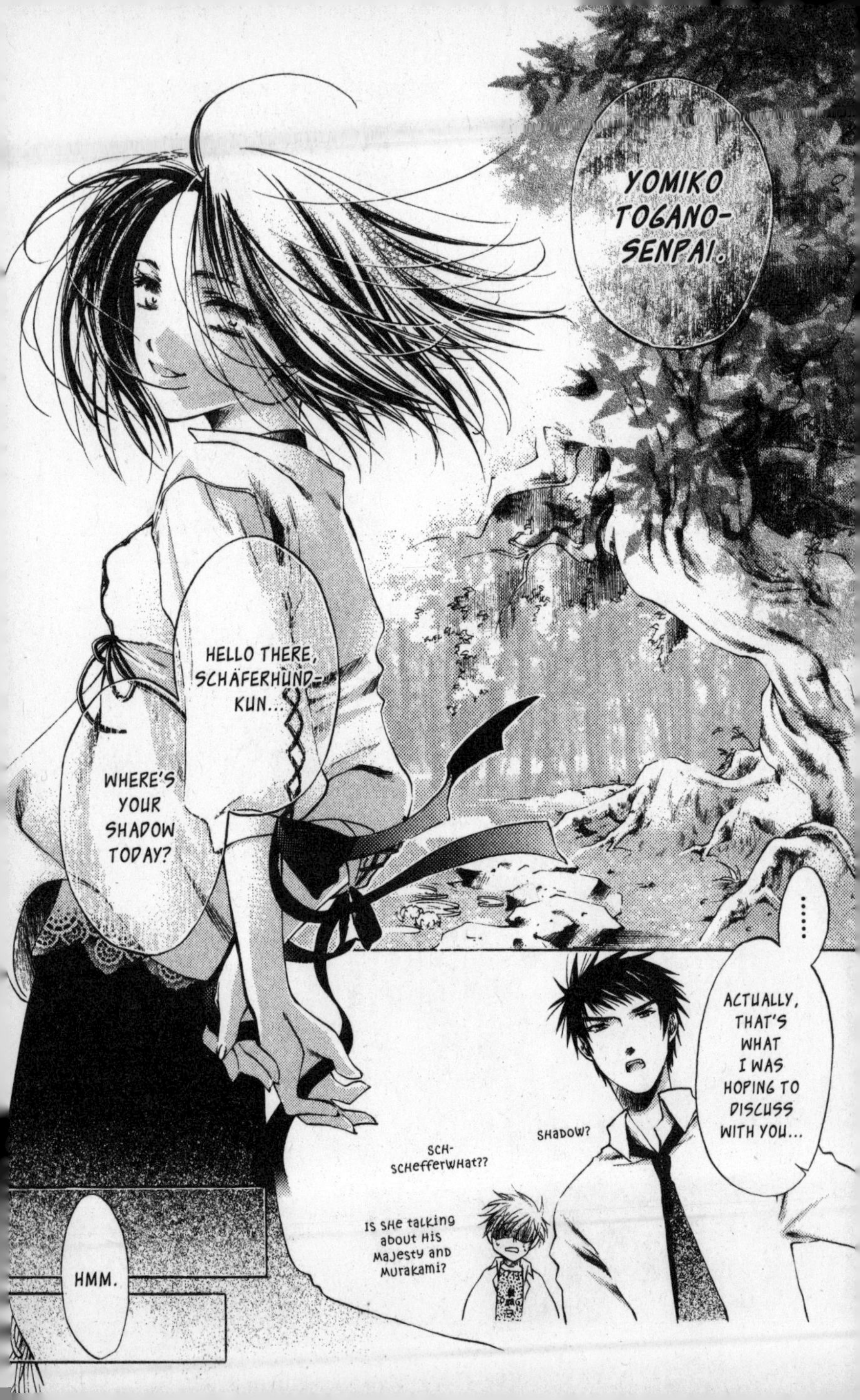
YOMIKO TOGANO-SENPAI.
HELLO THERE, SCHÄFERHUND-KUN...
WHERE'S YOUR SHADOW TODAY?
......
ACTUALLY, THAT'S WHAT I WAS HOPING TO DISCUSS WITH YOU...
SHADOW?
SCH-SCHEFFERWHAT??
IS SHE talking about His Majesty and Murakami?
HMM.

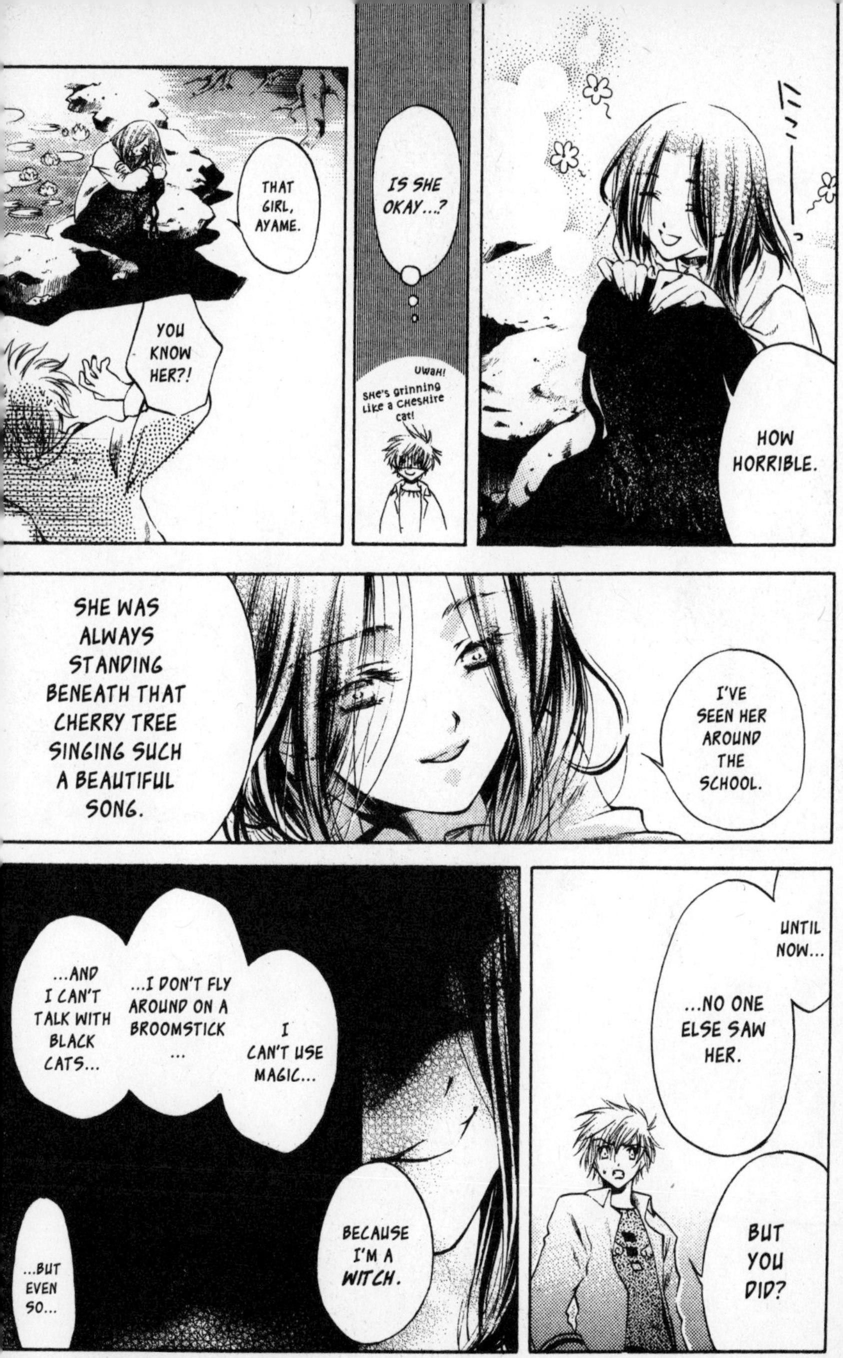
HOW HORRIBLE.
IS SHE OKAY...?
UWAH! SHE'S GRINNING LIKE A CHESHIRE CAT!
THAT GIRL, AYAME.
YOU KNOW HER?!
I'VE SEEN HER AROUND THE SCHOOL.
SHE WAS ALWAYS STANDING BENEATH THAT CHERRY TREE SINGING SUCH A BEAUTIFUL SONG.
UNTIL NOW...
...NO ONE ELSE SAW HER.
BUT YOU DID?
I CAN'T USE MAGIC...
...I DON'T FLY AROUND ON A BROOMSTICK...
...AND I CAN'T TALK WITH BLACK CATS...
BECAUSE I'M A WITCH.
...BUT EVEN SO...

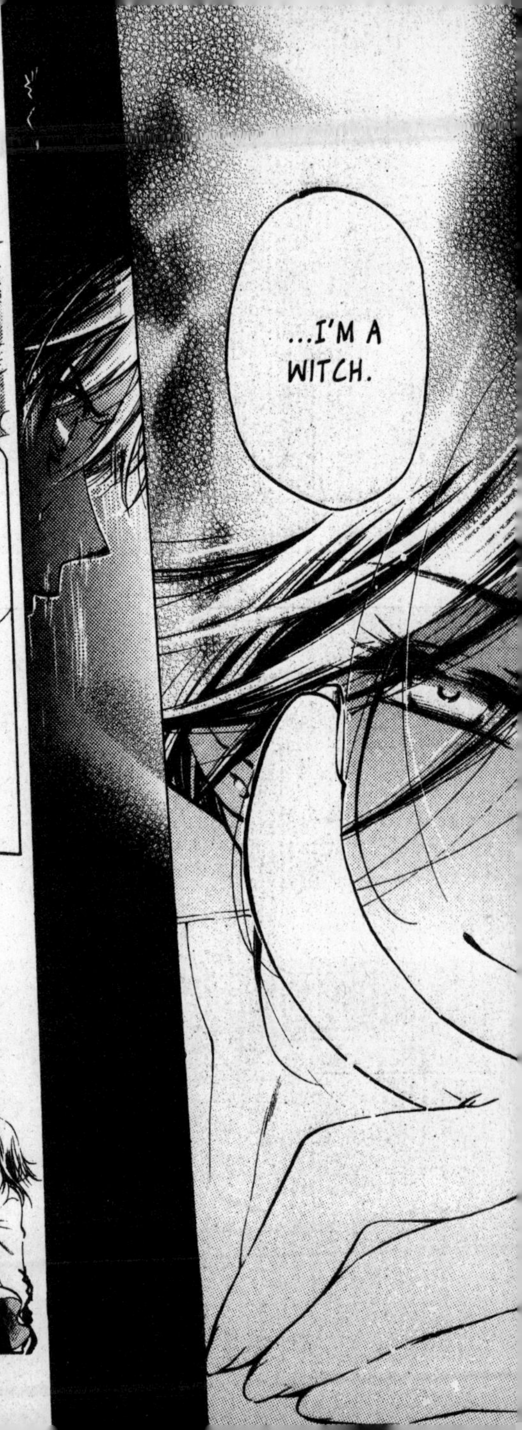
...I'M A WITCH.
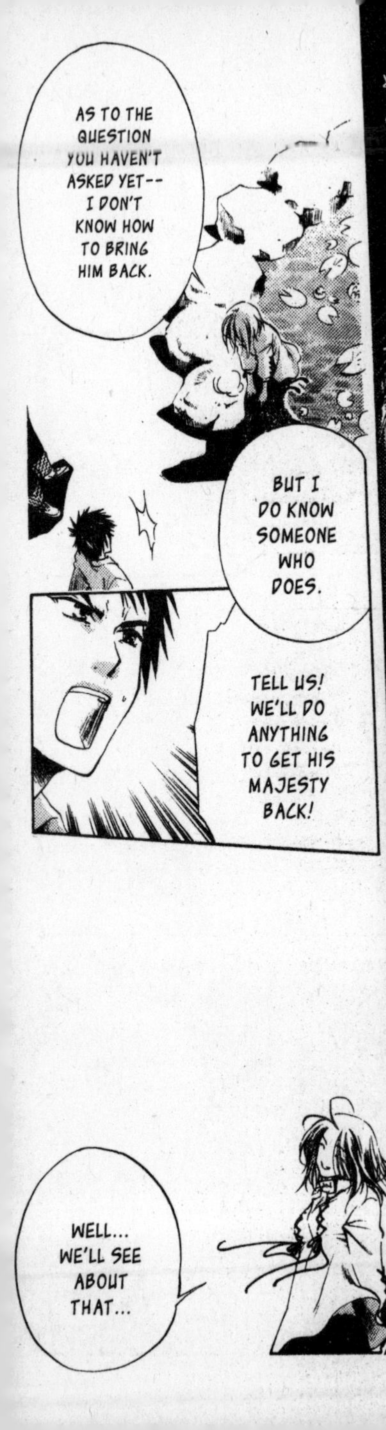
AS TO THE QUESTION YOU HAVEN'T ASKED YET-- I DON'T KNOW HOW TO BRING HIM BACK.
BUT I DO KNOW SOMEONE WHO DOES.
TELL US! WE'LL DO ANYTHING TO GET HIS MAJESTY BACK!
WELL... WE'LL SEE ABOUT THAT...

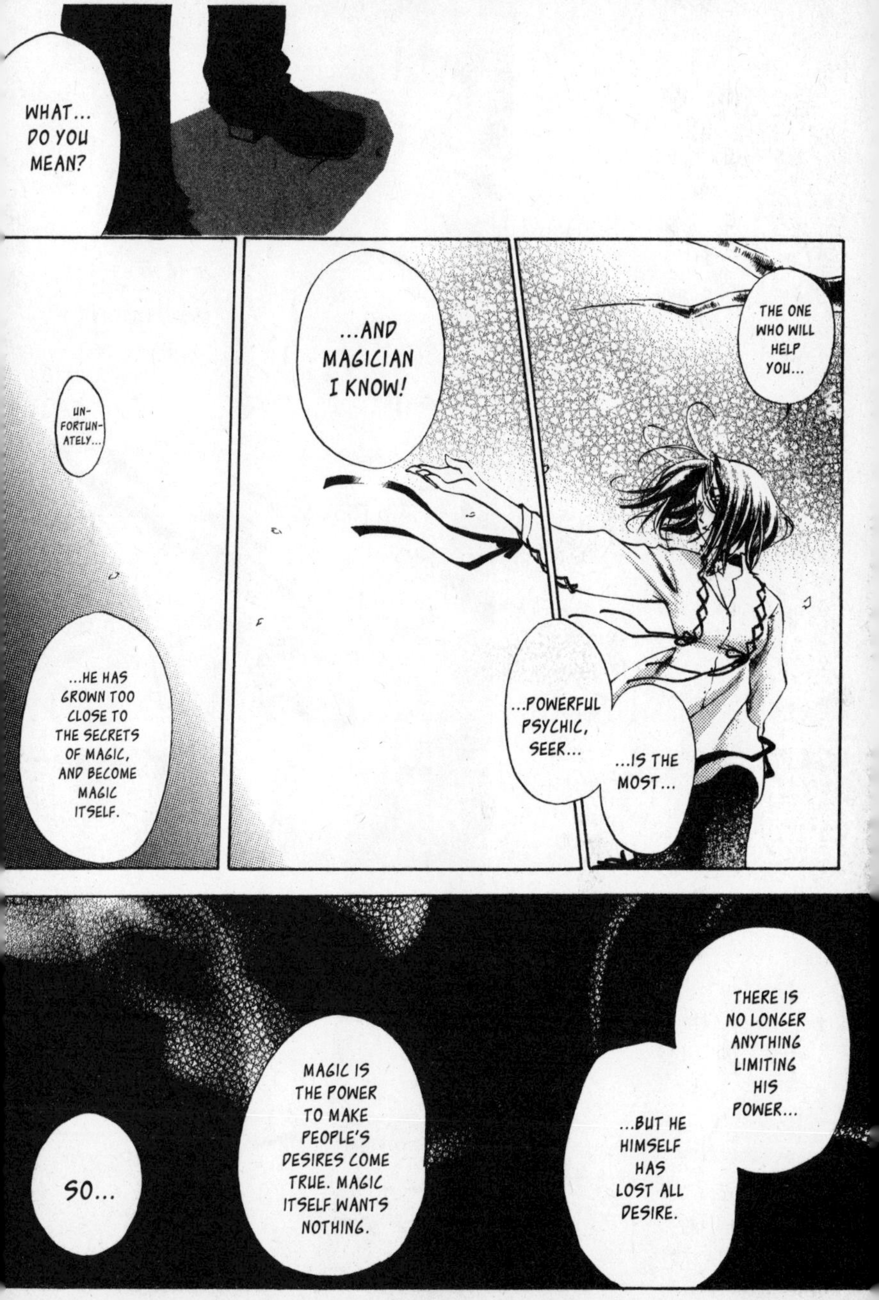
WHAT... DO YOU MEAN?
THE ONE WHO WILL HELP YOU...
...IS THE MOST...
...POWERFUL PSYCHIC, SEER...
...AND MAGICIAN I KNOW!
UN-FORTUN-ATELY...
...HE HAS GROWN TOO CLOSE TO THE SECRETS OF MAGIC, AND BECOME MAGIC ITSELF.
THERE IS NO LONGER ANYTHING LIMITING HIS POWER...
...BUT HE HIMSELF HAS LOST ALL DESIRE.
MAGIC IS THE POWER TO MAKE PEOPLE'S DESIRES COME TRUE. MAGIC ITSELF WANTS NOTHING.
SO...

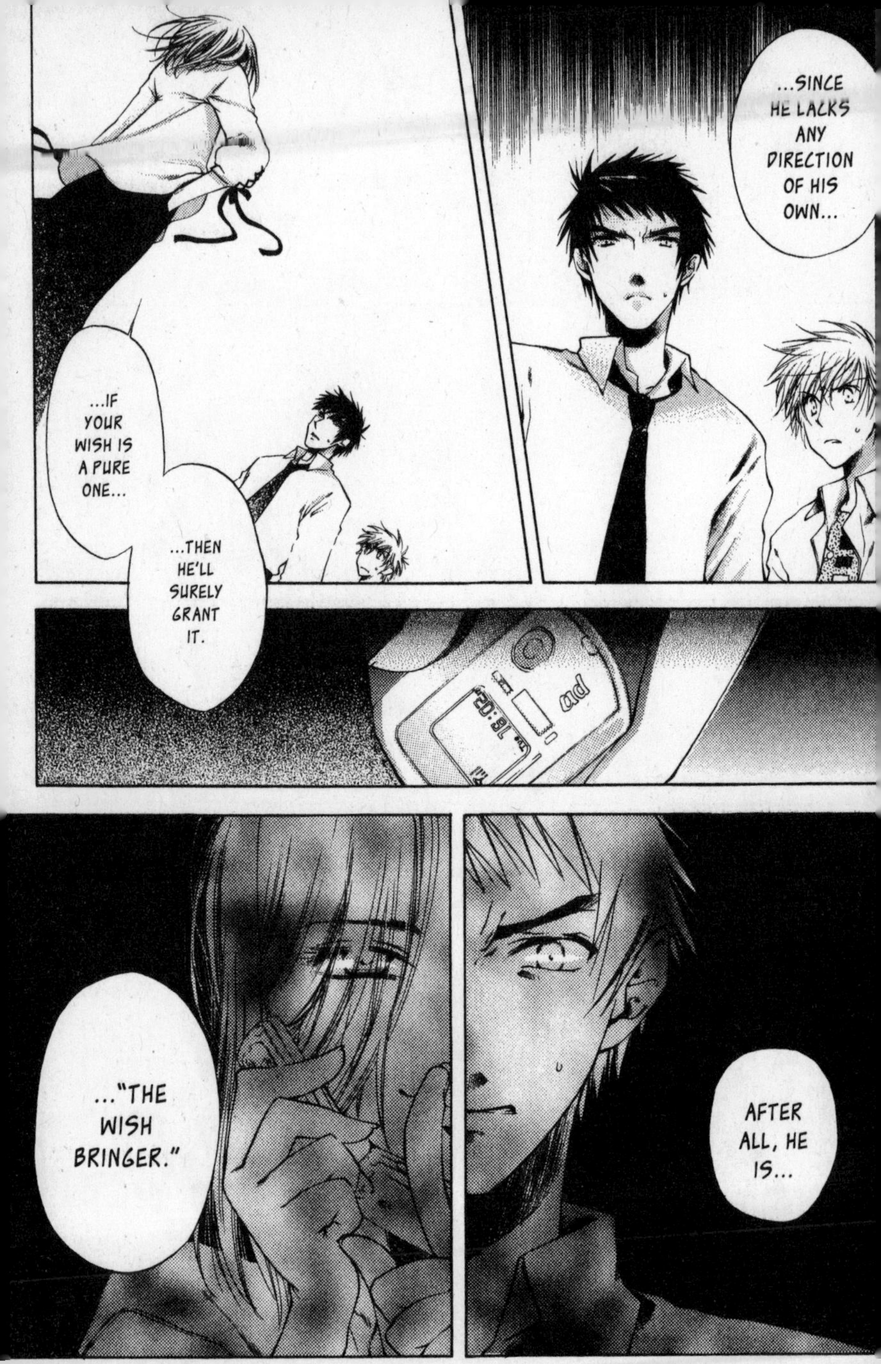
...SINCE HE LACKS ANY DIRECTION OF HIS OWN...
...IF YOUR WISH IS A PURE ONE...
...THEN HE'LL SURELY GRANT IT.
AFTER ALL, HE IS...
..."THE WISH BRINGER."

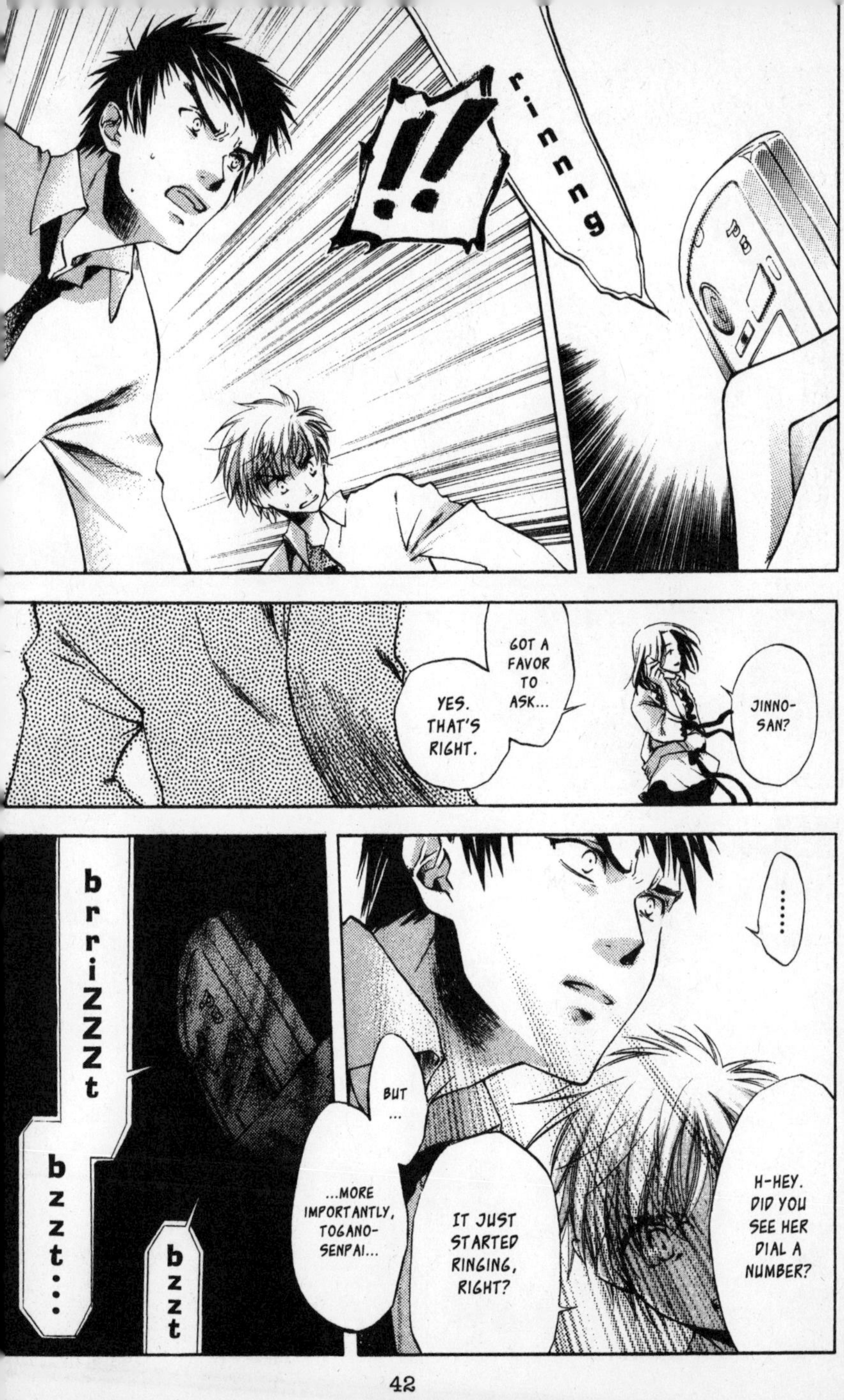
rinnng
!!
JINNO-SAN?
GOT A FAVOR TO ASK...
YES. THAT'S RIGHT.
......
H-HEY. DID YOU SEE HER DIAL A NUMBER?
IT JUST STARTED RINGING, RIGHT?
...MORE IMPORTANTLY, TOGANO-SENPAI...
BUT ...
brriZZZt
bzzt...
bzzt

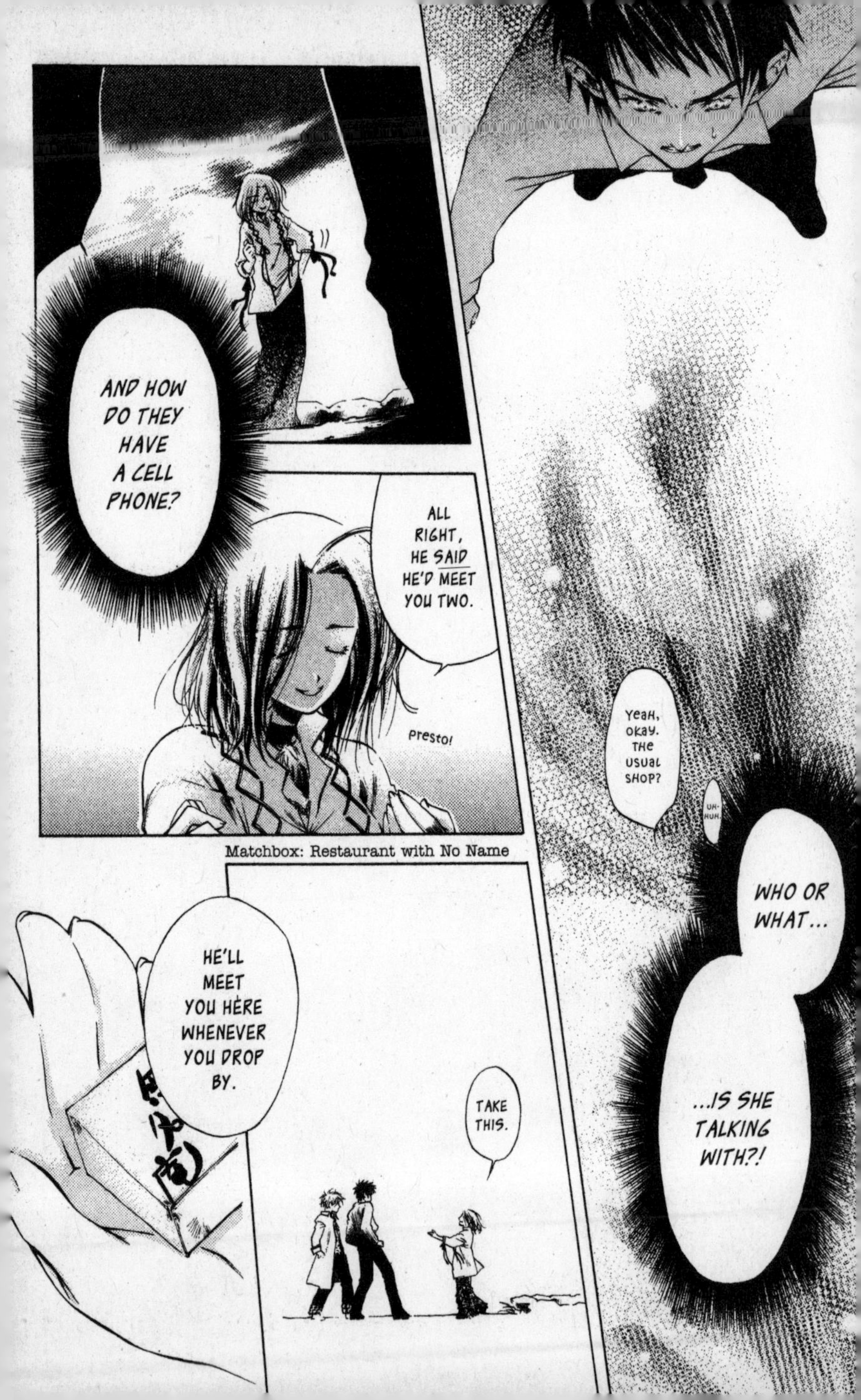
Yeah, okay. The usual shop?
UH-HUH.
WHO OR WHAT...
...IS SHE TALKING WITH?!
AND HOW DO THEY HAVE A CELL PHONE?
ALL RIGHT, HE SAID HE'D MEET YOU TWO.
presto!
Matchbox: Restaurant with No Name
TAKE THIS.
HE'LL MEET YOU HERE WHENEVER YOU DROP BY.

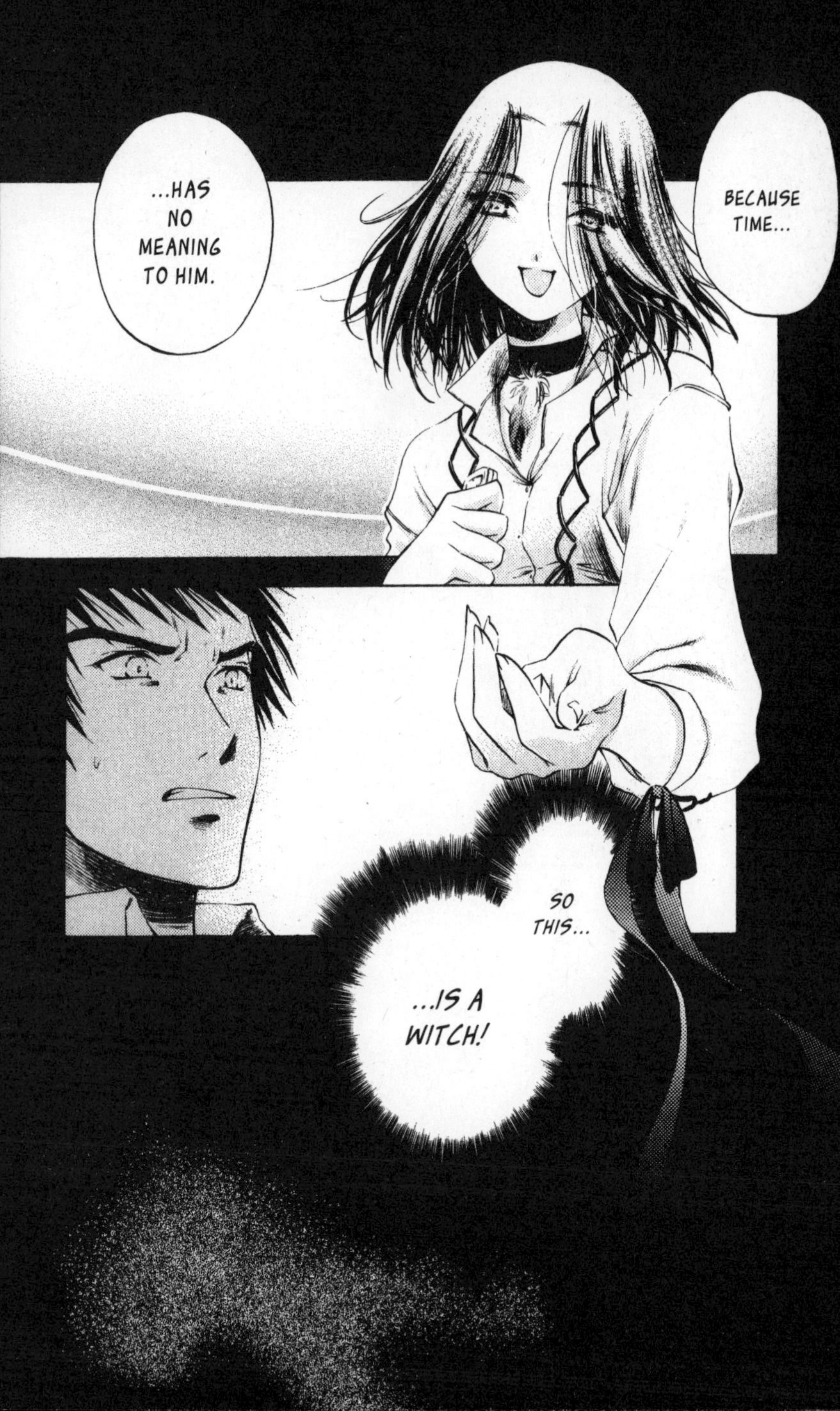
BECAUSE TIME...
...HAS NO MEANING TO HIM.
SO THIS...
...IS A WITCH!

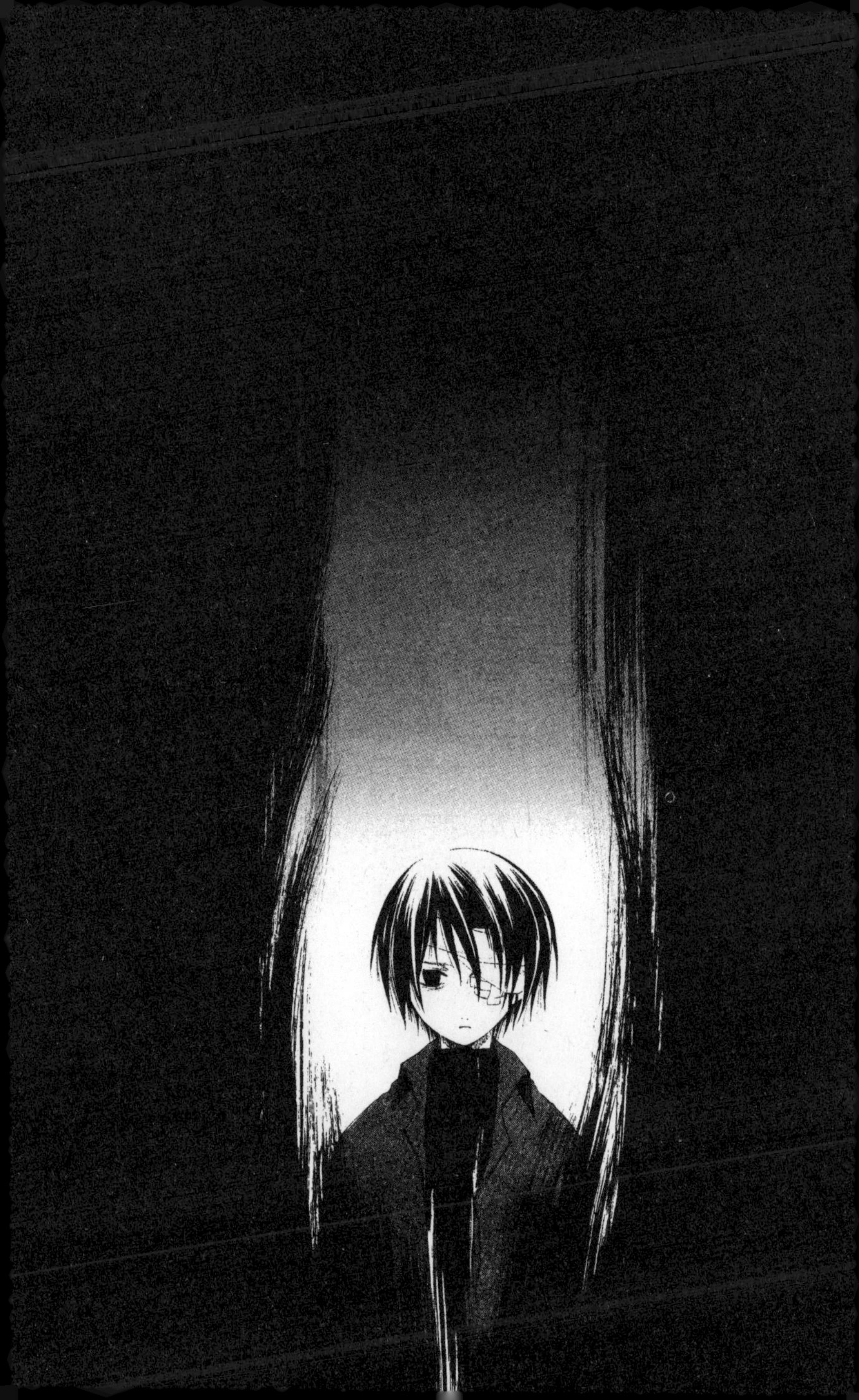

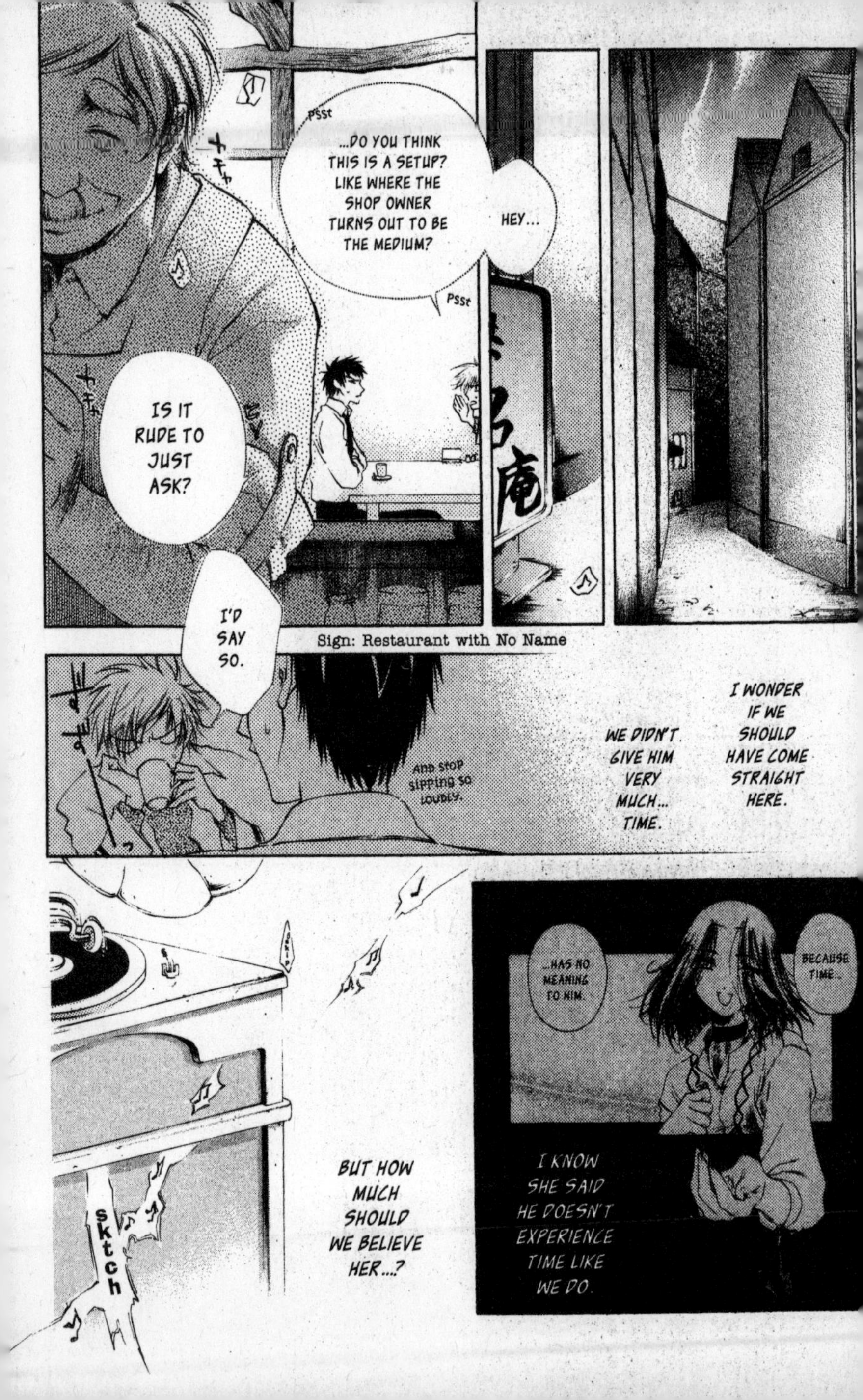
HEY...
Psst
...DO YOU THINK THIS IS A SETUP? LIKE WHERE THE SHOP OWNER TURNS OUT TO BE THE MEDIUM?
Psst
IS IT RUDE TO JUST ASK?
I'D SAY SO.
Sign: Restaurant with No Name
I WONDER IF WE SHOULD HAVE COME STRAIGHT HERE.
WE DIDN'T GIVE HIM VERY MUCH... TIME.
And stop sipping so loudly.
BECAUSE TIME...
...HAS NO MEANING TO HIM.
I KNOW SHE SAID HE DOESN'T EXPERIENCE TIME LIKE WE DO.
BUT HOW MUCH SHOULD WE BELIEVE HER...?
sktch

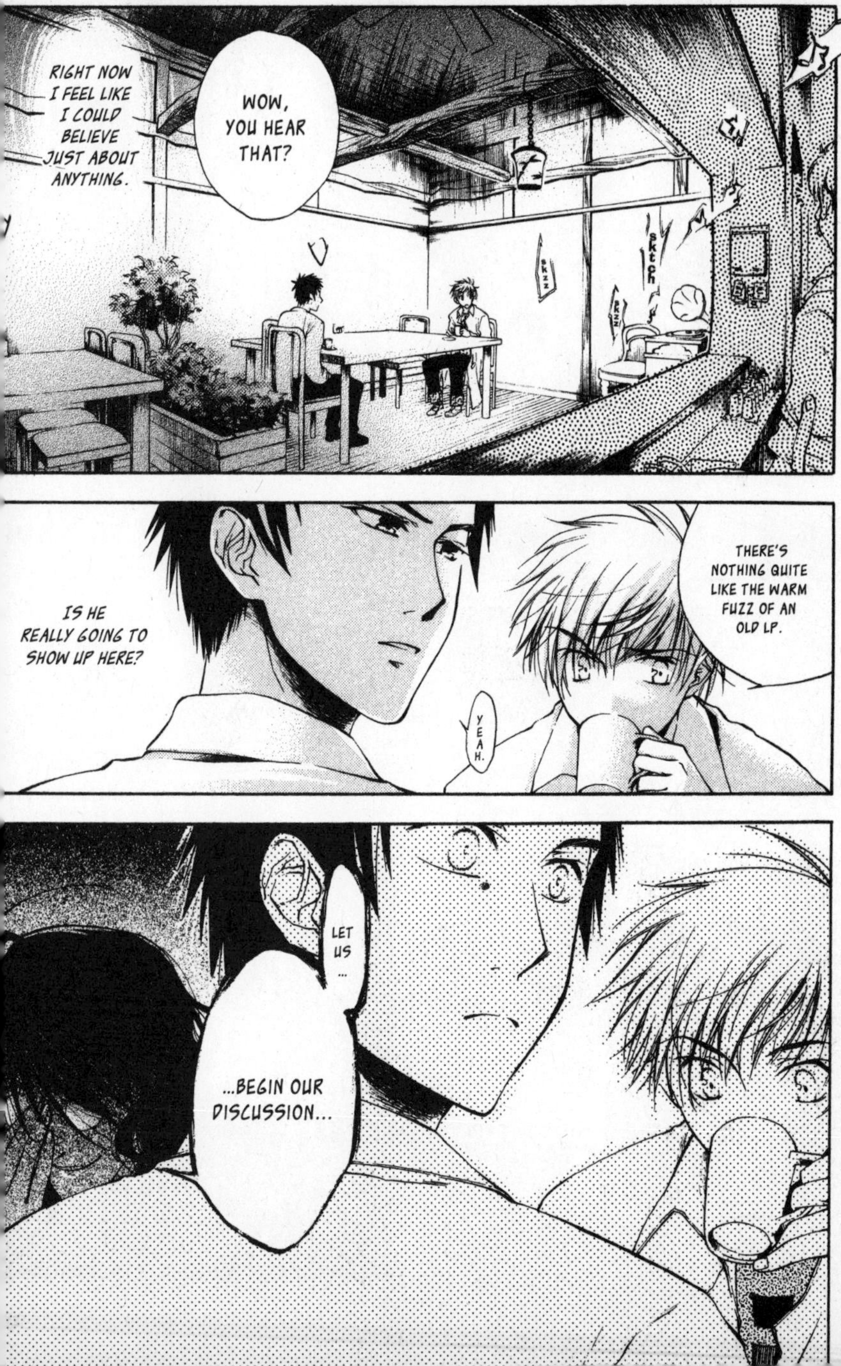
sktch
skzz
skzz
WOW, YOU HEAR THAT?
RIGHT NOW I FEEL LIKE I COULD BELIEVE JUST ABOUT ANYTHING.
THERE'S NOTHING QUITE LIKE THE WARM FUZZ OF AN OLD LP.
YEAH.
IS HE REALLY GOING TO SHOW UP HERE?
LET US...
...BEGIN OUR DISCUSSION...

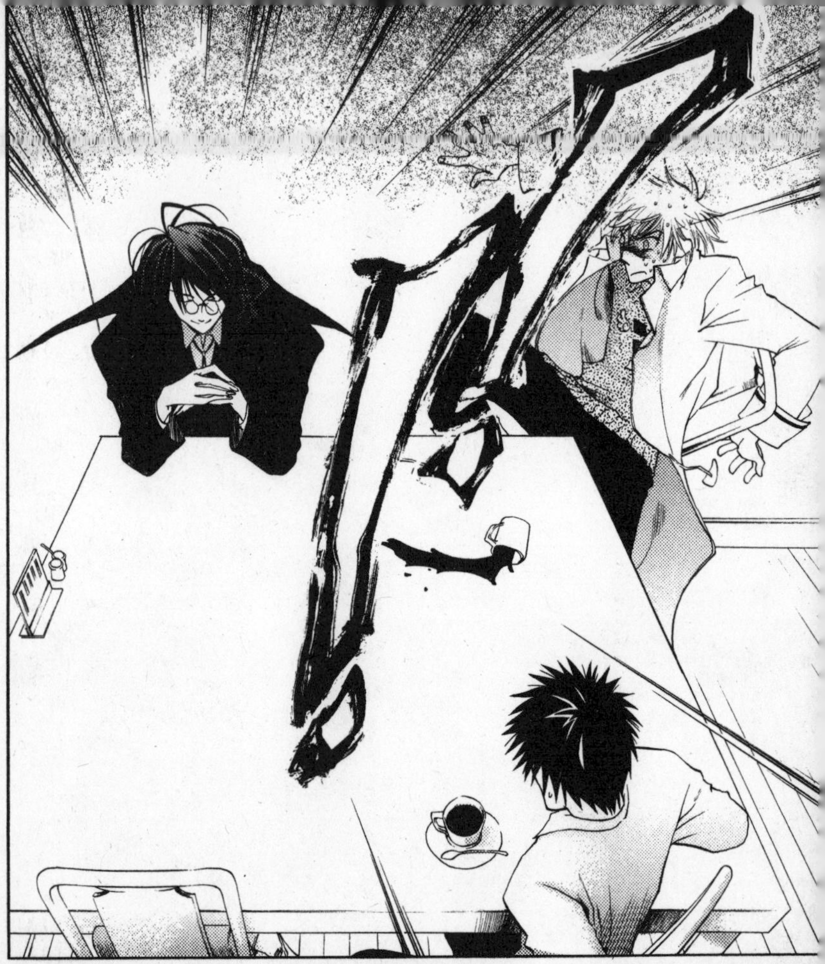

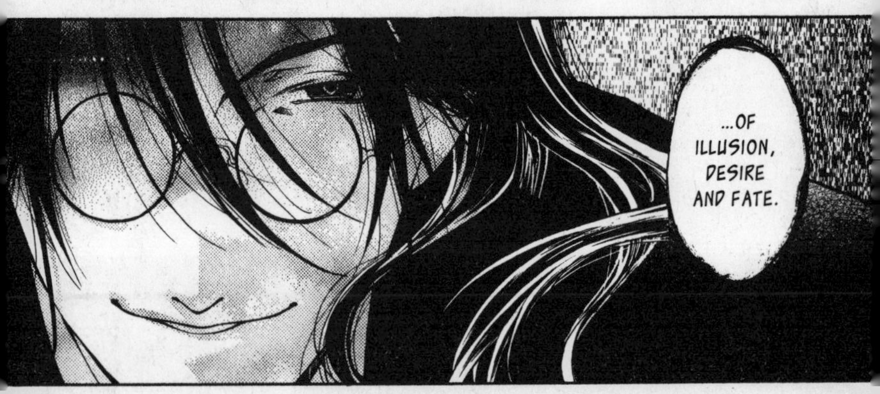
...OF ILLUSION, DESIRE AND FATE.

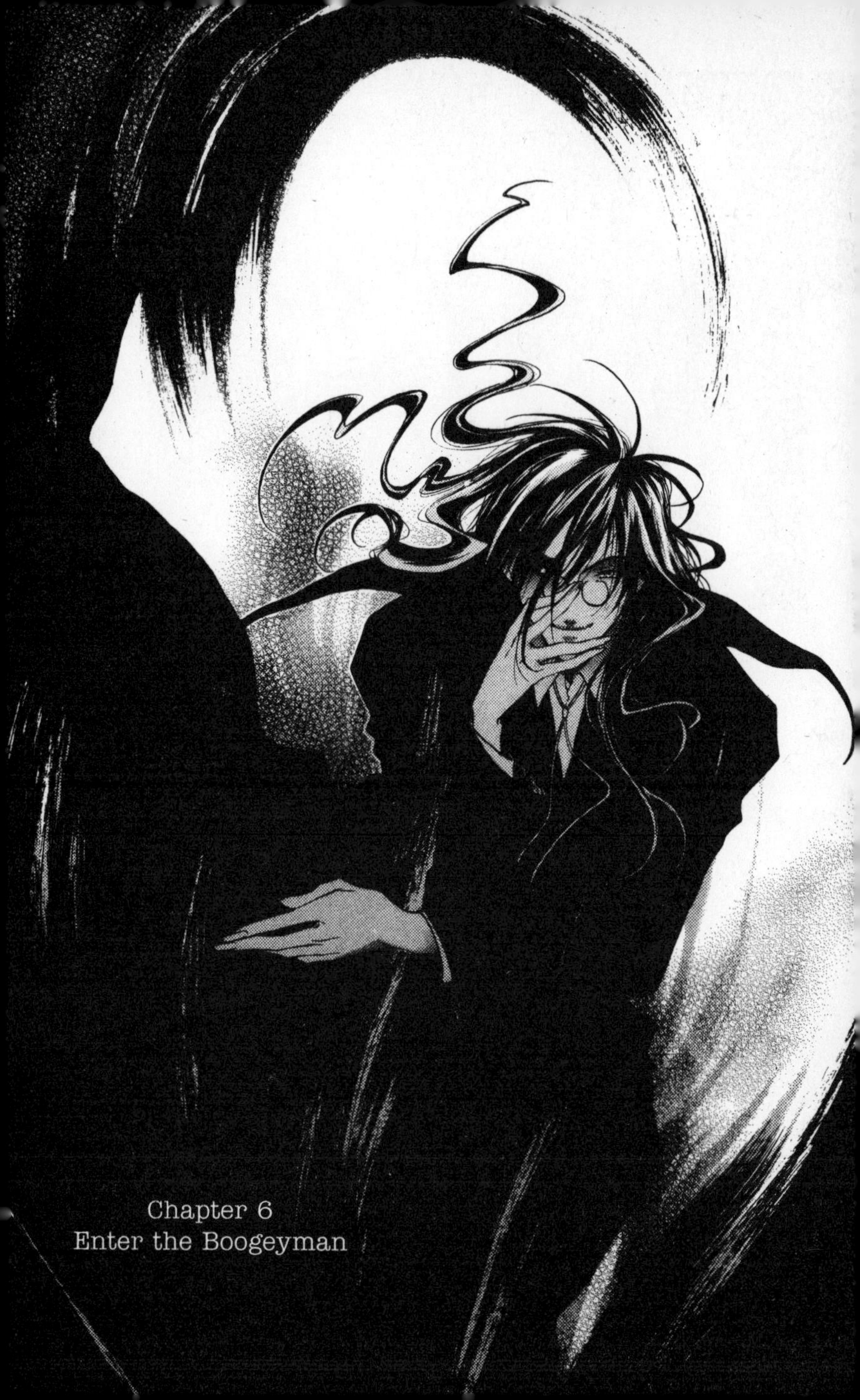
Chapter 6
Enter the Boogeyman

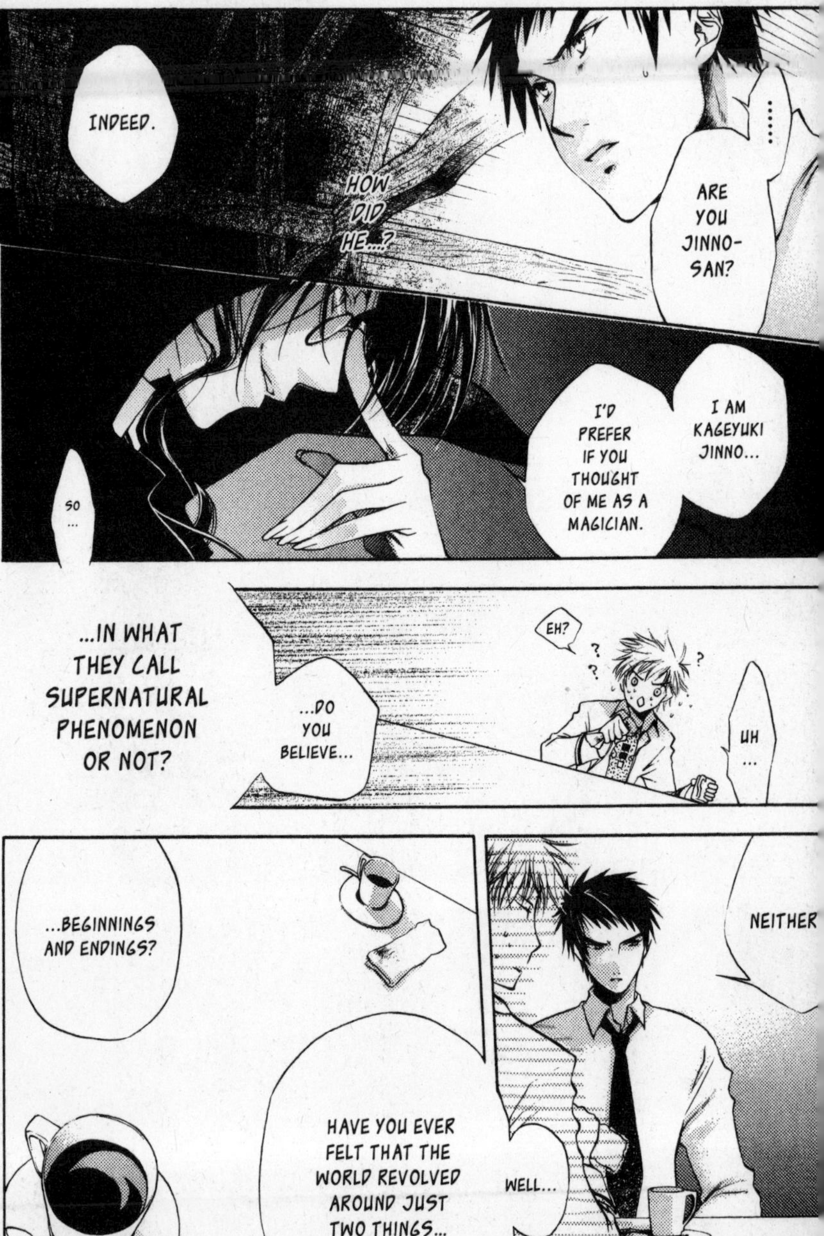
......
ARE YOU JINNO-SAN?
HOW DID HE...?
INDEED.
I AM KAGEYUKI JINNO...
I'D PREFER IF YOU THOUGHT OF ME AS A MAGICIAN.
SO ...
EH?
UH ...
...DO YOU BELIEVE...
...IN WHAT THEY CALL SUPERNATURAL PHENOMENON OR NOT?
NEITHER
WELL...
HAVE YOU EVER FELT THAT THE WORLD REVOLVED AROUND JUST TWO THINGS...
...BEGINNINGS AND ENDINGS?

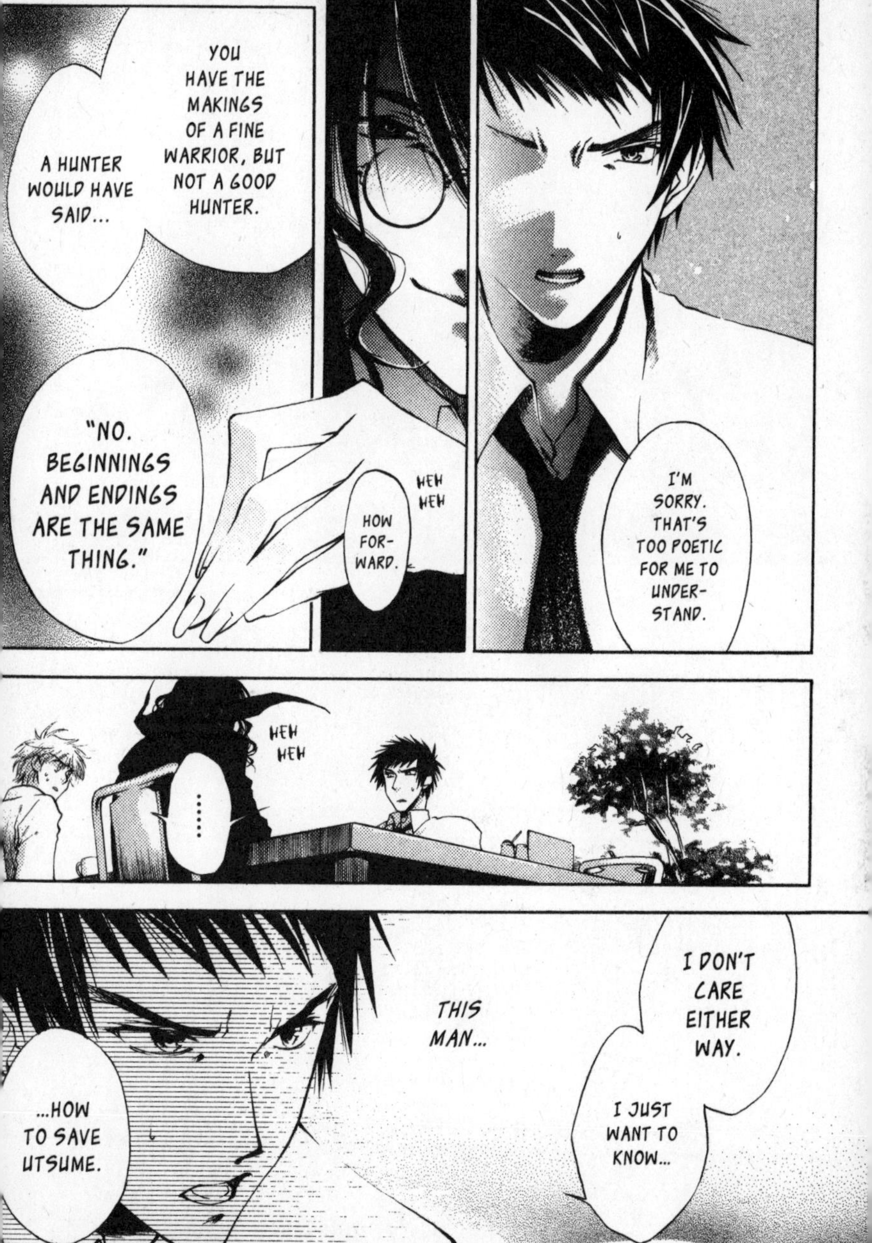
I'M SORRY. THAT'S TOO POETIC FOR ME TO UNDER-STAND.
HEH HEH
HOW FOR-WARD.
YOU HAVE THE MAKINGS OF A FINE WARRIOR, BUT NOT A GOOD HUNTER.
A HUNTER WOULD HAVE SAID...
"NO. BEGINNINGS AND ENDINGS ARE THE SAME THING."
HEH HEH
......
I DON'T CARE EITHER WAY.
I JUST WANT TO KNOW...
THIS MAN...
...HOW TO SAVE UTSUME.

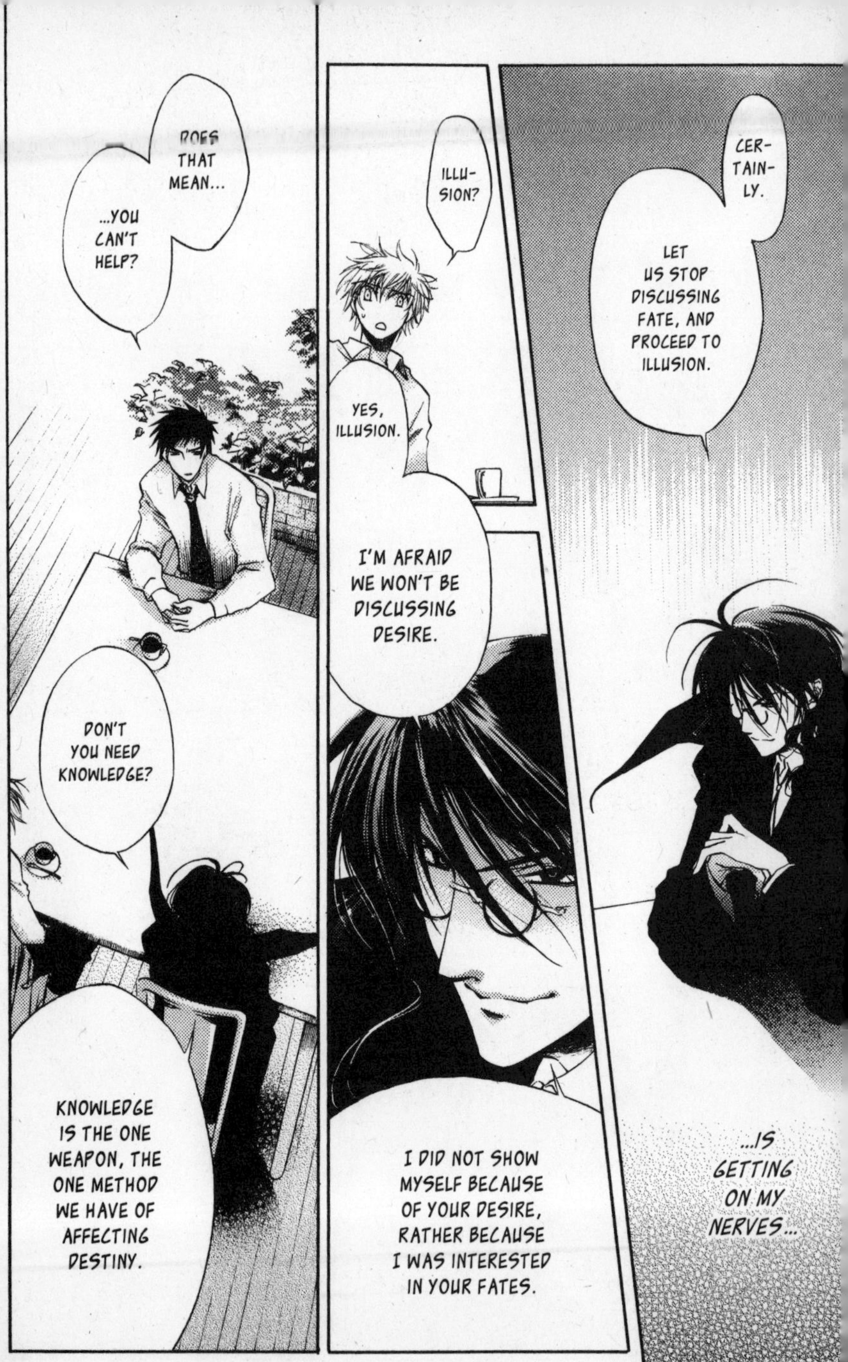
CER-TAIN-LY.
LET US STOP DISCUSSING FATE, AND PROCEED TO ILLUSION.
...IS GETTING ON MY NERVES...
ILLU-SION?
YES, ILLUSION.
I'M AFRAID WE WON'T BE DISCUSSING DESIRE.
I DID NOT SHOW MYSELF BECAUSE OF YOUR DESIRE, RATHER BECAUSE I WAS INTERESTED IN YOUR FATES.
DOES THAT MEAN...
...YOU CAN'T HELP?
DON'T YOU NEED KNOWLEDGE?
KNOWLEDGE IS THE ONE WEAPON, THE ONE METHOD WE HAVE OF AFFECTING DESTINY.

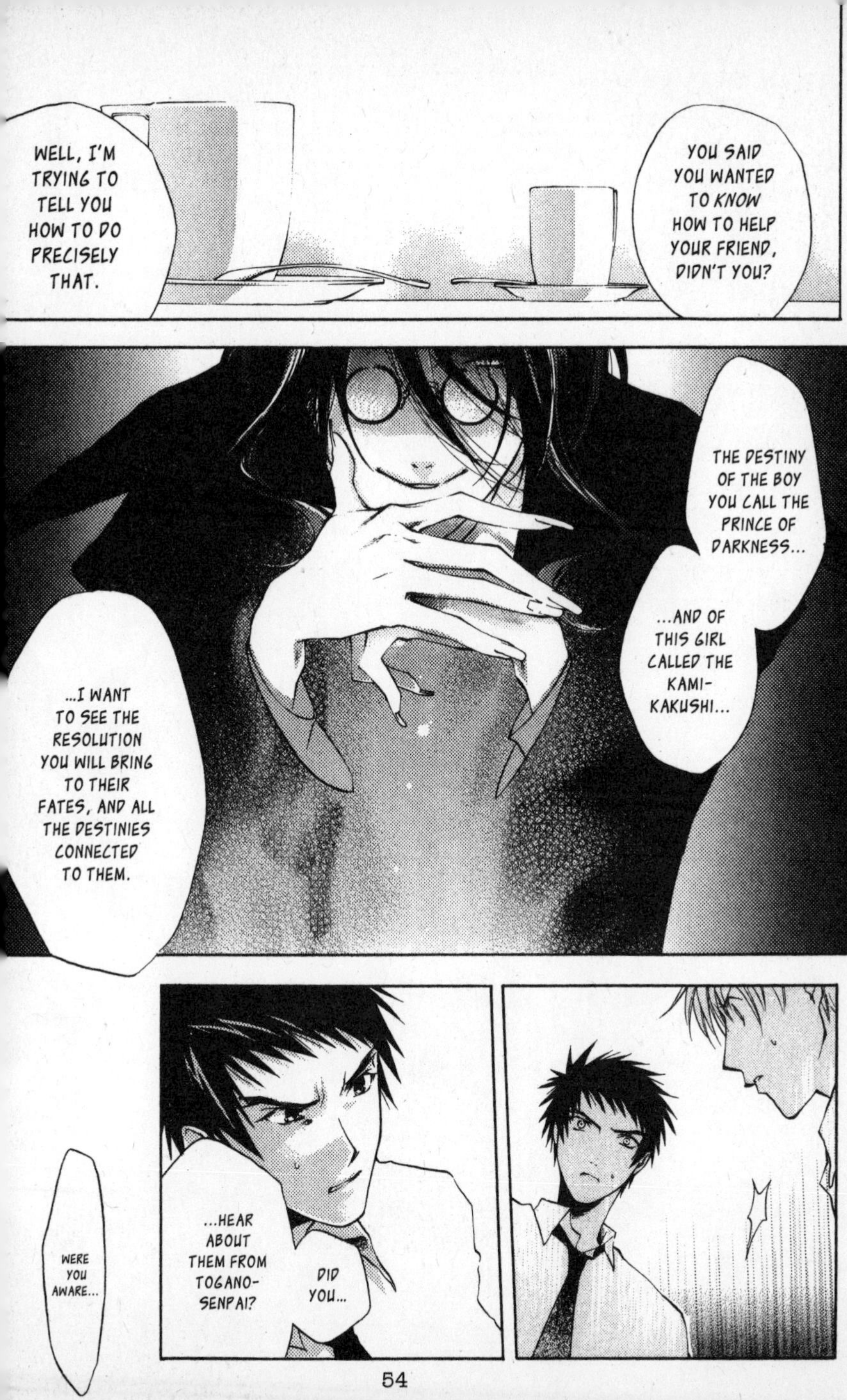
YOU SAID YOU WANTED TO KNOW HOW TO HELP YOUR FRIEND, DIDN'T YOU?
WELL, I'M TRYING TO TELL YOU HOW TO DO PRECISELY THAT.
THE DESTINY OF THE BOY YOU CALL THE PRINCE OF DARKNESS...
...AND OF THIS GIRL CALLED THE KAMI-KAKUSHI...
...I WANT TO SEE THE RESOLUTION YOU WILL BRING TO THEIR FATES, AND ALL THE DESTINIES CONNECTED TO THEM.
DID YOU...
...HEAR ABOUT THEM FROM TOGANO-SENPAI?
WERE YOU AWARE...

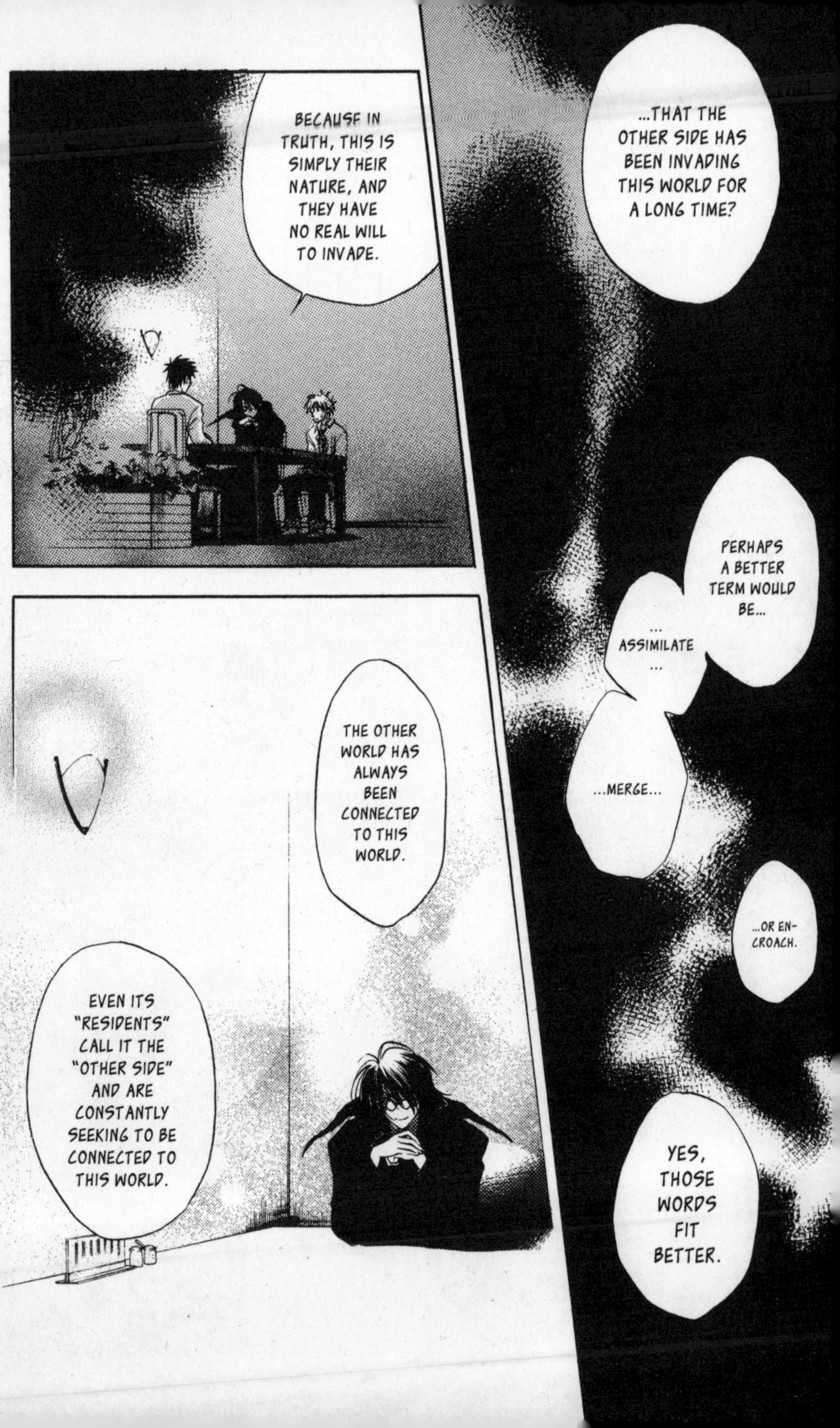
...THAT THE OTHER SIDE HAS BEEN INVADING THIS WORLD FOR A LONG TIME?
PERHAPS A BETTER TERM WOULD BE...
...ASSIMILATE...
...MERGE...
...OR EN-CROACH.
YES, THOSE WORDS FIT BETTER.
BECAUSE IN TRUTH, THIS IS SIMPLY THEIR NATURE, AND THEY HAVE NO REAL WILL TO INVADE.
THE OTHER WORLD HAS ALWAYS BEEN CONNECTED TO THIS WORLD.
EVEN ITS "RESIDENTS" CALL IT THE "OTHER SIDE" AND ARE CONSTANTLY SEEKING TO BE CONNECTED TO THIS WORLD.

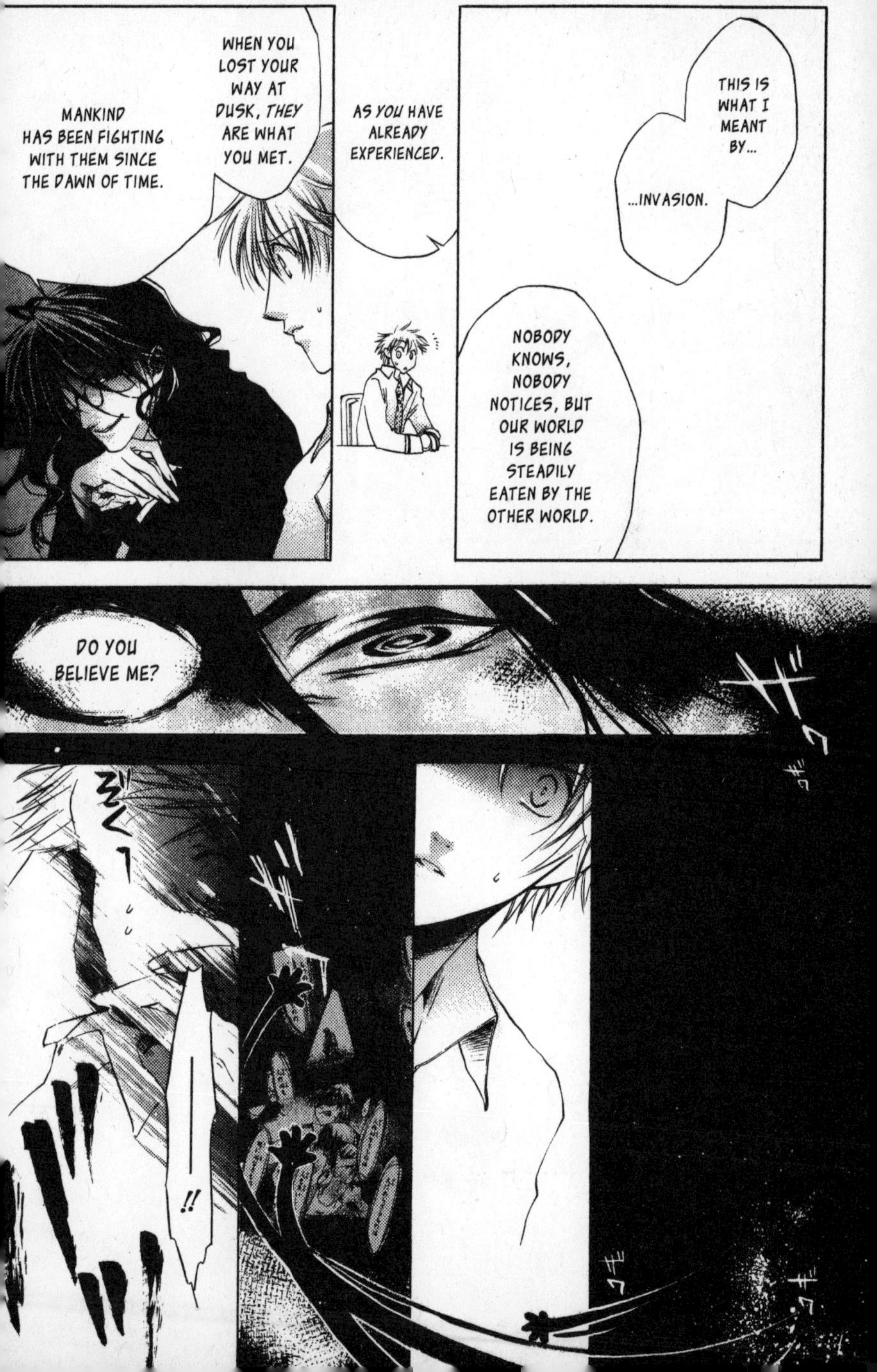
THIS IS WHAT I MEANT BY...
...INVASION.
NOBODY KNOWS, NOBODY NOTICES, BUT OUR WORLD IS BEING STEADILY EATEN BY THE OTHER WORLD.
AS YOU HAVE ALREADY EXPERIENCED.
WHEN YOU LOST YOUR WAY AT DUSK, THEY ARE WHAT YOU MET.
MANKIND HAS BEEN FIGHTING WITH THEM SINCE THE DAWN OF TIME.
DO YOU BELIEVE ME?
!!

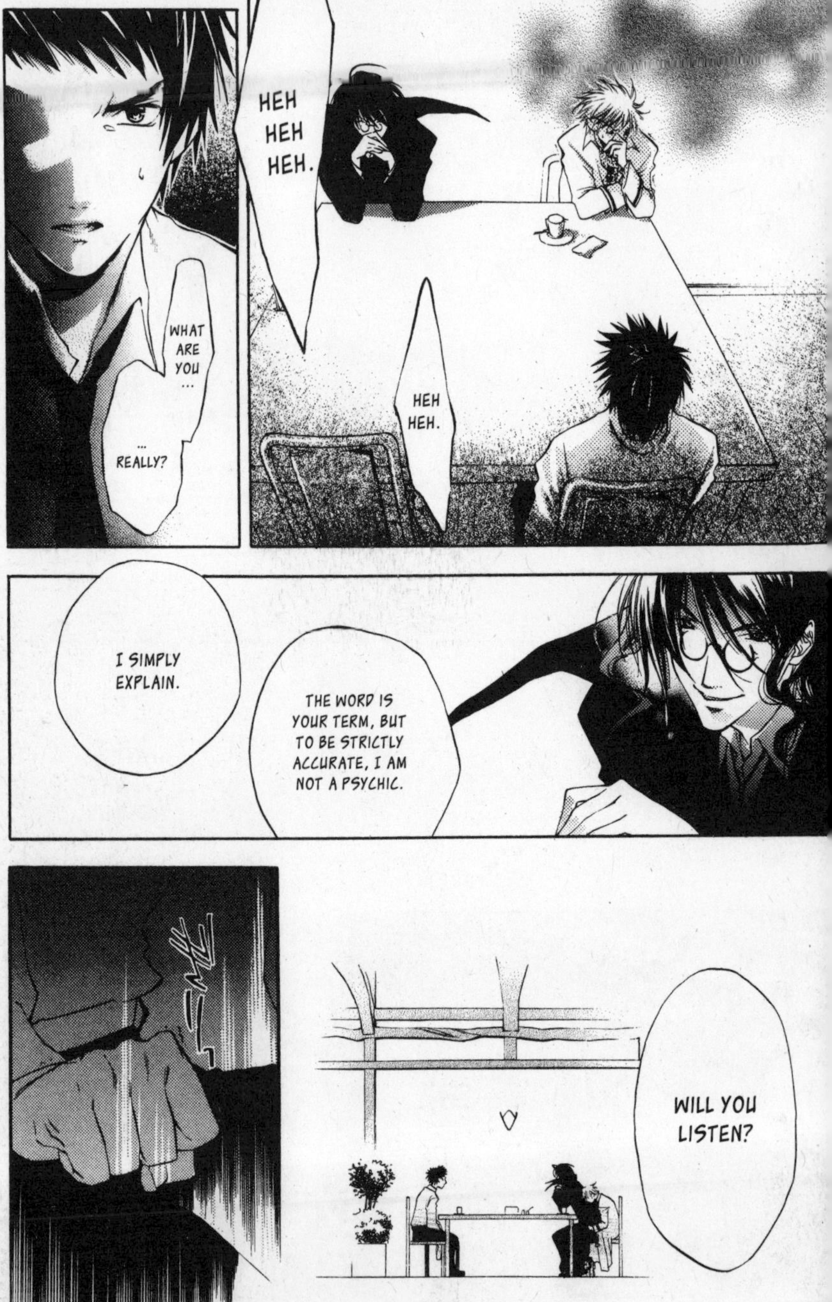
HEH HEH HEH.
HEH HEH.
WHAT ARE YOU ... ... REALLY?
THE WORD IS YOUR TERM, BUT TO BE STRICTLY ACCURATE, I AM NOT A PSYCHIC.
I SIMPLY EXPLAIN.
WILL YOU LISTEN?

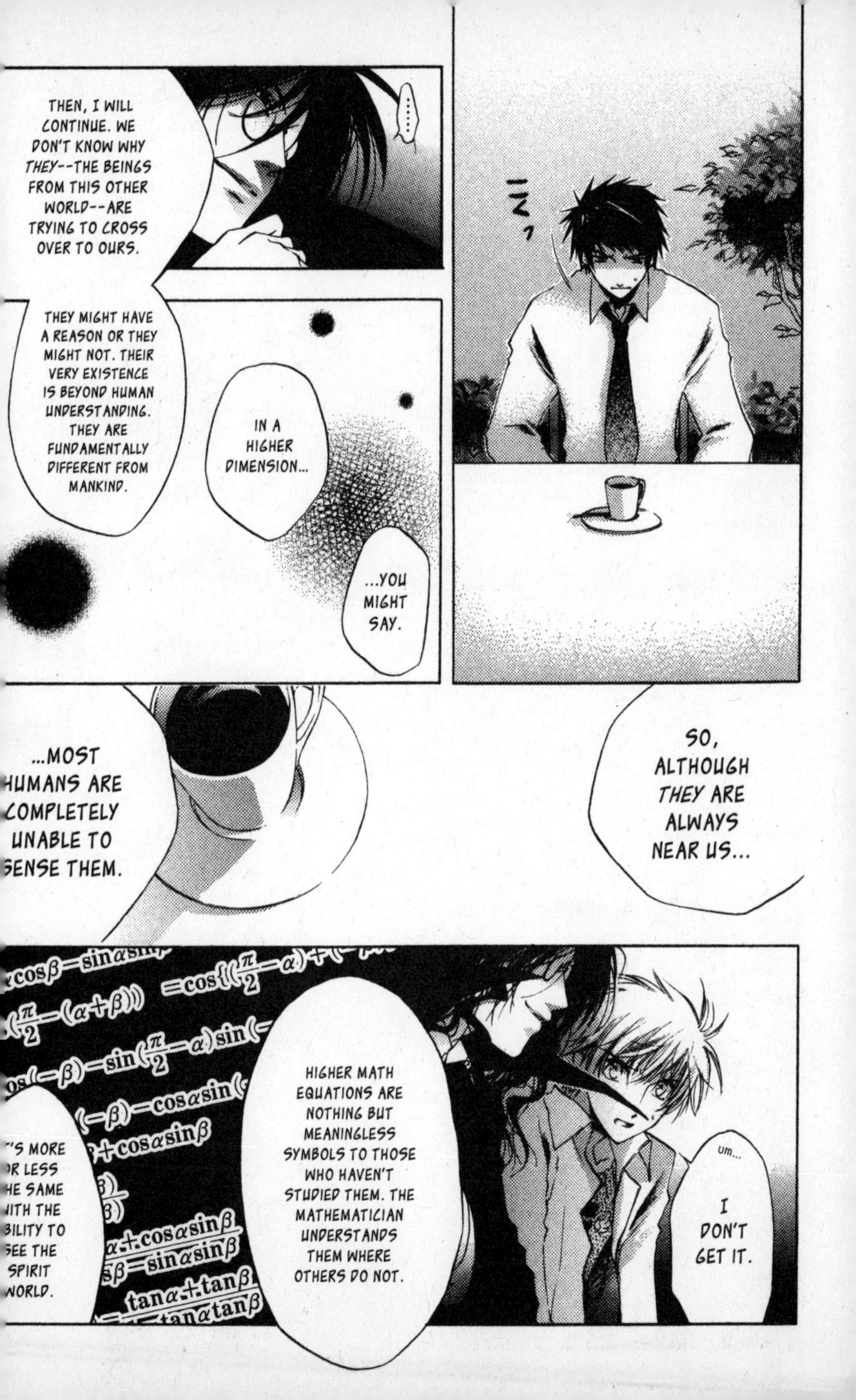
......
THEN, I WILL CONTINUE. WE DON'T KNOW WHY *THEY*--THE BEINGS FROM THIS OTHER WORLD--ARE TRYING TO CROSS OVER TO OURS.
THEY MIGHT HAVE A REASON OR THEY MIGHT NOT. THEIR VERY EXISTENCE IS BEYOND HUMAN UNDERSTANDING. THEY ARE FUNDAMENTALLY DIFFERENT FROM MANKIND.
IN A HIGHER DIMENSION...
...YOU MIGHT SAY.
SO, ALTHOUGH *THEY* ARE ALWAYS NEAR US...
...MOST HUMANS ARE COMPLETELY UNABLE TO SENSE THEM.
UM...
I DON'T GET IT.
HIGHER MATH EQUATIONS ARE NOTHING BUT MEANINGLESS SYMBOLS TO THOSE WHO HAVEN'T STUDIED THEM. THE MATHEMATICIAN UNDERSTANDS THEM WHERE OTHERS DO NOT.
'S MORE R LESS HE SAME ITH THE BILITY TO EE THE SPIRIT WORLD.

IMAGINE TWO PEOPLE LOOKING AT THE SAME SCENE. ONLY ONE OF THEM IS TUNED IN TO THE OTHER SIDE.
LIKE A MATHEMATICIAN ABLE TO MAKE SENSE OF A COMPLICATED QUESTION, THE TUNED PERSON SEES SOMETHING A NORMAL PERSON DOESN'T.
No sixth sense
A
Person A sees a normal summer day.
With sixth sense
B
Person B sees a normal summer day and something out of place.
NOW
THIS APTITUDE CAN BE RATHER UNFORTUNATE, AS YOU WELL KNOW.
SO YOU ARE ONE OF THESE UNFORTUNATE PEOPLE?
......

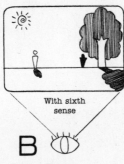

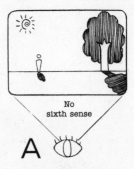

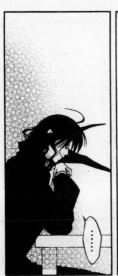

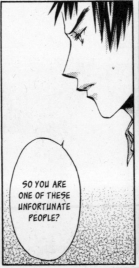

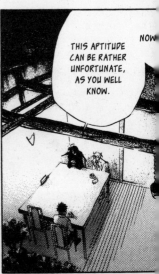

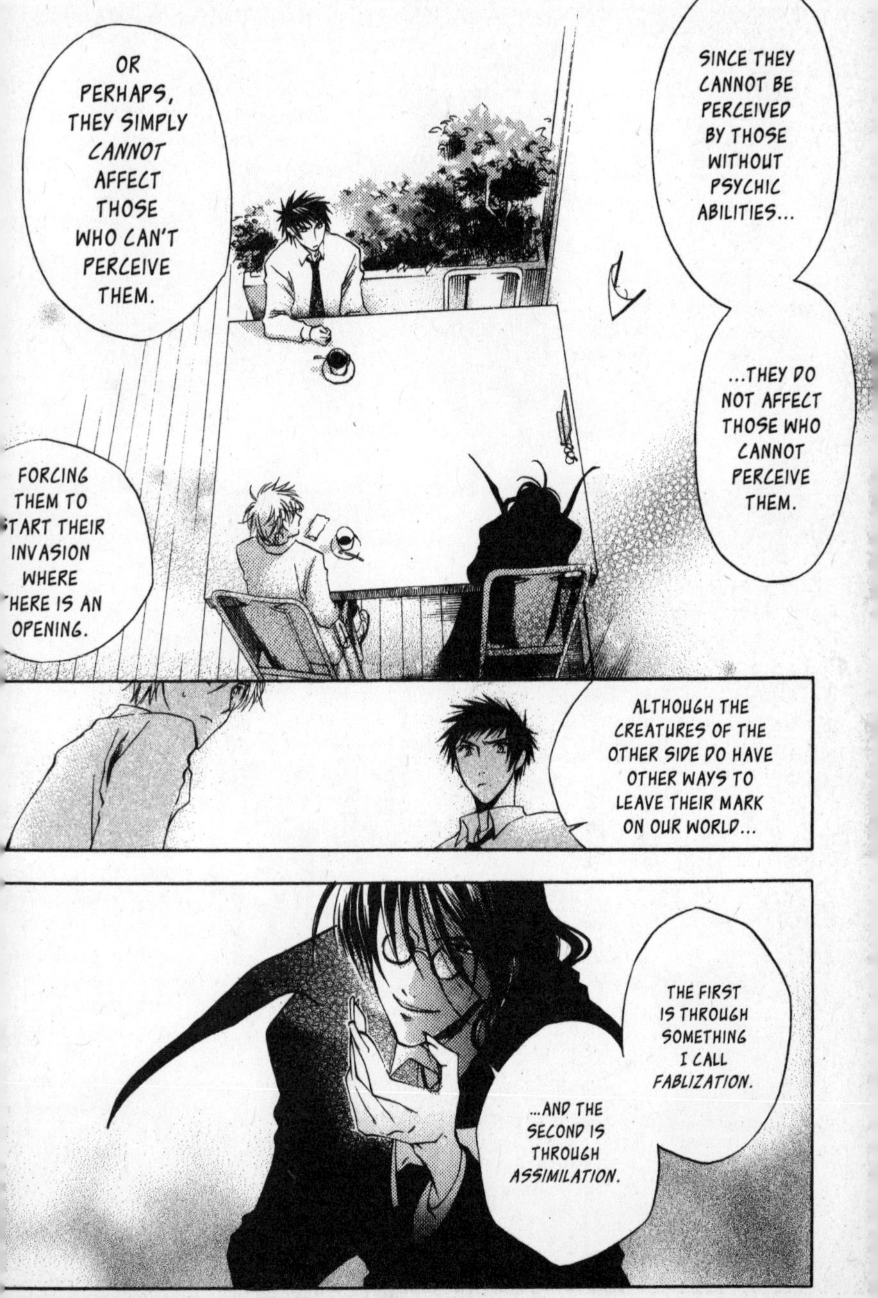
SINCE THEY CANNOT BE PERCEIVED BY THOSE WITHOUT PSYCHIC ABILITIES...
...THEY DO NOT AFFECT THOSE WHO CANNOT PERCEIVE THEM.
OR PERHAPS, THEY SIMPLY *CANNOT* AFFECT THOSE WHO CAN'T PERCEIVE THEM.
FORCING THEM TO TART THEIR INVASION WHERE HERE IS AN OPENING.
ALTHOUGH THE CREATURES OF THE OTHER SIDE DO HAVE OTHER WAYS TO LEAVE THEIR MARK ON OUR WORLD...
THE FIRST IS THROUGH SOMETHING I CALL *FABLIZATION*.
...AND THE SECOND IS THROUGH *ASSIMILATION*.

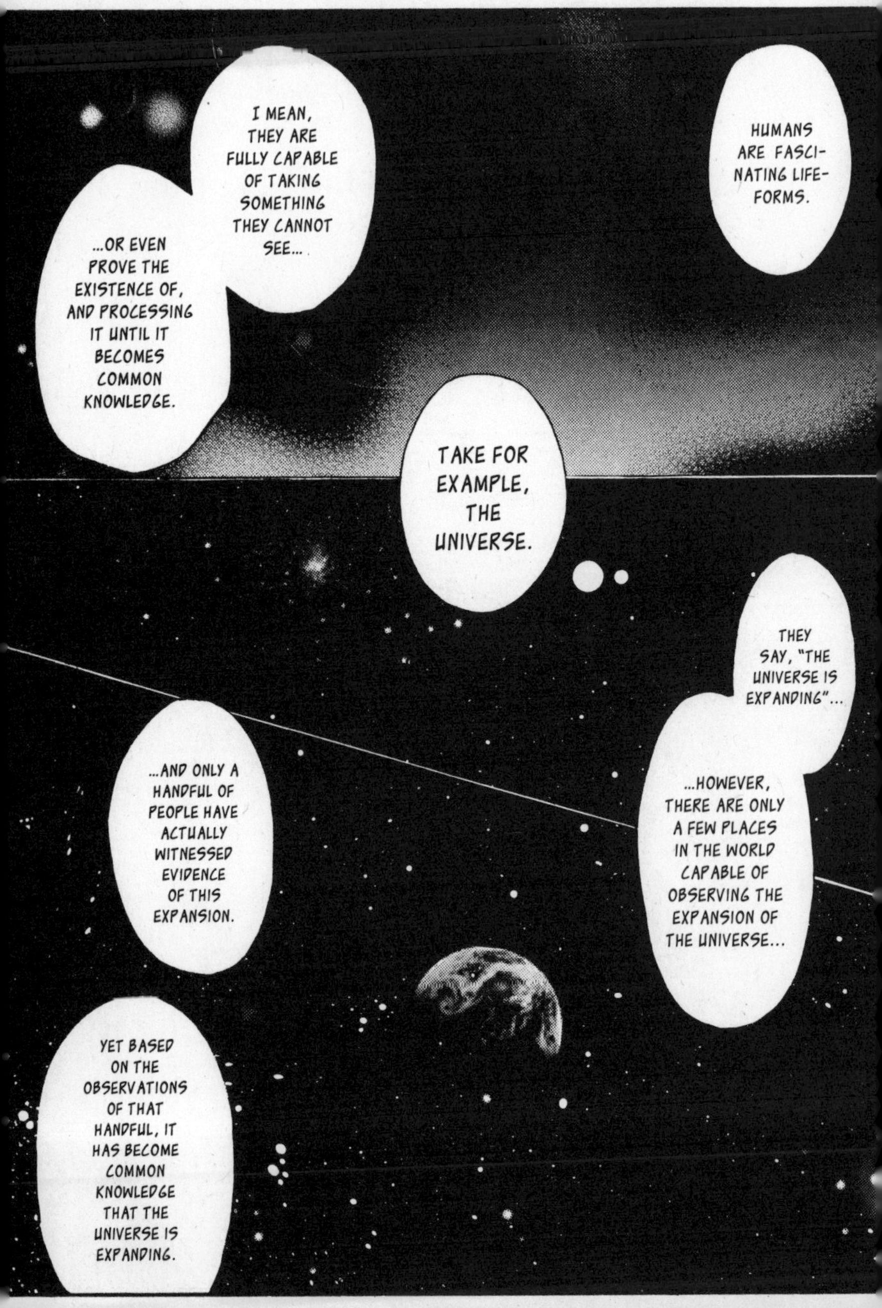
HUMANS ARE FASCINATING LIFE-FORMS.
I MEAN, THEY ARE FULLY CAPABLE OF TAKING SOMETHING THEY CANNOT SEE...
...OR EVEN PROVE THE EXISTENCE OF, AND PROCESSING IT UNTIL IT BECOMES COMMON KNOWLEDGE.
TAKE FOR EXAMPLE, THE UNIVERSE.
THEY SAY, "THE UNIVERSE IS EXPANDING"...
...HOWEVER, THERE ARE ONLY A FEW PLACES IN THE WORLD CAPABLE OF OBSERVING THE EXPANSION OF THE UNIVERSE...
...AND ONLY A HANDFUL OF PEOPLE HAVE ACTUALLY WITNESSED EVIDENCE OF THIS EXPANSION.
YET BASED ON THE OBSERVATIONS OF THAT HANDFUL, IT HAS BECOME COMMON KNOWLEDGE THAT THE UNIVERSE IS EXPANDING.

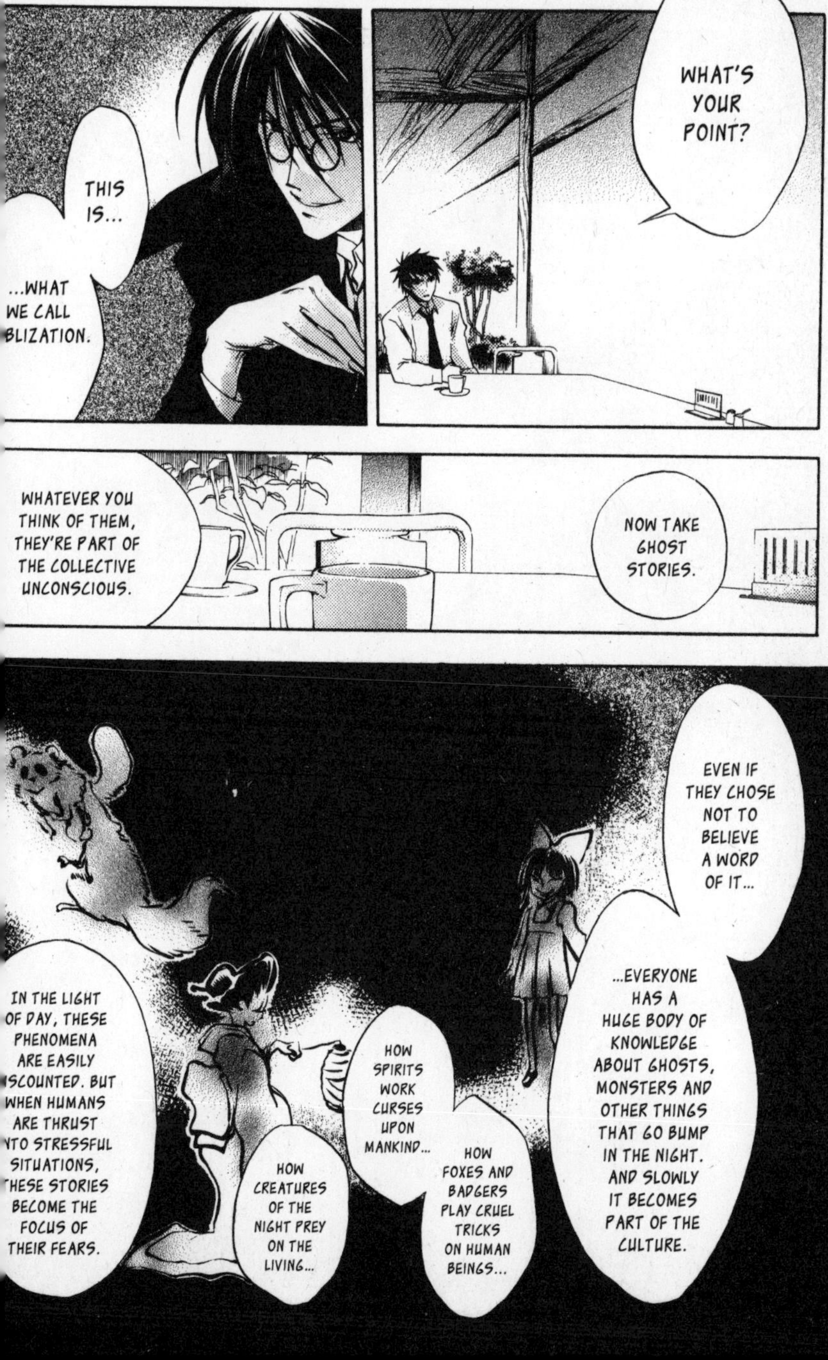
WHAT'S YOUR POINT?
THIS IS...
...WHAT WE CALL BLIZATION.
NOW TAKE GHOST STORIES.
WHATEVER YOU THINK OF THEM, THEY'RE PART OF THE COLLECTIVE UNCONSCIOUS.
EVEN IF THEY CHOSE NOT TO BELIEVE A WORD OF IT...
...EVERYONE HAS A HUGE BODY OF KNOWLEDGE ABOUT GHOSTS, MONSTERS AND OTHER THINGS THAT GO BUMP IN THE NIGHT. AND SLOWLY IT BECOMES PART OF THE CULTURE.
HOW FOXES AND BADGERS PLAY CRUEL TRICKS ON HUMAN BEINGS...
HOW SPIRITS WORK CURSES UPON MANKIND...
HOW CREATURES OF THE NIGHT PREY ON THE LIVING...
IN THE LIGHT OF DAY, THESE PHENOMENA ARE EASILY SCOUNTED. BUT WHEN HUMANS ARE THRUST NTO STRESSFUL SITUATIONS, HESE STORIES BECOME THE FOCUS OF THEIR FEARS.

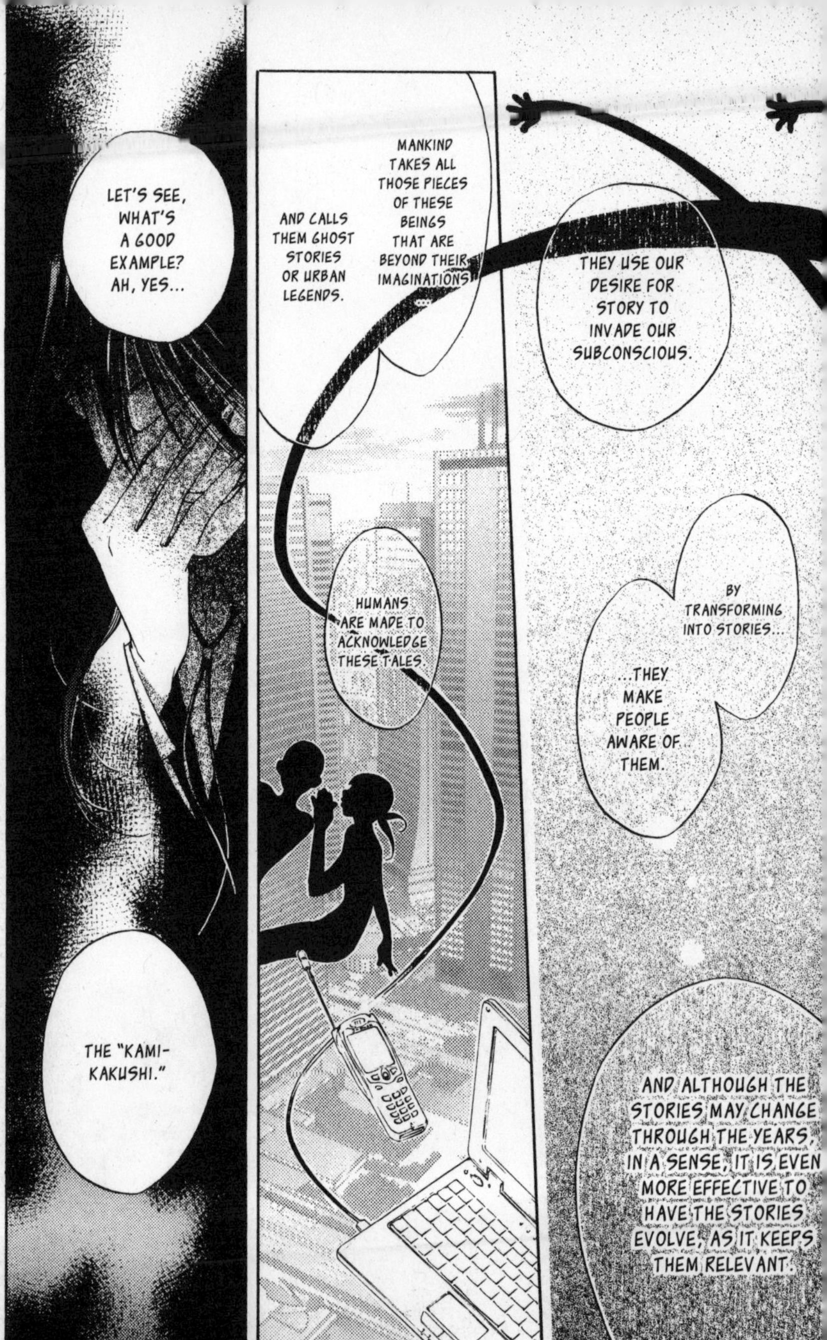
THEY USE OUR DESIRE FOR STORY TO INVADE OUR SUBCONSCIOUS.
BY TRANSFORMING INTO STORIES...
...THEY MAKE PEOPLE AWARE OF THEM.
AND ALTHOUGH THE STORIES MAY CHANGE THROUGH THE YEARS, IN A SENSE, IT IS EVEN MORE EFFECTIVE TO HAVE THE STORIES EVOLVE, AS IT KEEPS THEM RELEVANT.
MANKIND TAKES ALL THOSE PIECES OF THESE BEINGS THAT ARE BEYOND THEIR IMAGINATIONS
AND CALLS THEM GHOST STORIES OR URBAN LEGENDS.
HUMANS ARE MADE TO ACKNOWLEDGE THESE TALES.
LET'S SEE, WHAT'S A GOOD EXAMPLE? AH, YES...
THE "KAMI-KAKUSHI."

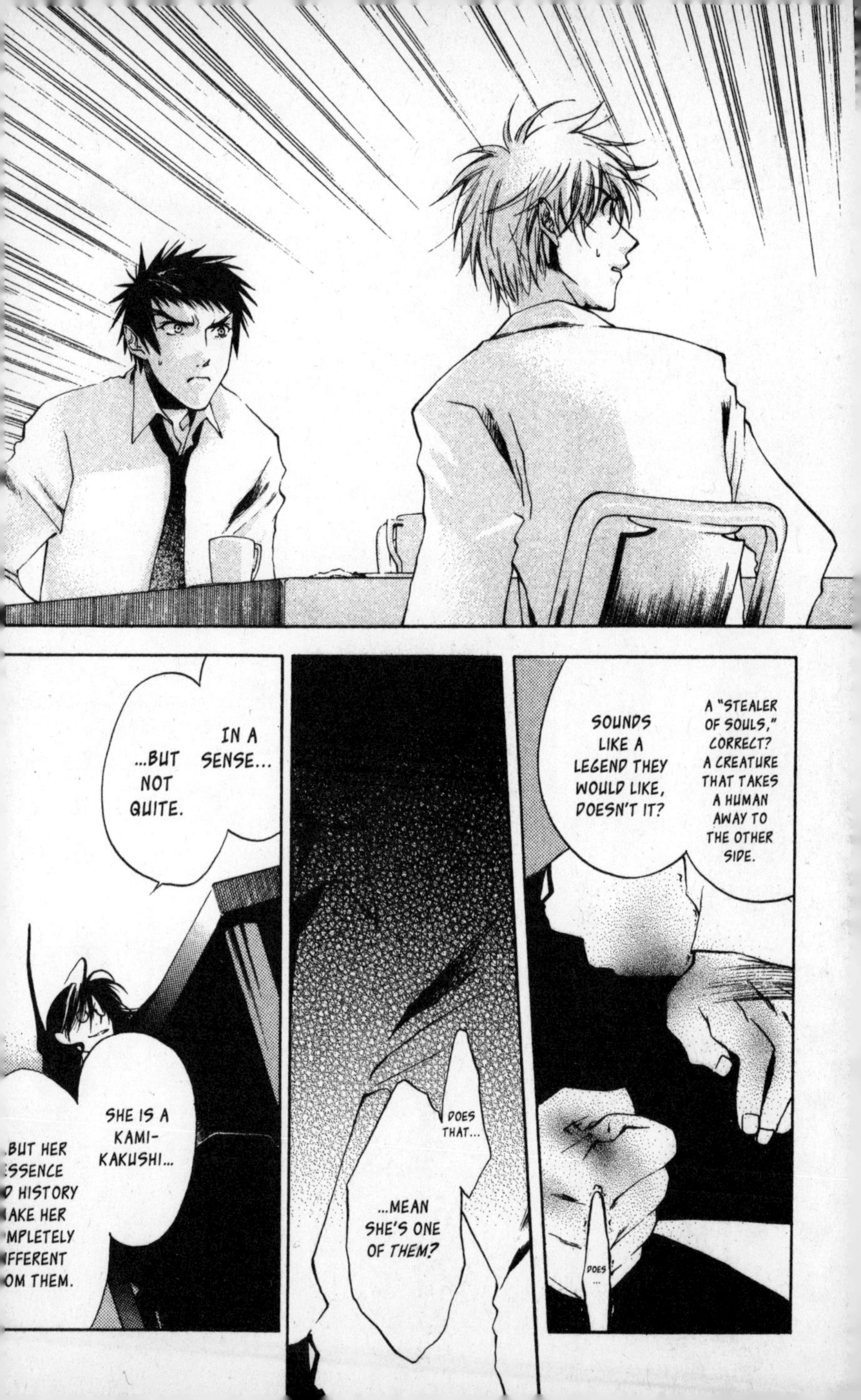
A "STEALER OF SOULS," CORRECT? A CREATURE THAT TAKES A HUMAN AWAY TO THE OTHER SIDE.
SOUNDS LIKE A LEGEND THEY WOULD LIKE, DOESN'T IT?
DOES...
DOES THAT...
...MEAN SHE'S ONE OF *THEM?*
IN A SENSE...
...BUT NOT QUITE.
SHE IS A KAMI-KAKUSHI...
BUT HER SSENCE D HISTORY AKE HER MPLETELY FFERENT OM THEM.

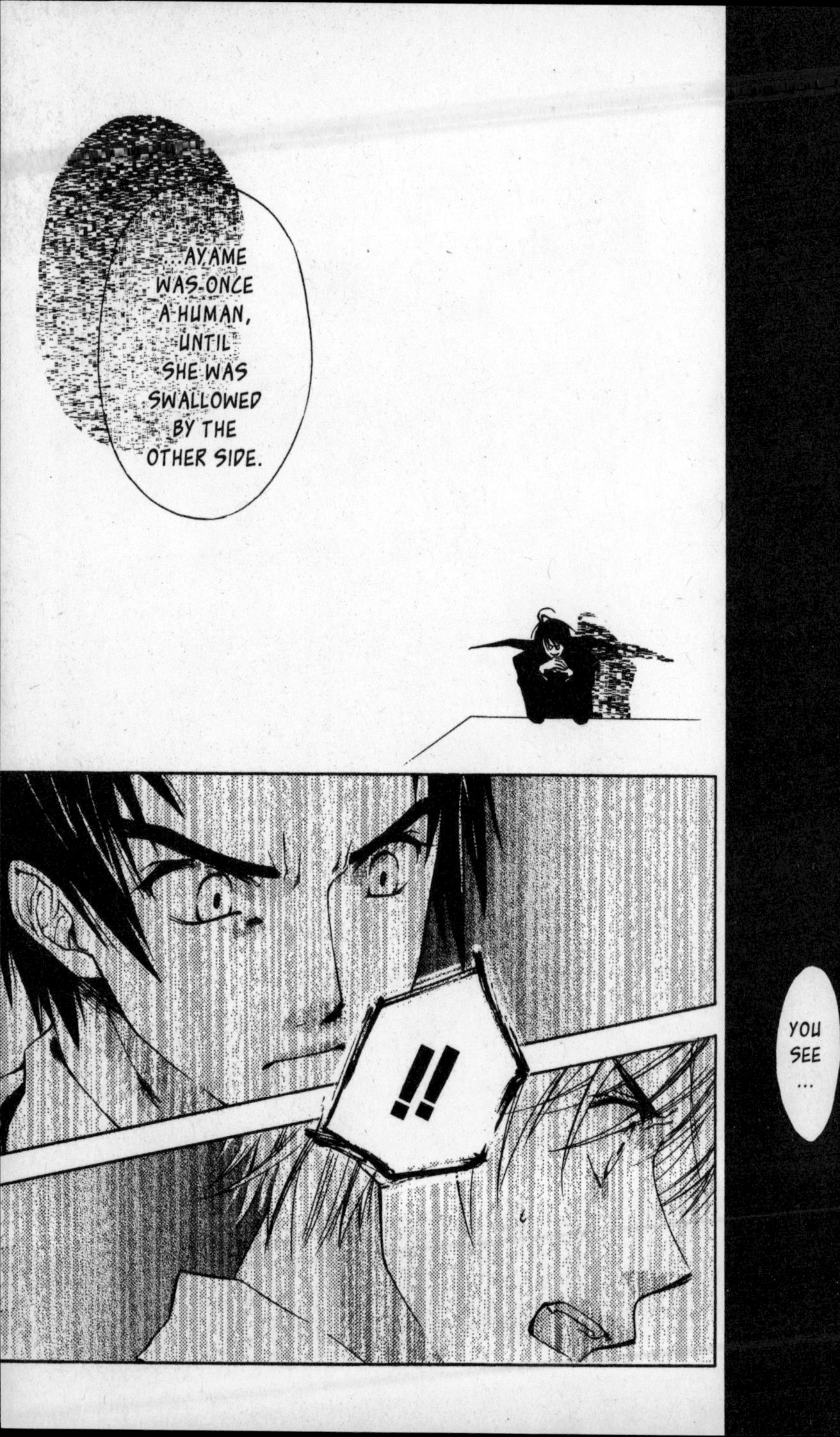
YOU SEE ...
...AYAME WAS ONCE A HUMAN, UNTIL SHE WAS SWALLOWED BY THE OTHER SIDE.
!!

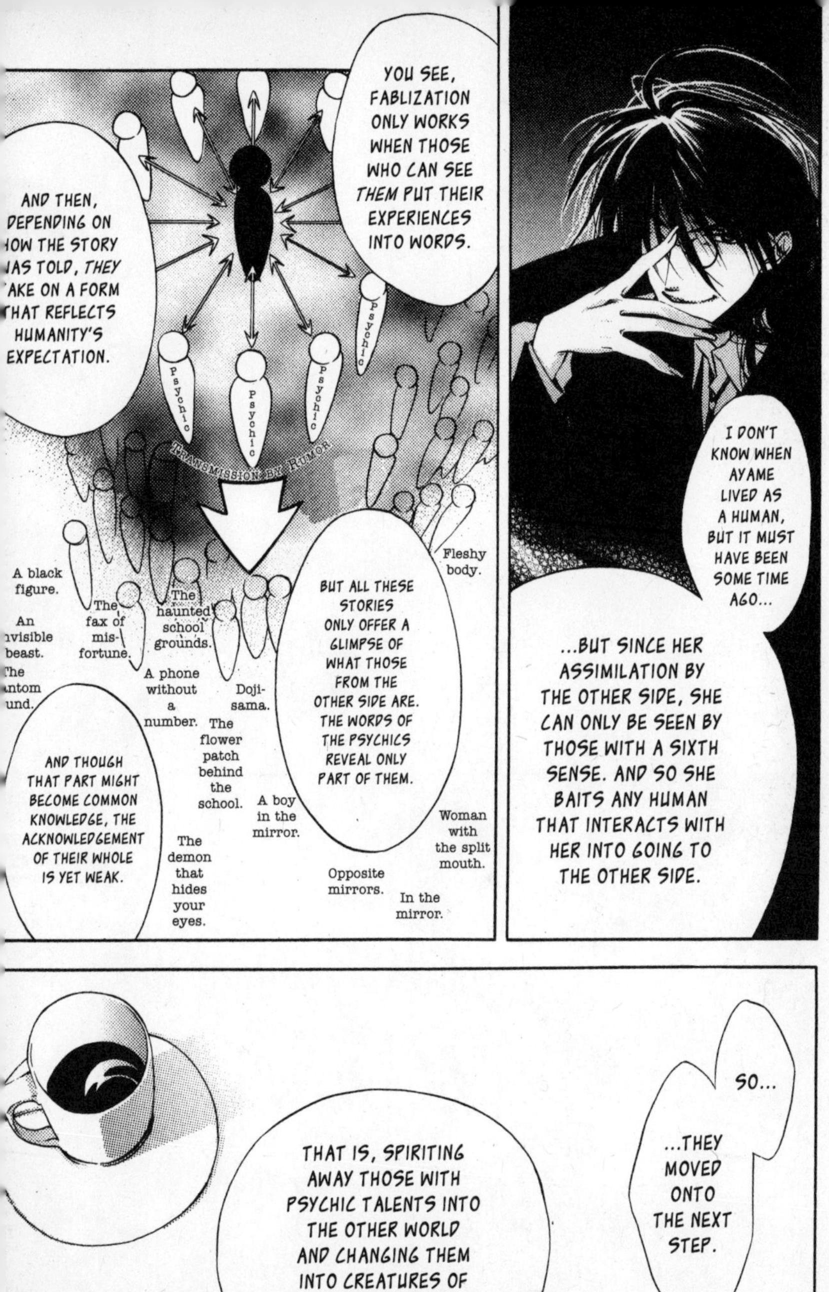
I DON'T KNOW WHEN AYAME LIVED AS A HUMAN, BUT IT MUST HAVE BEEN SOME TIME AGO...
...BUT SINCE HER ASSIMILATION BY THE OTHER SIDE, SHE CAN ONLY BE SEEN BY THOSE WITH A SIXTH SENSE. AND SO SHE BAITS ANY HUMAN THAT INTERACTS WITH HER INTO GOING TO THE OTHER SIDE.
YOU SEE, FABLIZATION ONLY WORKS WHEN THOSE WHO CAN SEE *THEM* PUT THEIR EXPERIENCES INTO WORDS.
Psychic
Psychic
Psychic
Psychic
TRANSMISSION BY RUMOR
Fleshy body.
A black figure.
The fax of mis-fortune.
The haunted school grounds.
A phone without a number.
Doji-sama.
The flower patch behind the school.
A boy in the mirror.
Woman with the split mouth.
The demon that hides your eyes.
Opposite mirrors.
In the mirror.
BUT ALL THESE STORIES ONLY OFFER A GLIMPSE OF WHAT THOSE FROM THE OTHER SIDE ARE. THE WORDS OF THE PSYCHICS REVEAL ONLY PART OF THEM.
AND THOUGH THAT PART MIGHT BECOME COMMON KNOWLEDGE, THE ACKNOWLEDGEMENT OF THEIR WHOLE IS YET WEAK.
SO...
...THEY MOVED ONTO THE NEXT STEP.
THAT IS, SPIRITING AWAY THOSE WITH PSYCHIC TALENTS INTO THE OTHER WORLD AND CHANGING THEM INTO CREATURES OF THE OTHER SIDE.

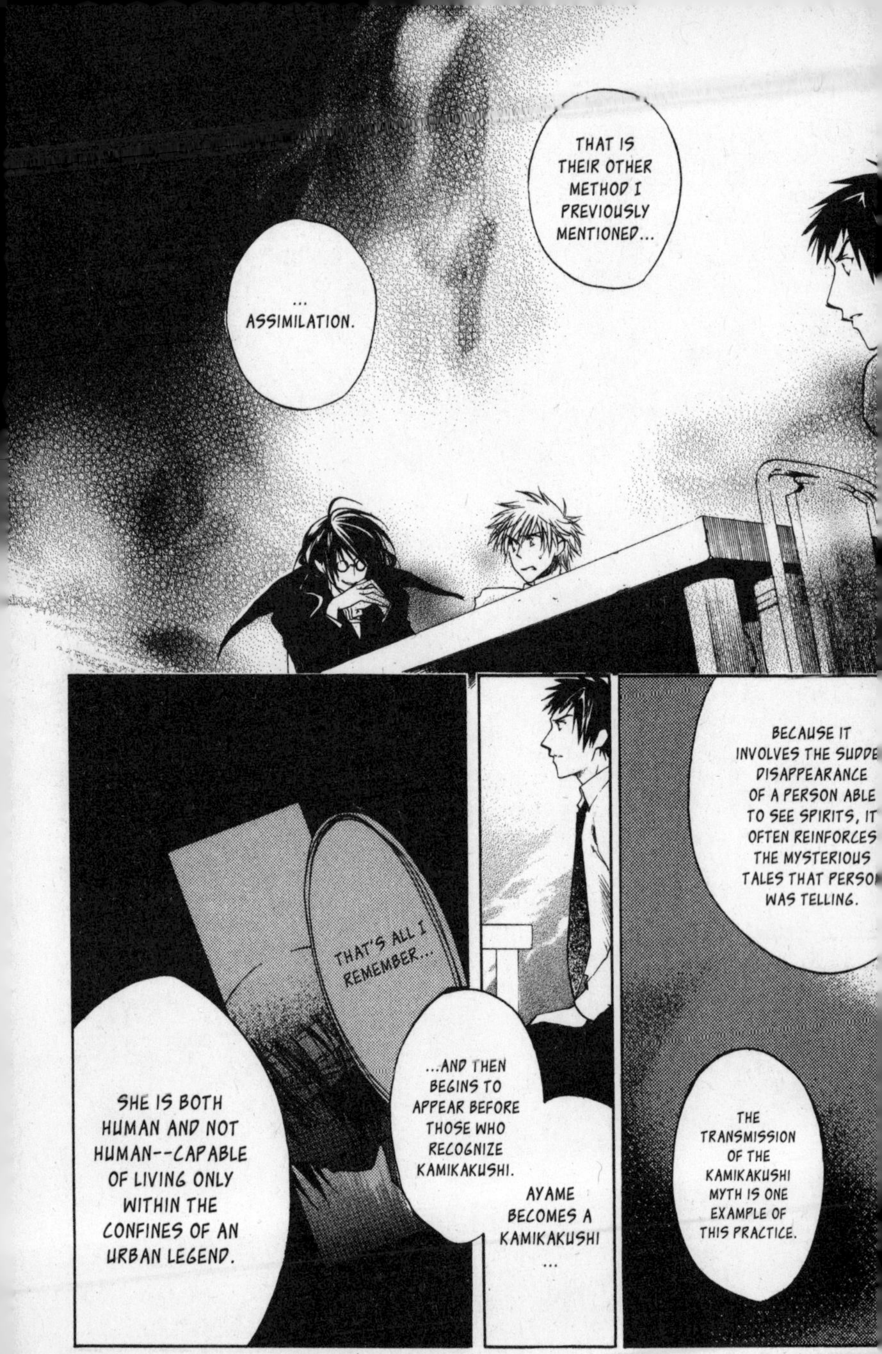
THAT IS THEIR OTHER METHOD I PREVIOUSLY MENTIONED...
... ASSIMILATION.
BECAUSE IT INVOLVES THE SUDDE DISAPPEARANCE OF A PERSON ABLE TO SEE SPIRITS, IT OFTEN REINFORCES THE MYSTERIOUS TALES THAT PERSO WAS TELLING.
THE TRANSMISSION OF THE KAMIKAKUSHI MYTH IS ONE EXAMPLE OF THIS PRACTICE.
AYAME BECOMES A KAMIKAKUSHI ...
...AND THEN BEGINS TO APPEAR BEFORE THOSE WHO RECOGNIZE KAMIKAKUSHI.
THAT'S ALL I REMEMBER...
SHE IS BOTH HUMAN AND NOT HUMAN--CAPABLE OF LIVING ONLY WITHIN THE CONFINES OF AN URBAN LEGEND.

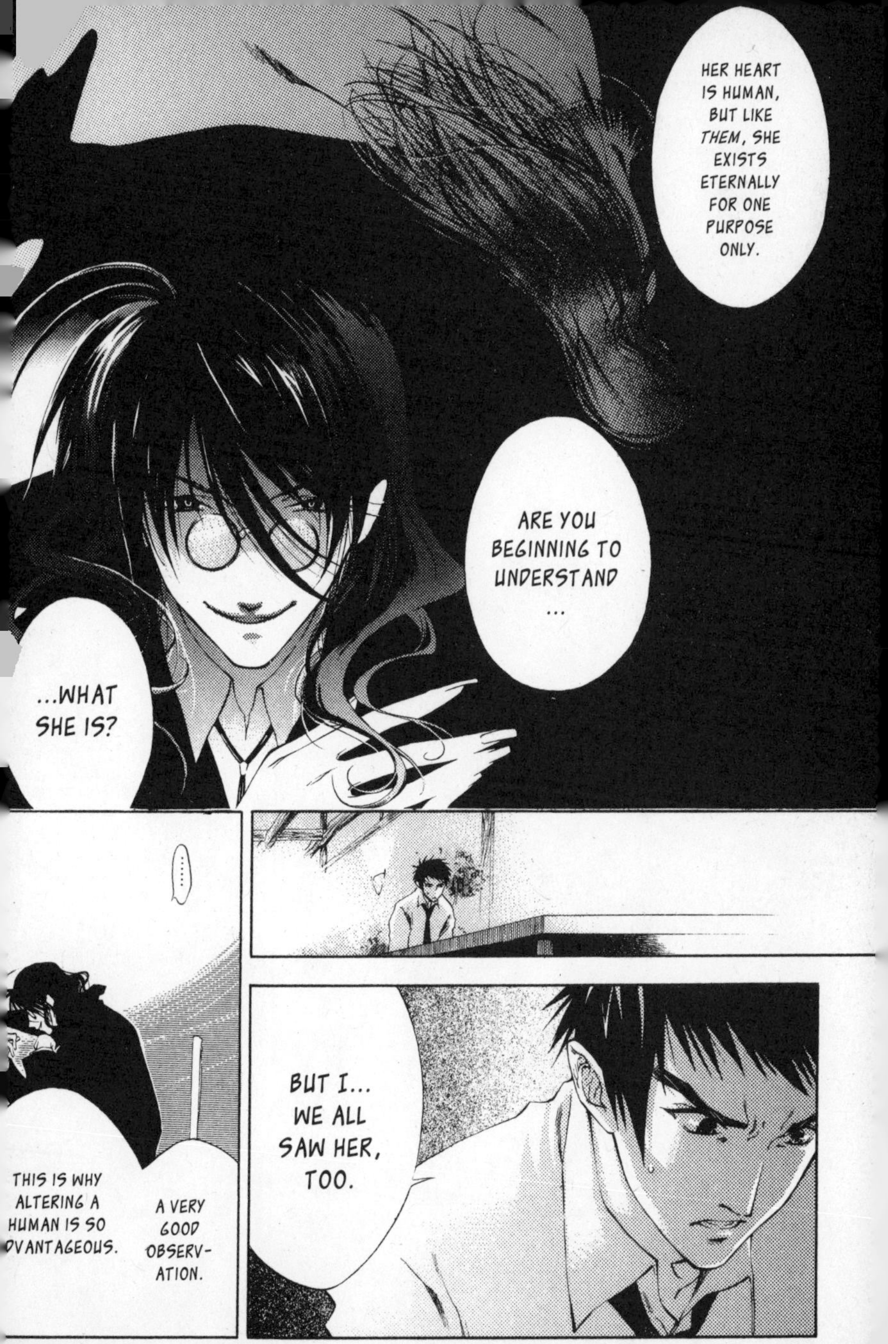
HER HEART IS HUMAN, BUT LIKE *THEM*, SHE EXISTS ETERNALLY FOR ONE PURPOSE ONLY.
ARE YOU BEGINNING TO UNDERSTAND ...
...WHAT SHE IS?
BUT I... WE ALL SAW HER, TOO.
.....
A VERY GOOD OBSERVATION.
THIS IS WHY ALTERING A HUMAN IS SO DVANTAGEOUS.

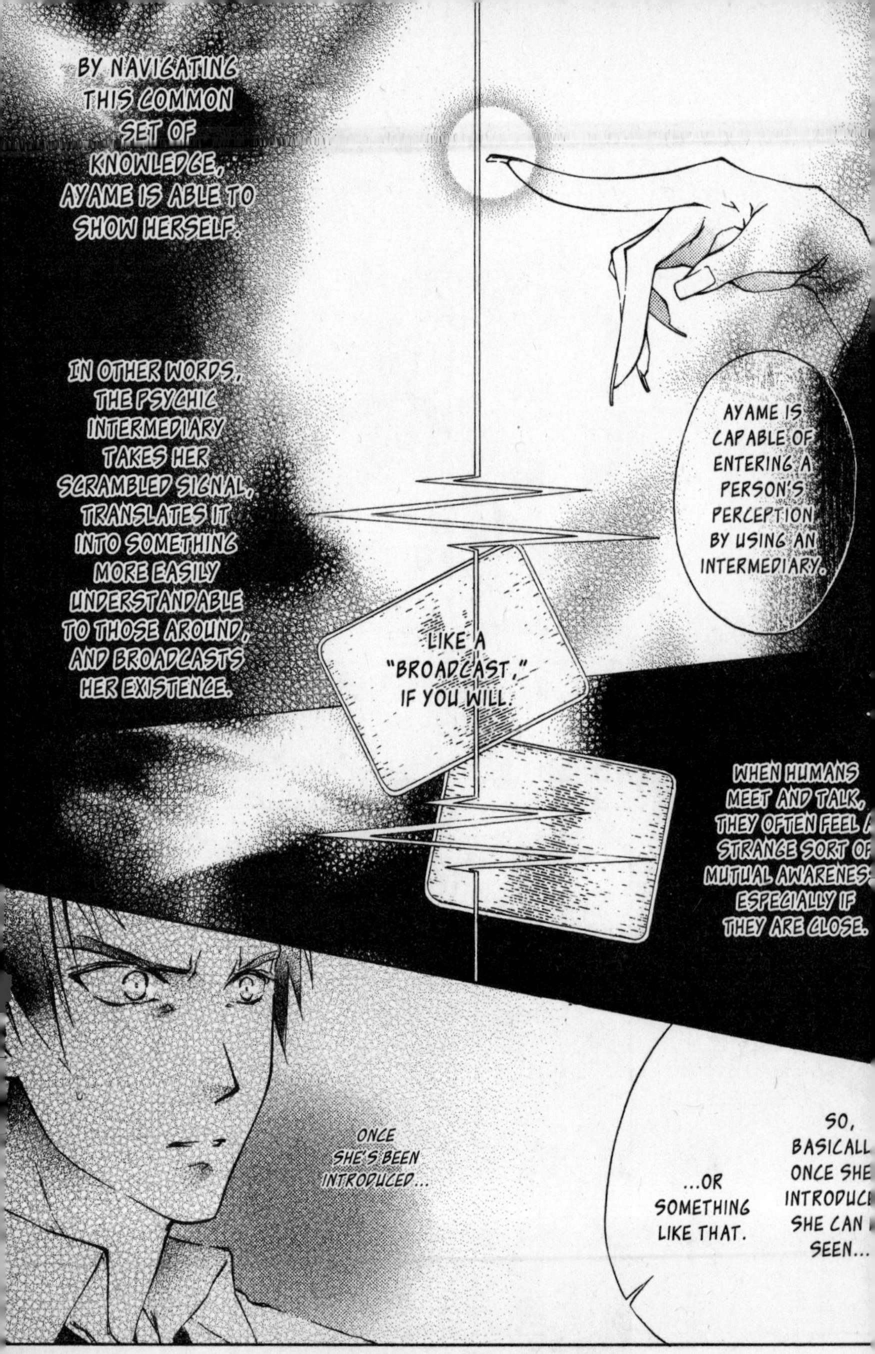
AYAME IS CAPABLE OF ENTERING A PERSON'S PERCEPTION BY USING AN INTERMEDIARY.
LIKE A "BROADCAST," IF YOU WILL.
IN OTHER WORDS, THE PSYCHIC INTERMEDIARY TAKES HER SCRAMBLED SIGNAL, TRANSLATES IT INTO SOMETHING MORE EASILY UNDERSTANDABLE TO THOSE AROUND, AND BROADCASTS HER EXISTENCE.
WHEN HUMANS MEET AND TALK, THEY OFTEN FEEL A STRANGE SORT OF MUTUAL AWARENES ESPECIALLY IF THEY ARE CLOSE.
BY NAVIGATING THIS COMMON SET OF KNOWLEDGE, AYAME IS ABLE TO SHOW HERSELF.
SO, BASICALL ONCE SHE INTRODUC SHE CAN SEEN...
...OR SOMETHING LIKE THAT.
ONCE SHE'S BEEN INTRODUCED...

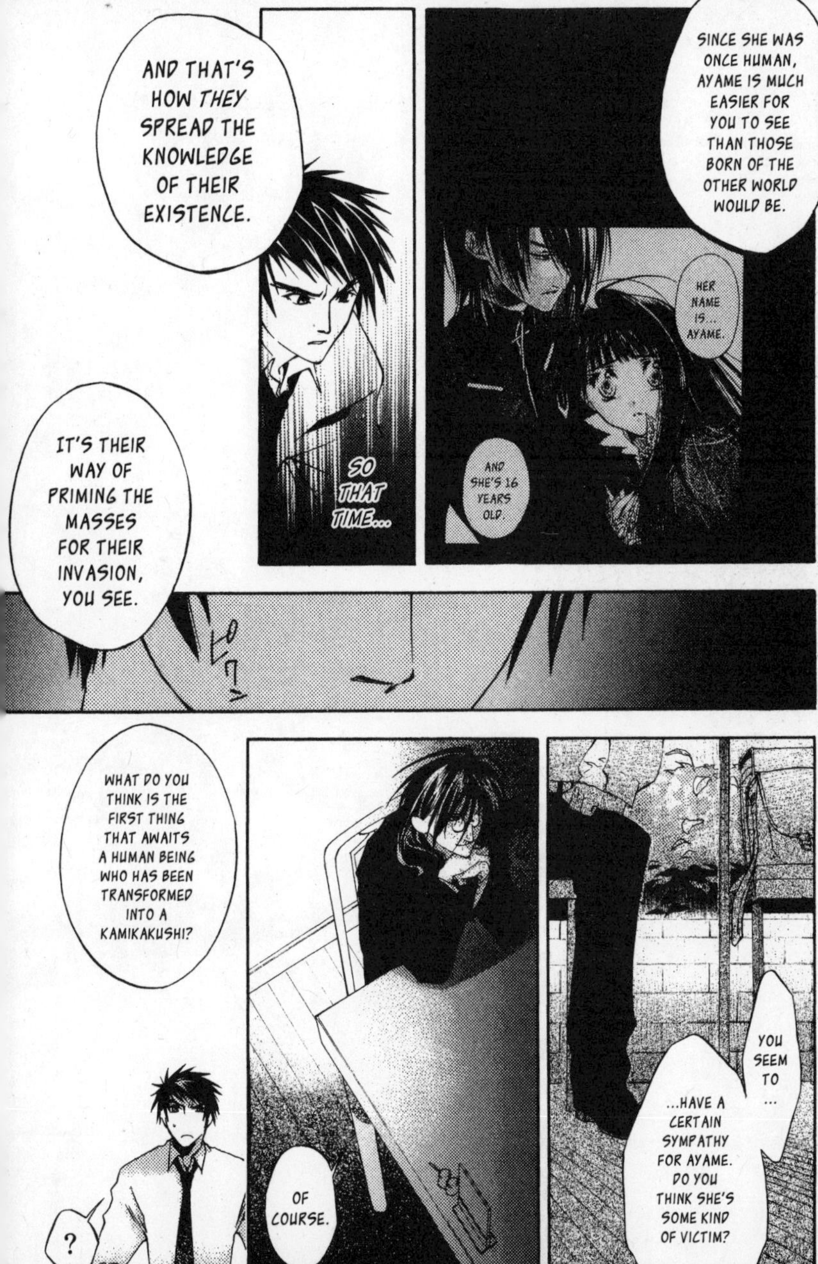
SINCE SHE WAS ONCE HUMAN, AYAME IS MUCH EASIER FOR YOU TO SEE THAN THOSE BORN OF THE OTHER WORLD WOULD BE.
HER NAME IS... AYAME.
AND SHE'S 16 YEARS OLD.
AND THAT'S HOW *THEY* SPREAD THE KNOWLEDGE OF THEIR EXISTENCE.
SO THAT TIME...
IT'S THEIR WAY OF PRIMING THE MASSES FOR THEIR INVASION, YOU SEE.
YOU SEEM TO ...
...HAVE A CERTAIN SYMPATHY FOR AYAME. DO YOU THINK SHE'S SOME KIND OF VICTIM?
OF COURSE.
WHAT DO YOU THINK IS THE FIRST THING THAT AWAITS A HUMAN BEING WHO HAS BEEN TRANSFORMED INTO A KAMIKAKUSHI?
?

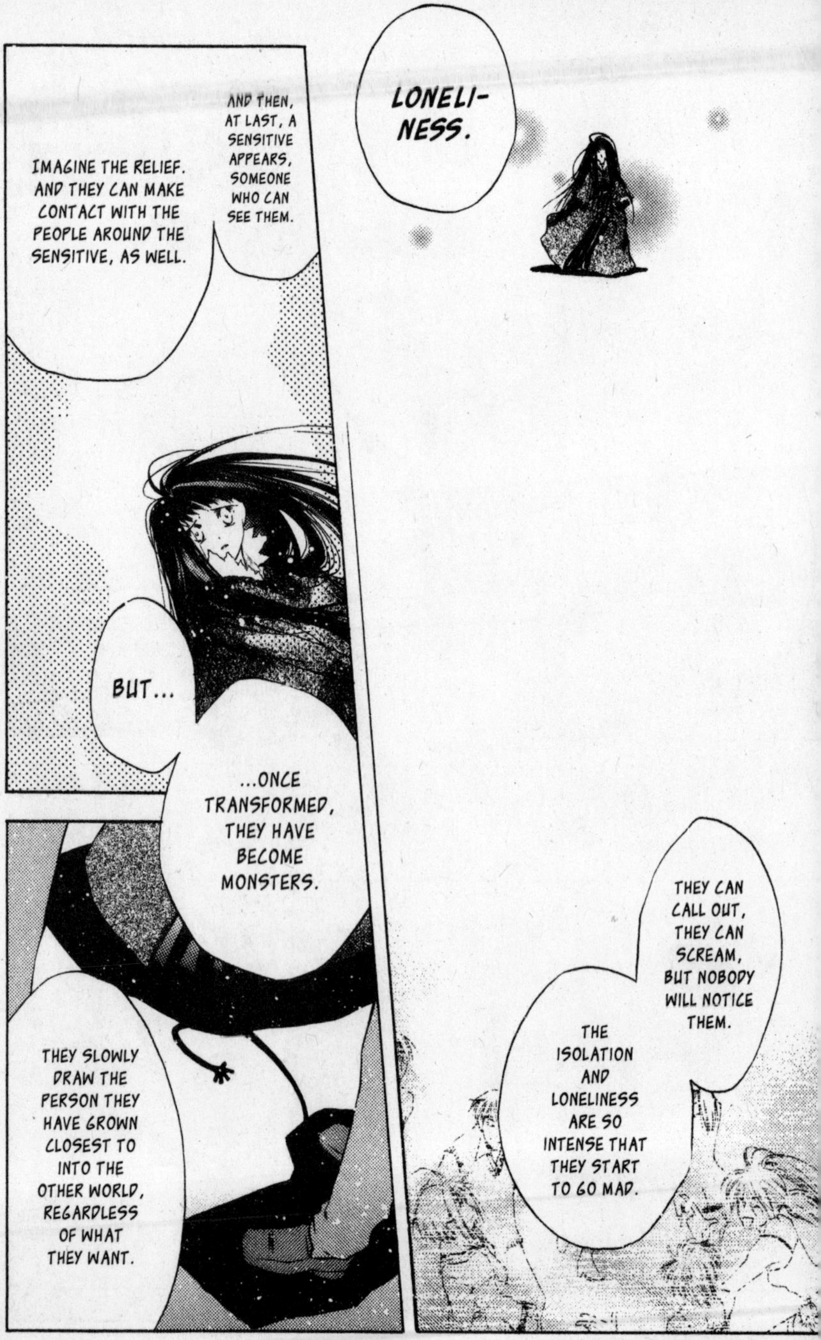
LONELI- NESS.
THEY CAN CALL OUT, THEY CAN SCREAM, BUT NOBODY WILL NOTICE THEM.
THE ISOLATION AND LONELINESS ARE SO INTENSE THAT THEY START TO GO MAD.
AND THEN, AT LAST, A SENSITIVE APPEARS, SOMEONE WHO CAN SEE THEM.
IMAGINE THE RELIEF. AND THEY CAN MAKE CONTACT WITH THE PEOPLE AROUND THE SENSITIVE, AS WELL.
BUT...
...ONCE TRANSFORMED, THEY HAVE BECOME MONSTERS.
THEY SLOWLY DRAW THE PERSON THEY HAVE GROWN CLOSEST TO INTO THE OTHER WORLD, REGARDLESS OF WHAT THEY WANT.

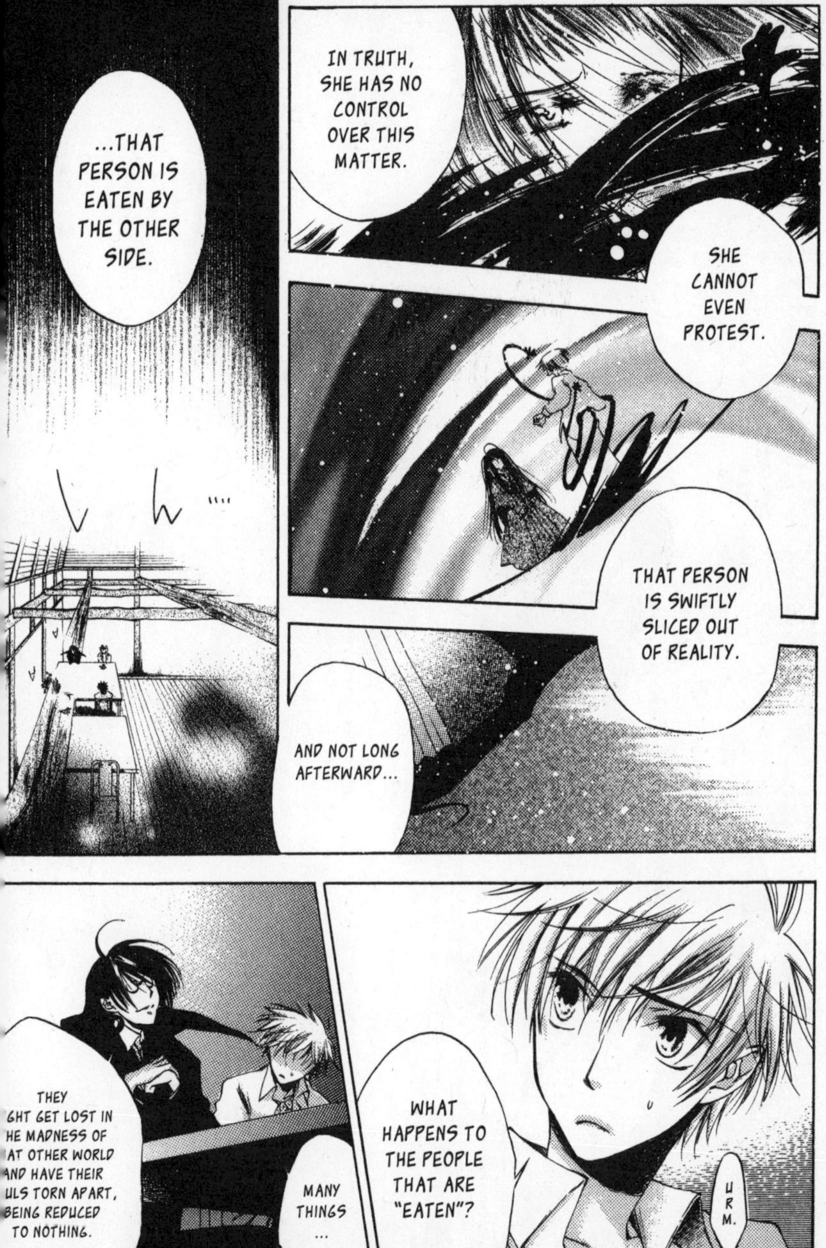
IN TRUTH, SHE HAS NO CONTROL OVER THIS MATTER.
SHE CANNOT EVEN PROTEST.
THAT PERSON IS SWIFTLY SLICED OUT OF REALITY.
AND NOT LONG AFTERWARD...
...THAT PERSON IS EATEN BY THE OTHER SIDE.
URM.
WHAT HAPPENS TO THE PEOPLE THAT ARE "EATEN"?
MANY THINGS ...
THEY GHT GET LOST IN HE MADNESS OF AT OTHER WORLD AND HAVE THEIR ULS TORN APART, BEING REDUCED TO NOTHING.

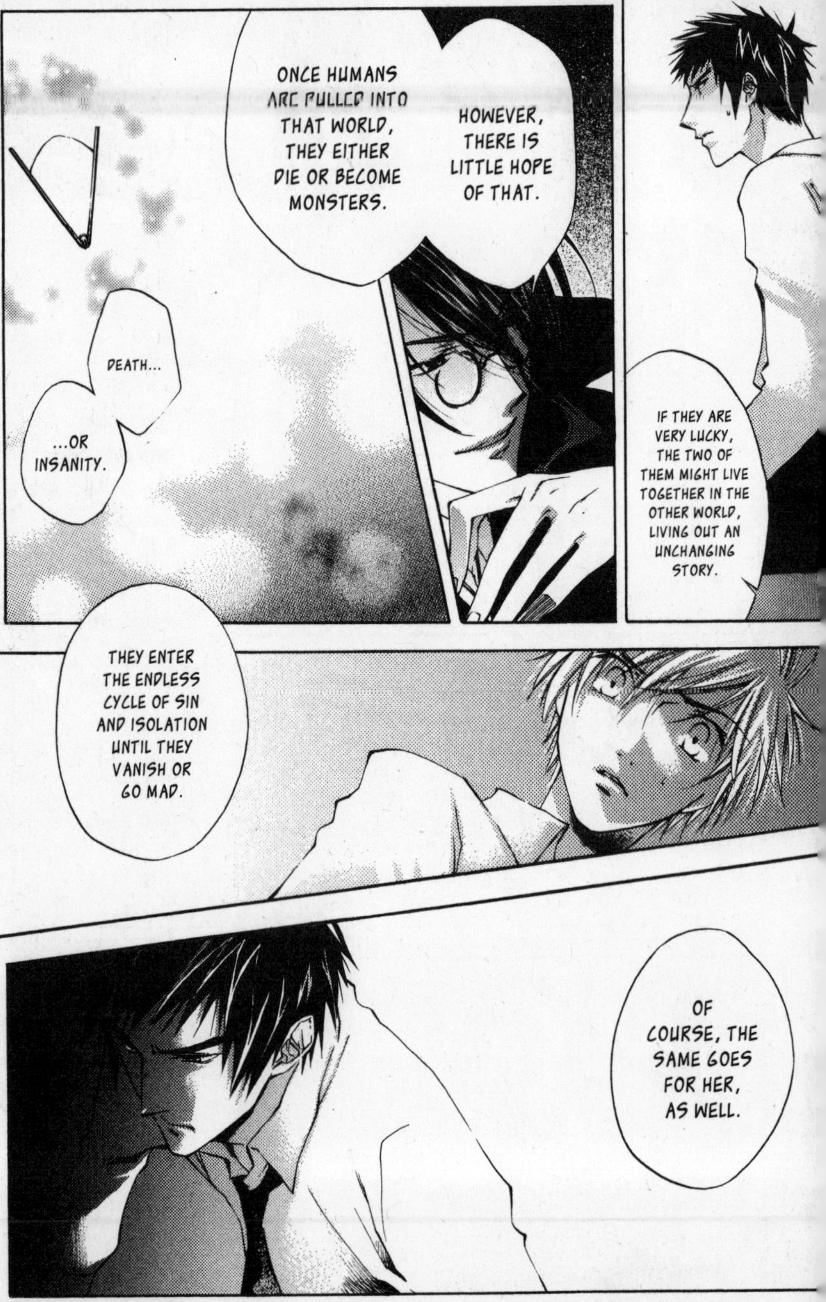

IF THEY ARE VERY LUCKY, THE TWO OF THEM MIGHT LIVE TOGETHER IN THE OTHER WORLD, LIVING OUT AN UNCHANGING STORY.
HOWEVER, THERE IS LITTLE HOPE OF THAT.
ONCE HUMANS ARE PULLED INTO THAT WORLD, THEY EITHER DIE OR BECOME MONSTERS.
DEATH...
...OR INSANITY.
THEY ENTER THE ENDLESS CYCLE OF SIN AND ISOLATION UNTIL THEY VANISH OR GO MAD.
OF COURSE, THE SAME GOES FOR HER, AS WELL.

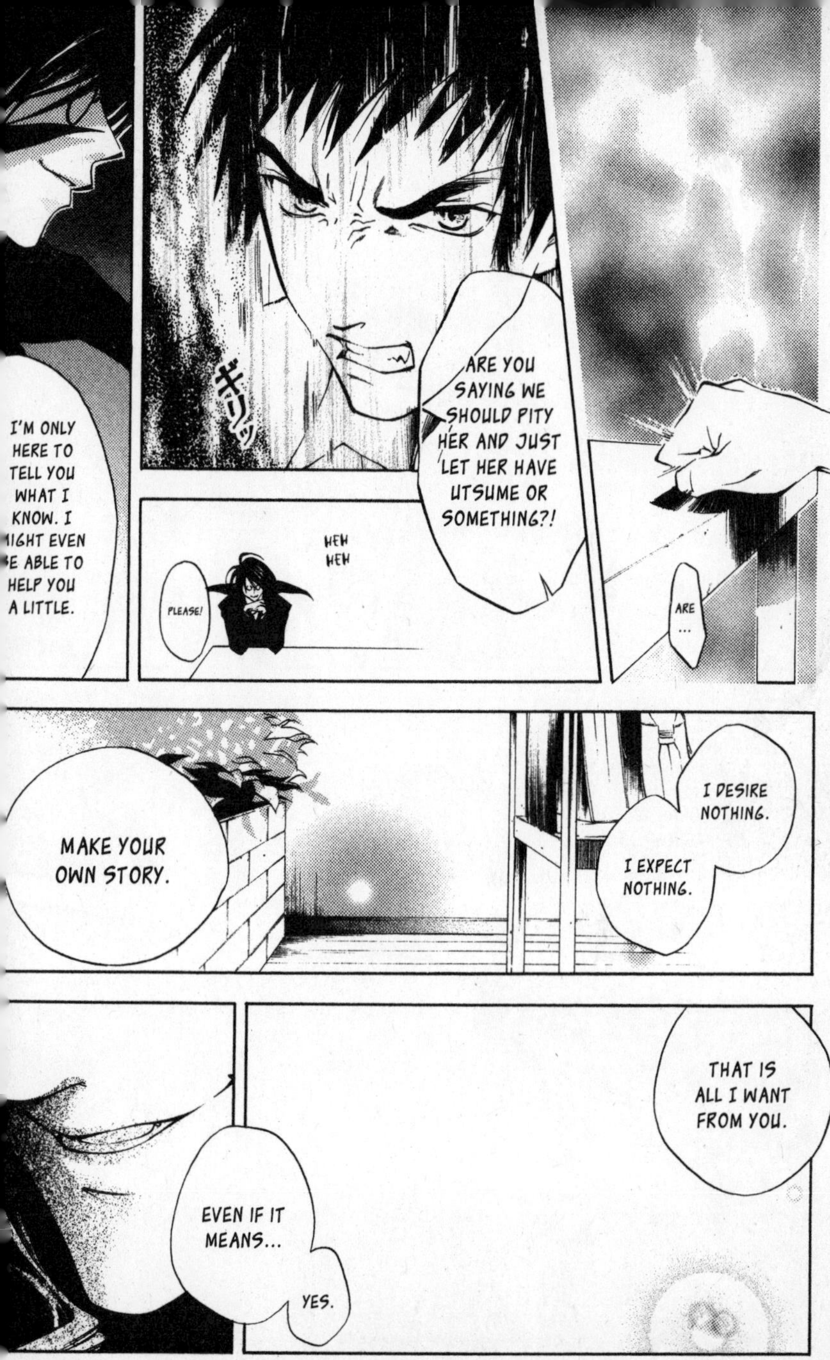
ARE ...
ギリッ
ARE YOU SAYING WE SHOULD PITY HER AND JUST LET HER HAVE UTSUME OR SOMETHING?!
HEH HEH
PLEASE!
I'M ONLY HERE TO TELL YOU WHAT I KNOW. I IGHT EVEN E ABLE TO HELP YOU A LITTLE.
I DESIRE NOTHING.
I EXPECT NOTHING.
MAKE YOUR OWN STORY.
THAT IS ALL I WANT FROM YOU.
EVEN IF IT MEANS...
YES.

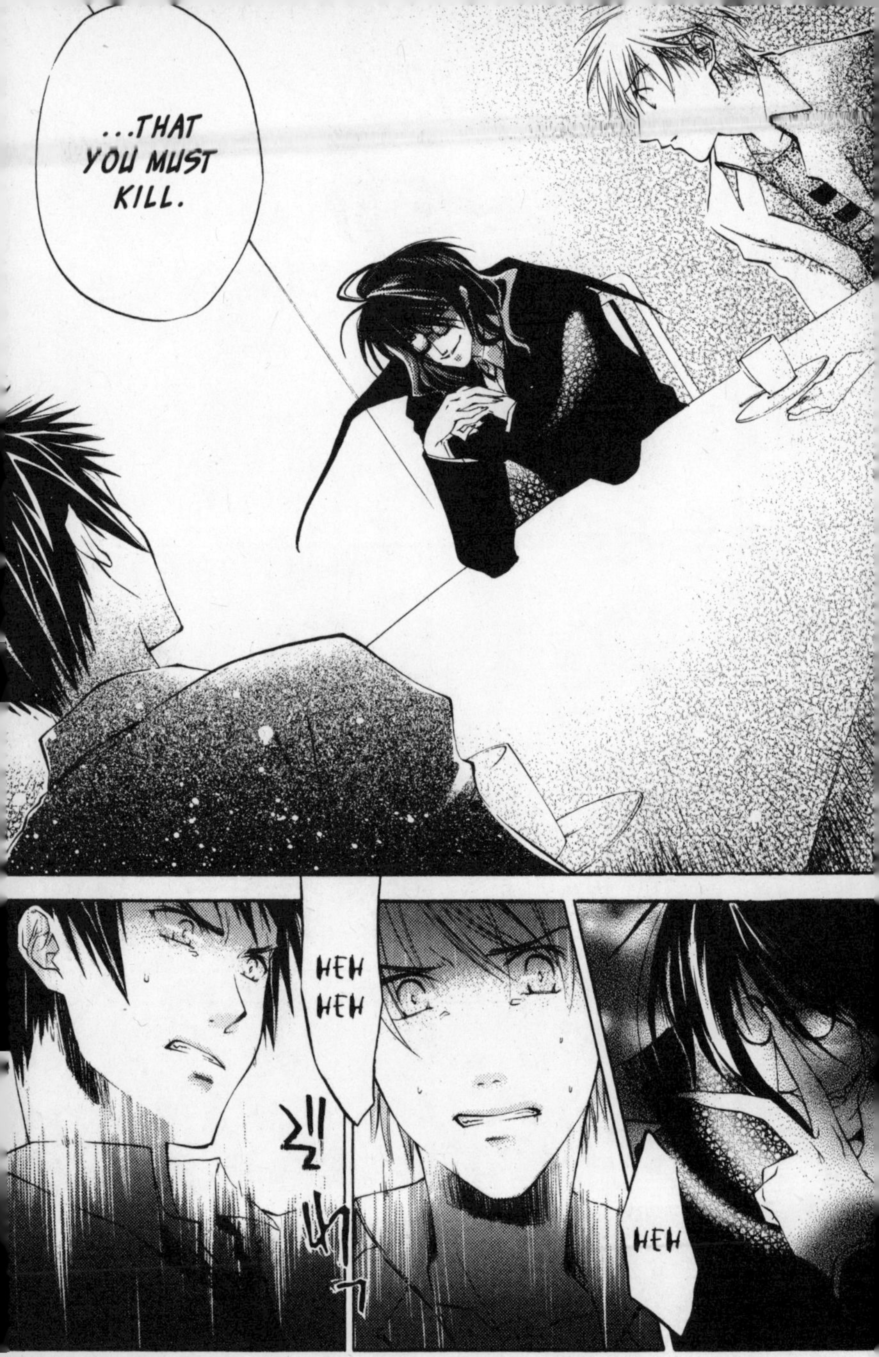
...THAT YOU MUST KILL.
HEH
HEH HEH

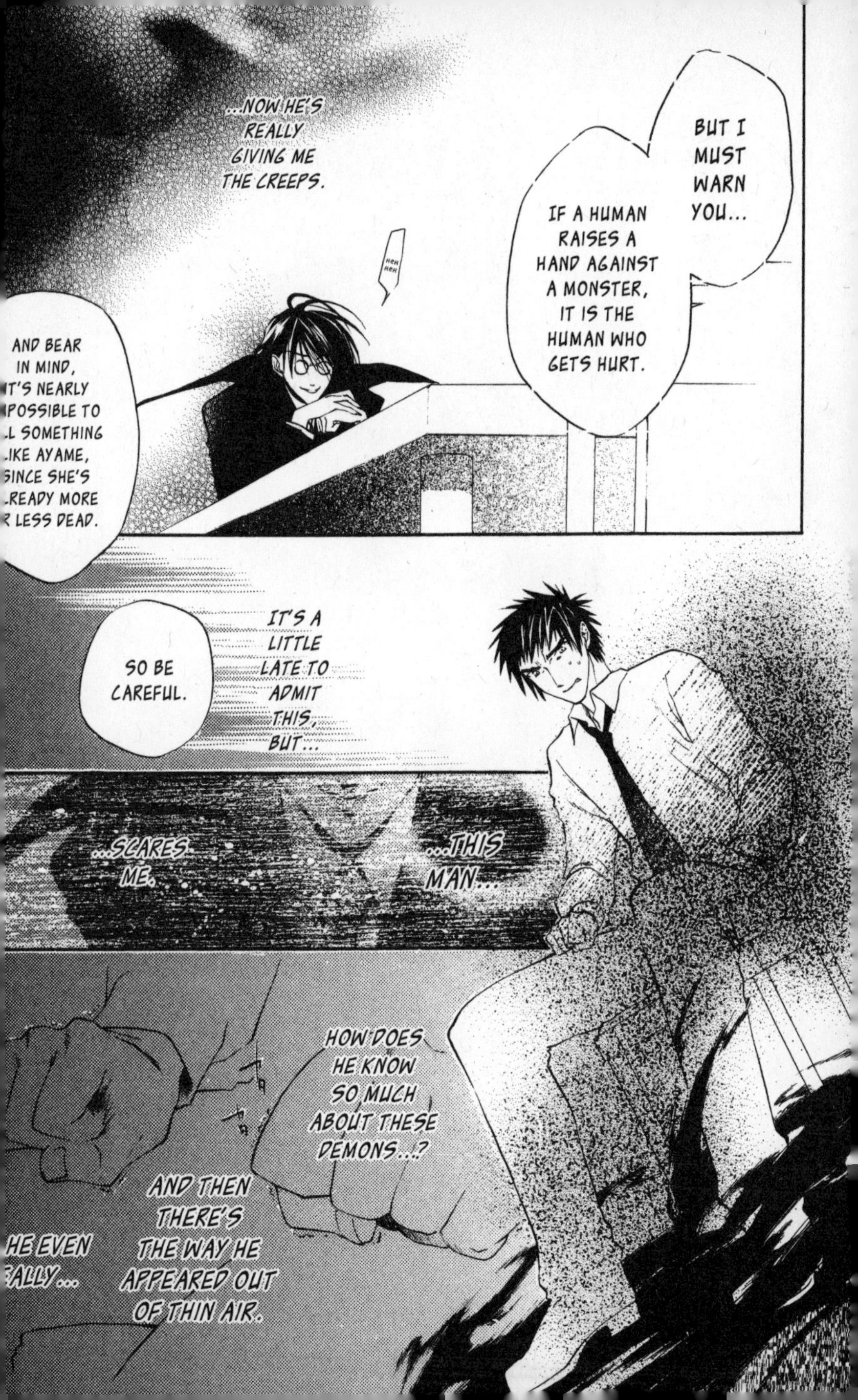
BUT I MUST WARN YOU...
IF A HUMAN RAISES A HAND AGAINST A MONSTER, IT IS THE HUMAN WHO GETS HURT.
...NOW HE'S REALLY GIVING ME THE CREEPS.
HEH HEH
AND BEAR IN MIND, T'S NEARLY POSSIBLE TO L SOMETHING IKE AYAME, INCE SHE'S READY MORE R LESS DEAD.
SO BE CAREFUL.
IT'S A LITTLE LATE TO ADMIT THIS, BUT...
...THIS MAN...
...SCARES ME.
HOW DOES HE KNOW SO MUCH ABOUT THESE DEMONS...?
AND THEN THERE'S THE WAY HE APPEARED OUT OF THIN AIR.
HE EVEN ALLY...

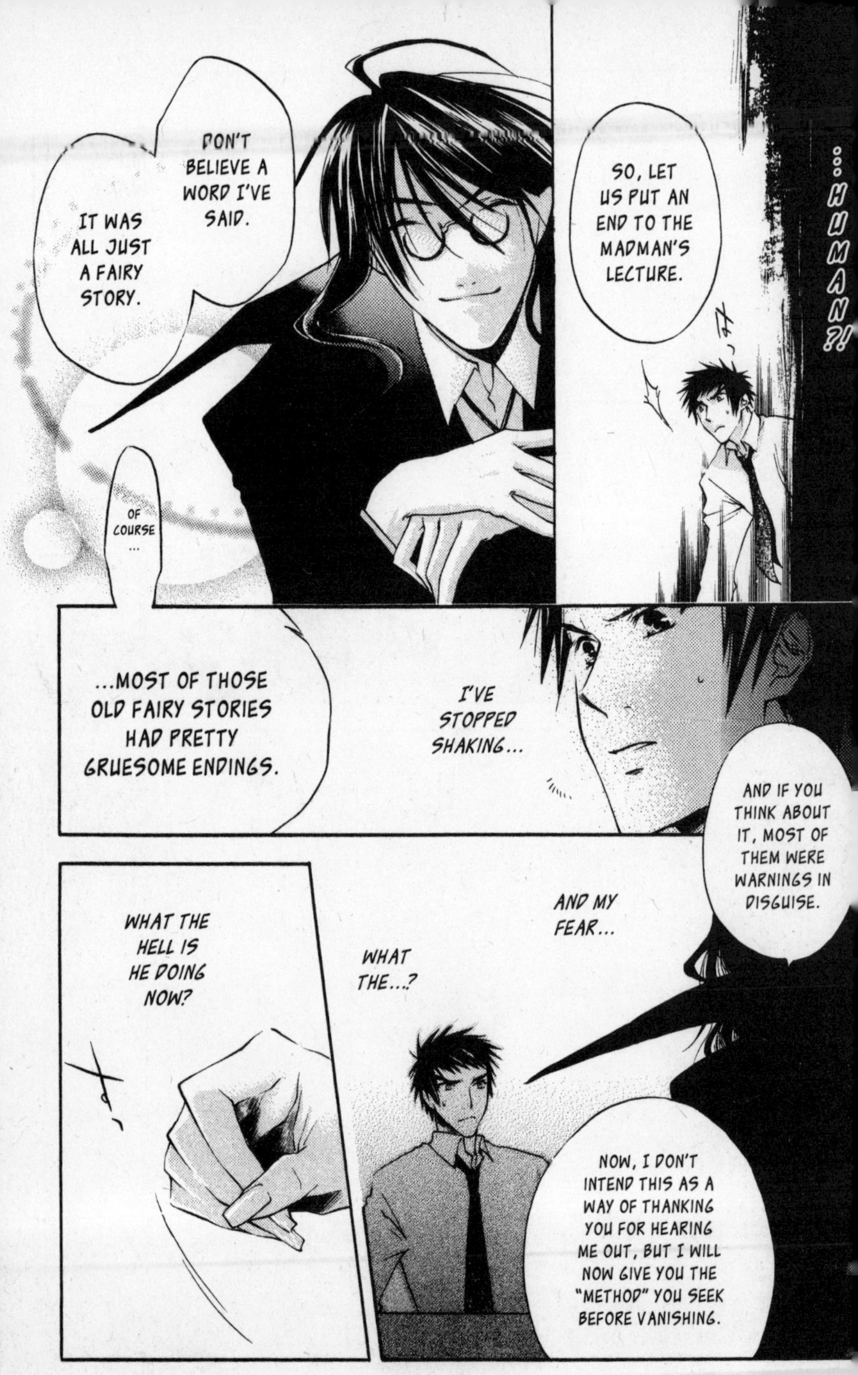
...HUMAN?!
SO, LET US PUT AN END TO THE MADMAN'S LECTURE.
はっ
DON'T BELIEVE A WORD I'VE SAID.
IT WAS ALL JUST A FAIRY STORY.
OF COURSE ...
...MOST OF THOSE OLD FAIRY STORIES HAD PRETTY GRUESOME ENDINGS.
I'VE STOPPED SHAKING...
AND IF YOU THINK ABOUT IT, MOST OF THEM WERE WARNINGS IN DISGUISE.
AND MY FEAR...
NOW, I DON'T INTEND THIS AS A WAY OF THANKING YOU FOR HEARING ME OUT, BUT I WILL NOW GIVE YOU THE "METHOD" YOU SEEK BEFORE VANISHING.
WHAT THE...?
WHAT THE HELL IS HE DOING NOW?

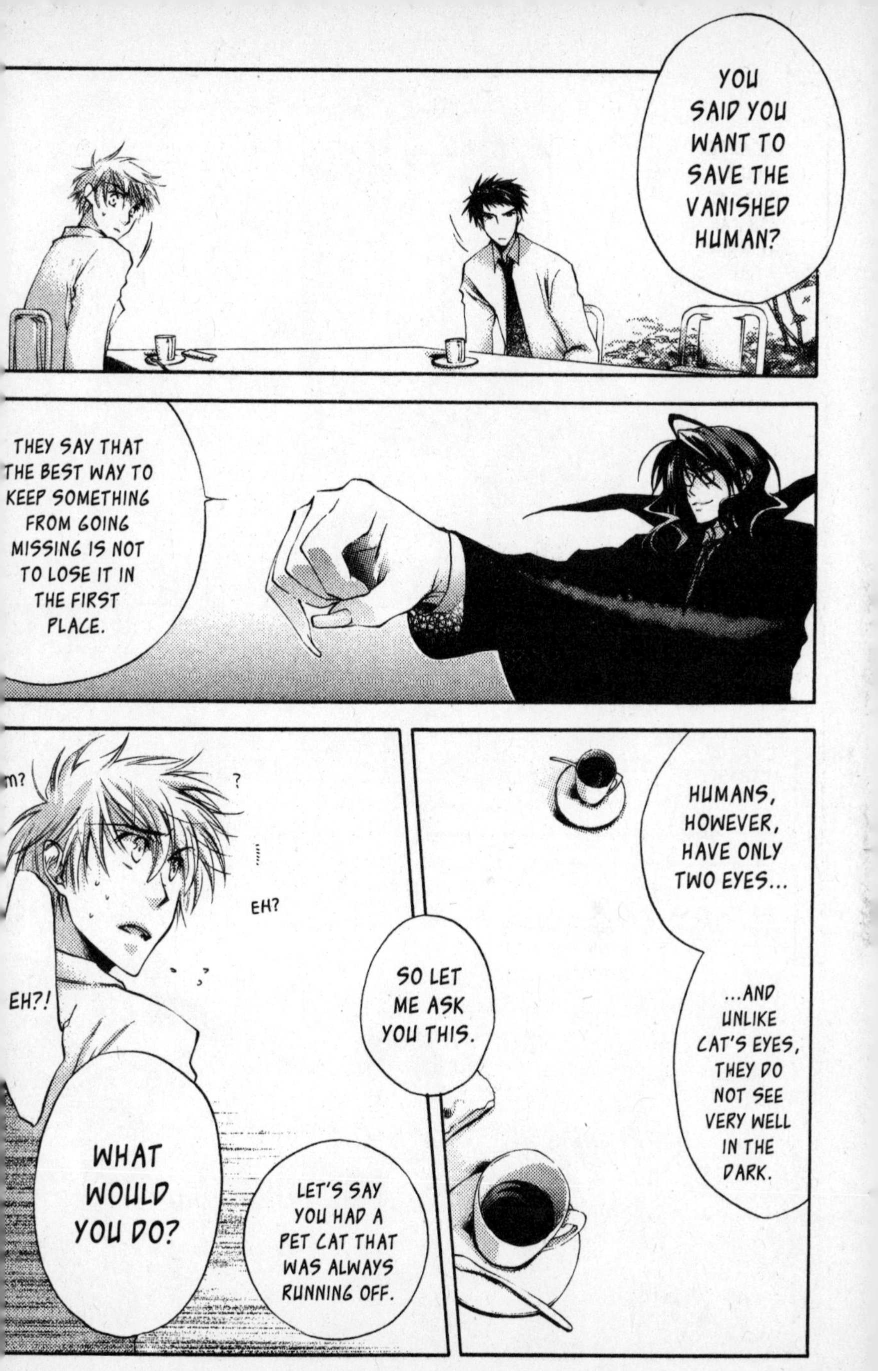
YOU SAID YOU WANT TO SAVE THE VANISHED HUMAN?
THEY SAY THAT THE BEST WAY TO KEEP SOMETHING FROM GOING MISSING IS NOT TO LOSE IT IN THE FIRST PLACE.
HUMANS, HOWEVER, HAVE ONLY TWO EYES...
...AND UNLIKE CAT'S EYES, THEY DO NOT SEE VERY WELL IN THE DARK.
SO LET ME ASK YOU THIS.
?
EH?
m?
EH?!
LET'S SAY YOU HAD A PET CAT THAT WAS ALWAYS RUNNING OFF.
WHAT WOULD YOU DO?

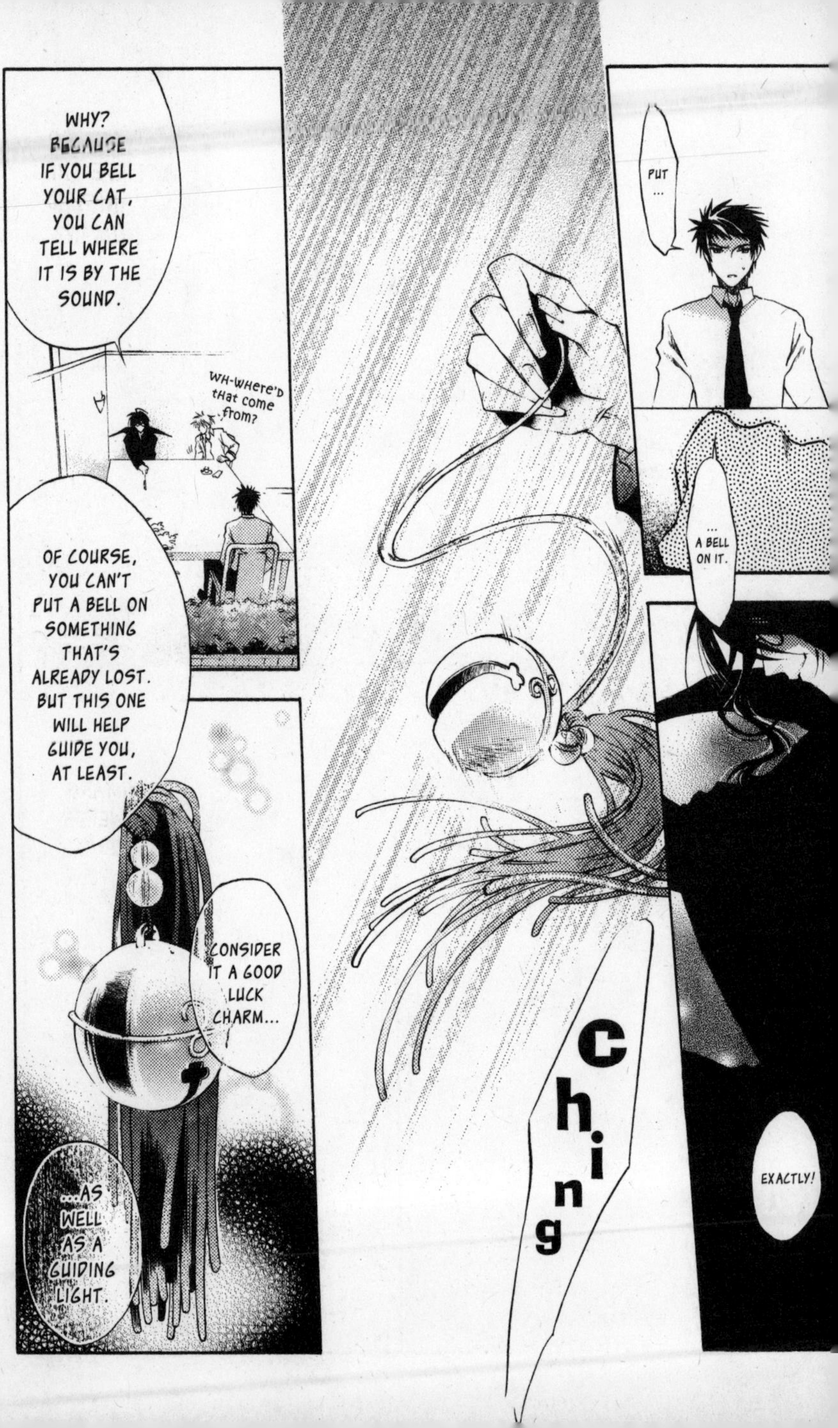
PUT ...
... A BELL ON IT.
EXACTLY!
ching
WHY? BECAUSE IF YOU BELL YOUR CAT, YOU CAN TELL WHERE IT IS BY THE SOUND.
WH-WHERE'D THAT COME FROM?
OF COURSE, YOU CAN'T PUT A BELL ON SOMETHING THAT'S ALREADY LOST. BUT THIS ONE WILL HELP GUIDE YOU, AT LEAST.
CONSIDER IT A GOOD LUCK CHARM...
...AS WELL AS A GUIDING LIGHT.

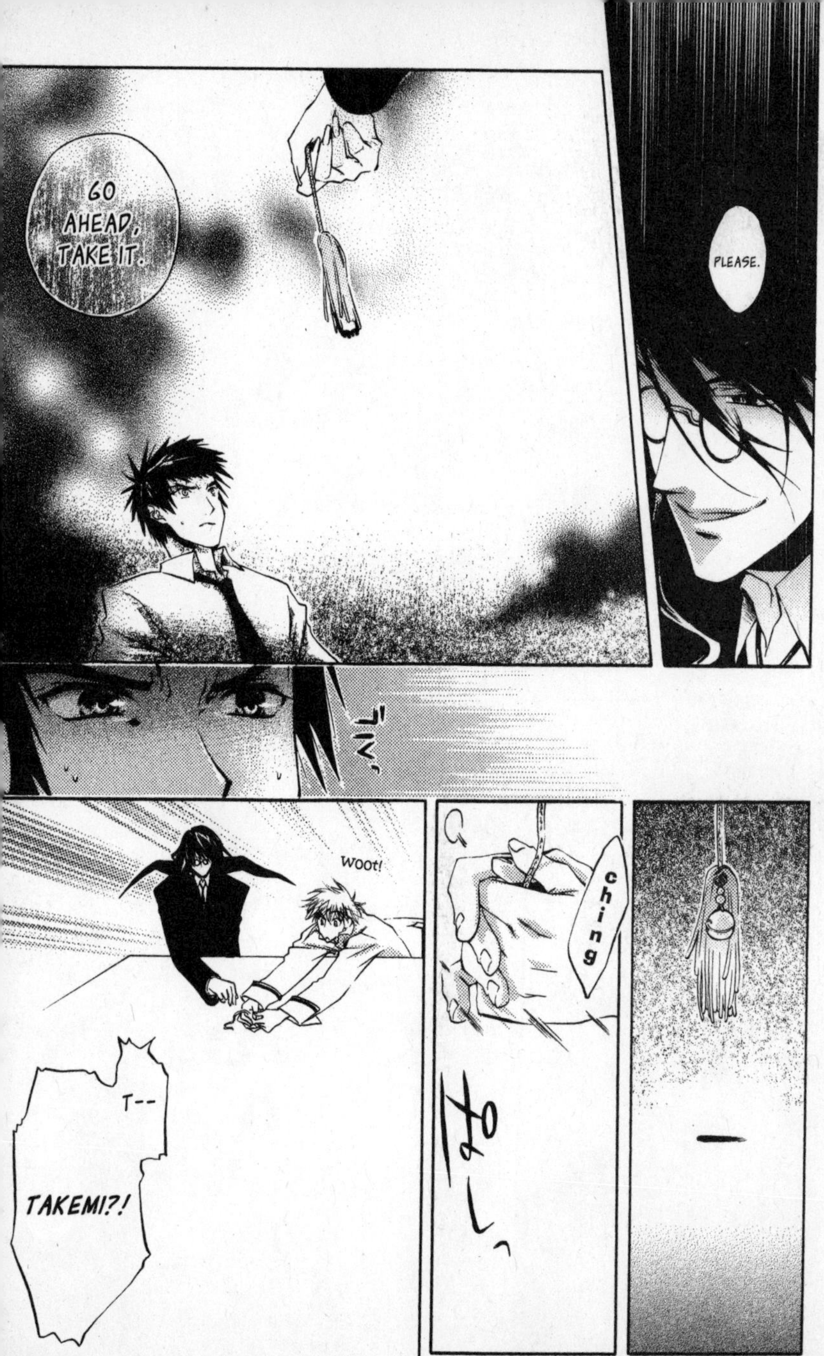
PLEASE.
GO AHEAD, TAKE IT.
ching
woot!
T--
TAKEMI?!

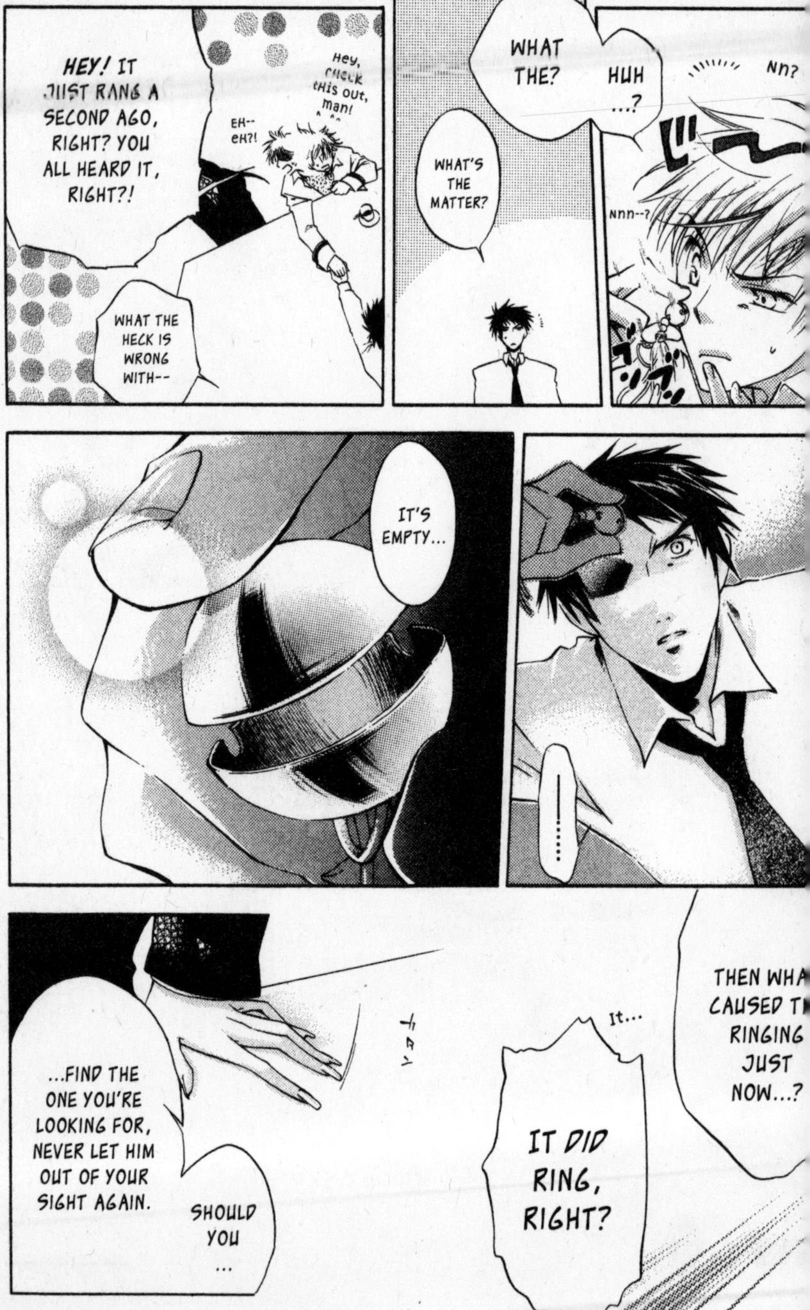
Nn?
HUH ...?
Nnn--?
WHAT THE?
WHAT'S THE MATTER?
HEY! IT JUST RANG A SECOND AGO, RIGHT? YOU ALL HEARD IT, RIGHT?!
Hey, check this out, man!
EH-- EH?!
WHAT THE HECK IS WRONG WITH--
......!
IT'S EMPTY...
THEN WHA CAUSED T RINGING JUST NOW...?
It...
IT DID RING, RIGHT?
SHOULD YOU ...
...FIND THE ONE YOU'RE LOOKING FOR, NEVER LET HIM OUT OF YOUR SIGHT AGAIN.

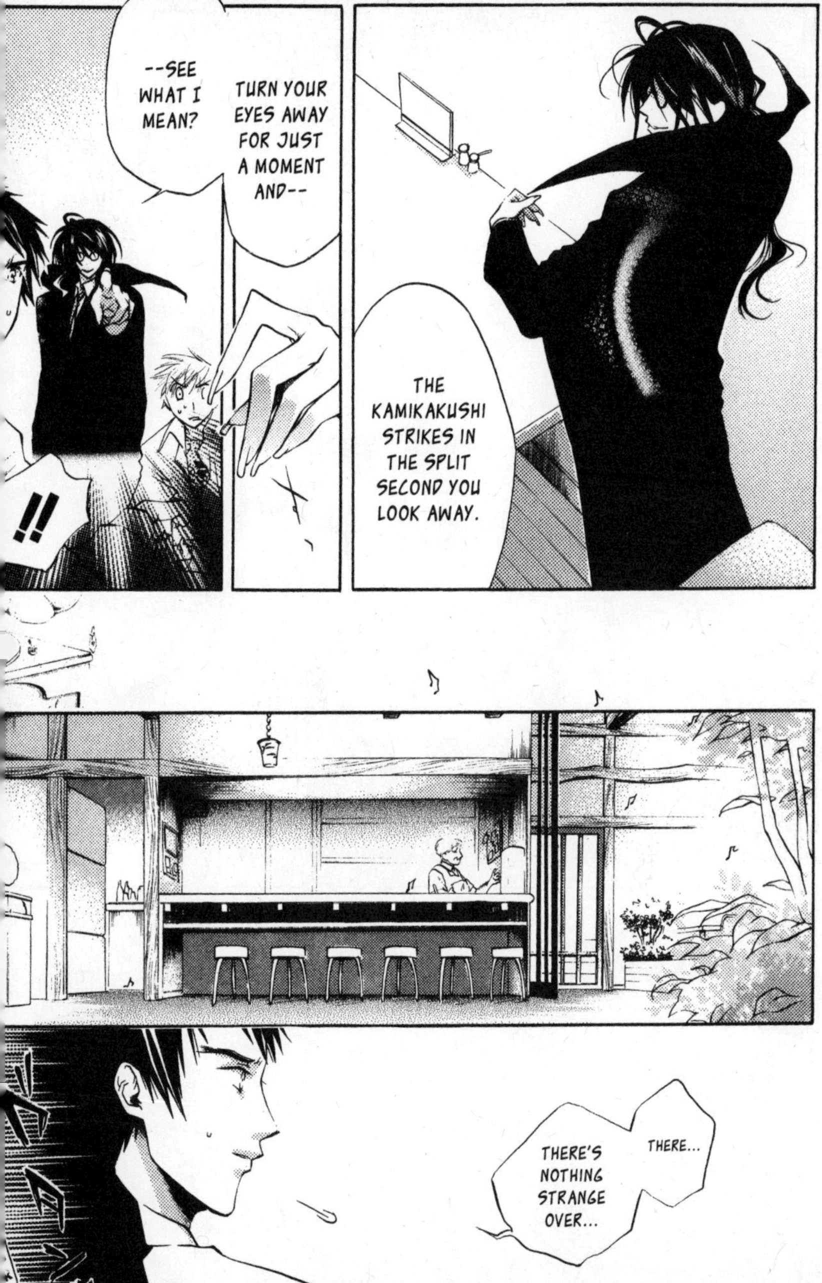
THE KAMIKAKUSHI STRIKES IN THE SPLIT SECOND YOU LOOK AWAY.
TURN YOUR EYES AWAY FOR JUST A MOMENT AND--
--SEE WHAT I MEAN?
!!
THERE...
THERE'S NOTHING STRANGE OVER...

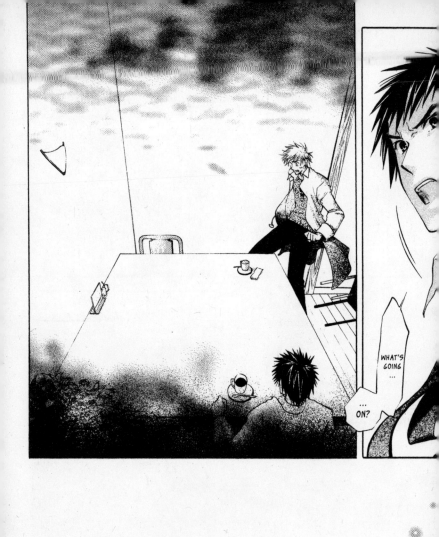

WHAT'S
GOING
...

... ON?

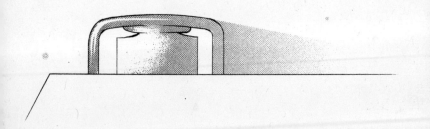

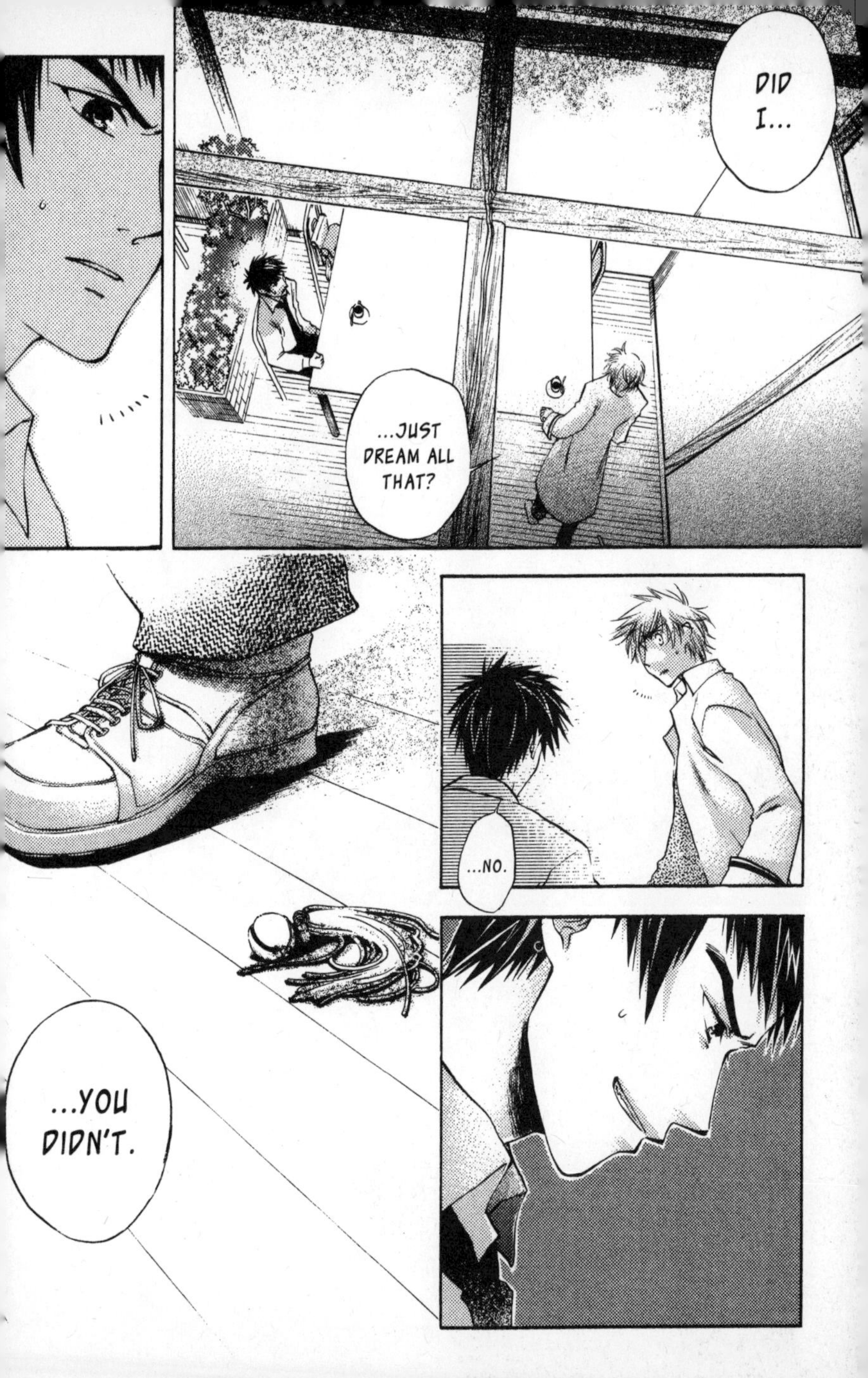
DID I...
...JUST DREAM ALL THAT?
...NO.
...YOU DIDN'T.

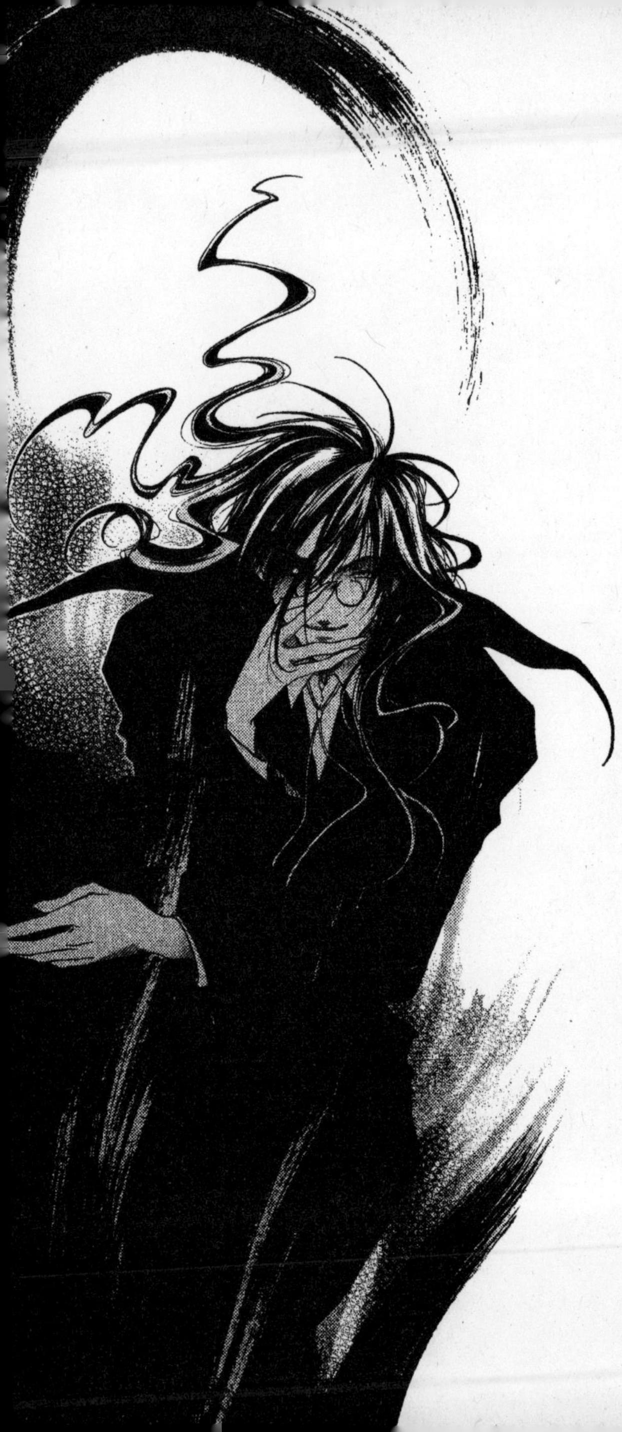

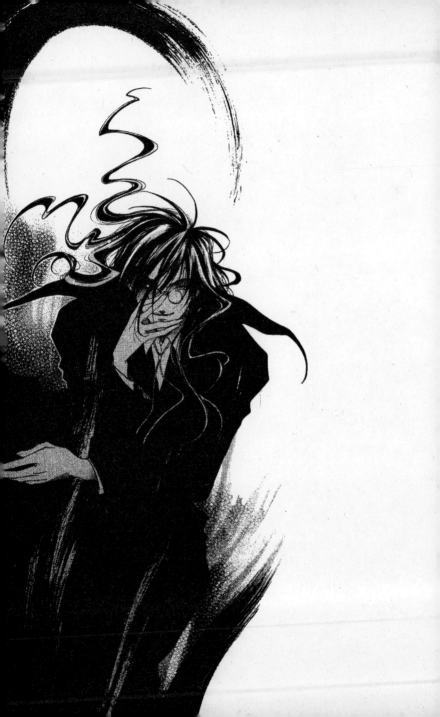

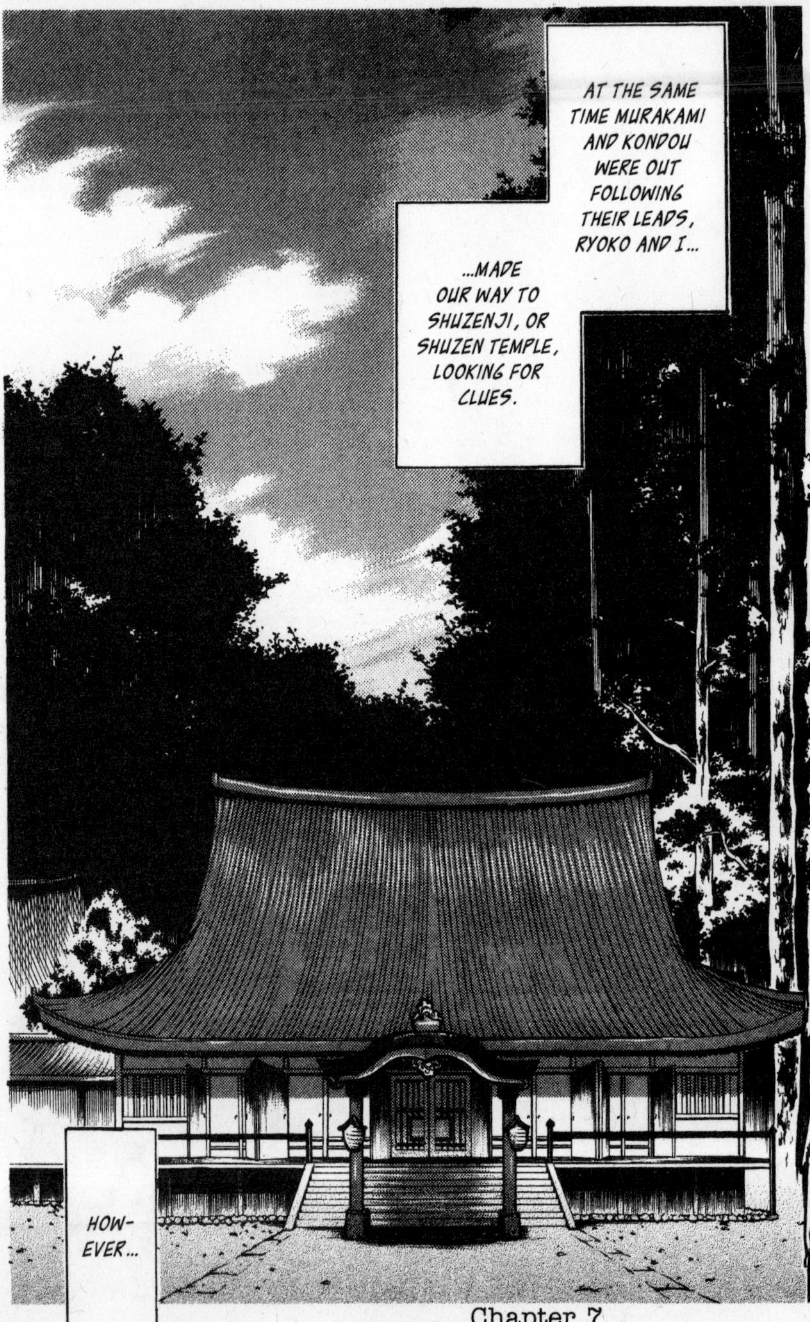
AT THE SAME TIME MURAKAMI AND KONDOU WERE OUT FOLLOWING THEIR LEADS, RYOKO AND I...
...MADE OUR WAY TO SHUZENJI, OR SHUZEN TEMPLE, LOOKING FOR CLUES.
HOW-EVER...

Chapter 7
Through the Looking Glass

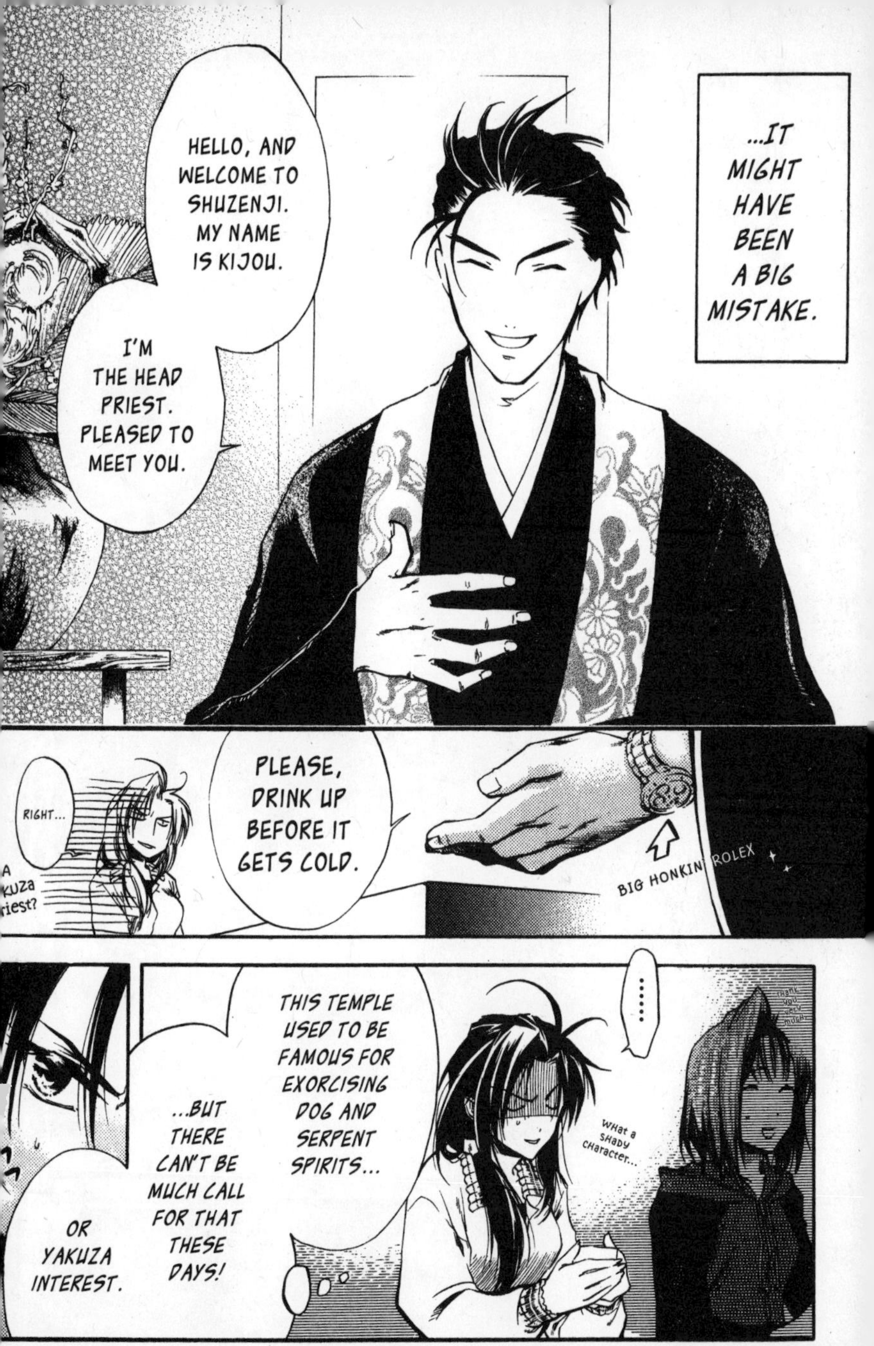
...IT MIGHT HAVE BEEN A BIG MISTAKE.
HELLO, AND WELCOME TO SHUZENJI. MY NAME IS KIJOU.
I'M THE HEAD PRIEST. PLEASED TO MEET YOU.
BIG HONKIN' ROLEX
PLEASE, DRINK UP BEFORE IT GETS COLD.
RIGHT...
Thank you very much.
What a shady character...
......
THIS TEMPLE USED TO BE FAMOUS FOR EXORCISING DOG AND SERPENT SPIRITS...
...BUT THERE CAN'T BE MUCH CALL FOR THAT THESE DAYS!
OR YAKUZA INTEREST.

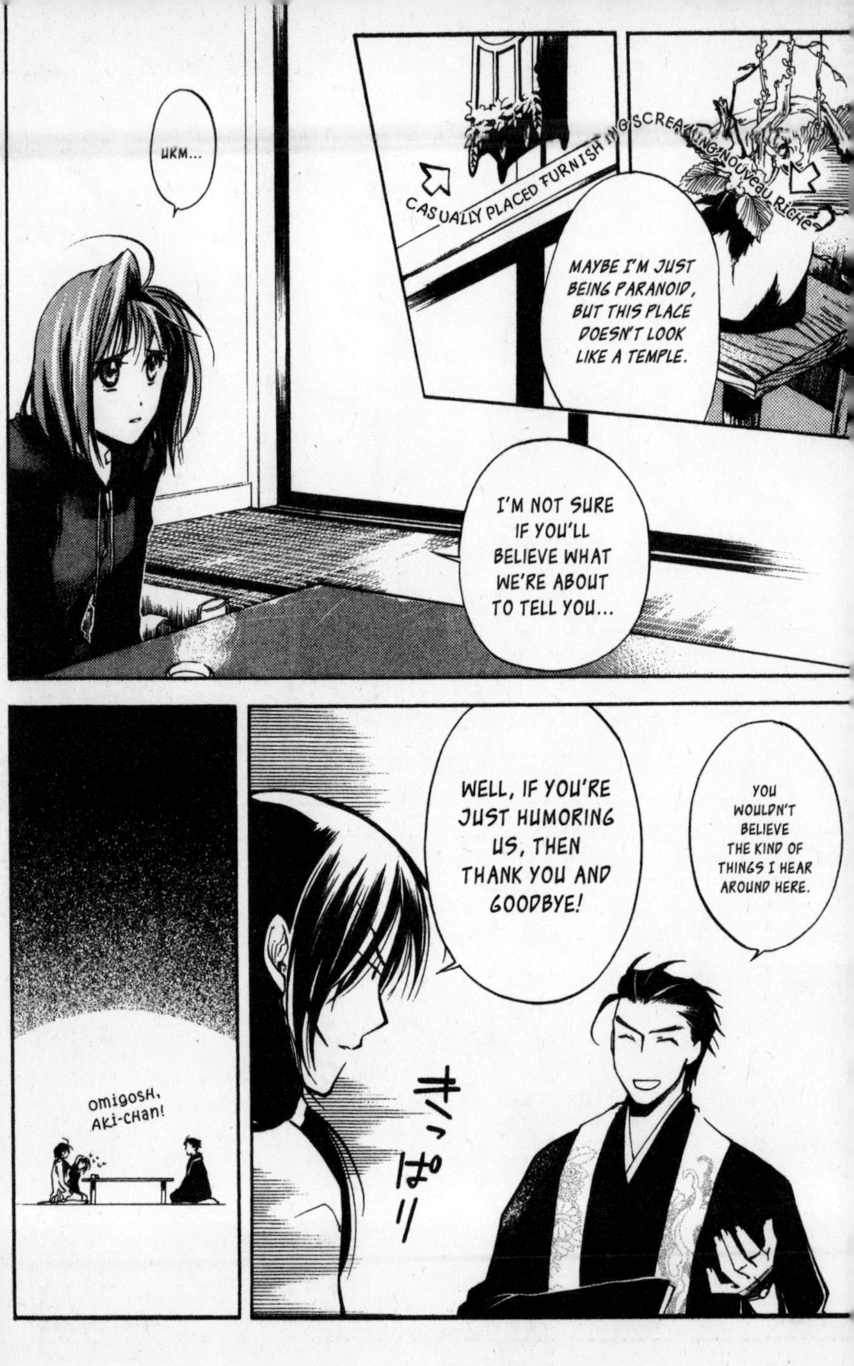
CASUALLY PLACED FURNISHING
SCREAMING NOUVEAU RICHE
MAYBE I'M JUST BEING PARANOID, BUT THIS PLACE DOESN'T LOOK LIKE A TEMPLE.
UKM...
I'M NOT SURE IF YOU'LL BELIEVE WHAT WE'RE ABOUT TO TELL YOU...
YOU WOULDN'T BELIEVE THE KIND OF THINGS I HEAR AROUND HERE.
WELL, IF YOU'RE JUST HUMORING US, THEN THANK YOU AND GOODBYE!
きっぱり
OMIGOSH, AKI-CHAN!

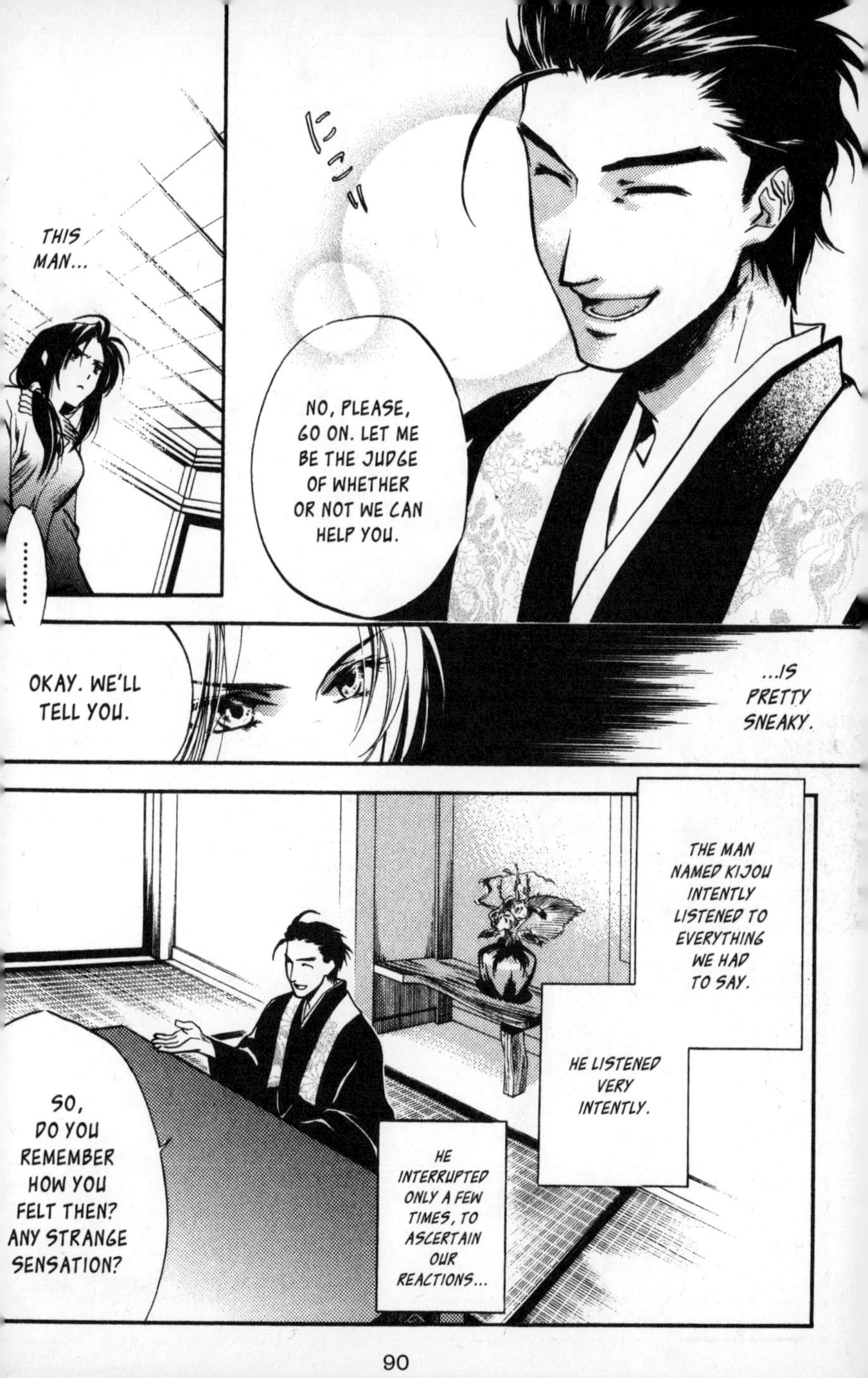
にこり
NO, PLEASE, GO ON. LET ME BE THE JUDGE OF WHETHER OR NOT WE CAN HELP YOU.
THIS MAN...
......
...IS PRETTY SNEAKY.
OKAY. WE'LL TELL YOU.
THE MAN NAMED KIJOU INTENTLY LISTENED TO EVERYTHING WE HAD TO SAY.
HE LISTENED VERY INTENTLY.
HE INTERRUPTED ONLY A FEW TIMES, TO ASCERTAIN OUR REACTIONS...
SO, DO YOU REMEMBER HOW YOU FELT THEN? ANY STRANGE SENSATION?

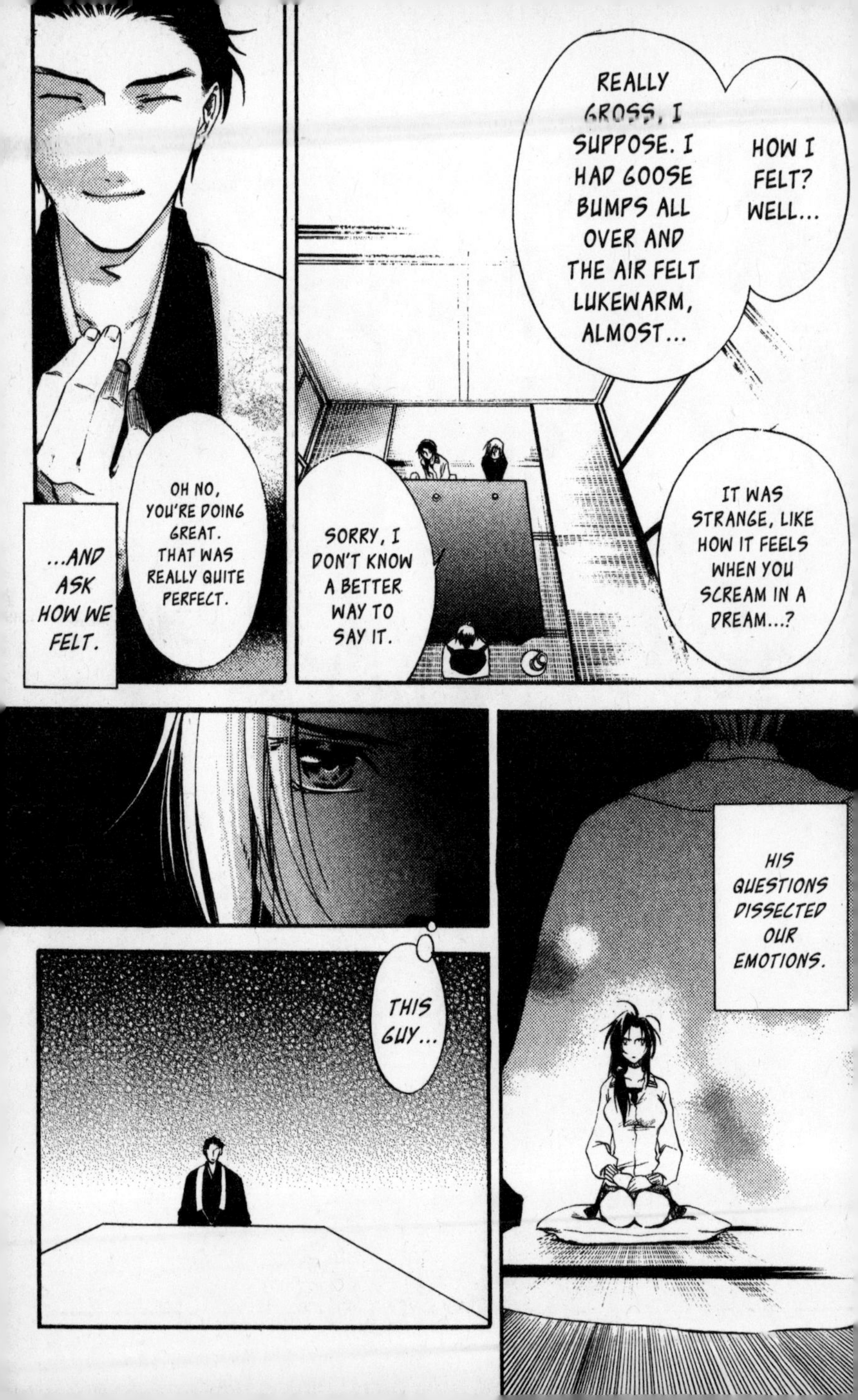
HOW I FELT? WELL...
REALLY GROSS, I SUPPOSE. I HAD GOOSE BUMPS ALL OVER AND THE AIR FELT LUKEWARM, ALMOST...
IT WAS STRANGE, LIKE HOW IT FEELS WHEN YOU SCREAM IN A DREAM...?
SORRY, I DON'T KNOW A BETTER WAY TO SAY IT.
OH NO, YOU'RE DOING GREAT. THAT WAS REALLY QUITE PERFECT.
...AND ASK HOW WE FELT.
HIS QUESTIONS DISSECTED OUR EMOTIONS.
THIS GUY...

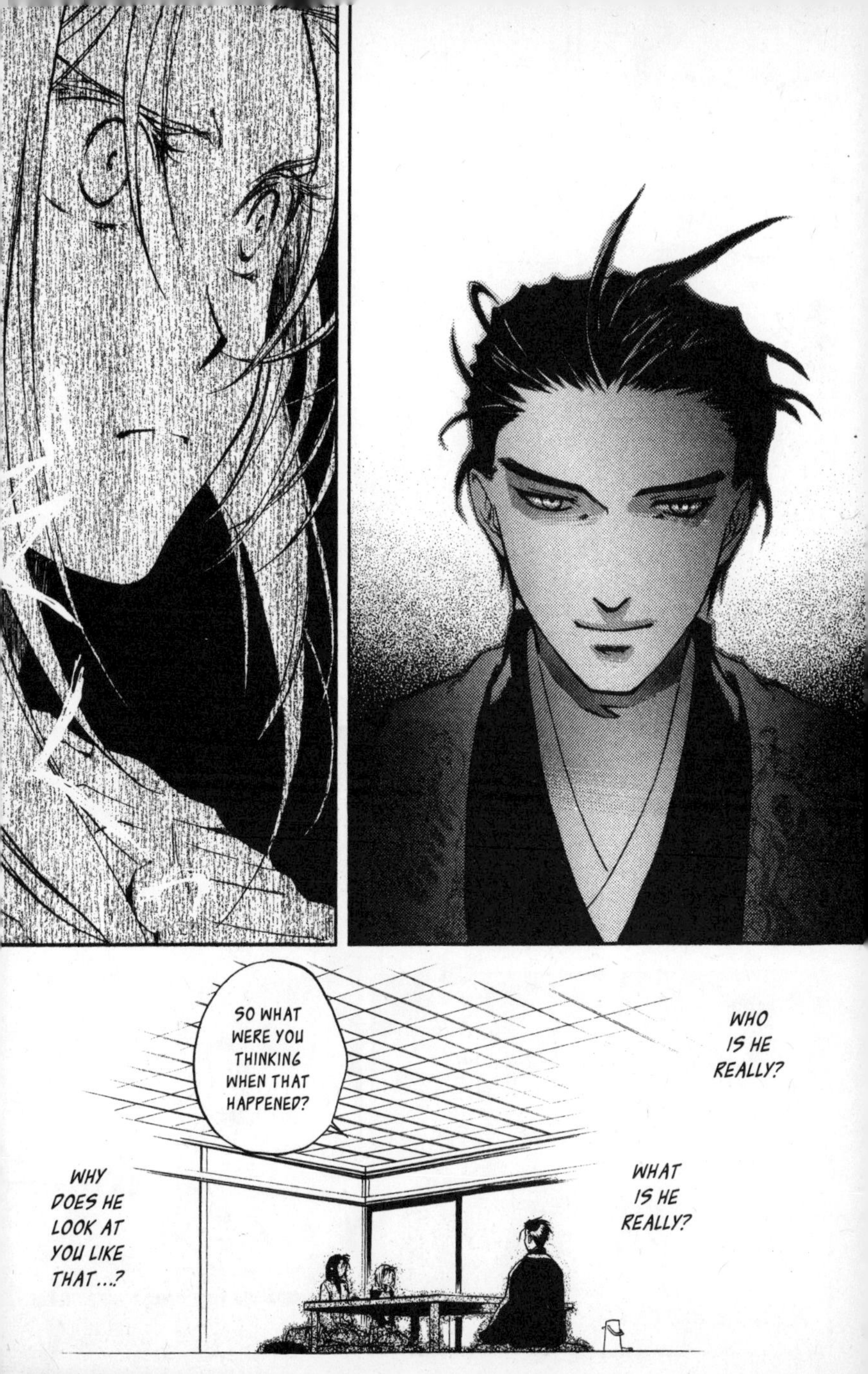
WHO IS HE REALLY?
SO WHAT WERE YOU THINKING WHEN THAT HAPPENED?
WHAT IS HE REALLY?
WHY DOES HE LOOK AT YOU LIKE THAT...?

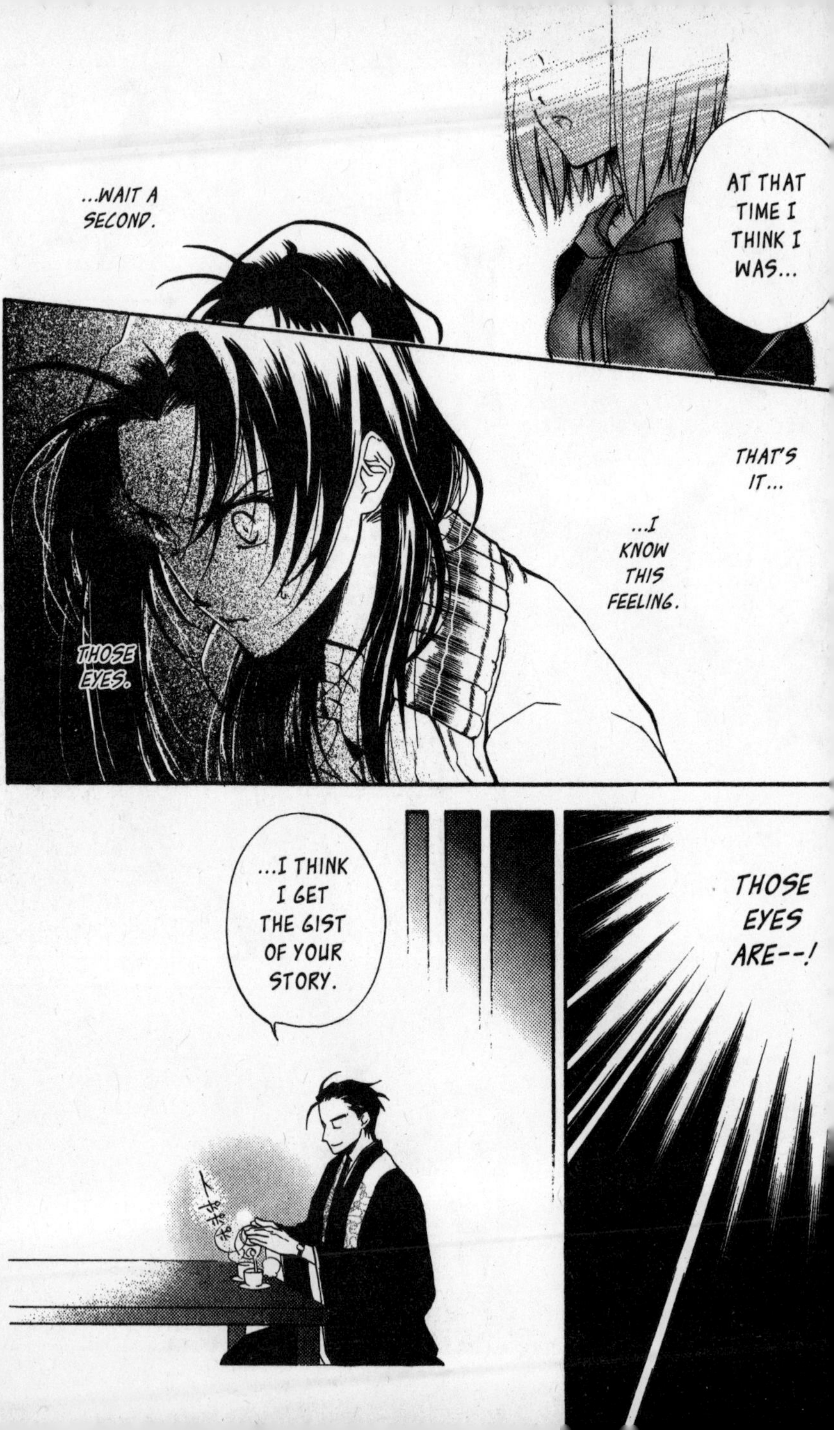
AT THAT TIME I THINK I WAS...
...WAIT A SECOND.
THAT'S IT...
...I KNOW THIS FEELING.
THOSE EYES.
THOSE EYES ARE--!
...I THINK I GET THE GIST OF YOUR STORY.

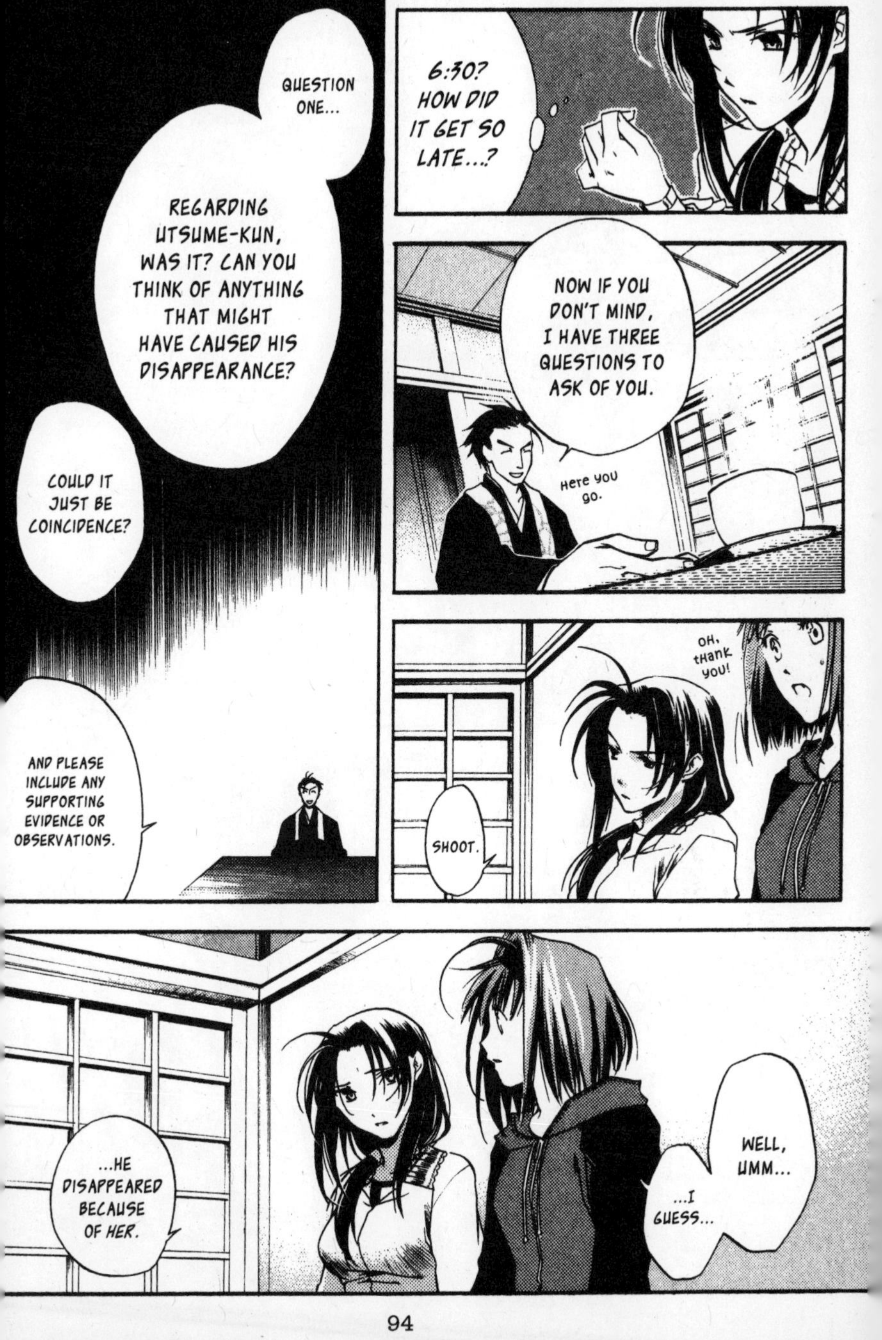
6:30? HOW DID IT GET SO LATE...?
NOW IF YOU DON'T MIND, I HAVE THREE QUESTIONS TO ASK OF YOU.
Here you go.
Oh, thank you!
SHOOT.
QUESTION ONE...
REGARDING UTSUME-KUN, WAS IT? CAN YOU THINK OF ANYTHING THAT MIGHT HAVE CAUSED HIS DISAPPEARANCE?
COULD IT JUST BE COINCIDENCE?
AND PLEASE INCLUDE ANY SUPPORTING EVIDENCE OR OBSERVATIONS.
WELL, UMM...
...I GUESS...
...HE DISAPPEARED BECAUSE OF HER.

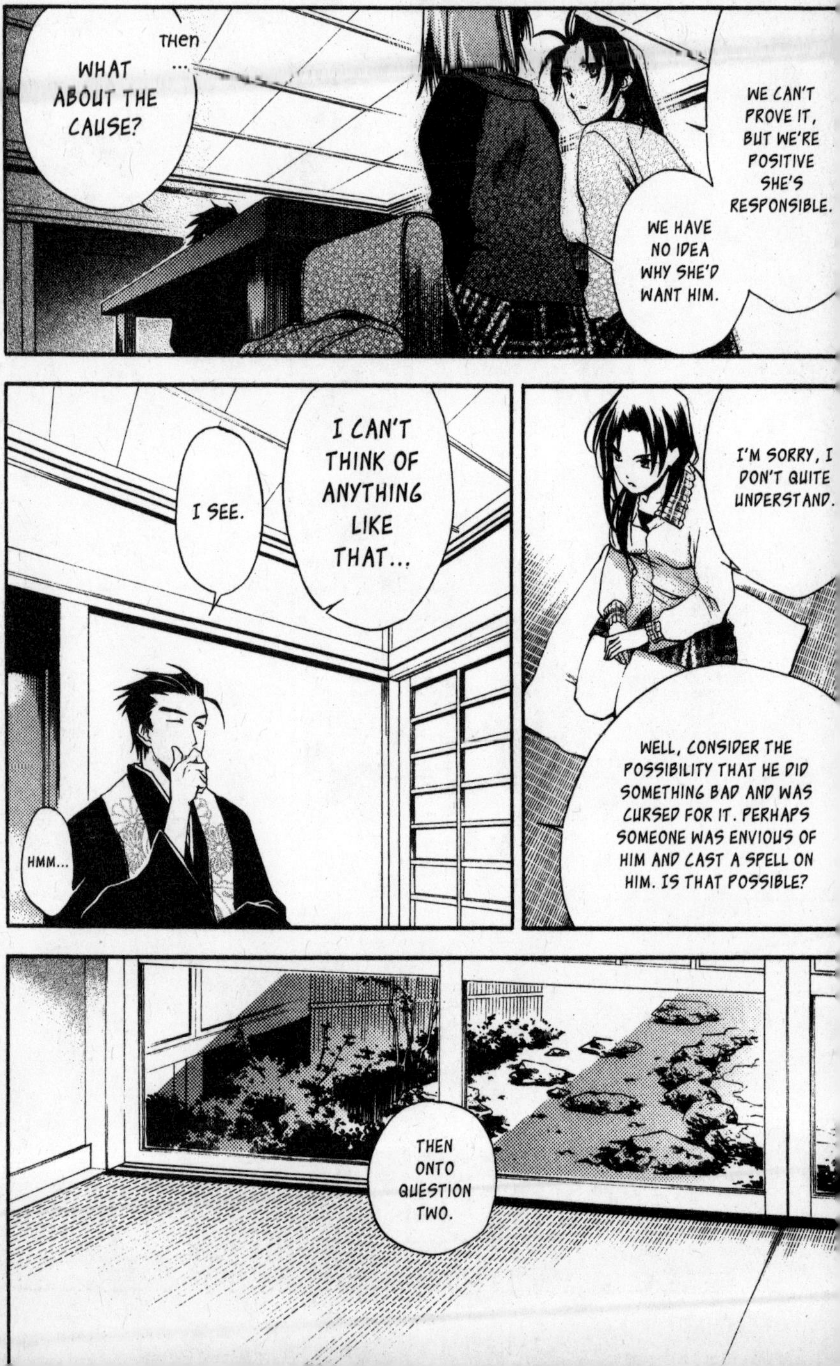
WE CAN'T PROVE IT, BUT WE'RE POSITIVE SHE'S RESPONSIBLE.
WE HAVE NO IDEA WHY SHE'D WANT HIM.
Then ...
WHAT ABOUT THE CAUSE?
I'M SORRY, I DON'T QUITE UNDERSTAND.
WELL, CONSIDER THE POSSIBILITY THAT HE DID SOMETHING BAD AND WAS CURSED FOR IT. PERHAPS SOMEONE WAS ENVIOUS OF HIM AND CAST A SPELL ON HIM. IS THAT POSSIBLE?
I CAN'T THINK OF ANYTHING LIKE THAT...
I SEE.
HMM...
THEN ONTO QUESTION TWO.

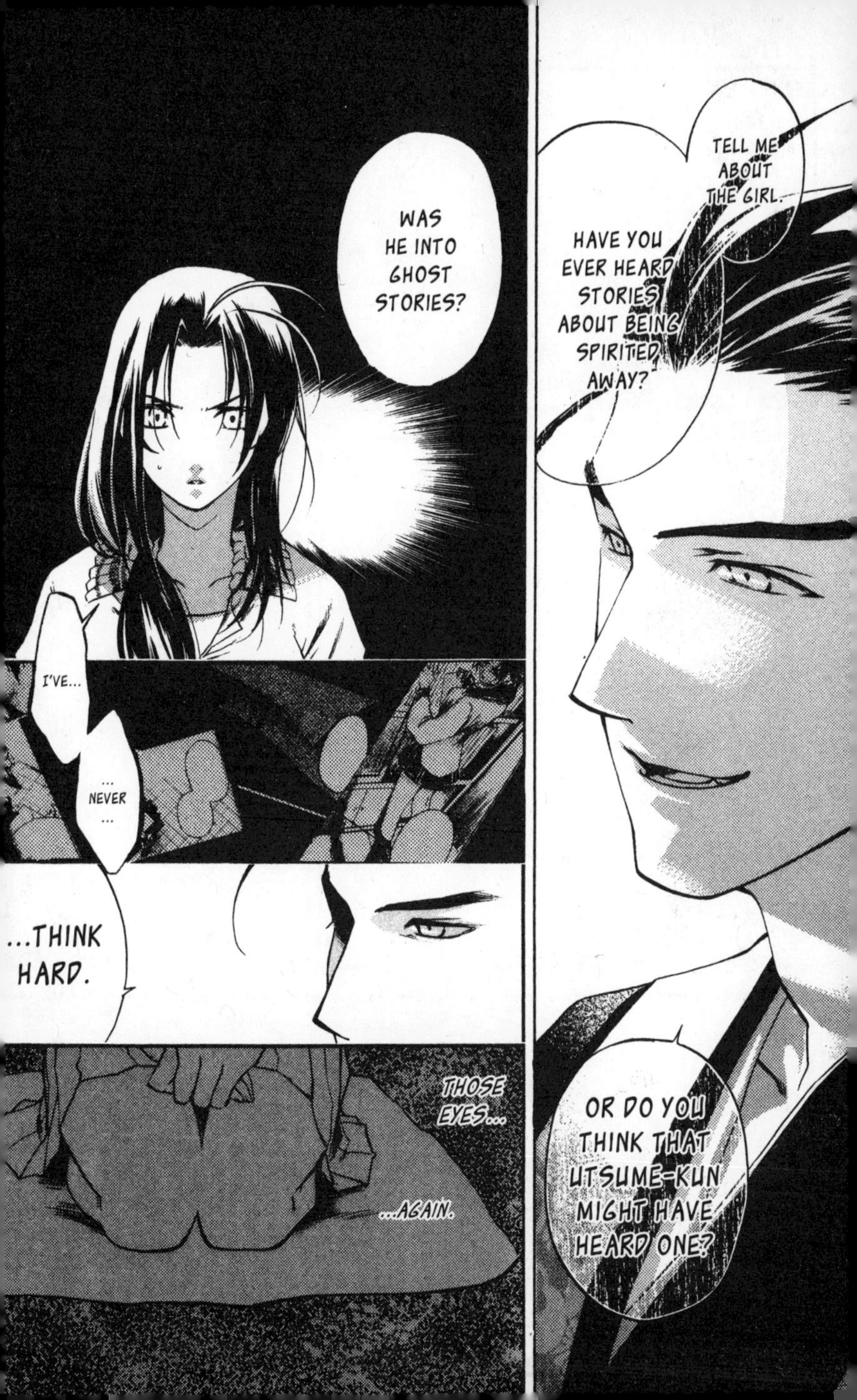
TELL ME ABOUT THE GIRL.
HAVE YOU EVER HEARD STORIES ABOUT BEING SPIRITED AWAY?
OR DO YOU THINK THAT UTSUME-KUN MIGHT HAVE HEARD ONE?
WAS HE INTO GHOST STORIES?
I'VE...
...NEVER...
...THINK HARD.
THOSE EYES...
...AGAIN.

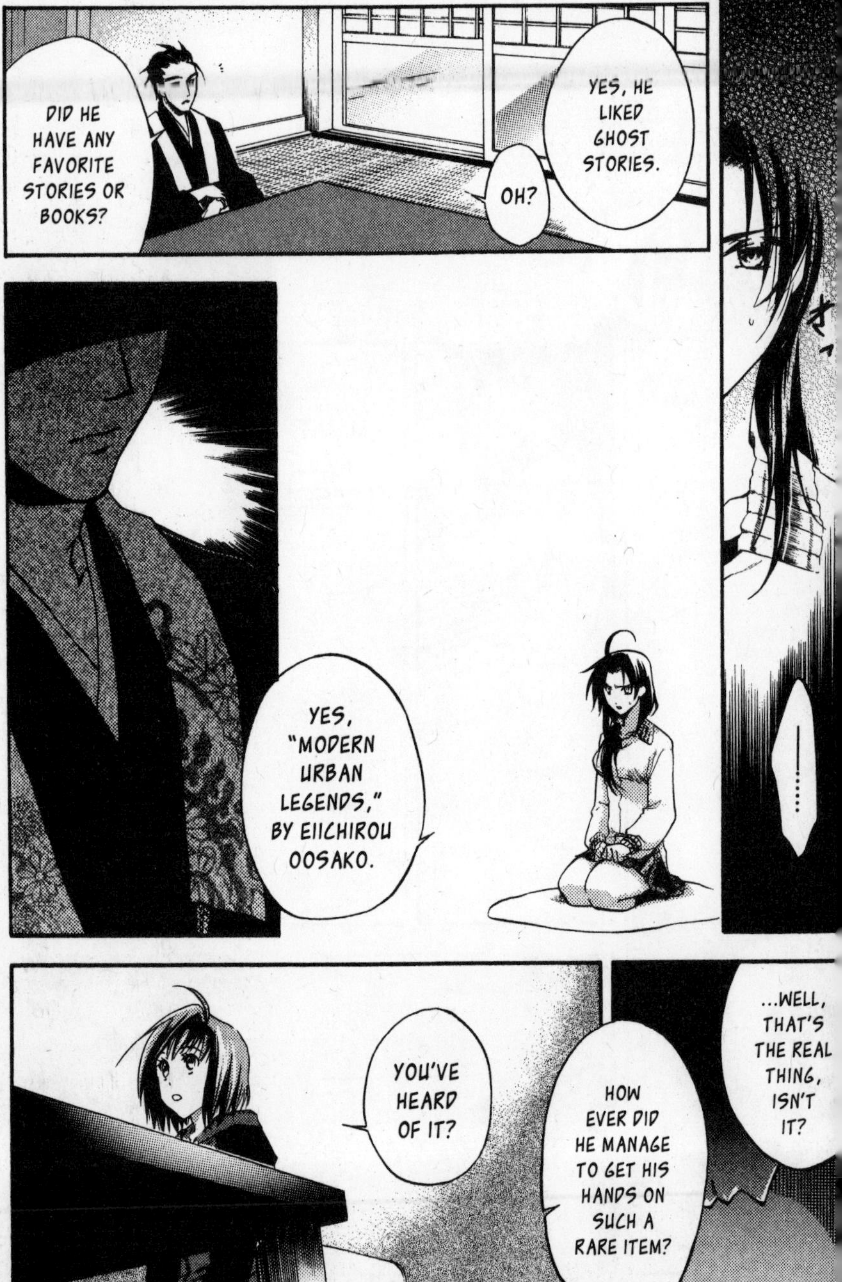
......
YES, HE LIKED GHOST STORIES.
OH?
DID HE HAVE ANY FAVORITE STORIES OR BOOKS?
YES, "MODERN URBAN LEGENDS," BY EIICHIROU OOSAKO.
...WELL, THAT'S THE REAL THING, ISN'T IT?
HOW EVER DID HE MANAGE TO GET HIS HANDS ON SUCH A RARE ITEM?
YOU'VE HEARD OF IT?

IS THIS BOOK YOURS?

......

I'M SORRY TO DO THIS, BUT, WOULD YOU MIND WAITING HERE FOR A MOMENT?

WE'LL GET TO THE THIRD QUESTION WHEN I RETURN.

THANK YOU.

MIGHT I HAVE THOSE?

NO, IT WAS PART OF UTSUME'S COLLECTION.

BUT I DO HAVE A FEW XEROXED PAGES WITH ME.

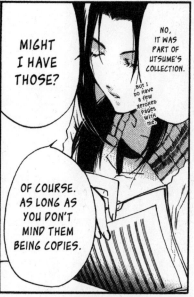

OF COURSE. AS LONG AS YOU DON'T MIND THEM BEING COPIES.

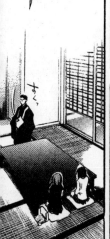

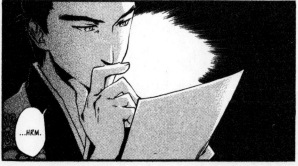

...HRM.

98

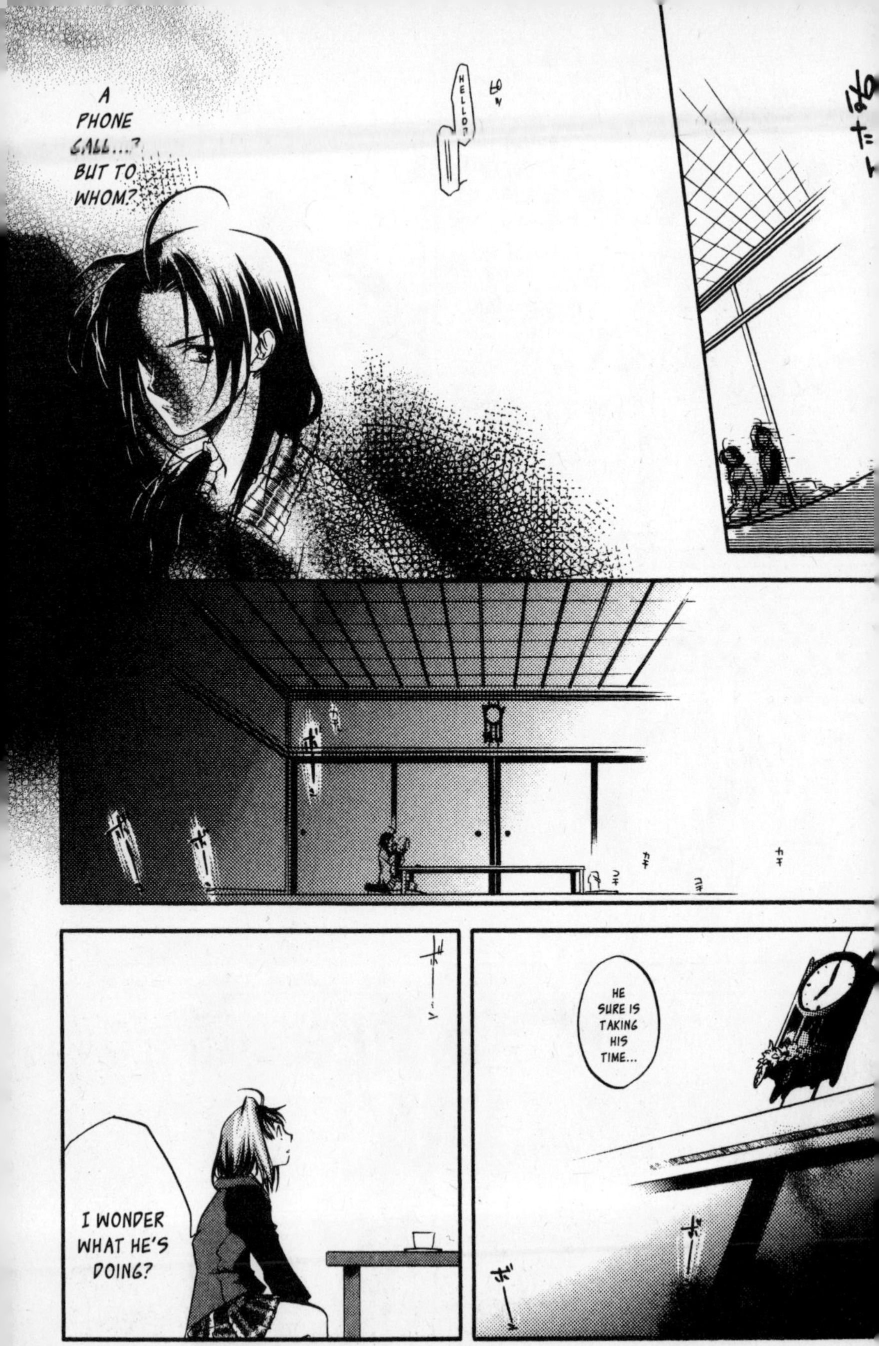
HELLO?
A PHONE CALL...? BUT TO WHOM?
HE SURE IS TAKING HIS TIME...
I WONDER WHAT HE'S DOING?

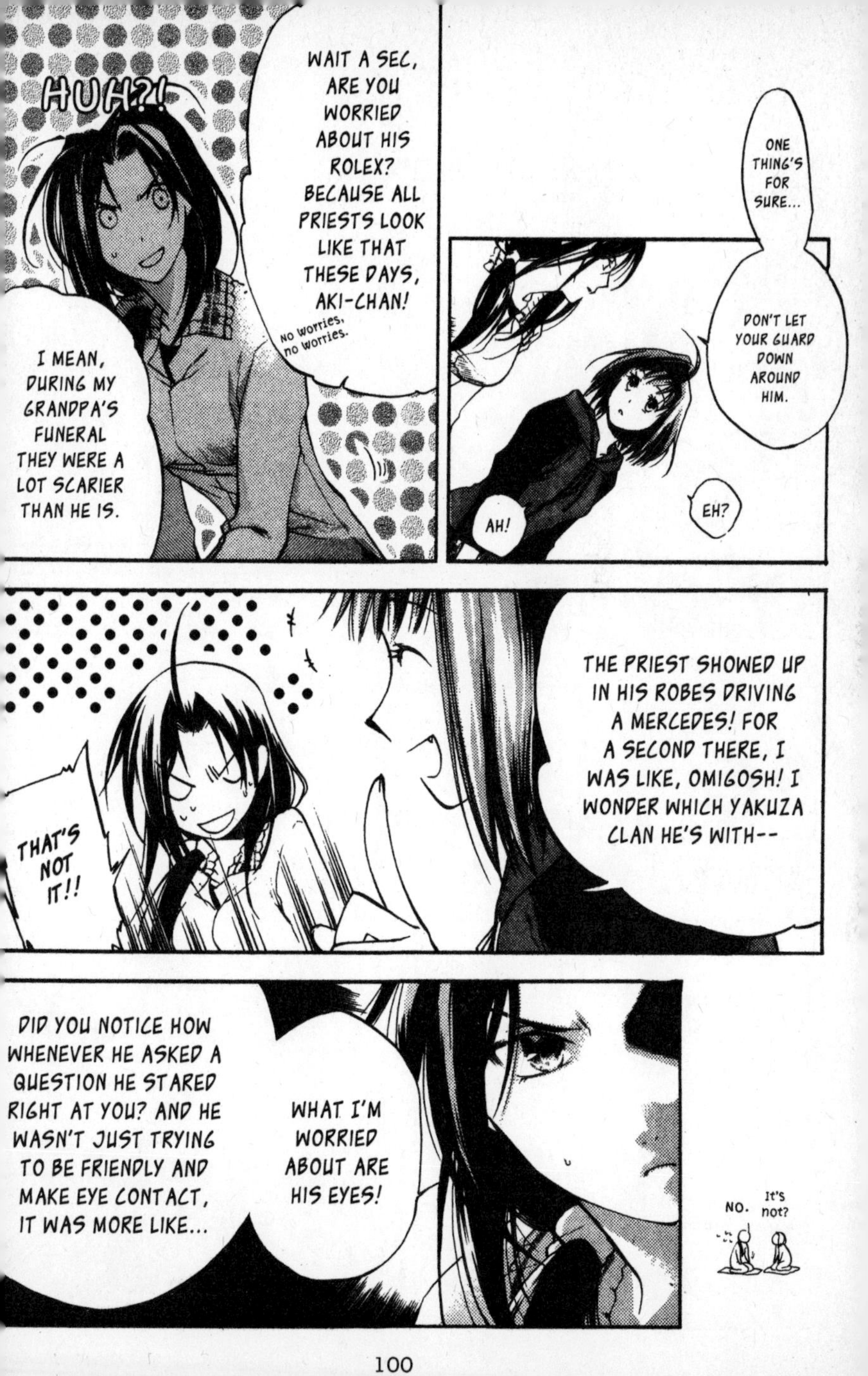
ONE THING'S FOR SURE...
DON'T LET YOUR GUARD DOWN AROUND HIM.
EH?
AH!
HUH?!
WAIT A SEC, ARE YOU WORRIED ABOUT HIS ROLEX? BECAUSE ALL PRIESTS LOOK LIKE THAT THESE DAYS, AKI-CHAN!
No worries, no worries.
I MEAN, DURING MY GRANDPA'S FUNERAL THEY WERE A LOT SCARIER THAN HE IS.
THE PRIEST SHOWED UP IN HIS ROBES DRIVING A MERCEDES! FOR A SECOND THERE, I WAS LIKE, OMIGOSH! I WONDER WHICH YAKUZA CLAN HE'S WITH--
THAT'S NOT IT!!
It's not?
NO.
WHAT I'M WORRIED ABOUT ARE HIS EYES!
DID YOU NOTICE HOW WHENEVER HE ASKED A QUESTION HE STARED RIGHT AT YOU? AND HE WASN'T JUST TRYING TO BE FRIENDLY AND MAKE EYE CONTACT, IT WAS MORE LIKE...

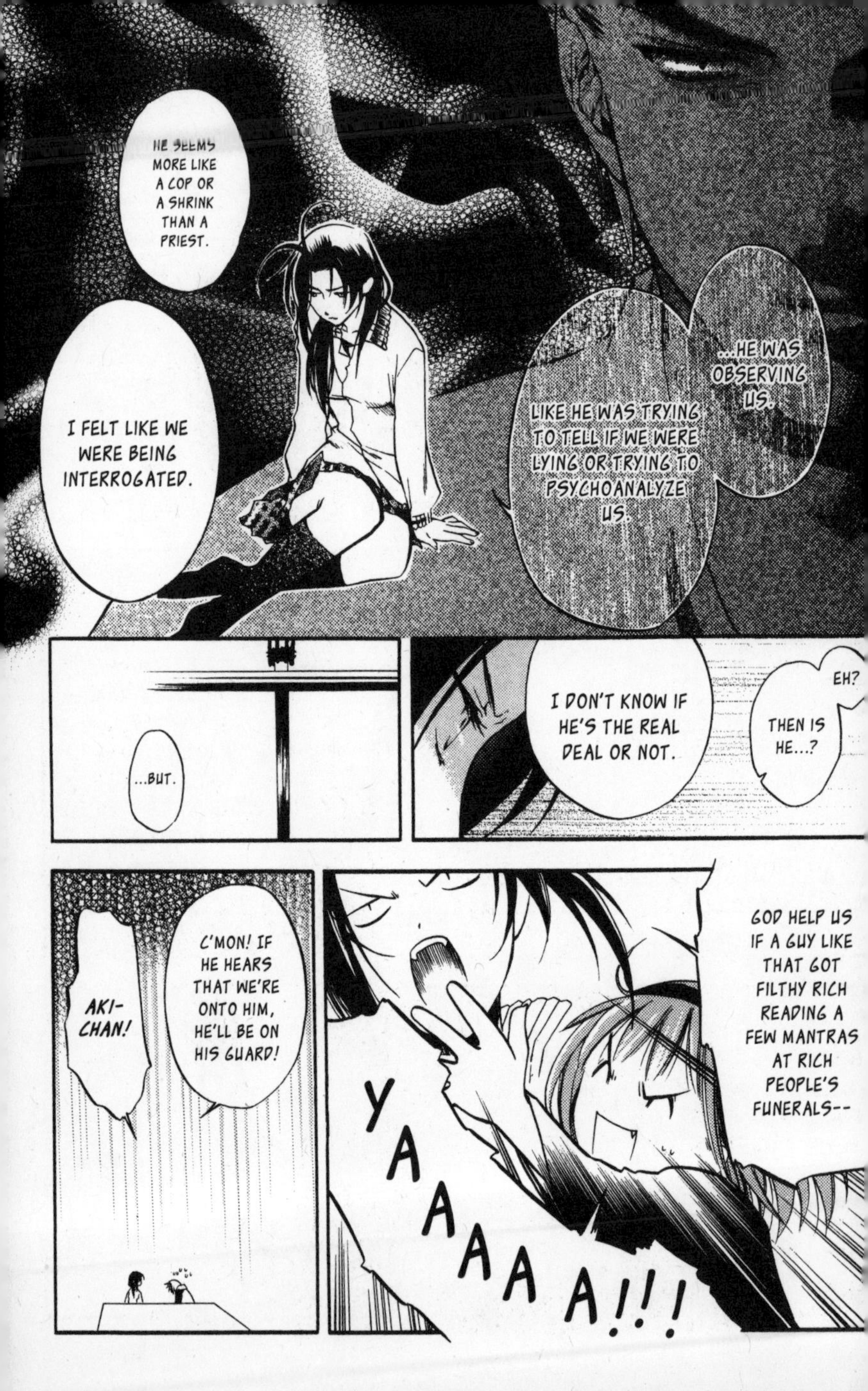
HE SEEMS MORE LIKE A COP OR A SHRINK THAN A PRIEST.
I FELT LIKE WE WERE BEING INTERROGATED.
LIKE HE WAS TRYING TO TELL IF WE WERE LYING OR TRYING TO PSYCHOANALYZE US.
...HE WAS OBSERVING US.
EH?
THEN IS HE...?
I DON'T KNOW IF HE'S THE REAL DEAL OR NOT.
...BUT.
GOD HELP US IF A GUY LIKE THAT GOT FILTHY RICH READING A FEW MANTRAS AT RICH PEOPLE'S FUNERALS--
YAAAAAA!!!
C'MON! IF HE HEARS THAT WE'RE ONTO HIM, HE'LL BE ON HIS GUARD!
AKI-CHAN!

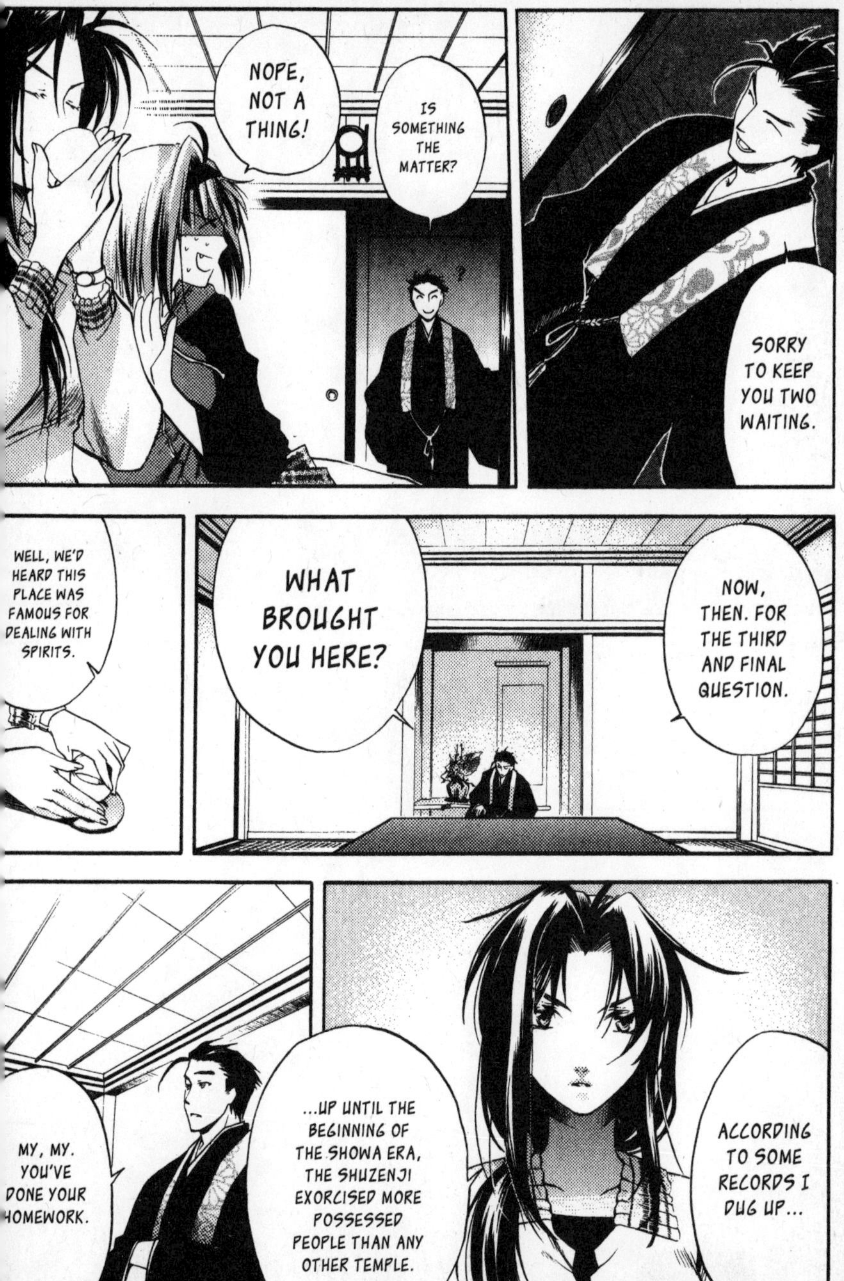
SORRY TO KEEP YOU TWO WAITING.
IS SOMETHING THE MATTER?
NOPE, NOT A THING!
NOW, THEN. FOR THE THIRD AND FINAL QUESTION.
WHAT BROUGHT YOU HERE?
WELL, WE'D HEARD THIS PLACE WAS FAMOUS FOR DEALING WITH SPIRITS.
ACCORDING TO SOME RECORDS I DUG UP...
...UP UNTIL THE BEGINNING OF THE SHOWA ERA, THE SHUZENJI EXORCISED MORE POSSESSED PEOPLE THAN ANY OTHER TEMPLE.
MY, MY. YOU'VE DONE YOUR HOMEWORK.

Showa Era: 1925-1989

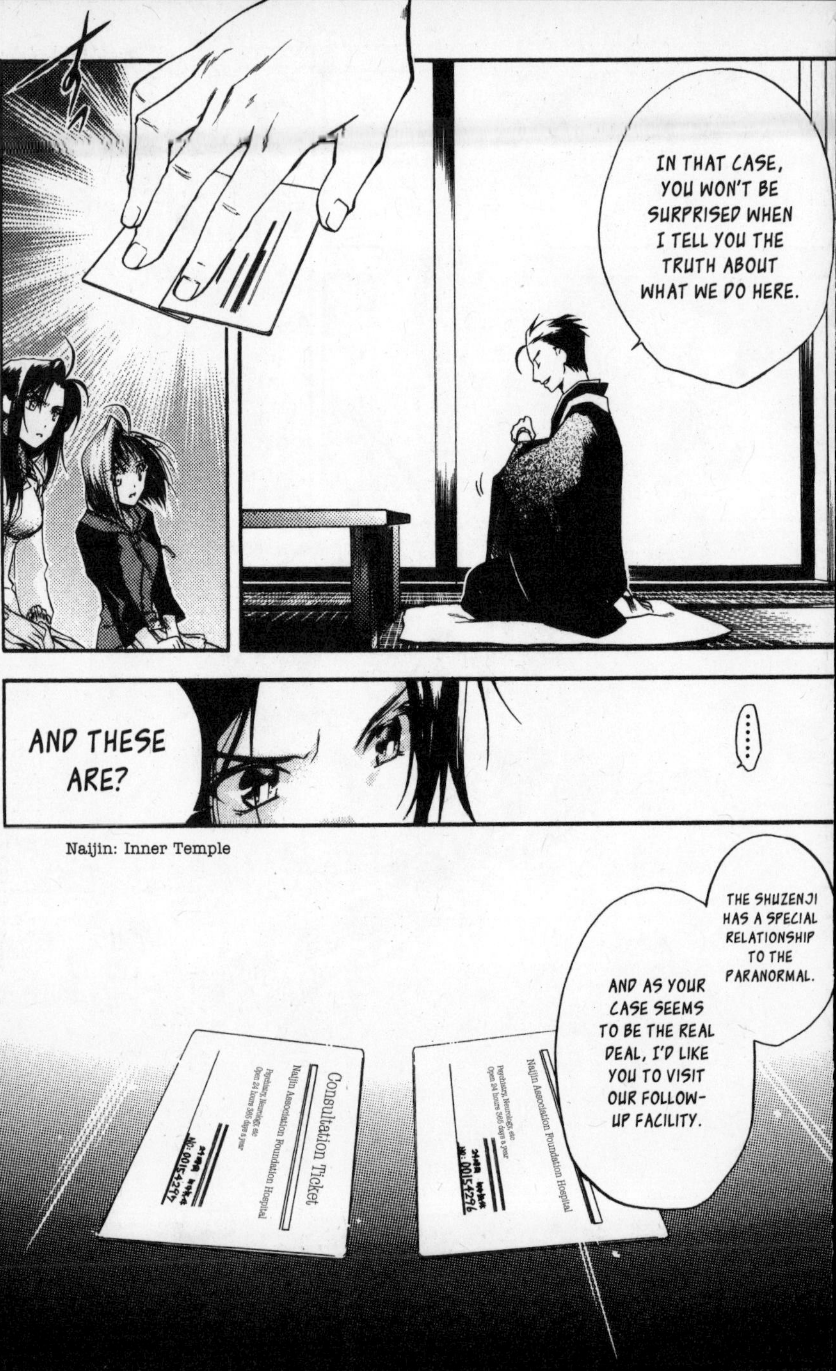
IN THAT CASE, YOU WON'T BE SURPRISED WHEN I TELL YOU THE TRUTH ABOUT WHAT WE DO HERE.
......
AND THESE ARE?
Naijin: Inner Temple
THE SHUZENJI HAS A SPECIAL RELATIONSHIP TO THE PARANORMAL.
AND AS YOUR CASE SEEMS TO BE THE REAL DEAL, I'D LIKE YOU TO VISIT OUR FOLLOW-UP FACILITY.
Naijin Association Foundation Hospital
Psychiatry, Neurology, etc
Open 24 hours 365 days a year
Consultation Ticket
Naijin Association Foundation Hospital
Psychiatry, Neurology, etc
Open 24 hours 365 days a year

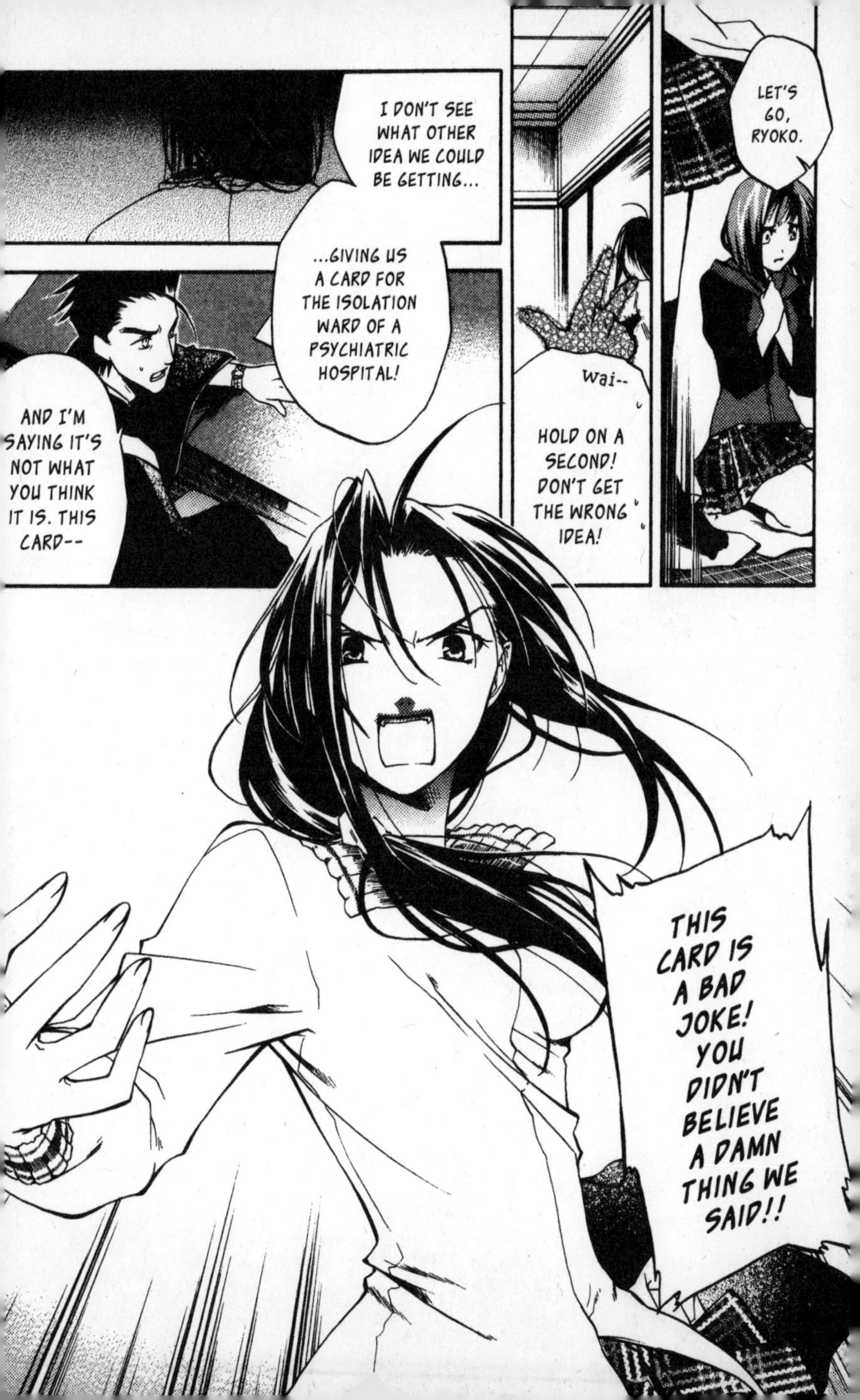
LET'S GO, RYOKO.
Wai--
HOLD ON A SECOND! DON'T GET THE WRONG IDEA!
I DON'T SEE WHAT OTHER IDEA WE COULD BE GETTING...
...GIVING US A CARD FOR THE ISOLATION WARD OF A PSYCHIATRIC HOSPITAL!
AND I'M SAYING IT'S NOT WHAT YOU THINK IT IS. THIS CARD--
THIS CARD IS A BAD JOKE! YOU DIDN'T BELIEVE A DAMN THING WE SAID!!

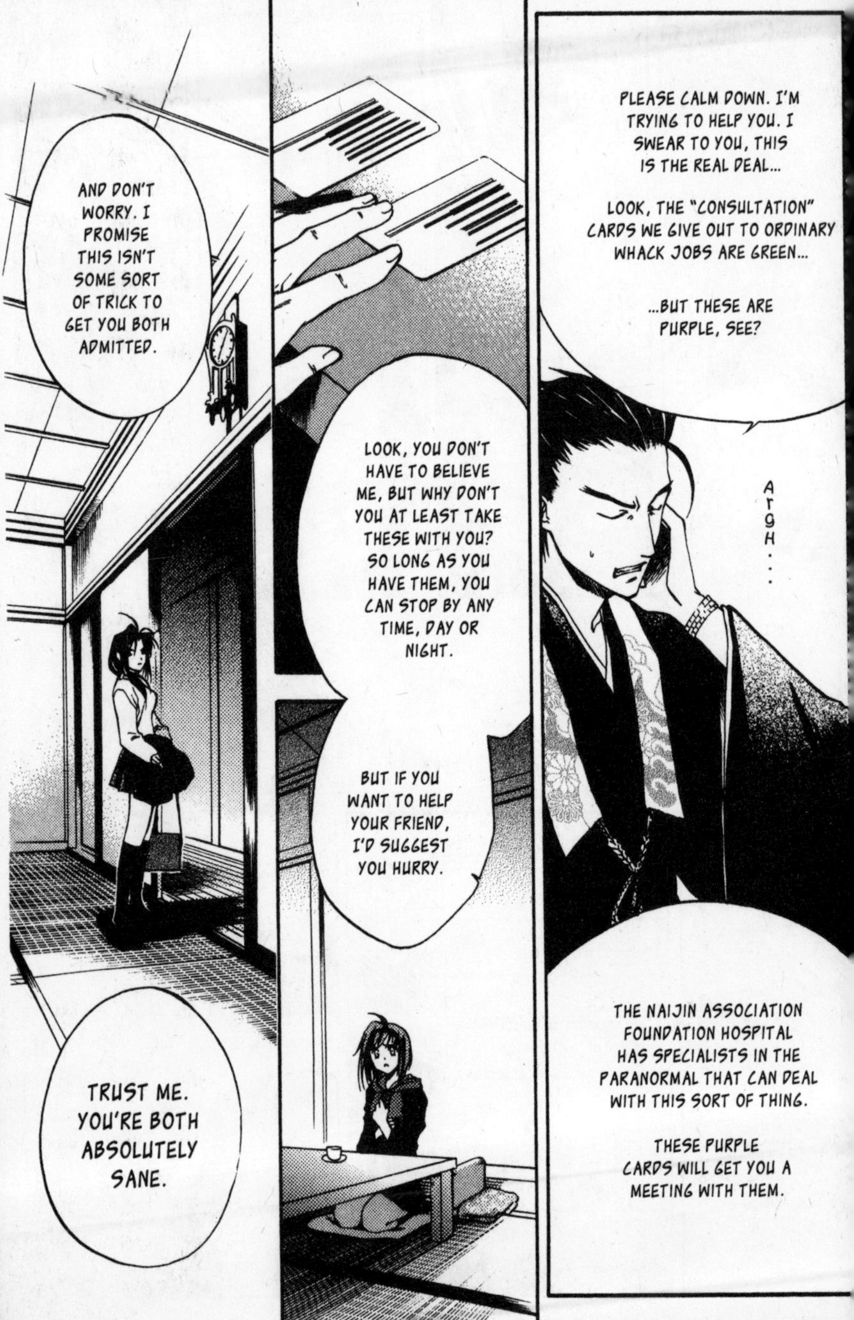
PLEASE CALM DOWN. I'M TRYING TO HELP YOU. I SWEAR TO YOU, THIS IS THE REAL DEAL...
LOOK, THE "CONSULTATION" CARDS WE GIVE OUT TO ORDINARY WHACK JOBS ARE GREEN...
...BUT THESE ARE PURPLE, SEE?
Argh...
THE NAIJIN ASSOCIATION FOUNDATION HOSPITAL HAS SPECIALISTS IN THE PARANORMAL THAT CAN DEAL WITH THIS SORT OF THING.
THESE PURPLE CARDS WILL GET YOU A MEETING WITH THEM.
LOOK, YOU DON'T HAVE TO BELIEVE ME, BUT WHY DON'T YOU AT LEAST TAKE THESE WITH YOU? SO LONG AS YOU HAVE THEM, YOU CAN STOP BY ANY TIME, DAY OR NIGHT.
BUT IF YOU WANT TO HELP YOUR FRIEND, I'D SUGGEST YOU HURRY.
AND DON'T WORRY. I PROMISE THIS ISN'T SOME SORT OF TRICK TO GET YOU BOTH ADMITTED.
TRUST ME. YOU'RE BOTH ABSOLUTELY SANE.

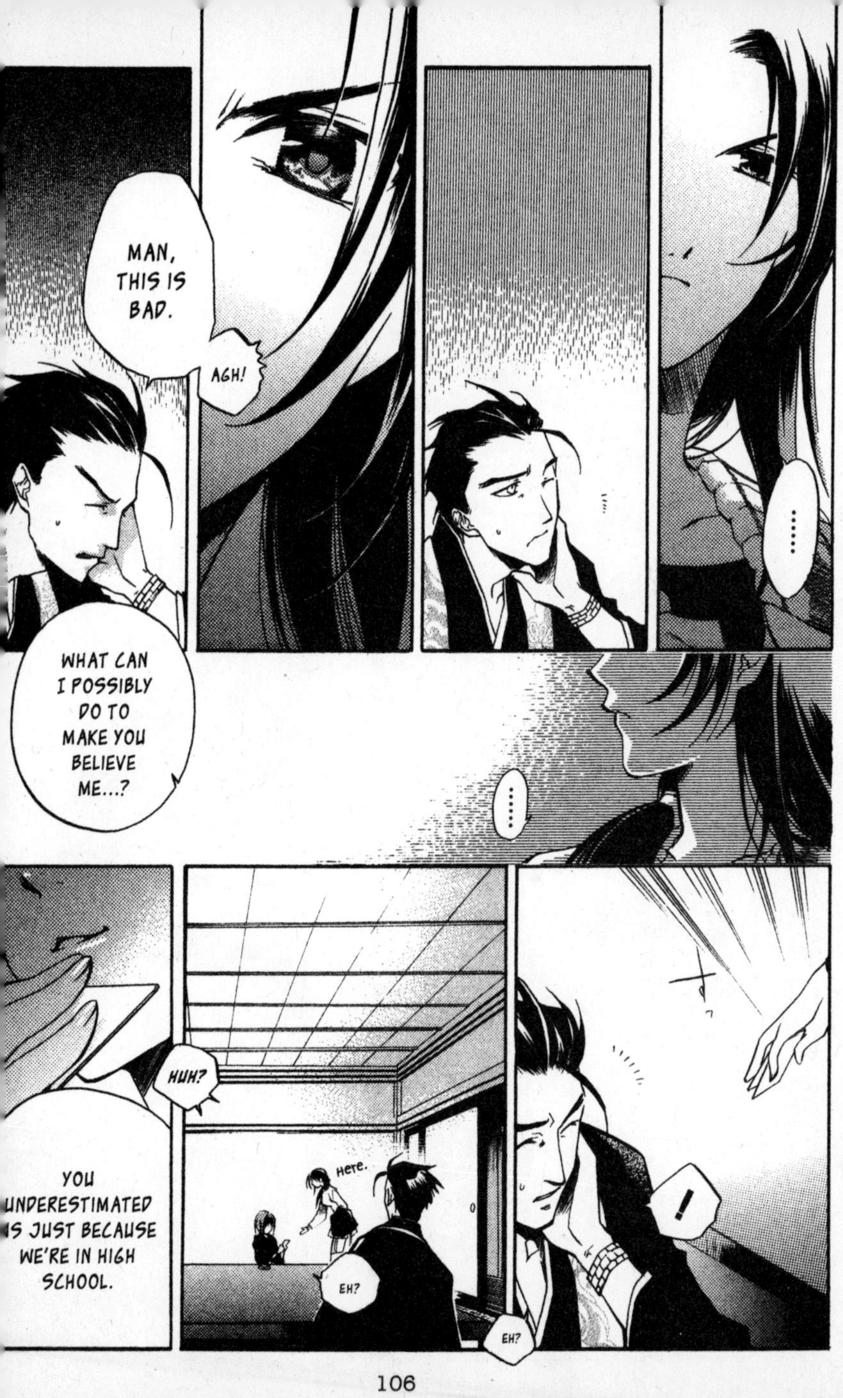
......
AGH!
MAN, THIS IS BAD.
......
WHAT CAN I POSSIBLY DO TO MAKE YOU BELIEVE ME...?
!
Here.
EH?
EH?
HUH?
YOU UNDERESTIMATED US JUST BECAUSE WE'RE IN HIGH SCHOOL.

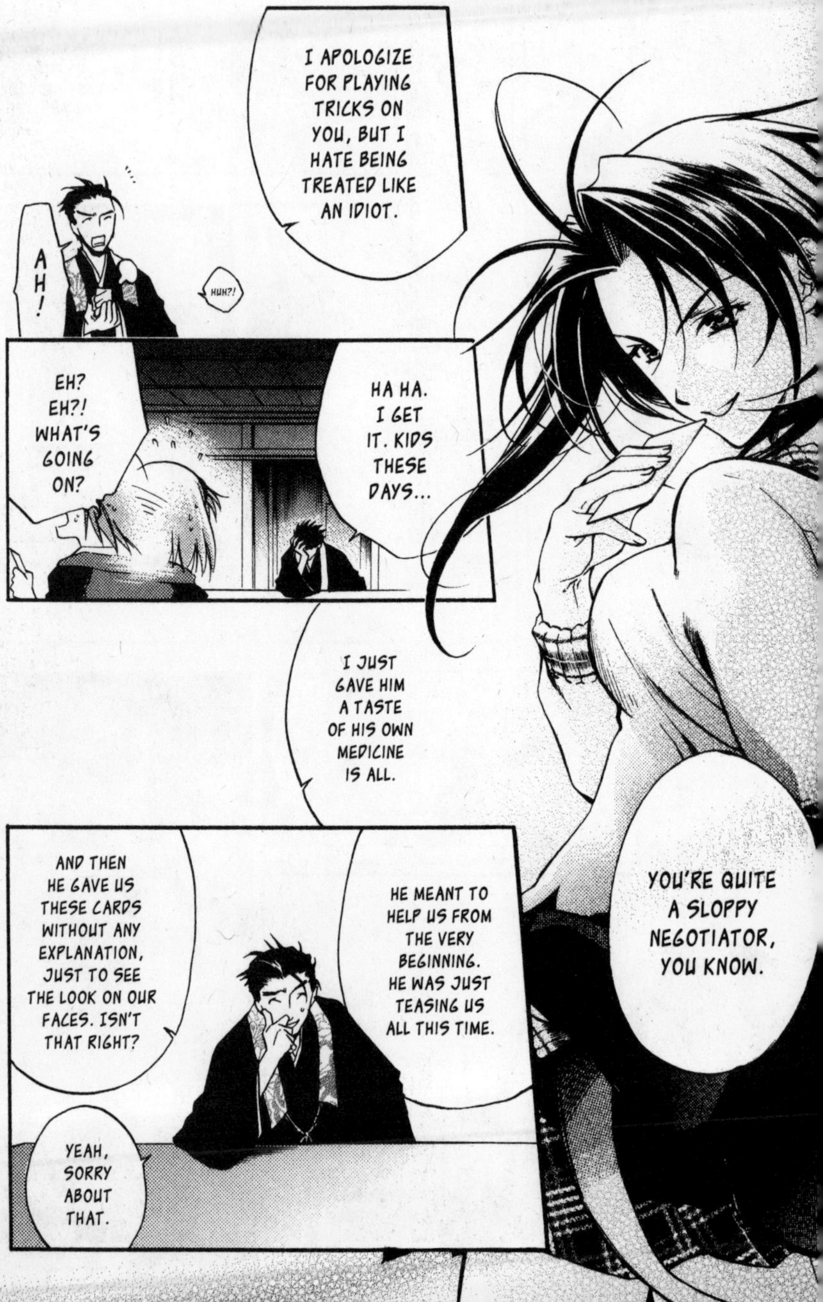

I APOLOGIZE FOR PLAYING TRICKS ON YOU, BUT I HATE BEING TREATED LIKE AN IDIOT.
AH!
HUH?!
HA HA. I GET IT. KIDS THESE DAYS...
EH? EH?! WHAT'S GOING ON?
I JUST GAVE HIM A TASTE OF HIS OWN MEDICINE IS ALL.
YOU'RE QUITE A SLOPPY NEGOTIATOR, YOU KNOW.
HE MEANT TO HELP US FROM THE VERY BEGINNING. HE WAS JUST TEASING US ALL THIS TIME.
AND THEN HE GAVE US THESE CARDS WITHOUT ANY EXPLANATION, JUST TO SEE THE LOOK ON OUR FACES. ISN'T THAT RIGHT?
YEAH, SORRY ABOUT THAT.

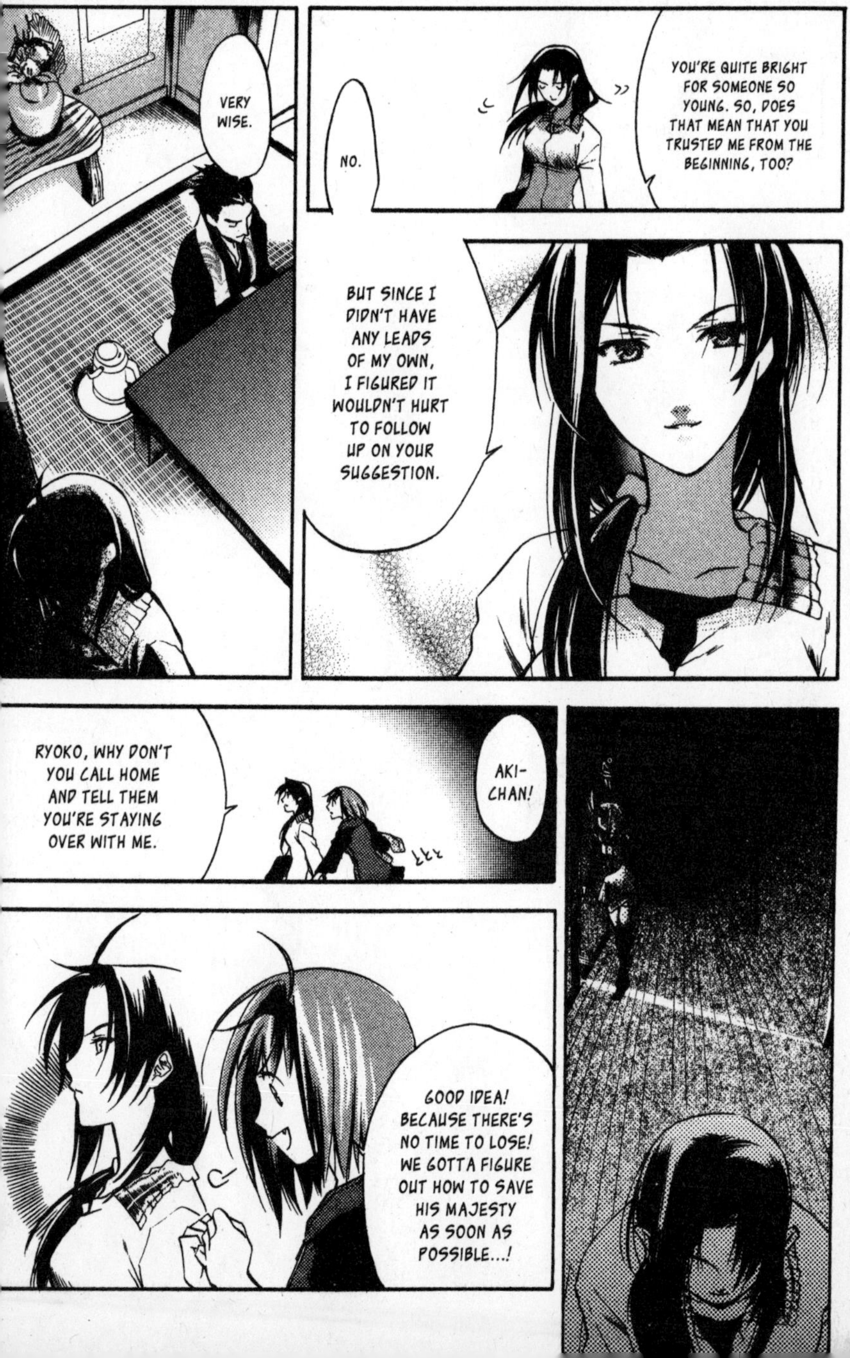
YOU'RE QUITE BRIGHT FOR SOMEONE SO YOUNG. SO, DOES THAT MEAN THAT YOU TRUSTED ME FROM THE BEGINNING, TOO?
NO.
BUT SINCE I DIDN'T HAVE ANY LEADS OF MY OWN, I FIGURED IT WOULDN'T HURT TO FOLLOW UP ON YOUR SUGGESTION.
VERY WISE.
AKI-CHAN!
RYOKO, WHY DON'T YOU CALL HOME AND TELL THEM YOU'RE STAYING OVER WITH ME.
GOOD IDEA! BECAUSE THERE'S NO TIME TO LOSE! WE GOTTA FIGURE OUT HOW TO SAVE HIS MAJESTY AS SOON AS POSSIBLE...!

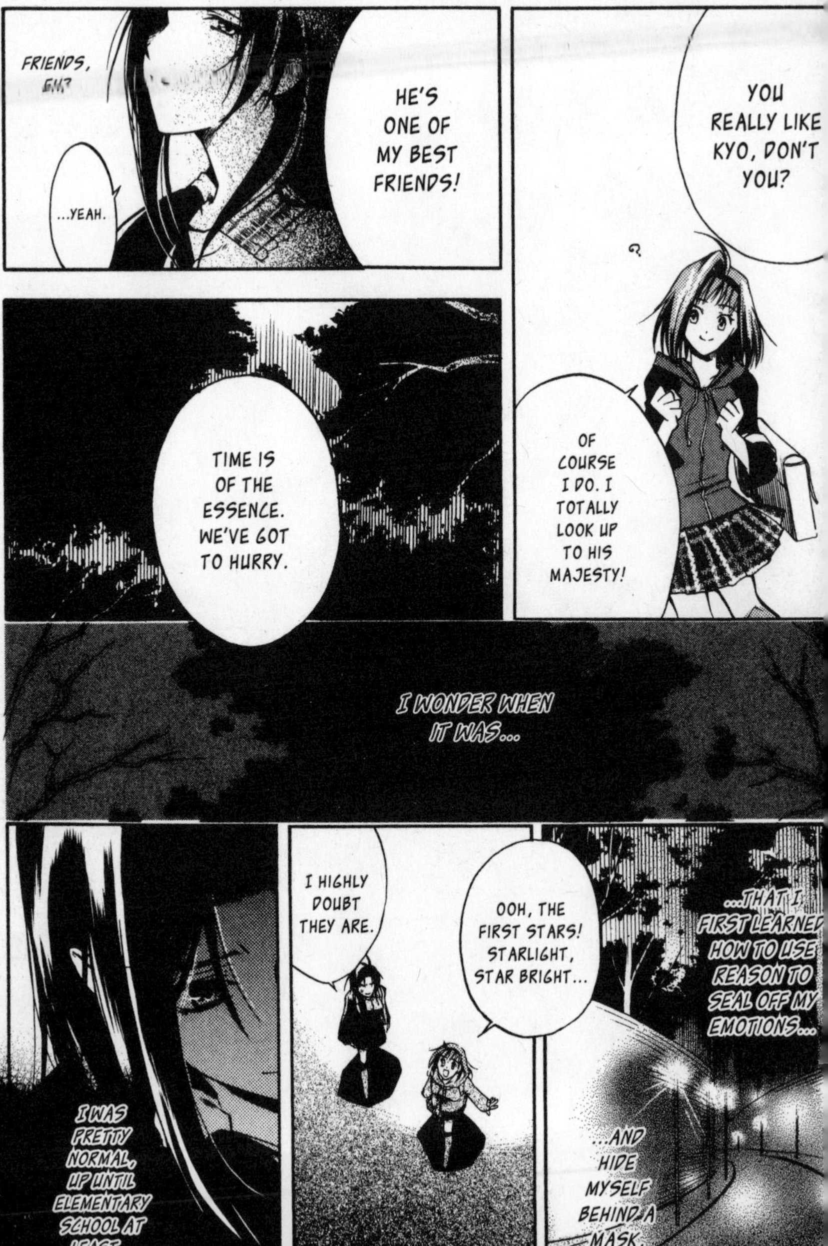
YOU REALLY LIKE KYO, DON'T YOU?
?
OF COURSE I DO. I TOTALLY LOOK UP TO HIS MAJESTY!
HE'S ONE OF MY BEST FRIENDS!
FRIENDS, EH?
...YEAH.
TIME IS OF THE ESSENCE. WE'VE GOT TO HURRY.
I WONDER WHEN IT WAS...
...THAT I FIRST LEARNED HOW TO USE REASON TO SEAL OFF MY EMOTIONS...
...AND HIDE MYSELF BEHIND A MASK.
OOH, THE FIRST STARS! STARLIGHT, STAR BRIGHT...
I HIGHLY DOUBT THEY ARE.
I WAS PRETTY NORMAL, UP UNTIL ELEMENTARY SCHOOL AT LEAST...

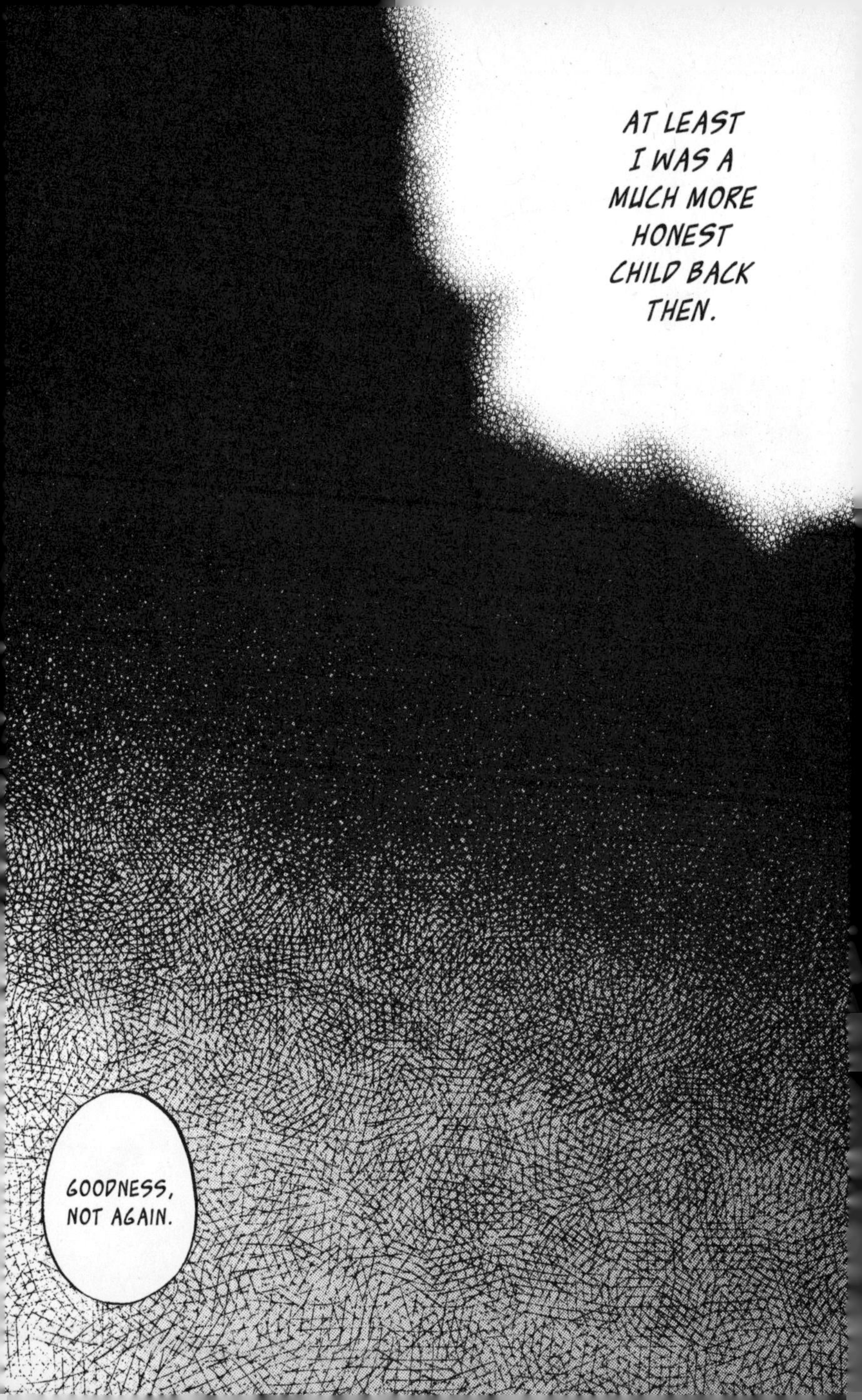
AT LEAST I WAS A MUCH MORE HONEST CHILD BACK THEN.
GOODNESS, NOT AGAIN.

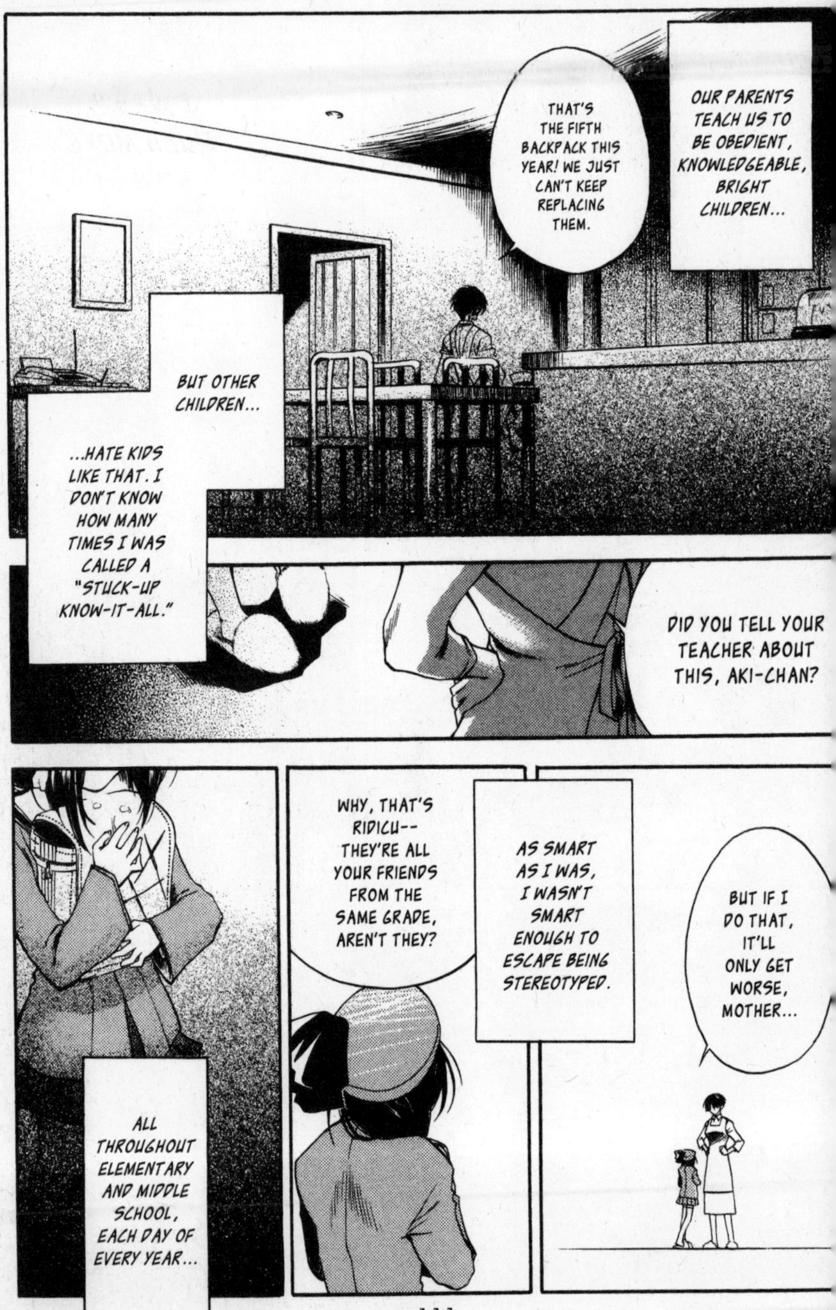
OUR PARENTS TEACH US TO BE OBEDIENT, KNOWLEDGEABLE, BRIGHT CHILDREN...
THAT'S THE FIFTH BACKPACK THIS YEAR! WE JUST CAN'T KEEP REPLACING THEM.
BUT OTHER CHILDREN...
...HATE KIDS LIKE THAT. I DON'T KNOW HOW MANY TIMES I WAS CALLED A "STUCK-UP KNOW-IT-ALL."
DID YOU TELL YOUR TEACHER ABOUT THIS, AKI-CHAN?
BUT IF I DO THAT, IT'LL ONLY GET WORSE, MOTHER...
AS SMART AS I WAS, I WASN'T SMART ENOUGH TO ESCAPE BEING STEREOTYPED.
WHY, THAT'S RIDICU-- THEY'RE ALL YOUR FRIENDS FROM THE SAME GRADE, AREN'T THEY?
ALL THROUGHOUT ELEMENTARY AND MIDDLE SCHOOL, EACH DAY OF EVERY YEAR...

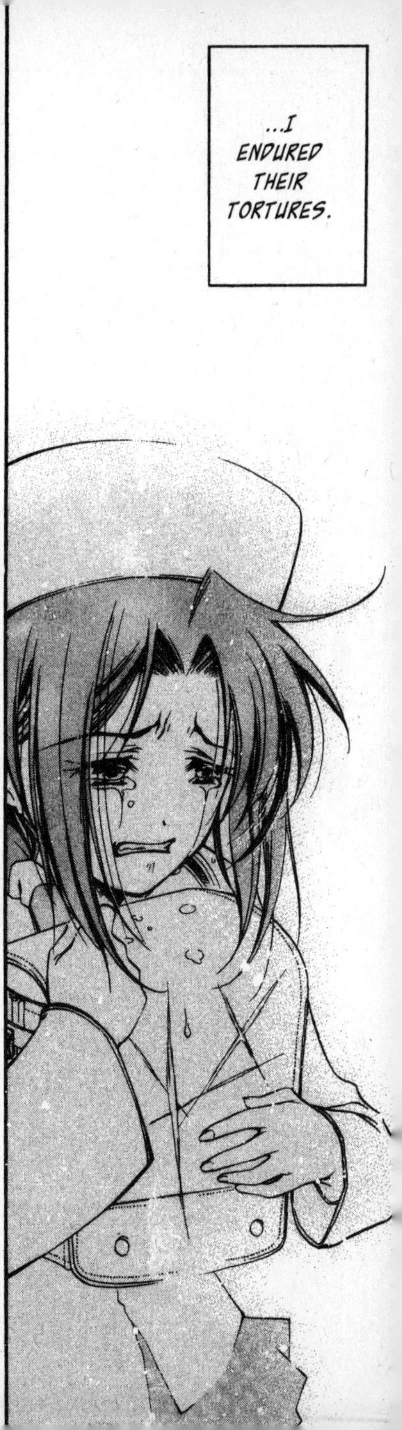
...I ENDURED THEIR TORTURES.

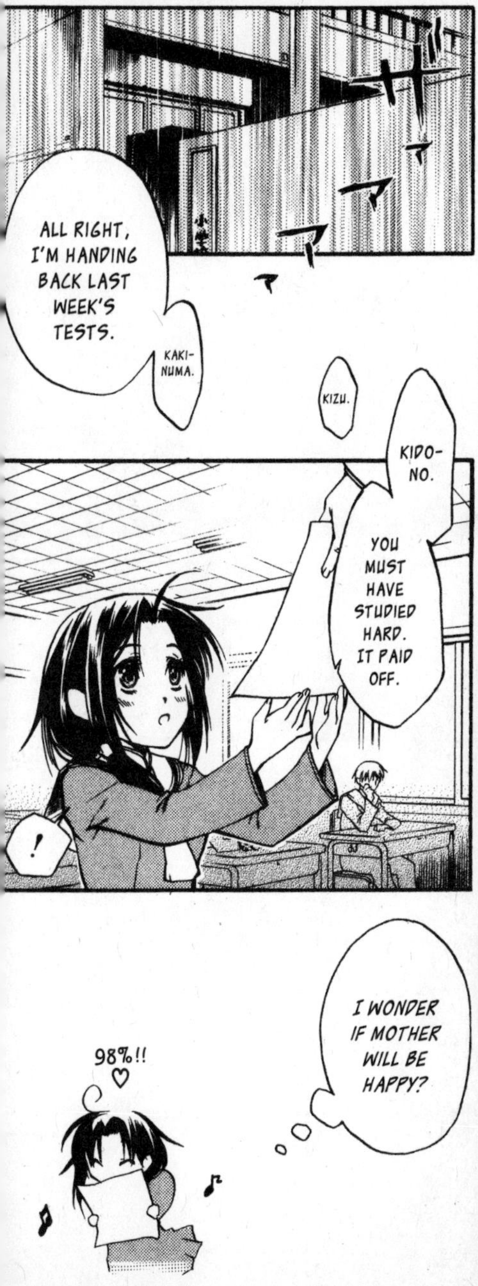
ALL RIGHT, I'M HANDING BACK LAST WEEK'S TESTS.
KAKI-NUMA.
KIZU.
KIDO-NO.
YOU MUST HAVE STUDIED HARD. IT PAID OFF.
!
I WONDER IF MOTHER WILL BE HAPPY?
98%!! ♡

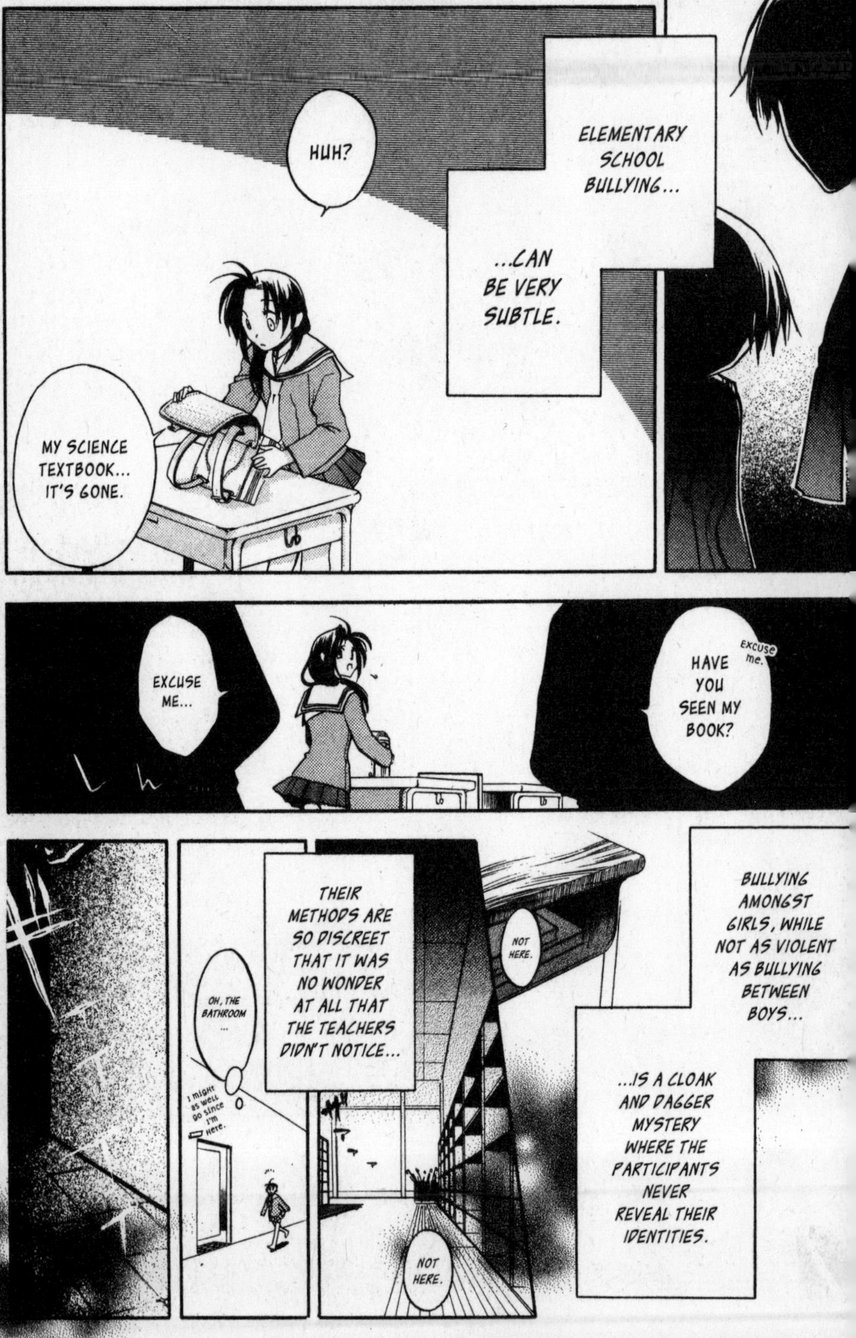
ELEMENTARY SCHOOL BULLYING...
...CAN BE VERY SUBTLE.
HUH?
MY SCIENCE TEXTBOOK... IT'S GONE.
HAVE YOU SEEN MY BOOK?
EXCUSE ME.
EXCUSE ME...
BULLYING AMONGST GIRLS, WHILE NOT AS VIOLENT AS BULLYING BETWEEN BOYS...
...IS A CLOAK AND DAGGER MYSTERY WHERE THE PARTICIPANTS NEVER REVEAL THEIR IDENTITIES.
NOT HERE.
NOT HERE.
THEIR METHODS ARE SO DISCREET THAT IT WAS NO WONDER AT ALL THAT THE TEACHERS DIDN'T NOTICE...
OH, THE BATHROOM ...
I might as well go since I'm here.

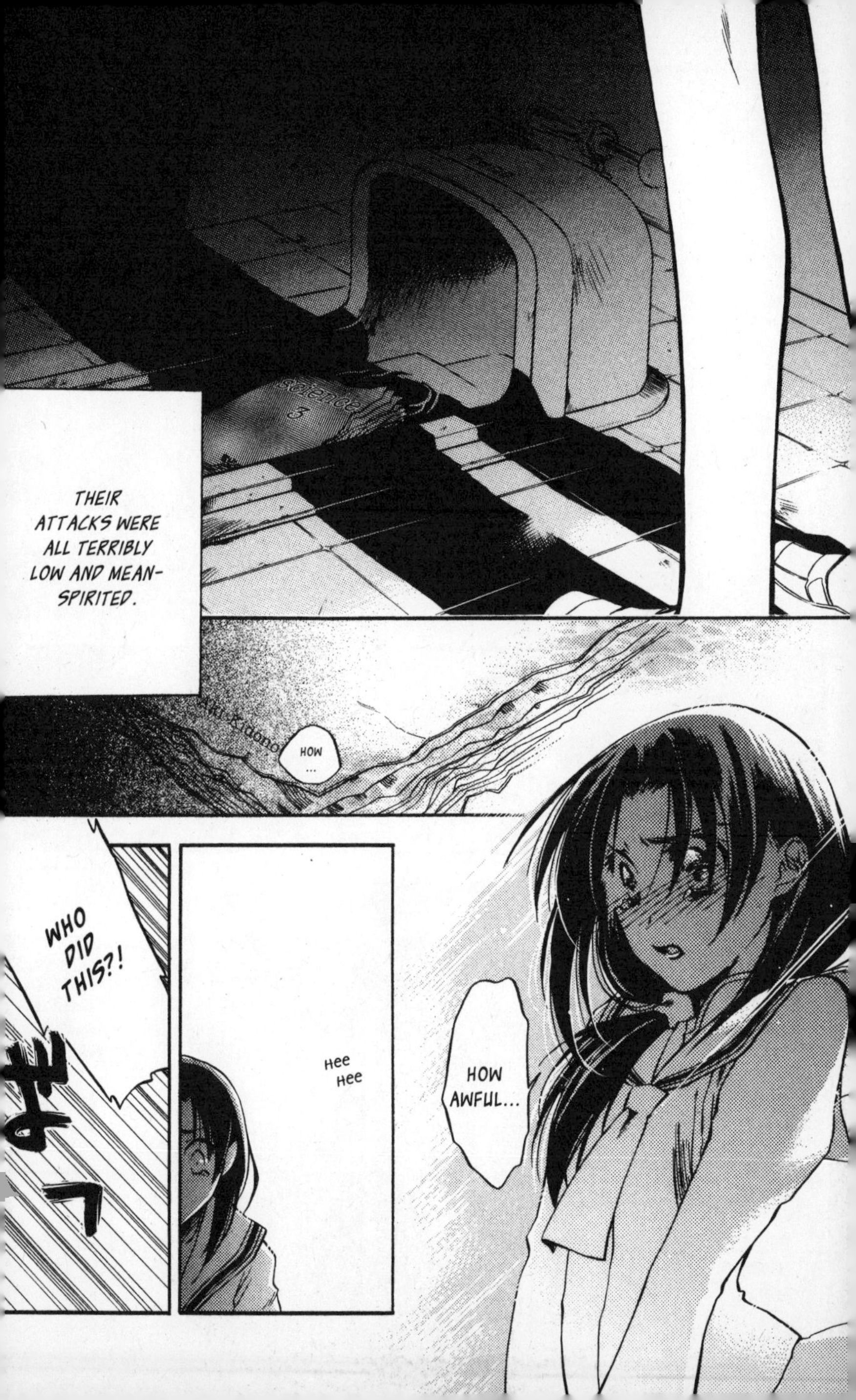
science
3
THEIR ATTACKS WERE ALL TERRIBLY LOW AND MEAN-SPIRITED.
HOW ...
HOW AWFUL...
Hee Hee
WHO DID THIS?!

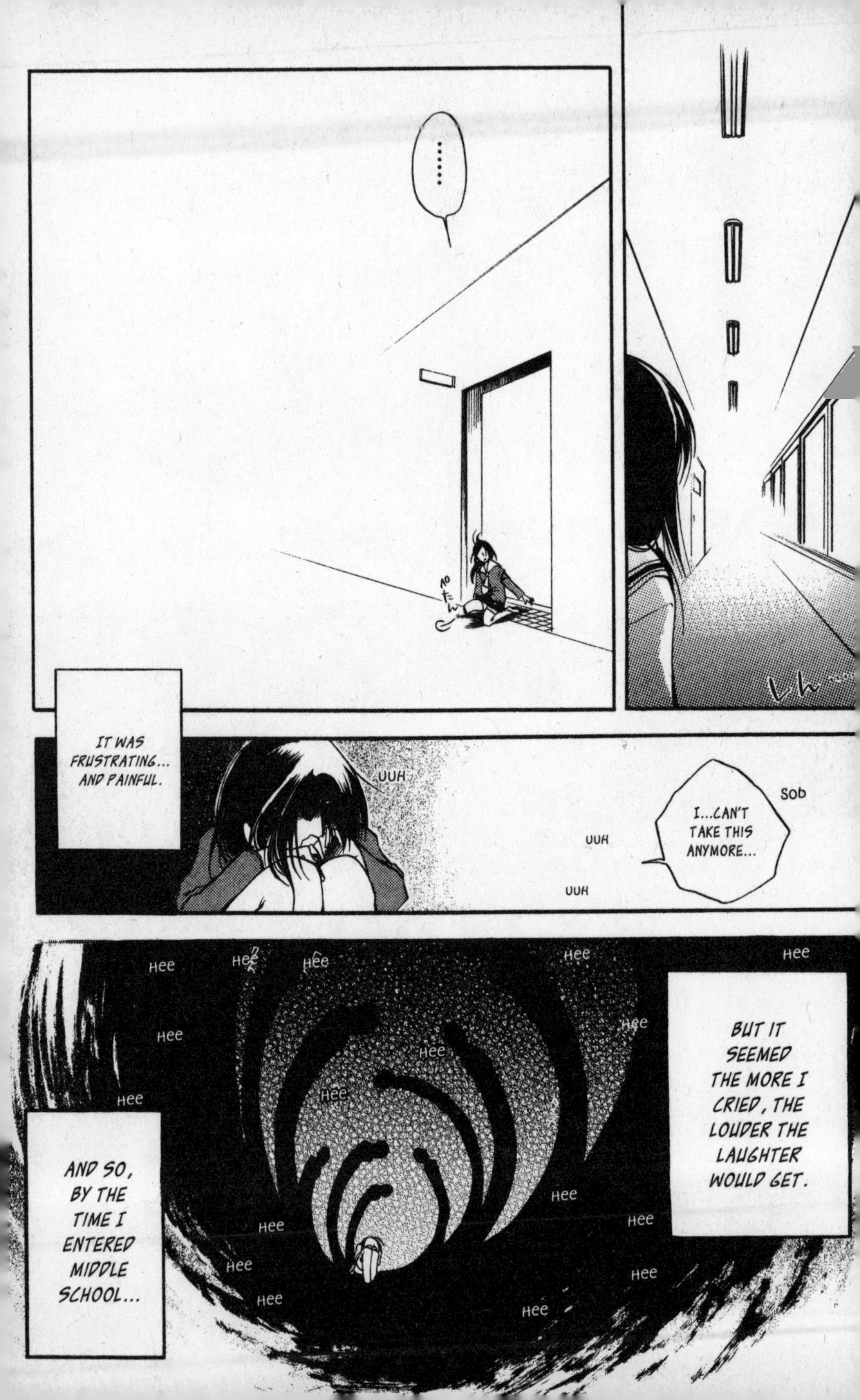
しん…
……
Sob
I...CAN'T TAKE THIS ANYMORE...
UUH
UUH
UUH
IT WAS FRUSTRATING... AND PAINFUL.
BUT IT SEEMED THE MORE I CRIED, THE LOUDER THE LAUGHTER WOULD GET.
Hee
Hee
Hee
Hee
Hee
Hee
Hee
Hee
Hee
Hee
Hee
Hee
Hee
Hee
Hee
Hee
Hee
Hee
AND SO, BY THE TIME I ENTERED MIDDLE SCHOOL...

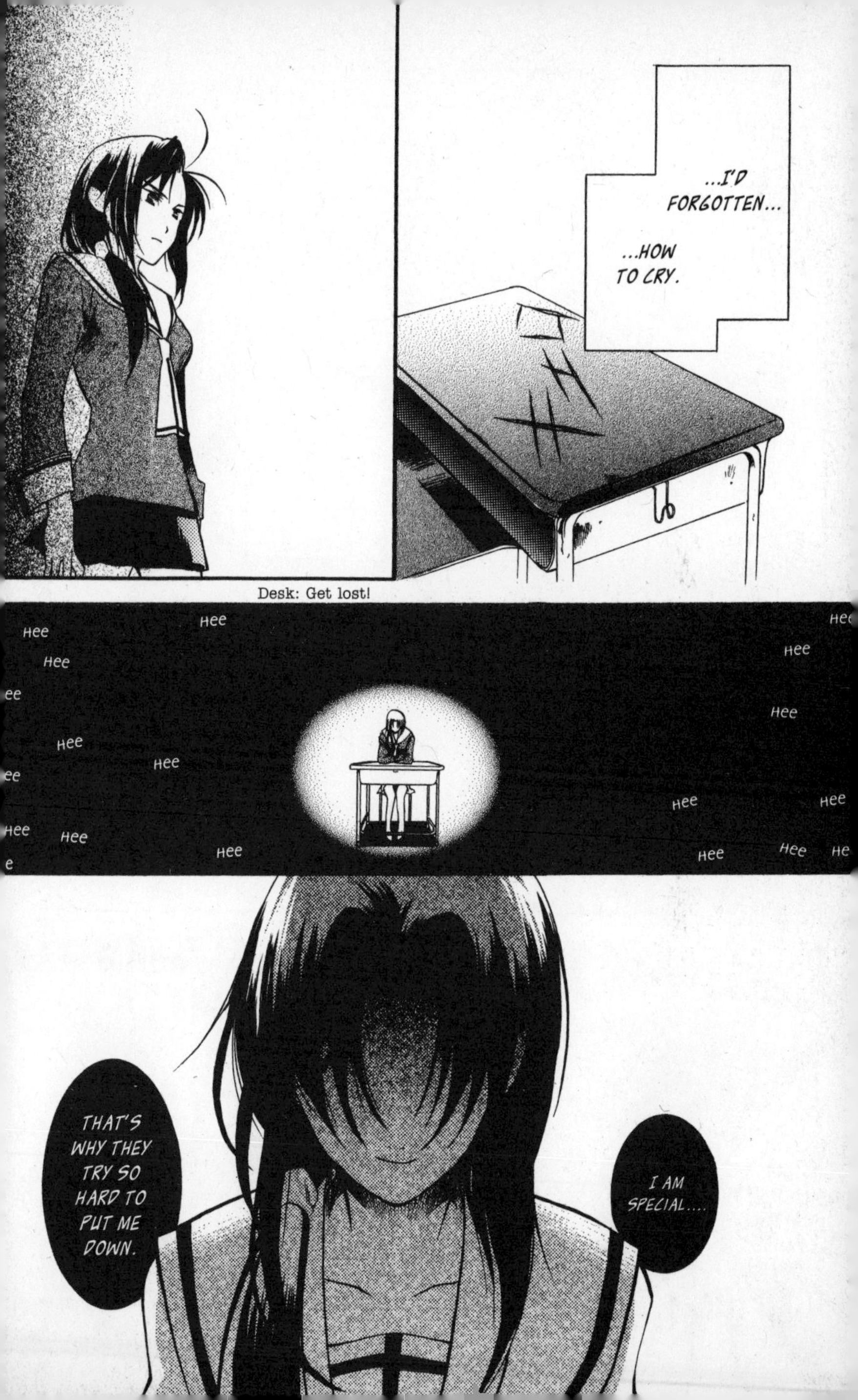
...I'D FORGOTTEN...
...HOW TO CRY.
Desk: Get lost!
Hee
Hee
Hee
Hee
Hee
Hee
Hee
Hee
Hee
Hee
Hee
Hee
Hee
I AM SPECIAL....
THAT'S WHY THEY TRY SO HARD TO PUT ME DOWN.

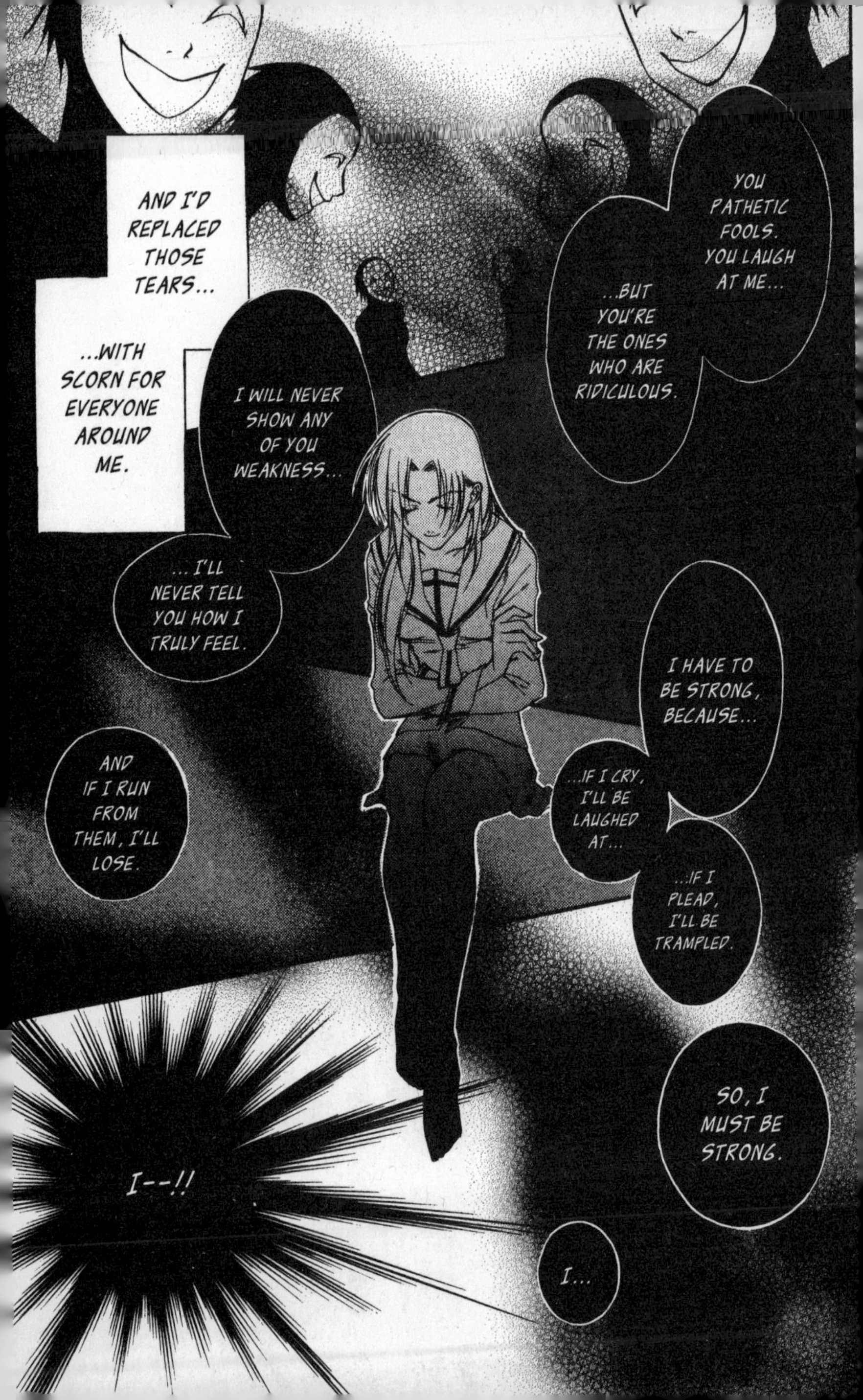
YOU PATHETIC FOOLS. YOU LAUGH AT ME...
AND I'D REPLACED THOSE TEARS...
...BUT YOU'RE THE ONES WHO ARE RIDICULOUS.
...WITH SCORN FOR EVERYONE AROUND ME.
I WILL NEVER SHOW ANY OF YOU WEAKNESS...
...I'LL NEVER TELL YOU HOW I TRULY FEEL.
I HAVE TO BE STRONG, BECAUSE...
...IF I CRY, I'LL BE LAUGHED AT...
...IF I PLEAD, I'LL BE TRAMPLED.
AND IF I RUN FROM THEM, I'LL LOSE.
SO, I MUST BE STRONG.
I...
I--!!

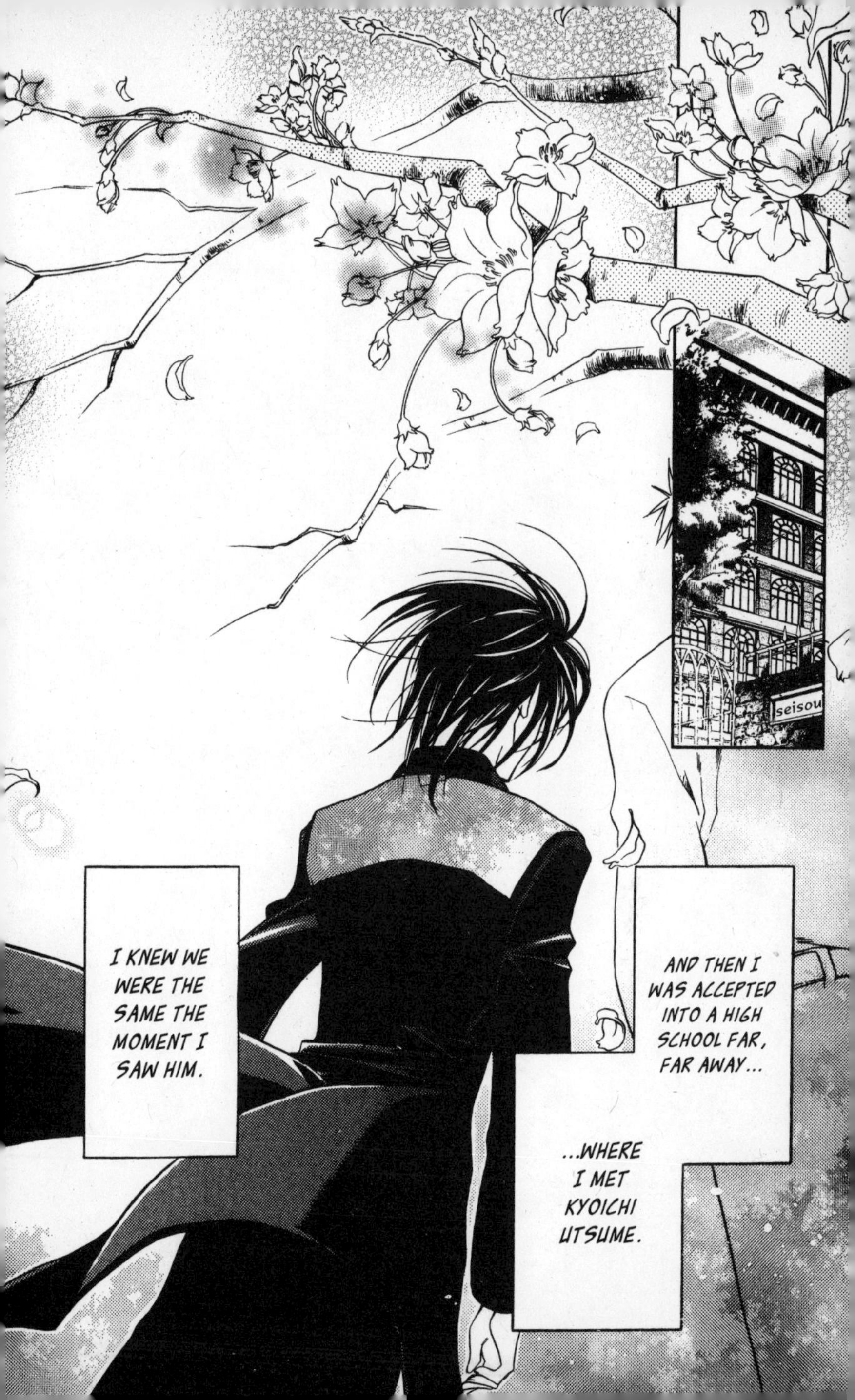
seisou
AND THEN I WAS ACCEPTED INTO A HIGH SCHOOL FAR, FAR AWAY...
...WHERE I MET KYOICHI UTSUME.
I KNEW WE WERE THE SAME THE MOMENT I SAW HIM.

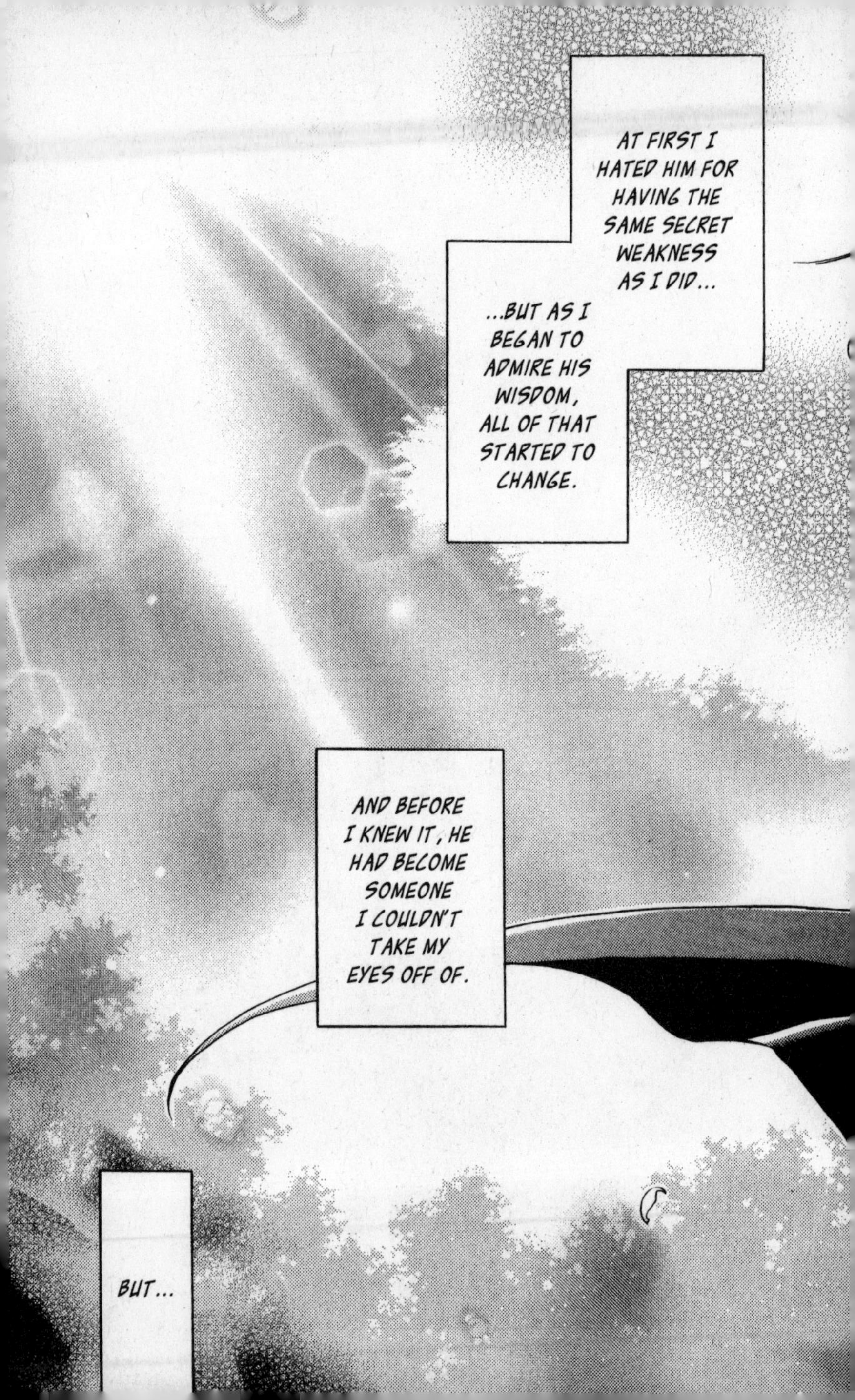
AT FIRST I HATED HIM FOR HAVING THE SAME SECRET WEAKNESS AS I DID...
...BUT AS I BEGAN TO ADMIRE HIS WISDOM, ALL OF THAT STARTED TO CHANGE.
AND BEFORE I KNEW IT, HE HAD BECOME SOMEONE I COULDN'T TAKE MY EYES OFF OF.
BUT...

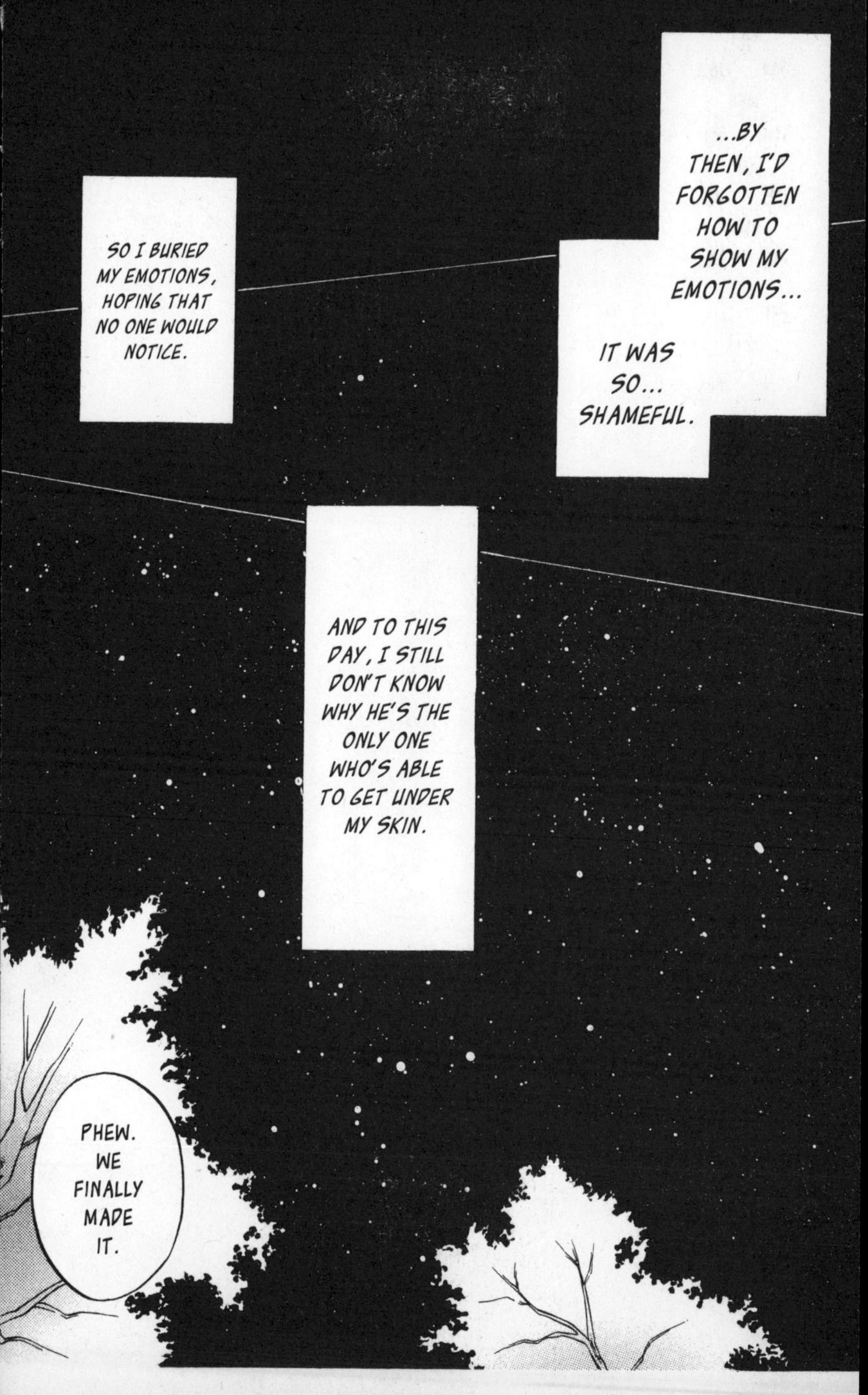
...BY THEN, I'D FORGOTTEN HOW TO SHOW MY EMOTIONS...
IT WAS SO... SHAMEFUL.
SO I BURIED MY EMOTIONS, HOPING THAT NO ONE WOULD NOTICE.
AND TO THIS DAY, I STILL DON'T KNOW WHY HE'S THE ONLY ONE WHO'S ABLE TO GET UNDER MY SKIN.
PHEW. WE FINALLY MADE IT.

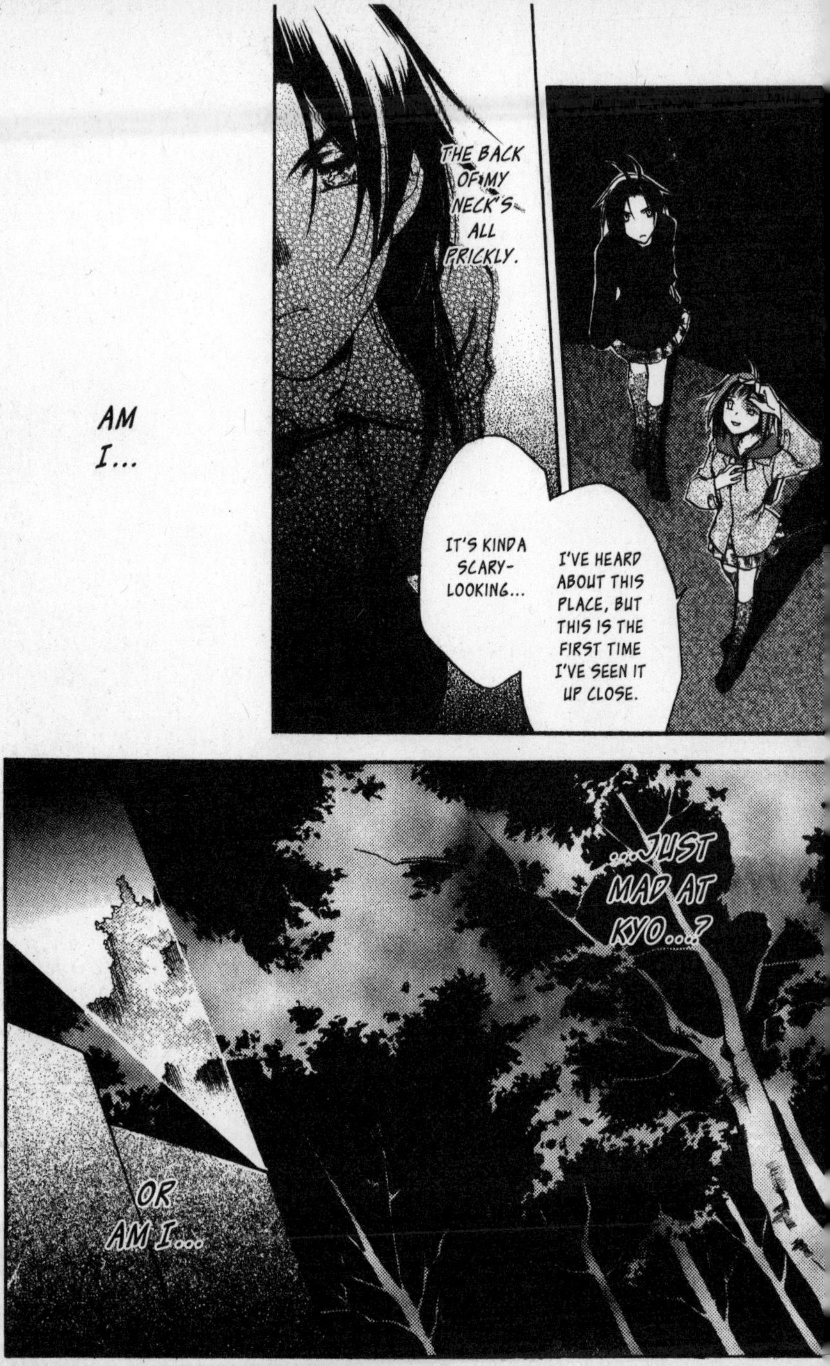
I'VE HEARD ABOUT THIS PLACE, BUT THIS IS THE FIRST TIME I'VE SEEN IT UP CLOSE.
IT'S KINDA SCARY-LOOKING...
THE BACK OF MY NECK'S ALL PRICKLY.
AM I...
...JUST MAD AT KYO...?
OR AM I...

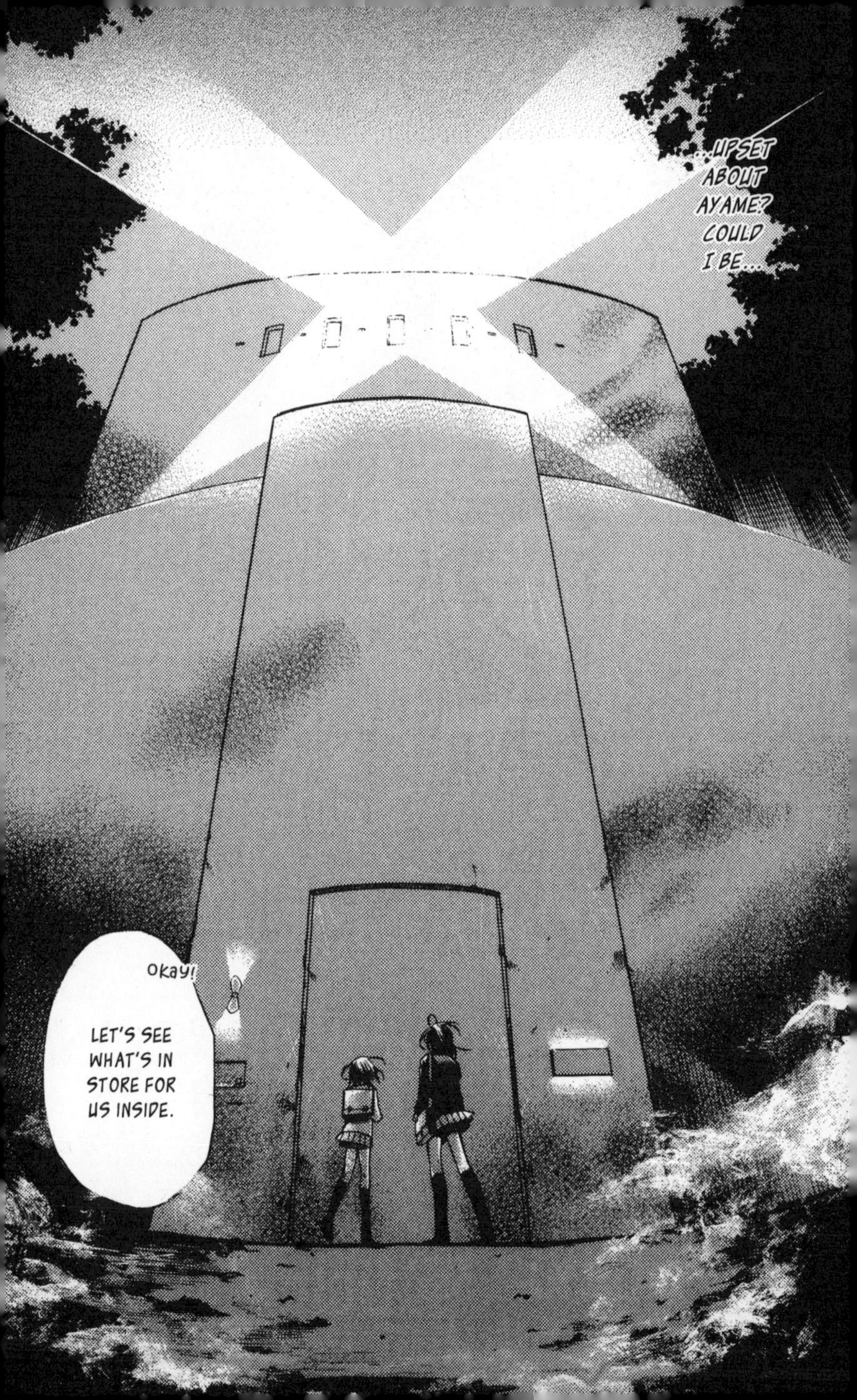
...UPSET ABOUT AYAME? COULD I BE...
Okay!
LET'S SEE WHAT'S IN STORE FOR US INSIDE.

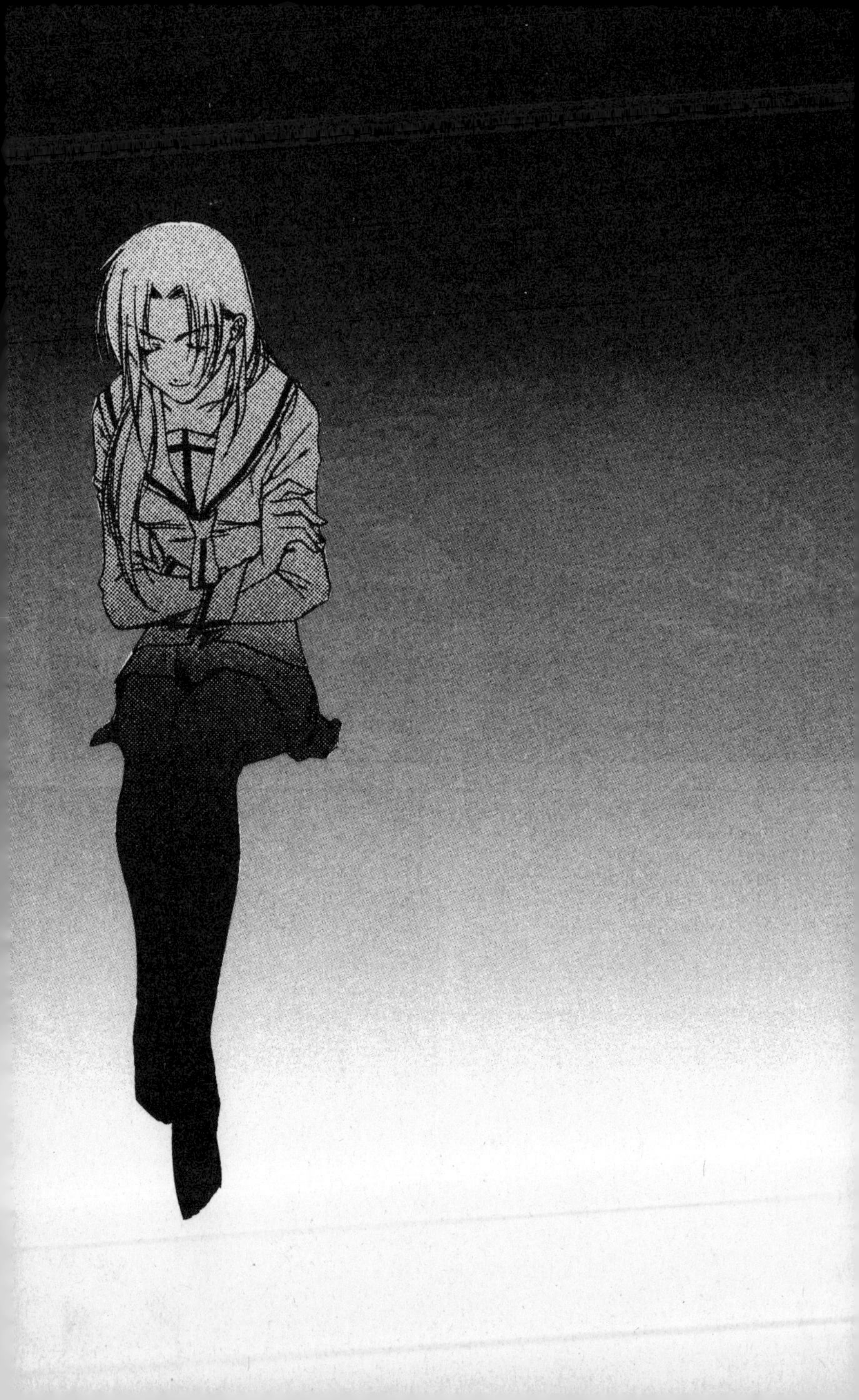

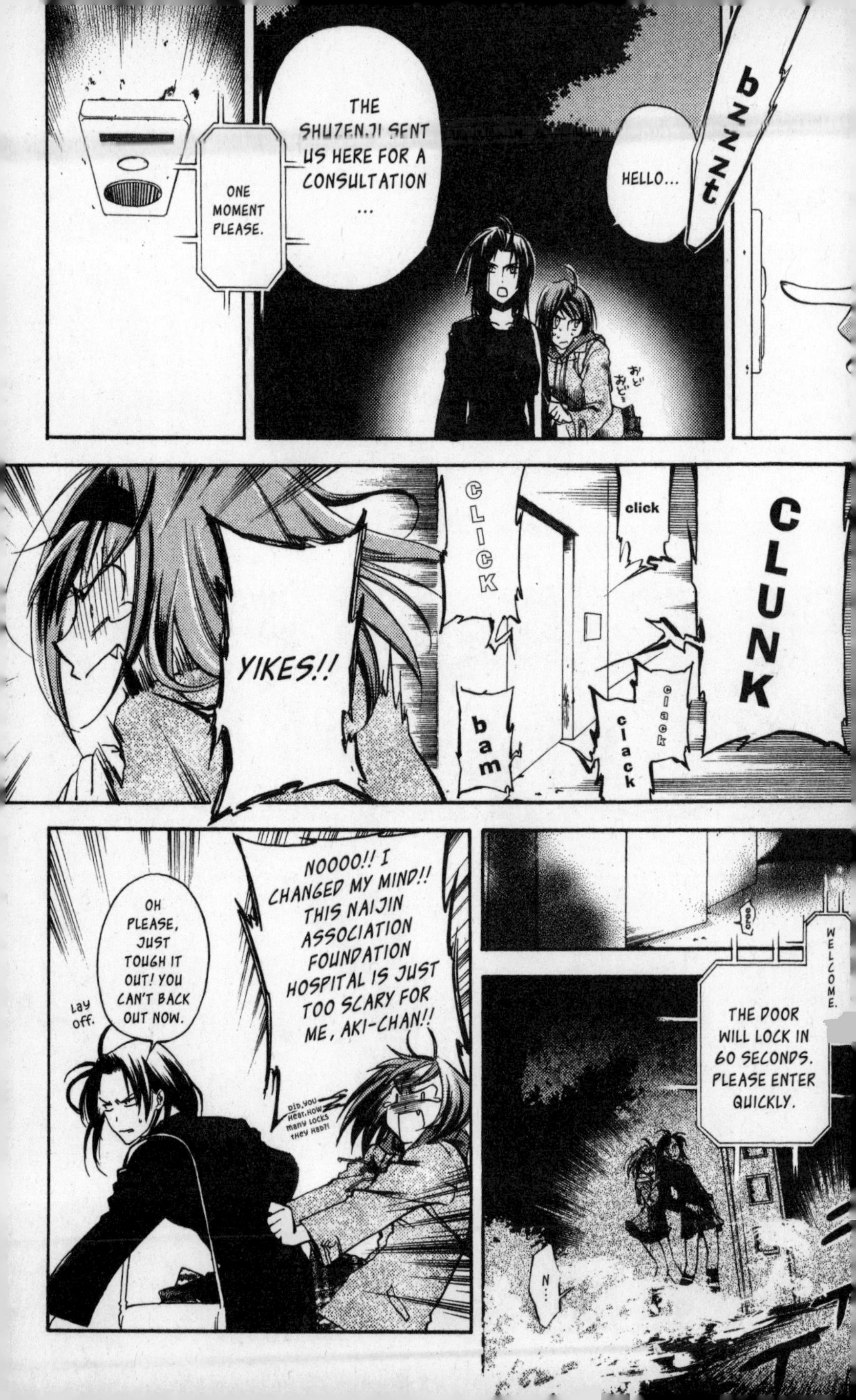
bzzzt
HELLO...
THE SHUZENJI SENT US HERE FOR A CONSULTATION ...
おどおど
ONE MOMENT PLEASE.
CLUNK
click
CLICK
clack
clack
bam
YIKES!!
cree
WELCOME.
THE DOOR WILL LOCK IN 60 SECONDS. PLEASE ENTER QUICKLY.
N...
NOOOO!! I CHANGED MY MIND!! THIS NAIJIN ASSOCIATION FOUNDATION HOSPITAL IS JUST TOO SCARY FOR ME, AKI-CHAN!!
DID YOU HEAR HOW MANY LOCKS THEY HAD?!
OH PLEASE, JUST TOUGH IT OUT! YOU CAN'T BACK OUT NOW.
Lay off.

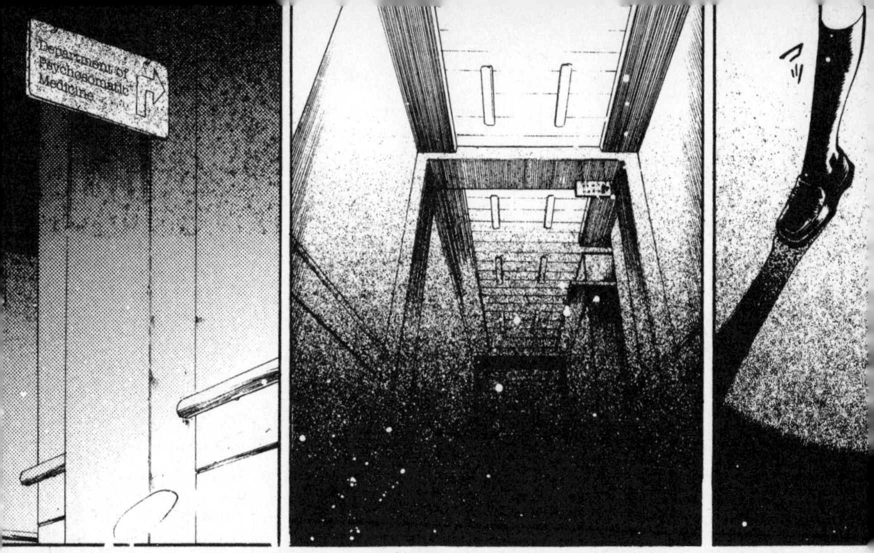
Department of Psychosomatic Medicine

Chapter 8
The Hunter

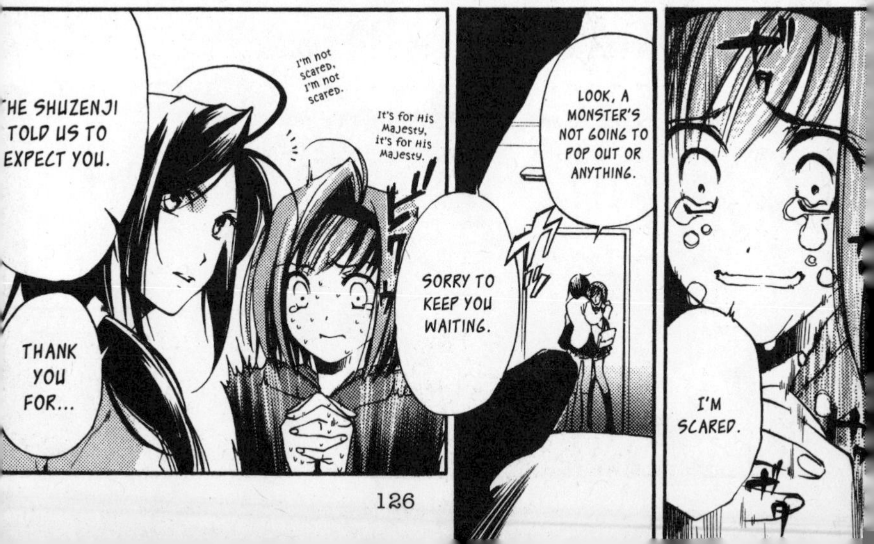
I'M SCARED.
LOOK, A MONSTER'S NOT GOING TO POP OUT OR ANYTHING.
SORRY TO KEEP YOU WAITING.
It's for His Majesty, it's for His Majesty.
I'm not scared, I'm not scared.
HE SHUZENJI TOLD US TO EXPECT YOU.
THANK YOU FOR...

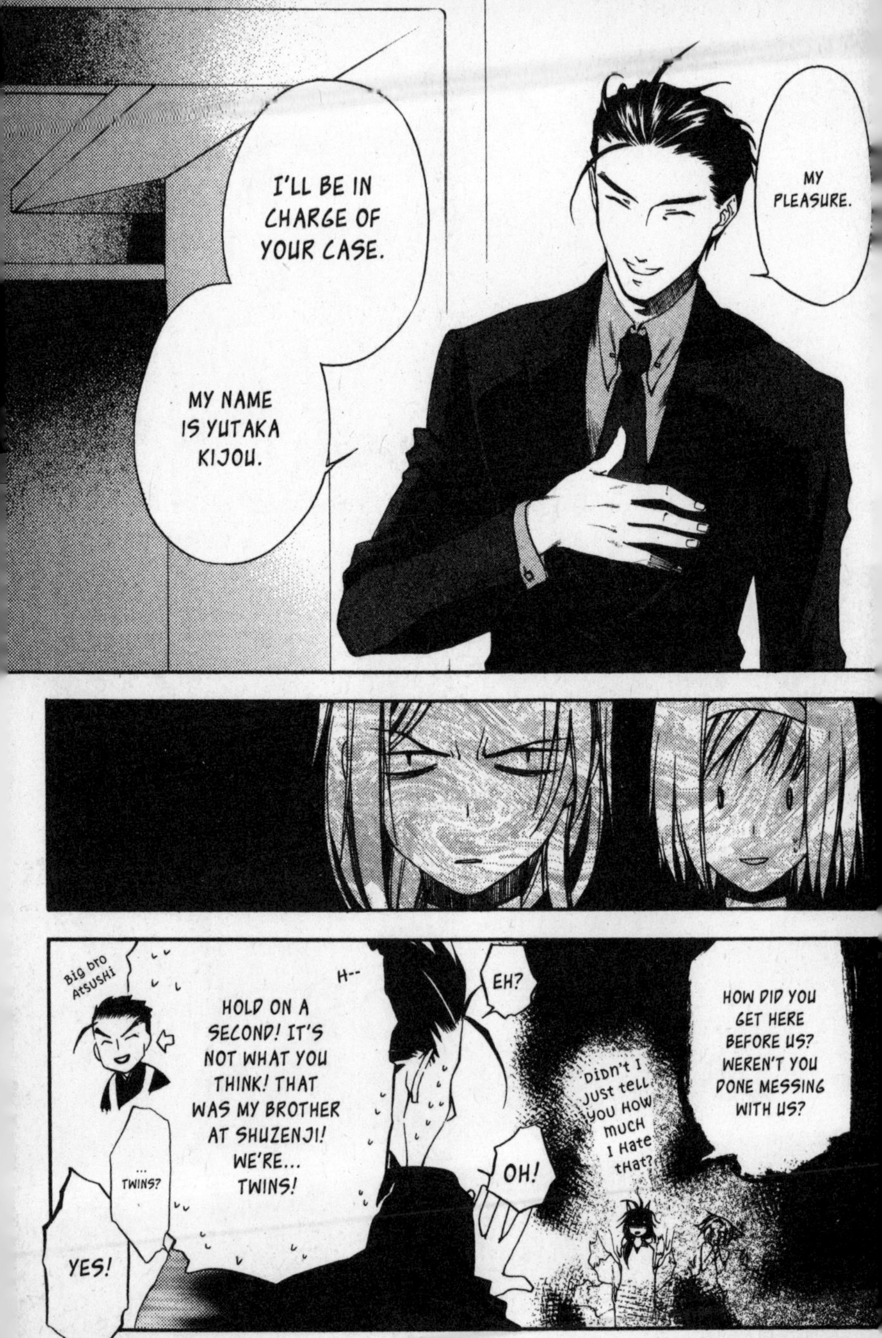
MY PLEASURE.
I'LL BE IN CHARGE OF YOUR CASE.
MY NAME IS YUTAKA KIJOU.
HOW DID YOU GET HERE BEFORE US? WEREN'T YOU DONE MESSING WITH US?
Didn't I just tell you how much I Hate that?
EH?
H--
OH!
HOLD ON A SECOND! IT'S NOT WHAT YOU THINK! THAT WAS MY BROTHER AT SHUZENJI! WE'RE... TWINS!
Big bro Atsushi
...TWINS?
YES!

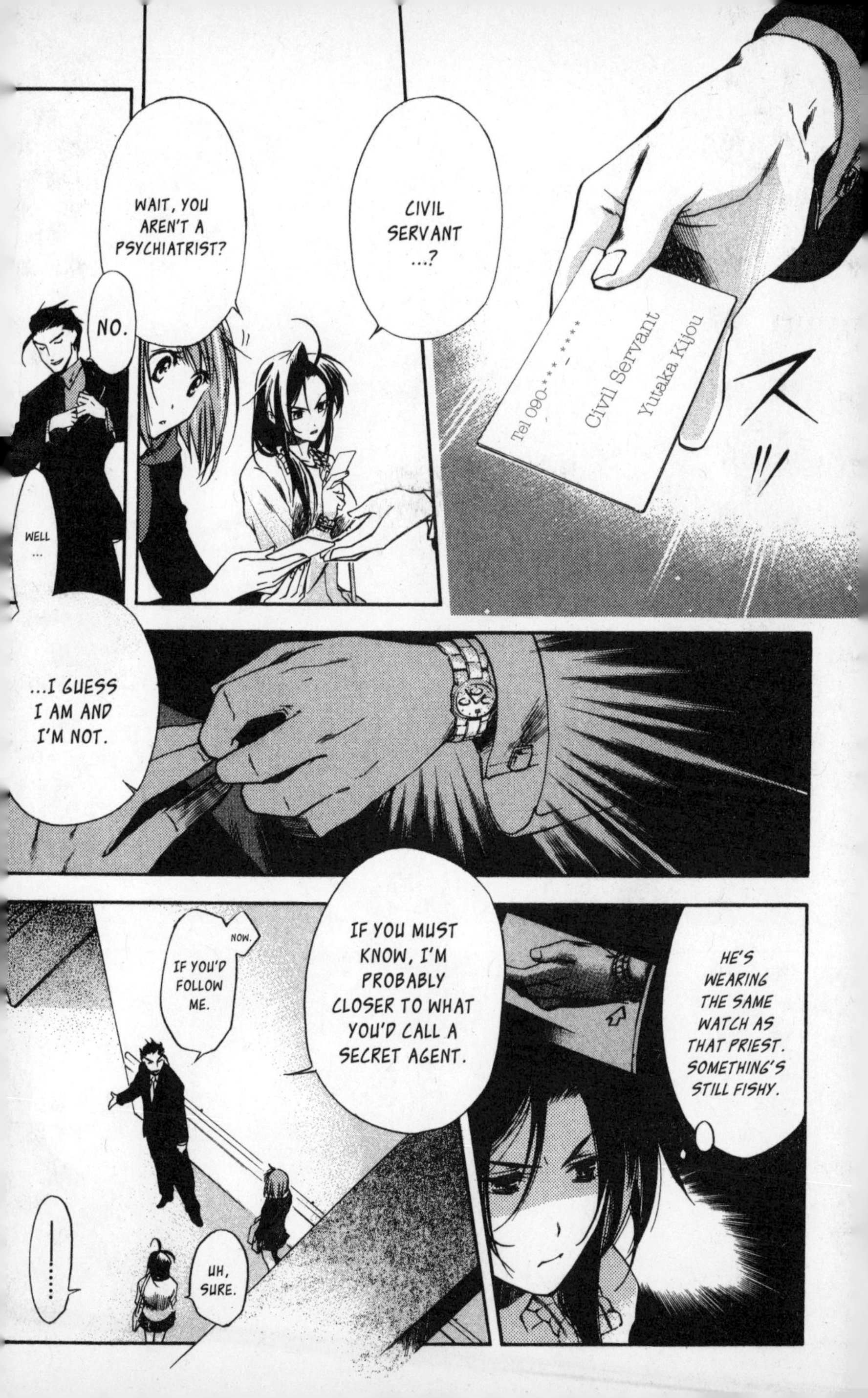
Civil Servant
Yutaka Kijou
Tel 090-****_****
ス
CIVIL SERVANT ...?
WAIT, YOU AREN'T A PSYCHIATRIST?
NO.
WELL ...
...I GUESS I AM AND I'M NOT.
HE'S WEARING THE SAME WATCH AS THAT PRIEST. SOMETHING'S STILL FISHY.
IF YOU MUST KNOW, I'M PROBABLY CLOSER TO WHAT YOU'D CALL A SECRET AGENT.
NOW.
IF YOU'D FOLLOW ME.
UH, SURE.
......!

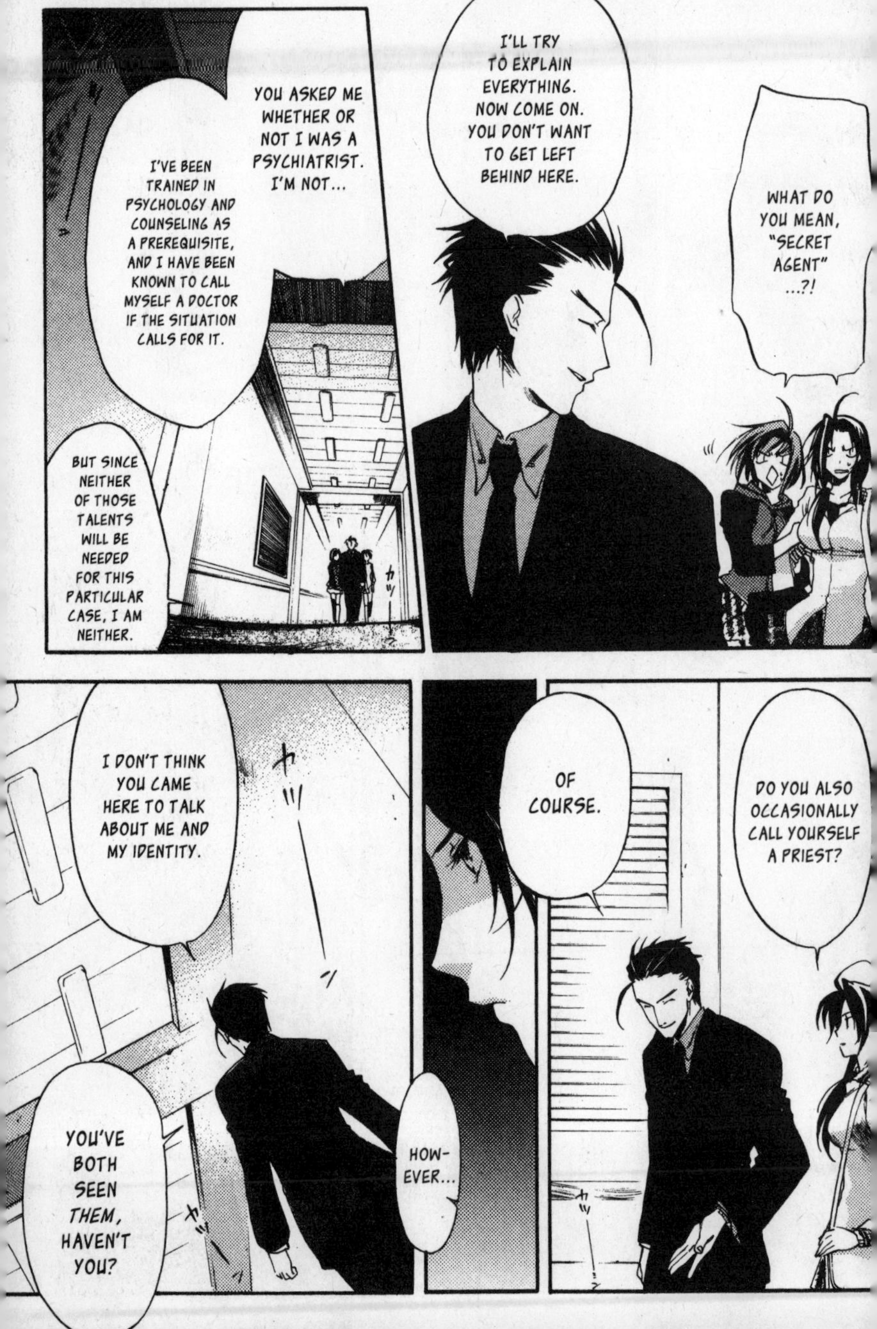
WHAT DO YOU MEAN, "SECRET AGENT" ...?!
I'LL TRY TO EXPLAIN EVERYTHING. NOW COME ON. YOU DON'T WANT TO GET LEFT BEHIND HERE.
YOU ASKED ME WHETHER OR NOT I WAS A PSYCHIATRIST. I'M NOT...
I'VE BEEN TRAINED IN PSYCHOLOGY AND COUNSELING AS A PREREQUISITE, AND I HAVE BEEN KNOWN TO CALL MYSELF A DOCTOR IF THE SITUATION CALLS FOR IT.
BUT SINCE NEITHER OF THOSE TALENTS WILL BE NEEDED FOR THIS PARTICULAR CASE, I AM NEITHER.
DO YOU ALSO OCCASIONALLY CALL YOURSELF A PRIEST?
OF COURSE.
HOW-EVER...
I DON'T THINK YOU CAME HERE TO TALK ABOUT ME AND MY IDENTITY.
YOU'VE BOTH SEEN THEM, HAVEN'T YOU?

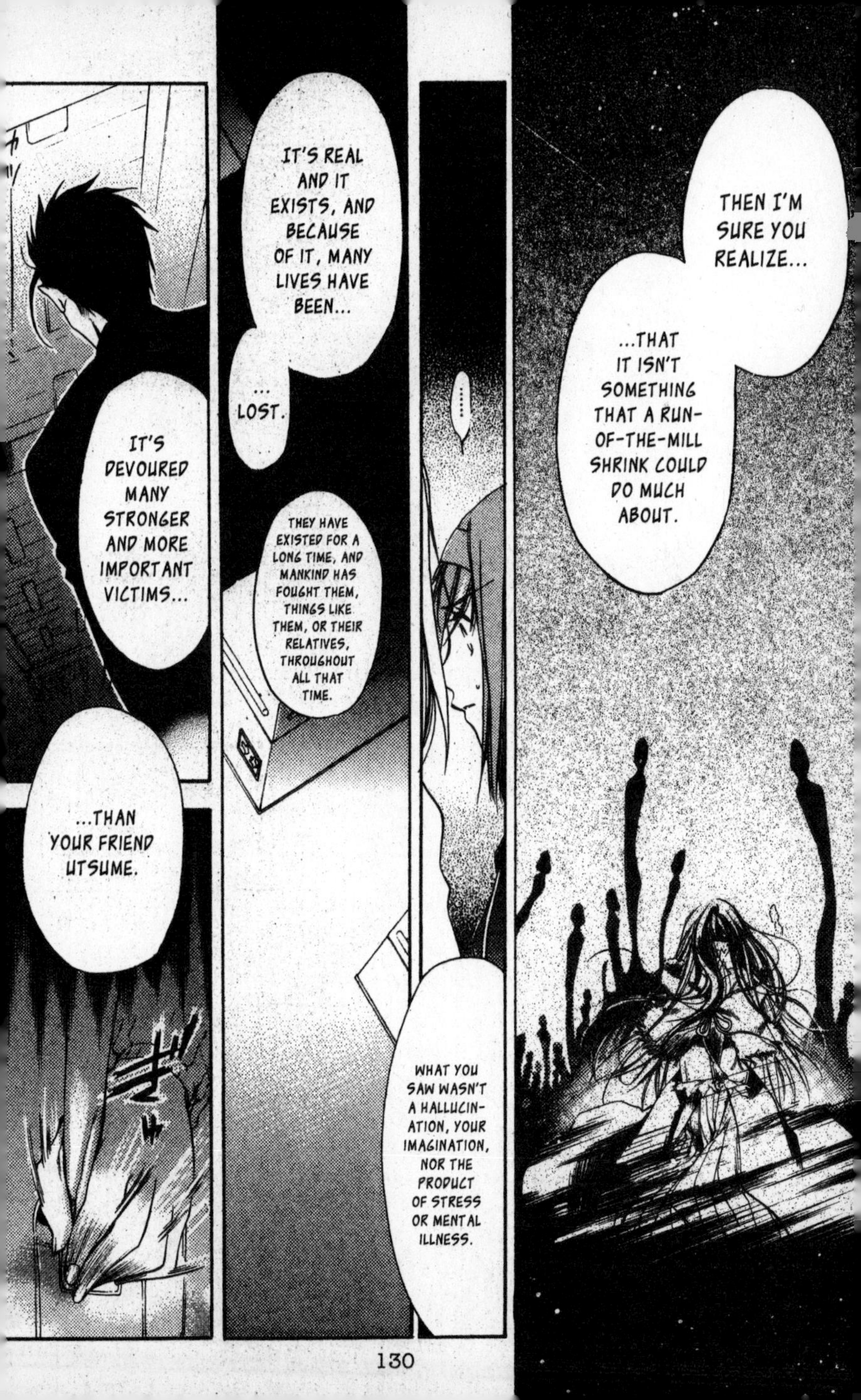
THEN I'M SURE YOU REALIZE...
...THAT IT ISN'T SOMETHING THAT A RUN-OF-THE-MILL SHRINK COULD DO MUCH ABOUT.
......
WHAT YOU SAW WASN'T A HALLUCIN-ATION, YOUR IMAGINATION, NOR THE PRODUCT OF STRESS OR MENTAL ILLNESS.
IT'S REAL AND IT EXISTS, AND BECAUSE OF IT, MANY LIVES HAVE BEEN...
...LOST.
THEY HAVE EXISTED FOR A LONG TIME, AND MANKIND HAS FOUGHT THEM, THINGS LIKE THEM, OR THEIR RELATIVES, THROUGHOUT ALL THAT TIME.
IT'S DEVOURED MANY STRONGER AND MORE IMPORTANT VICTIMS...
...THAN YOUR FRIEND UTSUME.

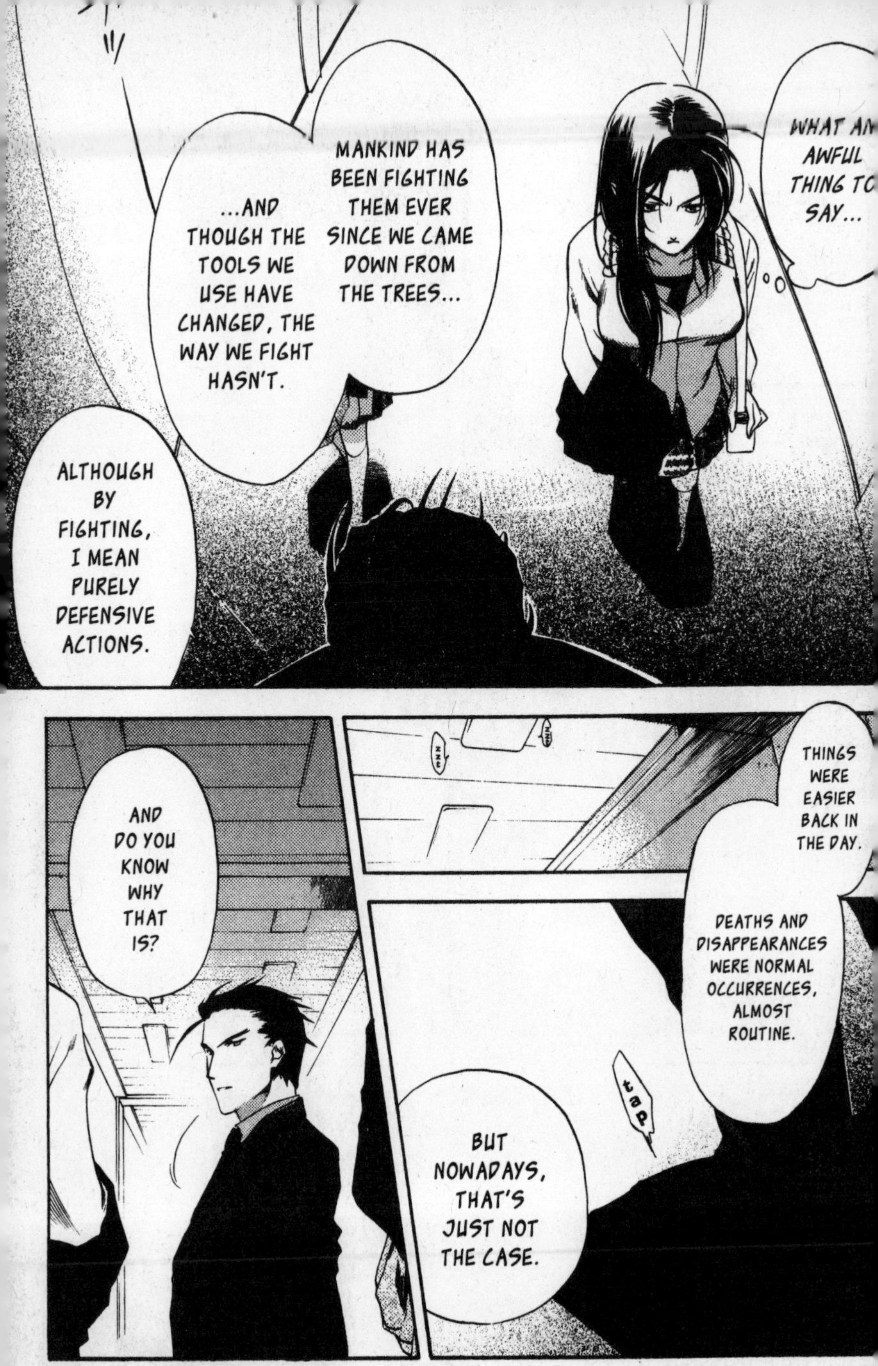
WHAT AN AWFUL THING TO SAY...
MANKIND HAS BEEN FIGHTING THEM EVER SINCE WE CAME DOWN FROM THE TREES...
...AND THOUGH THE TOOLS WE USE HAVE CHANGED, THE WAY WE FIGHT HASN'T.
ALTHOUGH BY FIGHTING, I MEAN PURELY DEFENSIVE ACTIONS.
THINGS WERE EASIER BACK IN THE DAY.
DEATHS AND DISAPPEARANCES WERE NORMAL OCCURRENCES, ALMOST ROUTINE.
tap
BUT NOWADAYS, THAT'S JUST NOT THE CASE.
AND DO YOU KNOW WHY THAT IS?

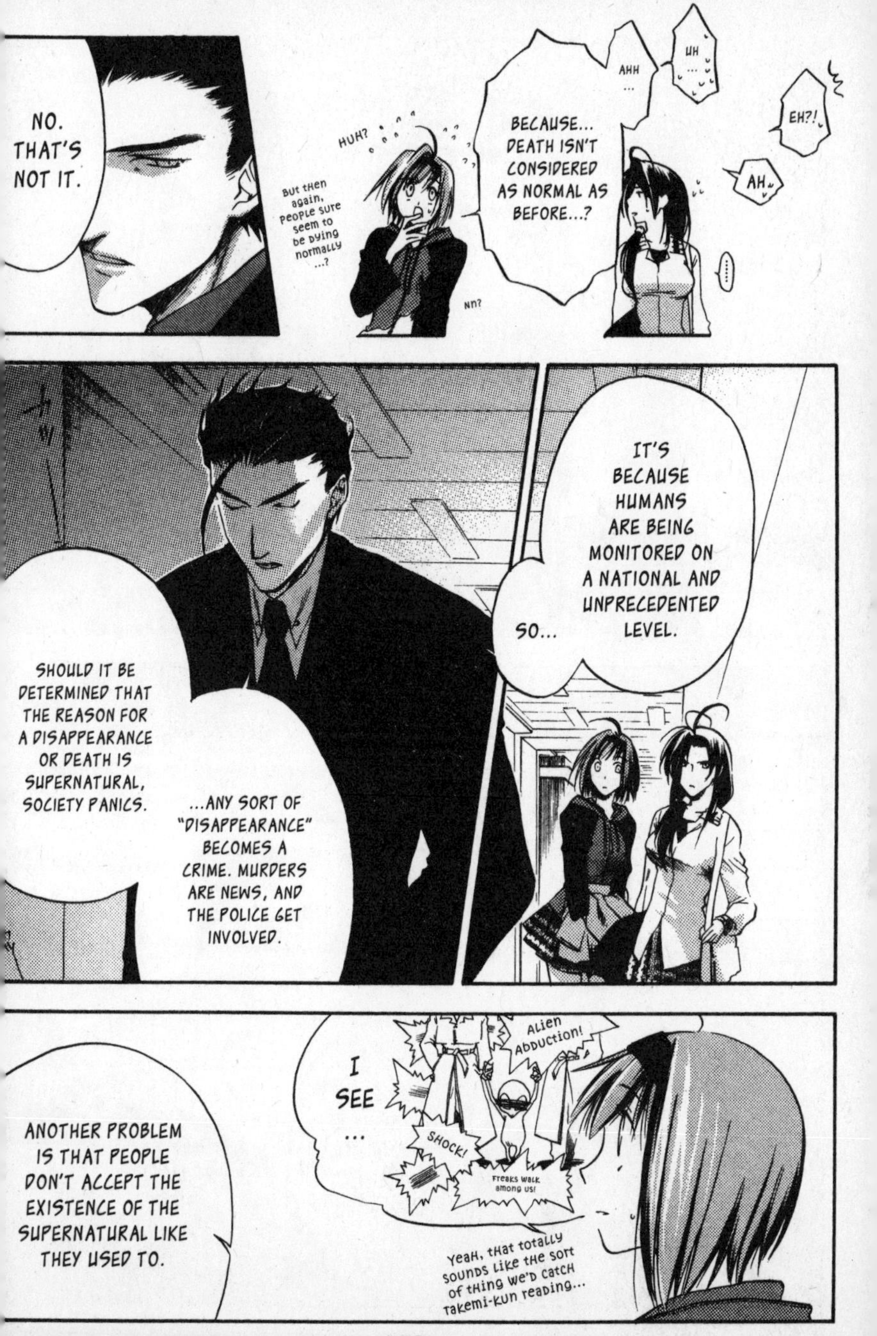
EH?!
AH
UH...
AHH...
BECAUSE... DEATH ISN'T CONSIDERED AS NORMAL AS BEFORE...?
...
NN?
HUH?
But then again, people sure seem to be dying normally ...?
NO. THAT'S NOT IT.
IT'S BECAUSE HUMANS ARE BEING MONITORED ON A NATIONAL AND UNPRECEDENTED LEVEL.
SO...
...ANY SORT OF "DISAPPEARANCE" BECOMES A CRIME. MURDERS ARE NEWS, AND THE POLICE GET INVOLVED.
SHOULD IT BE DETERMINED THAT THE REASON FOR A DISAPPEARANCE OR DEATH IS SUPERNATURAL, SOCIETY PANICS.
I SEE ...
Alien Abduction!
SHOCK!
Freaks walk among us!
Yeah, that totally sounds like the sort of thing we'd catch Takemi-kun reading...
ANOTHER PROBLEM IS THAT PEOPLE DON'T ACCEPT THE EXISTENCE OF THE SUPERNATURAL LIKE THEY USED TO.

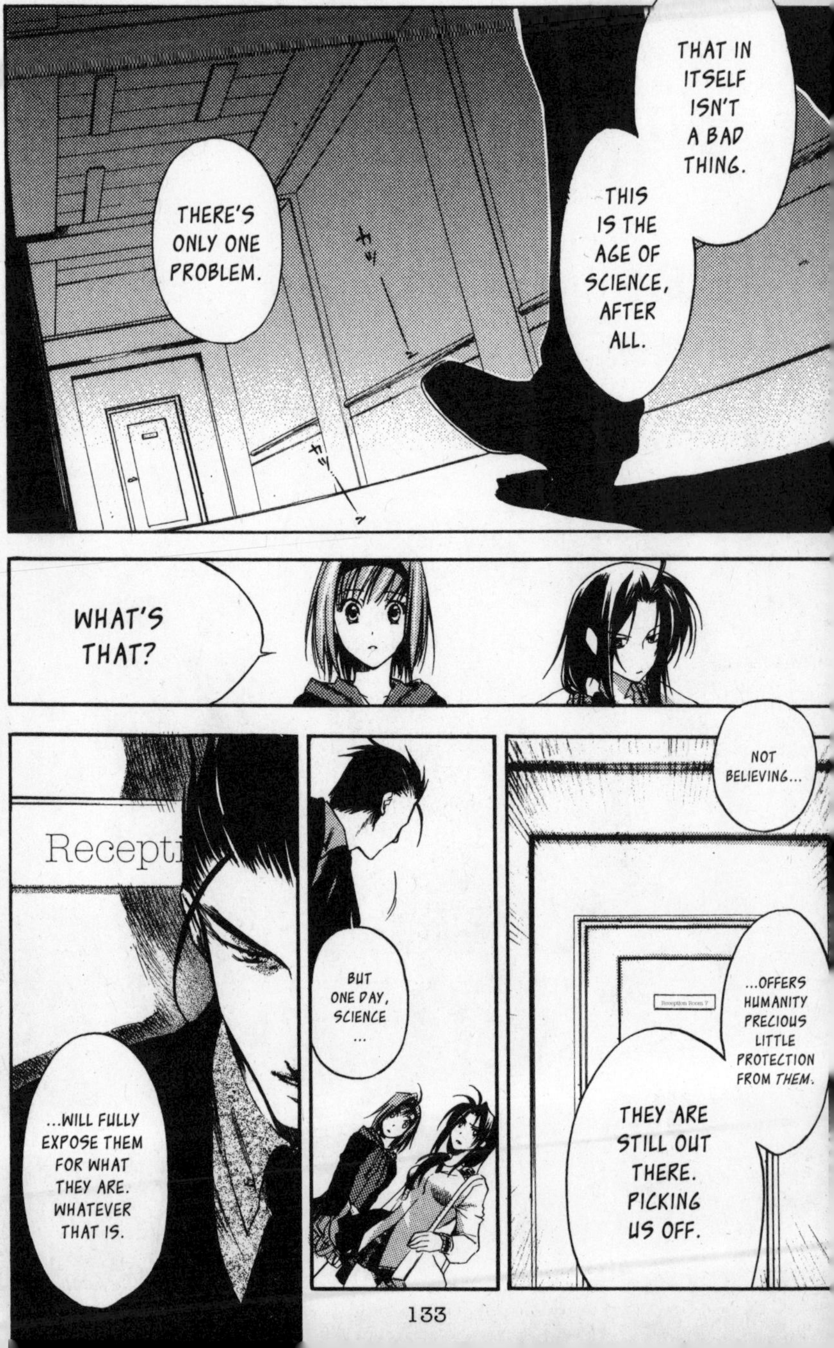
THAT IN ITSELF ISN'T A BAD THING.
THIS IS THE AGE OF SCIENCE, AFTER ALL.
THERE'S ONLY ONE PROBLEM.
WHAT'S THAT?
NOT BELIEVING...
...OFFERS HUMANITY PRECIOUS LITTLE PROTECTION FROM *THEM*.
THEY ARE STILL OUT THERE. PICKING US OFF.
BUT ONE DAY, SCIENCE ...
Recepti
...WILL FULLY EXPOSE THEM FOR WHAT THEY ARE. WHATEVER THAT IS.

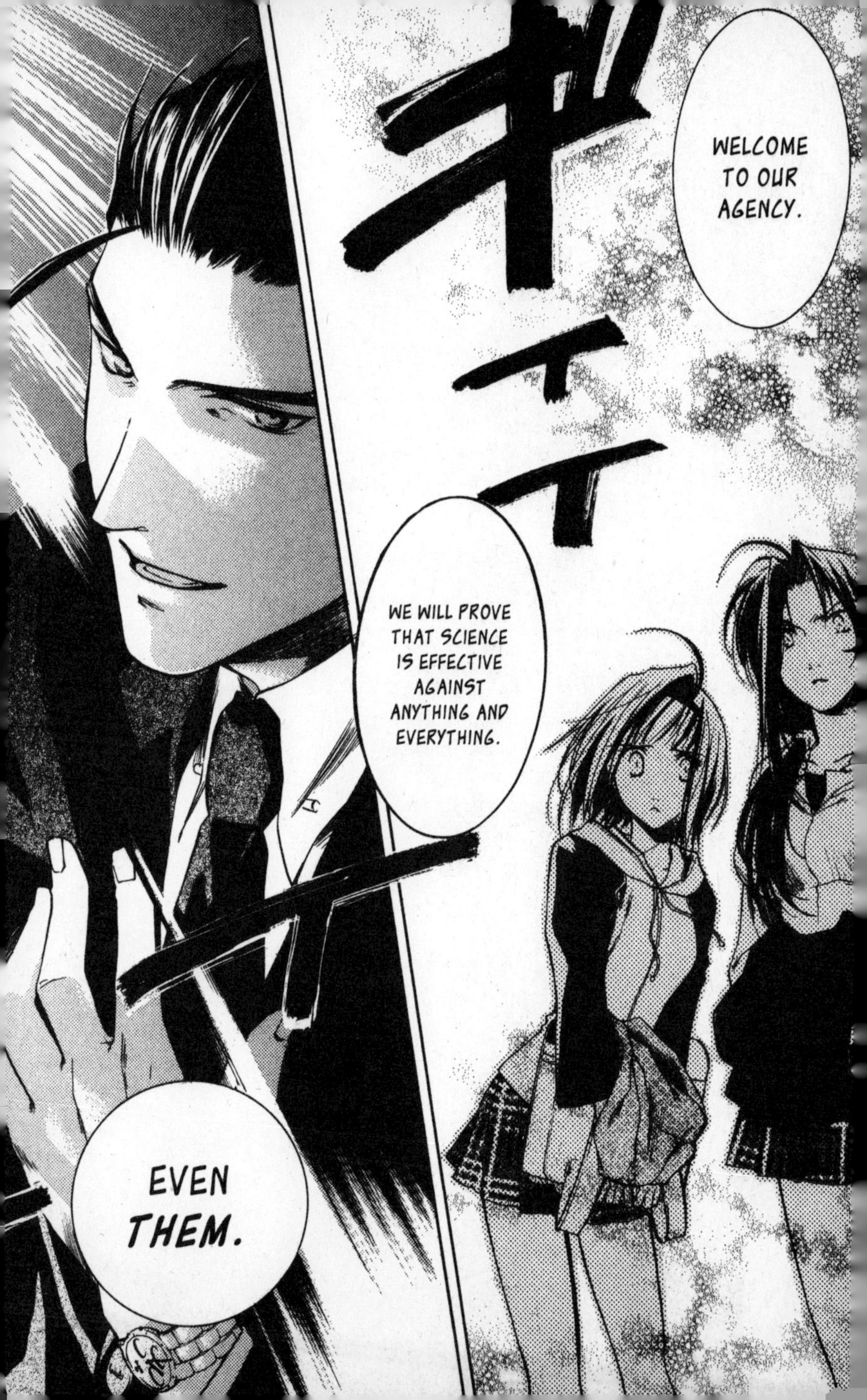
WELCOME TO OUR AGENCY.
WE WILL PROVE THAT SCIENCE IS EFFECTIVE AGAINST ANYTHING AND EVERYTHING.
EVEN THEM.

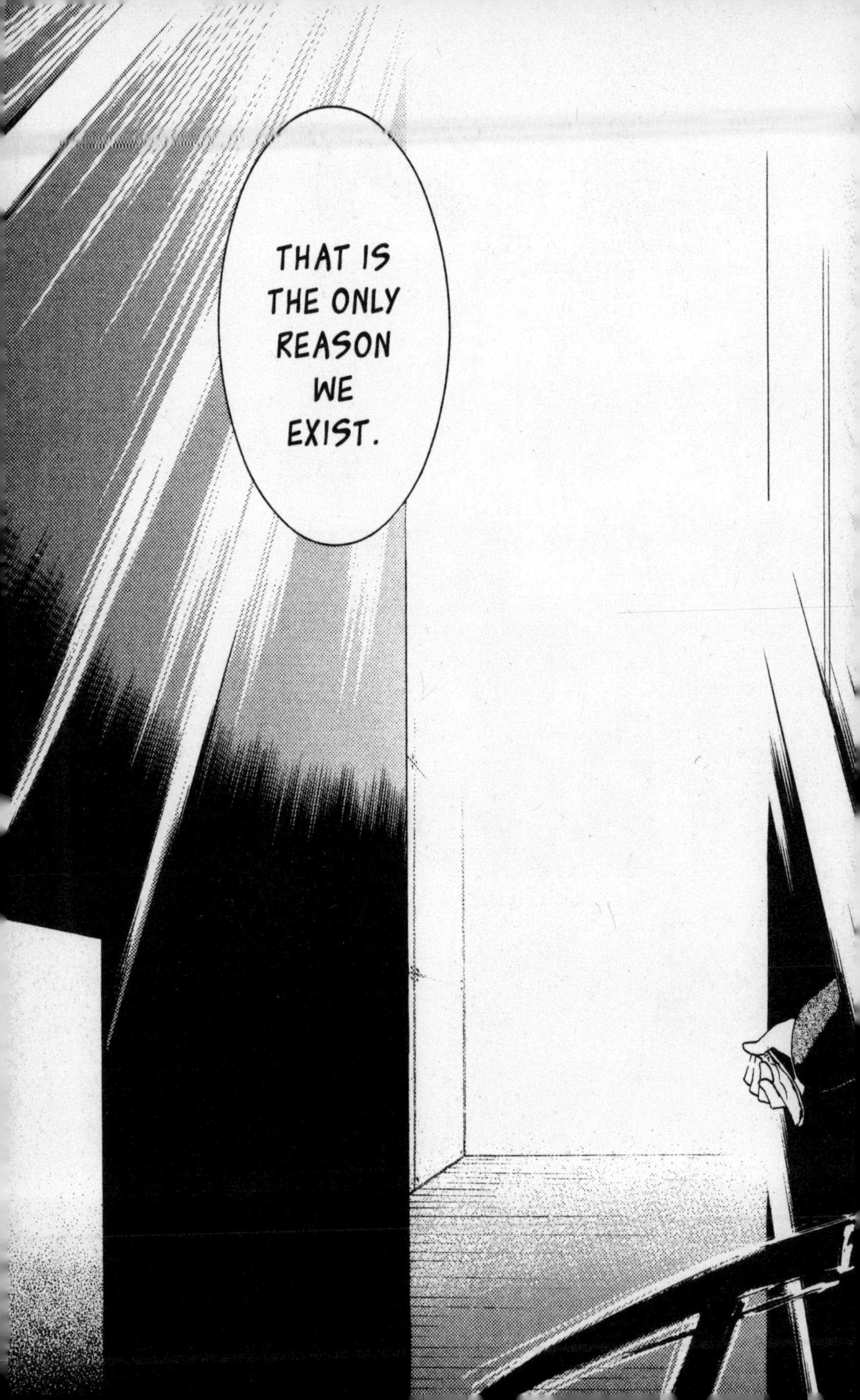
THAT IS THE ONLY REASON WE EXIST.

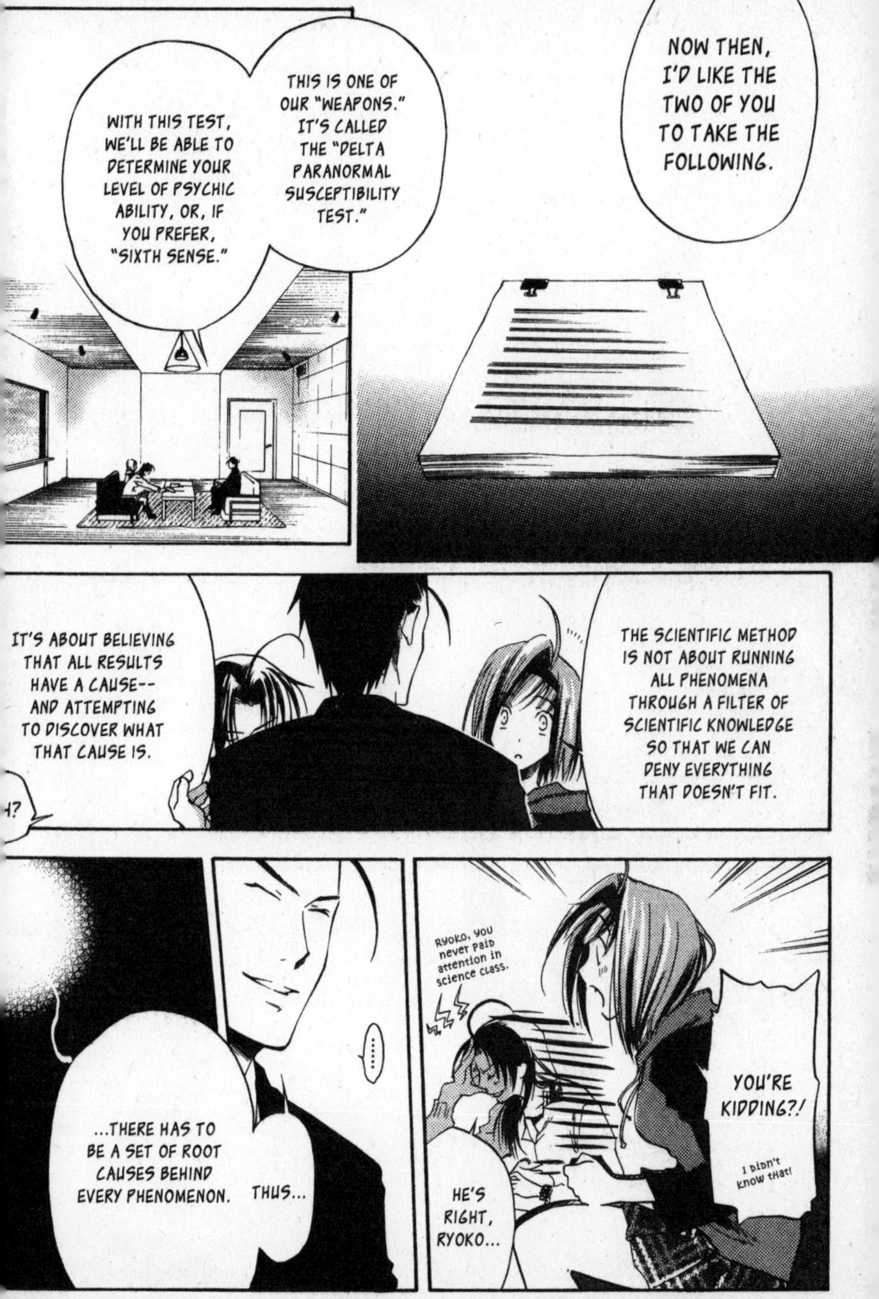
NOW THEN, I'D LIKE THE TWO OF YOU TO TAKE THE FOLLOWING.
THIS IS ONE OF OUR "WEAPONS." IT'S CALLED THE "DELTA PARANORMAL SUSCEPTIBILITY TEST."
WITH THIS TEST, WE'LL BE ABLE TO DETERMINE YOUR LEVEL OF PSYCHIC ABILITY, OR, IF YOU PREFER, "SIXTH SENSE."
THE SCIENTIFIC METHOD IS NOT ABOUT RUNNING ALL PHENOMENA THROUGH A FILTER OF SCIENTIFIC KNOWLEDGE SO THAT WE CAN DENY EVERYTHING THAT DOESN'T FIT.
IT'S ABOUT BELIEVING THAT ALL RESULTS HAVE A CAUSE-- AND ATTEMPTING TO DISCOVER WHAT THAT CAUSE IS.
YOU'RE KIDDING?!
Ryoko, you never paid attention in science class.
I didn't know that!
HE'S RIGHT, RYOKO...
......
THUS...
...THERE HAS TO BE A SET OF ROOT CAUSES BEHIND EVERY PHENOMENON.

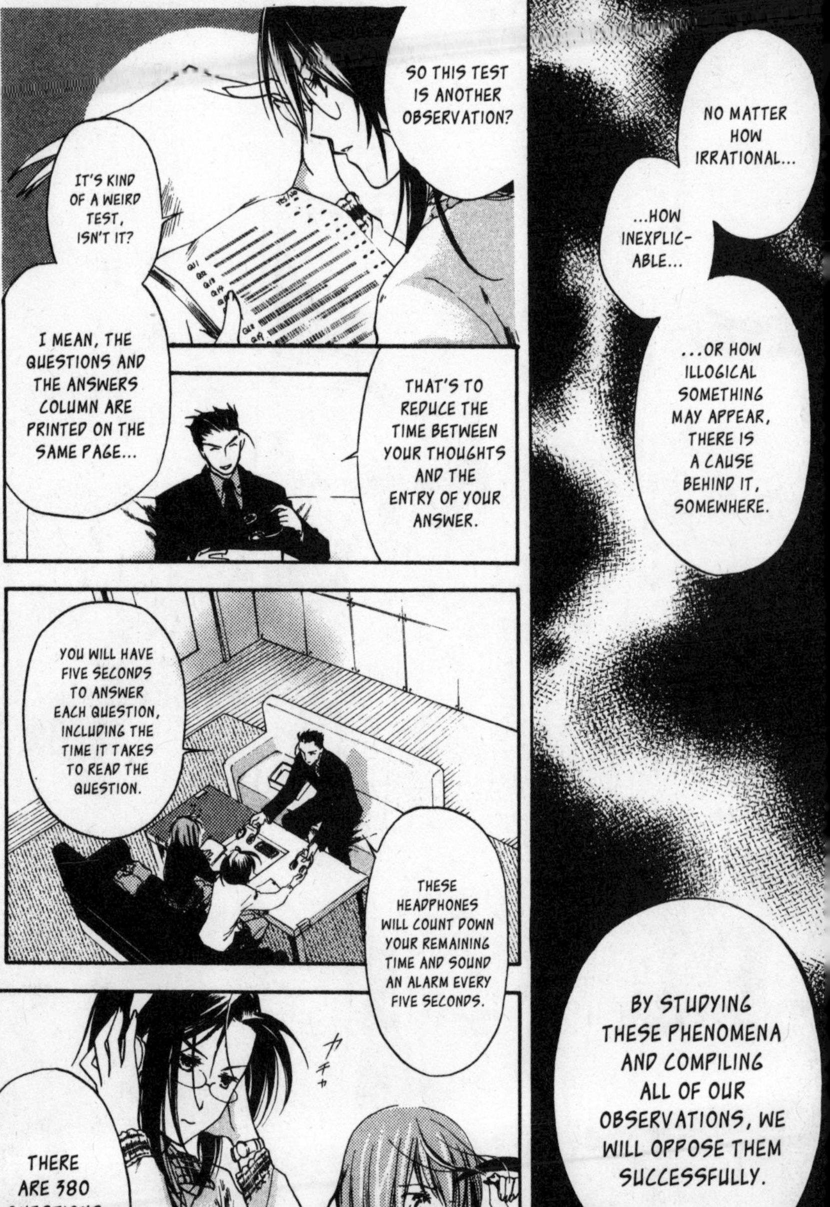
NO MATTER HOW IRRATIONAL...
...HOW INEXPLIC-ABLE...
...OR HOW ILLOGICAL SOMETHING MAY APPEAR, THERE IS A CAUSE BEHIND IT, SOMEWHERE.
BY STUDYING THESE PHENOMENA AND COMPILING ALL OF OUR OBSERVATIONS, WE WILL OPPOSE THEM SUCCESSFULLY.
SO THIS TEST IS ANOTHER OBSERVATION?
IT'S KIND OF A WEIRD TEST, ISN'T IT?
I MEAN, THE QUESTIONS AND THE ANSWERS COLUMN ARE PRINTED ON THE SAME PAGE...
THAT'S TO REDUCE THE TIME BETWEEN YOUR THOUGHTS AND THE ENTRY OF YOUR ANSWER.
YOU WILL HAVE FIVE SECONDS TO ANSWER EACH QUESTION, INCLUDING THE TIME IT TAKES TO READ THE QUESTION.
THESE HEADPHONES WILL COUNT DOWN YOUR REMAINING TIME AND SOUND AN ALARM EVERY FIVE SECONDS.
カチャ
THERE ARE 380 QUESTIONS IN TOTAL.

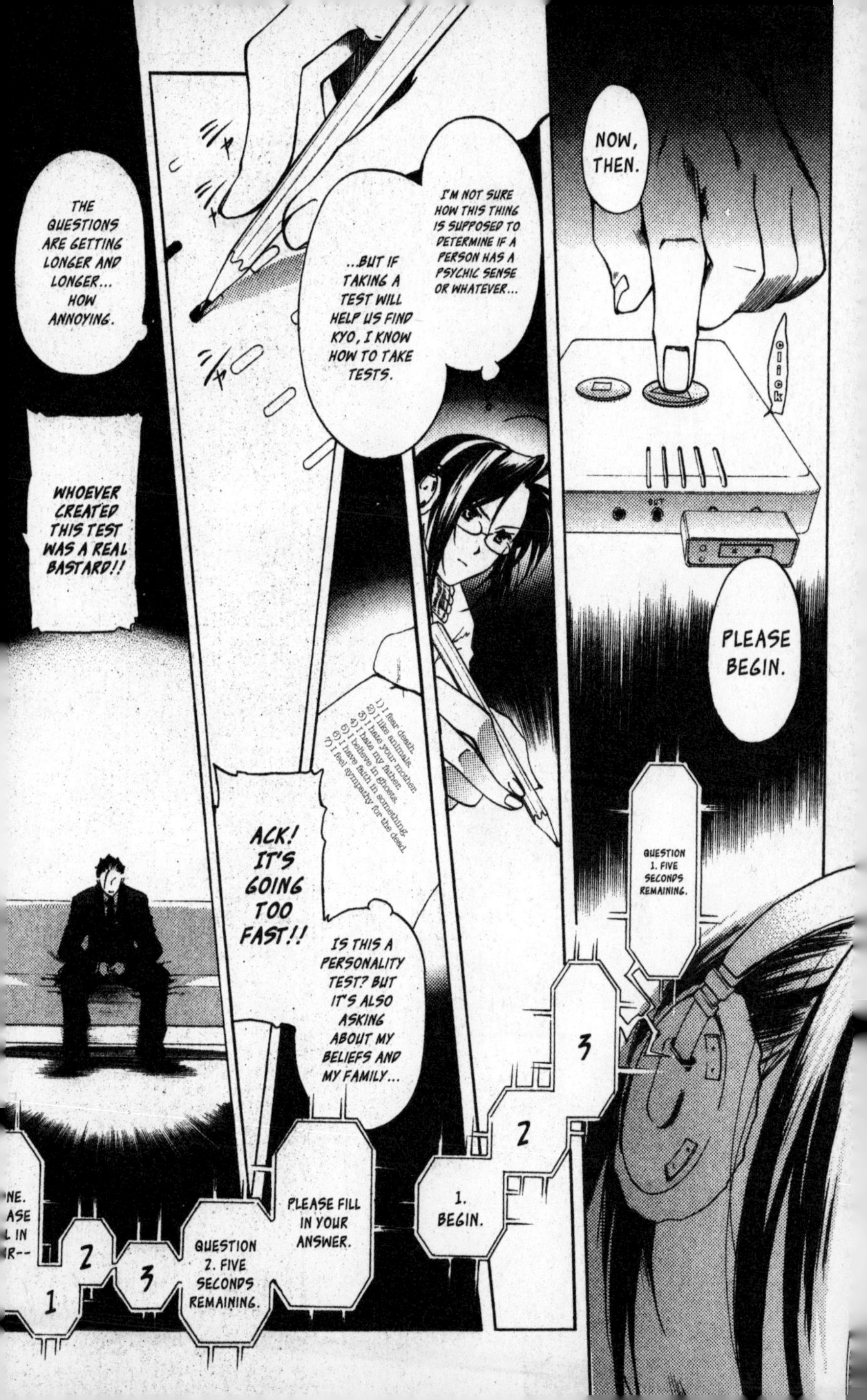
NOW, THEN.
click
PLEASE BEGIN.
QUESTION 1. FIVE SECONDS REMAINING.
3
2
1. BEGIN.
I'M NOT SURE HOW THIS THING IS SUPPOSED TO DETERMINE IF A PERSON HAS A PSYCHIC SENSE OR WHATEVER...
...BUT IF TAKING A TEST WILL HELP US FIND KYO, I KNOW HOW TO TAKE TESTS.
1) I fear death.
2) I like animals.
3) I hate your mother.
4) I hate my father.
5) I believe in ghosts.
6) I have faith in something.
7) I feel sympathy for the dead.
ACK! IT'S GOING TOO FAST!!
IS THIS A PERSONALITY TEST? BUT IT'S ALSO ASKING ABOUT MY BELIEFS AND MY FAMILY...
PLEASE FILL IN YOUR ANSWER.
QUESTION 2. FIVE SECONDS REMAINING.
3
2
1
THE QUESTIONS ARE GETTING LONGER AND LONGER... HOW ANNOYING.
WHOEVER CREATED THIS TEST WAS A REAL BASTARD!!

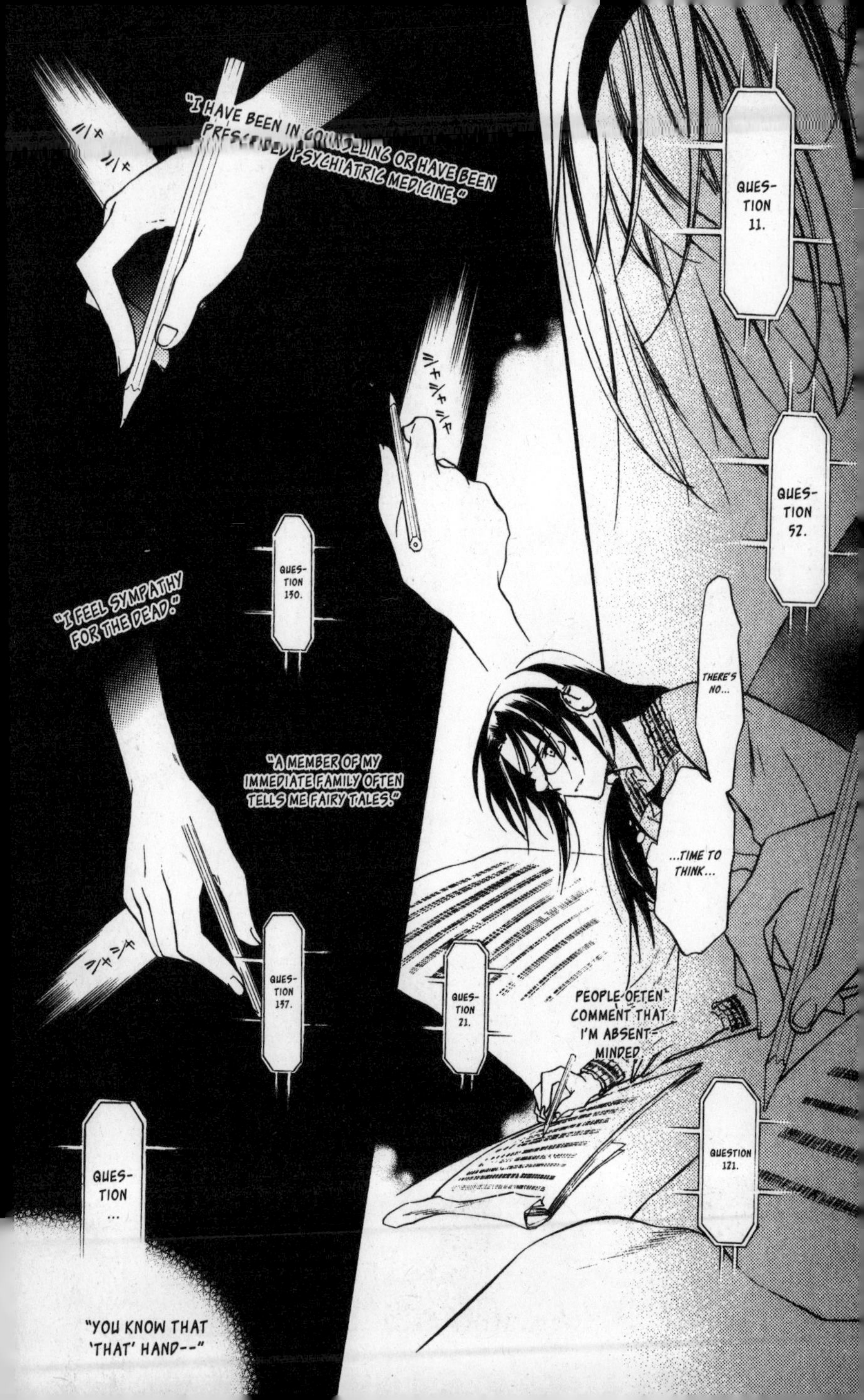
QUESTION 11.
QUESTION 52.
THERE'S NO...
...TIME TO THINK...
QUESTION 121.
PEOPLE OFTEN COMMENT THAT I'M ABSENT-MINDED.
QUESTION 21.
"I HAVE BEEN IN COUNSELING OR HAVE BEEN PRESCRIBED PSYCHIATRIC MEDICINE."
QUESTION 130.
"I FEEL SYMPATHY FOR THE DEAD."
"A MEMBER OF MY IMMEDIATE FAMILY OFTEN TELLS ME FAIRY TALES."
QUESTION 137.
QUESTION...
"YOU KNOW THAT 'THAT' HAND--"

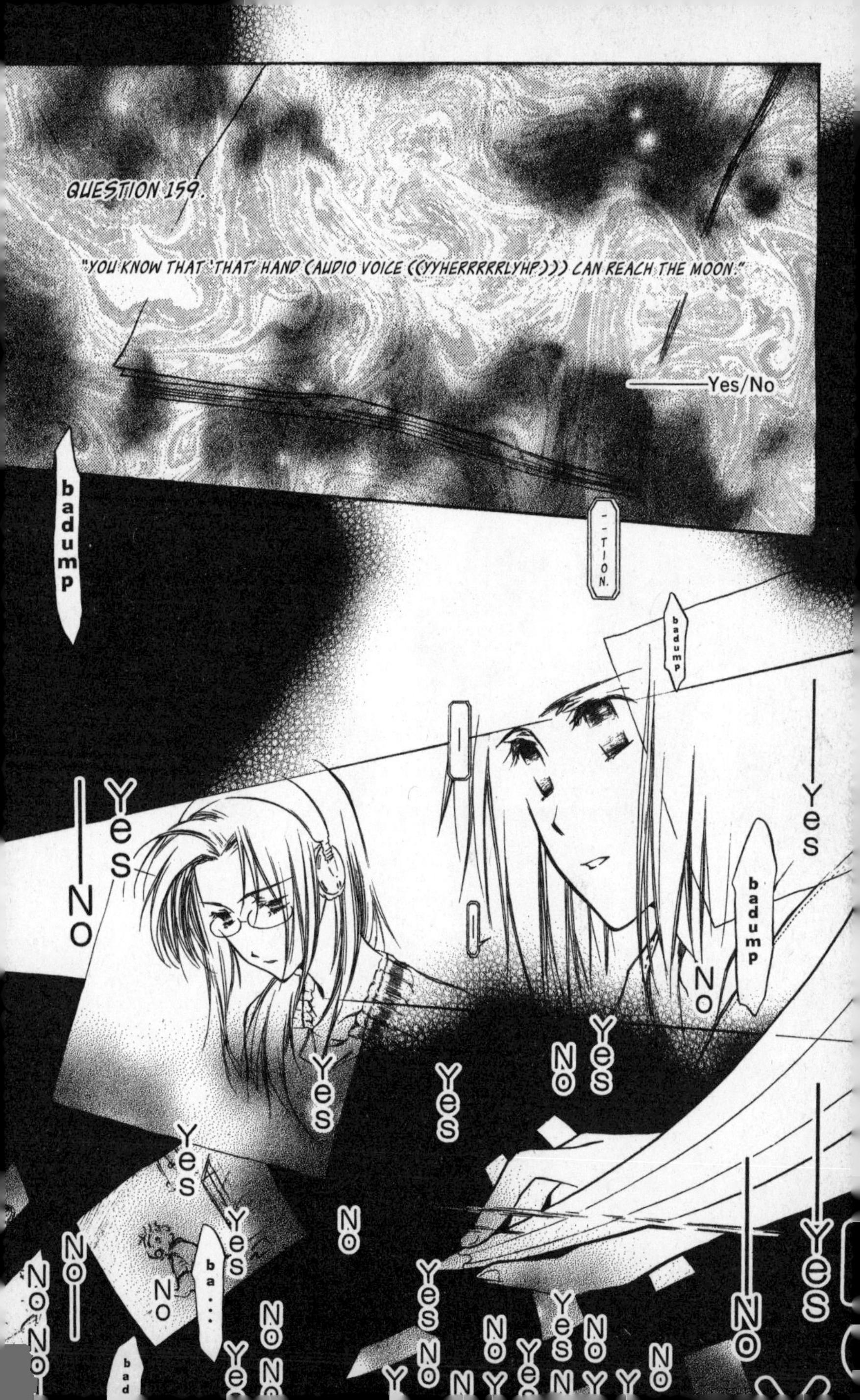
QUESTION 159.
"YOU KNOW THAT 'THAT' HAND (AUDIO VOICE ((YYHERRRRRLYHP))) CAN REACH THE MOON."
——Yes/No
——TION.
badump
badump
—
—Yes
badump
NO
Yes
NO
Yes
Yes
Yes
—NO
—Yes
Yes
—NO
ba...
NO
Yes
NO
NO
—NO
NO
—NO

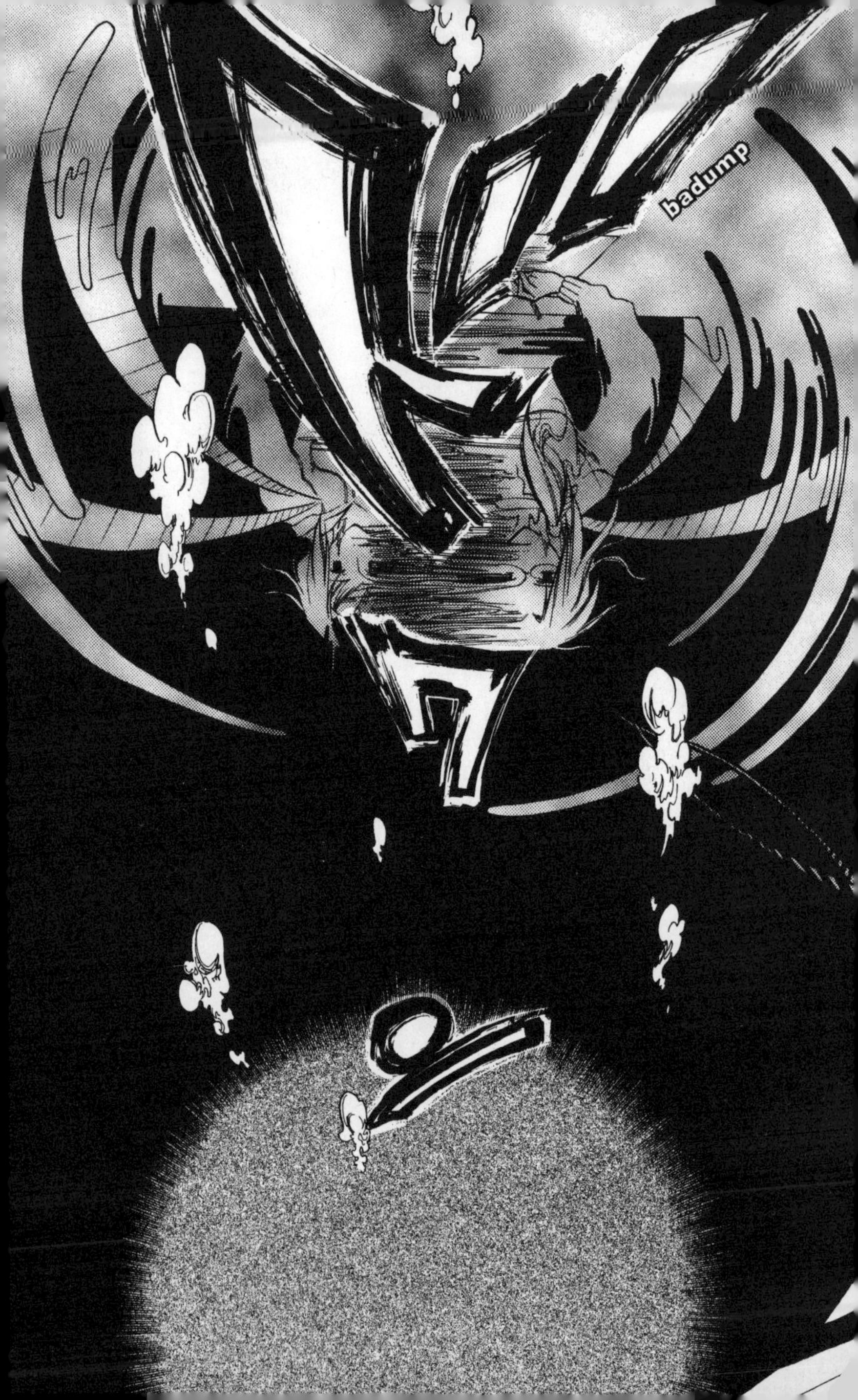
badump

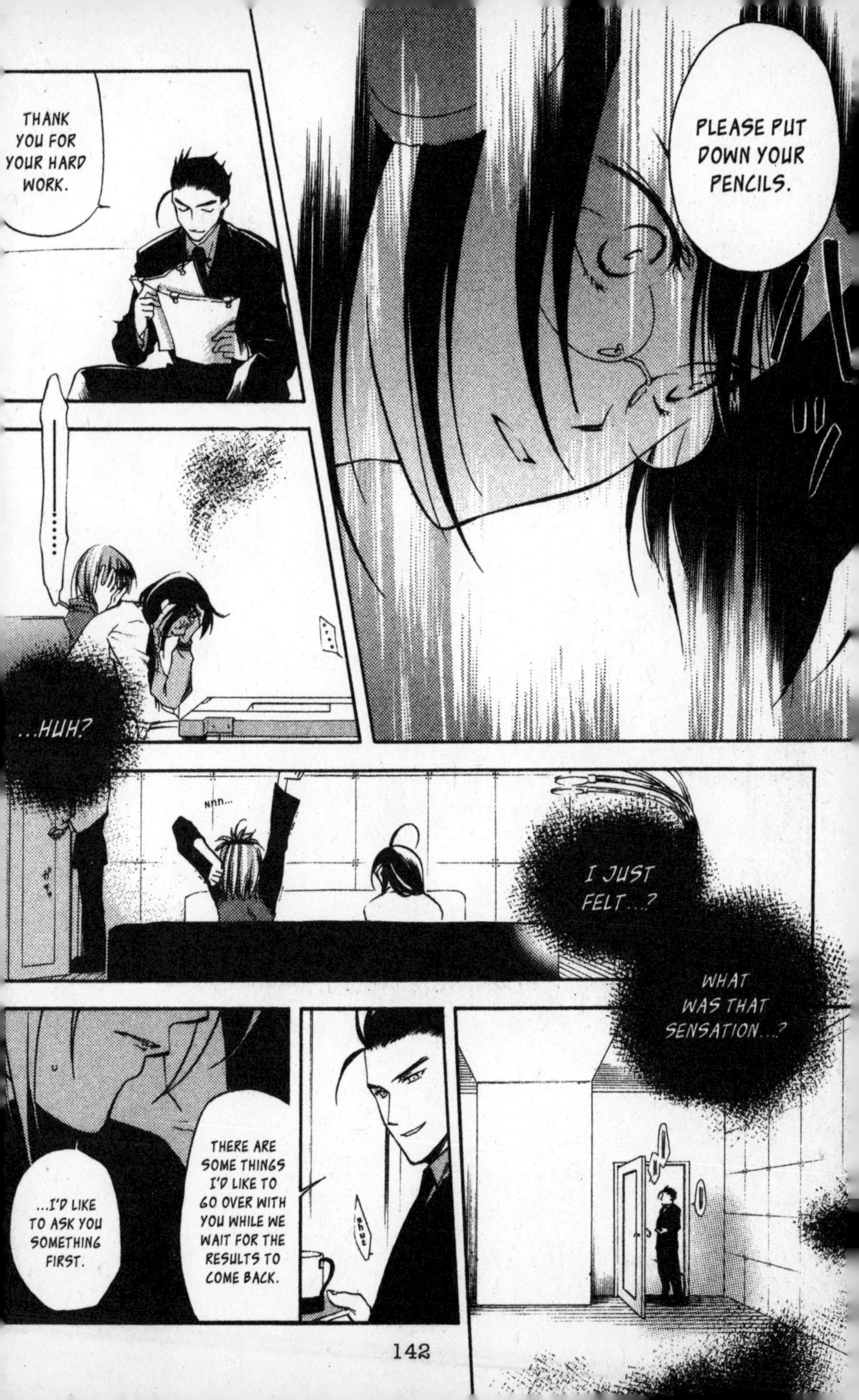
PLEASE PUT DOWN YOUR PENCILS.
THANK YOU FOR YOUR HARD WORK.
......
...HUH?
I JUST FELT...?
nnn...
WHAT WAS THAT SENSATION...?
shut
THERE ARE SOME THINGS I'D LIKE TO GO OVER WITH YOU WHILE WE WAIT FOR THE RESULTS TO COME BACK.
...I'D LIKE TO ASK YOU SOMETHING FIRST.

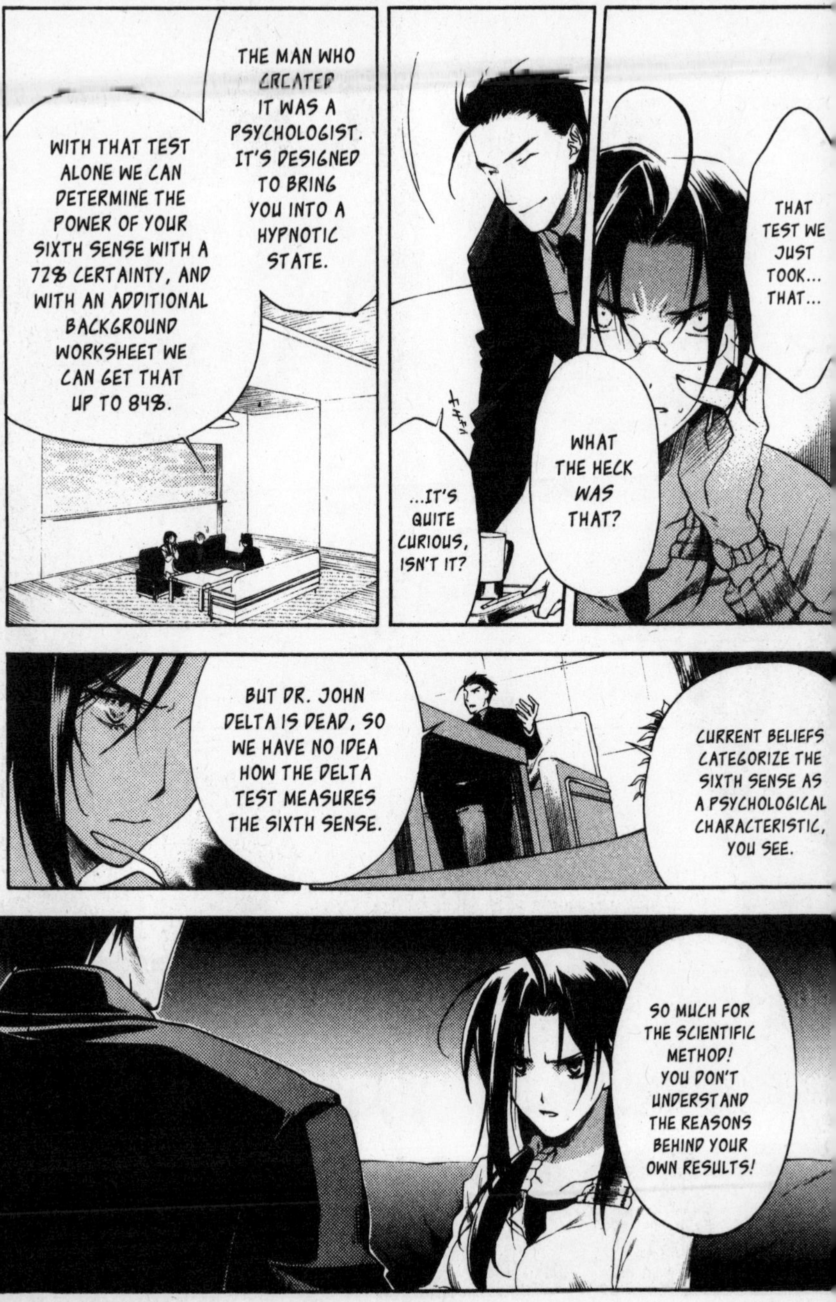
THAT TEST WE JUST TOOK... THAT...
WHAT THE HECK WAS THAT?
...IT'S QUITE CURIOUS, ISN'T IT?
THE MAN WHO CREATED IT WAS A PSYCHOLOGIST. IT'S DESIGNED TO BRING YOU INTO A HYPNOTIC STATE.
WITH THAT TEST ALONE WE CAN DETERMINE THE POWER OF YOUR SIXTH SENSE WITH A 72% CERTAINTY, AND WITH AN ADDITIONAL BACKGROUND WORKSHEET WE CAN GET THAT UP TO 84%.
CURRENT BELIEFS CATEGORIZE THE SIXTH SENSE AS A PSYCHOLOGICAL CHARACTERISTIC, YOU SEE.
BUT DR. JOHN DELTA IS DEAD, SO WE HAVE NO IDEA HOW THE DELTA TEST MEASURES THE SIXTH SENSE.
SO MUCH FOR THE SCIENTIFIC METHOD! YOU DON'T UNDERSTAND THE REASONS BEHIND YOUR OWN RESULTS!

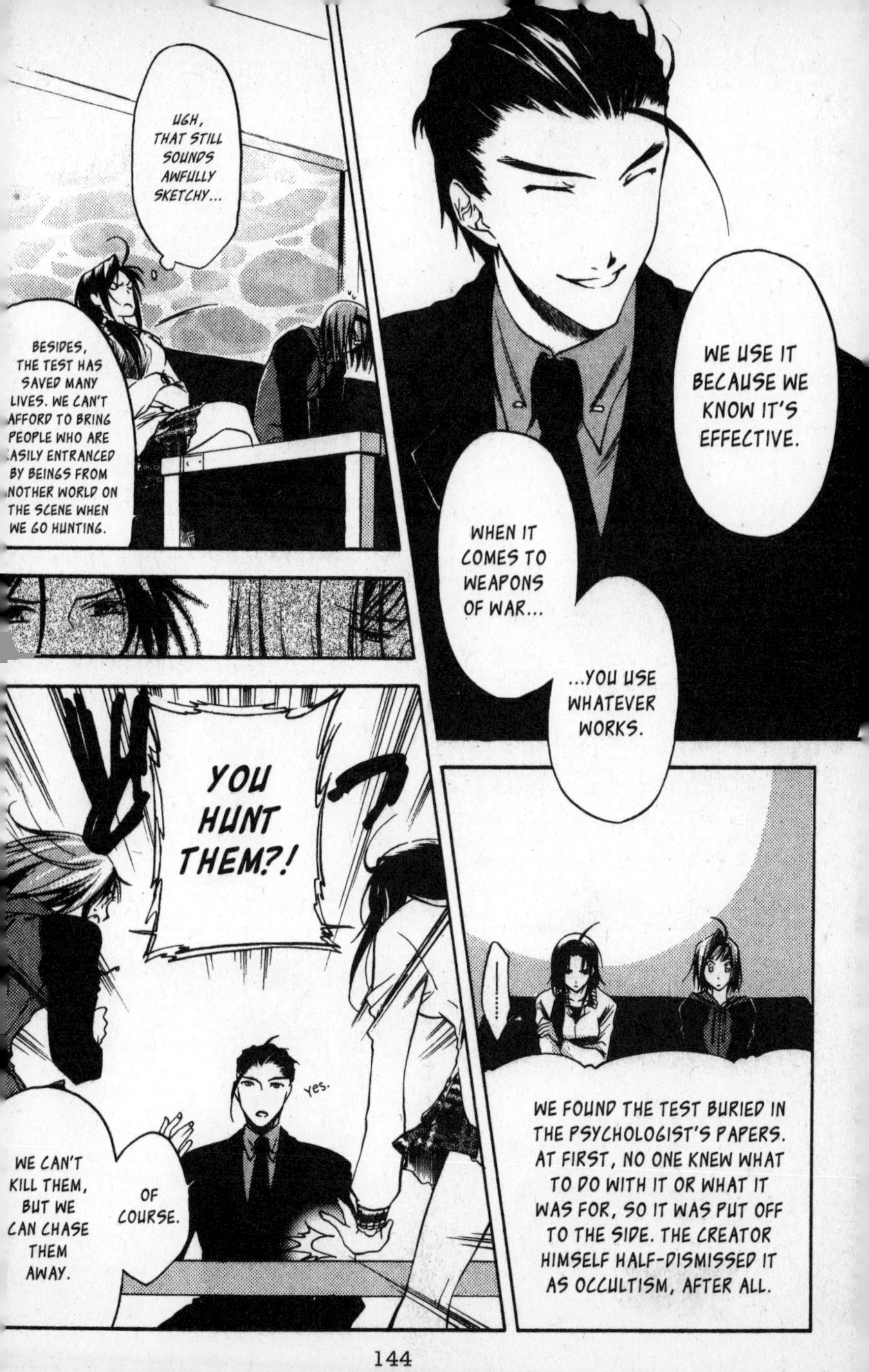
WE USE IT BECAUSE WE KNOW IT'S EFFECTIVE.
WHEN IT COMES TO WEAPONS OF WAR...
...YOU USE WHATEVER WORKS.
UGH, THAT STILL SOUNDS AWFULLY SKETCHY...
BESIDES, THE TEST HAS SAVED MANY LIVES. WE CAN'T AFFORD TO BRING PEOPLE WHO ARE EASILY ENTRANCED BY BEINGS FROM ANOTHER WORLD ON THE SCENE WHEN WE GO HUNTING.
YOU HUNT THEM?!
YES.
OF COURSE.
WE CAN'T KILL THEM, BUT WE CAN CHASE THEM AWAY.
...
WE FOUND THE TEST BURIED IN THE PSYCHOLOGIST'S PAPERS. AT FIRST, NO ONE KNEW WHAT TO DO WITH IT OR WHAT IT WAS FOR, SO IT WAS PUT OFF TO THE SIDE. THE CREATOR HIMSELF HALF-DISMISSED IT AS OCCULTISM, AFTER ALL.

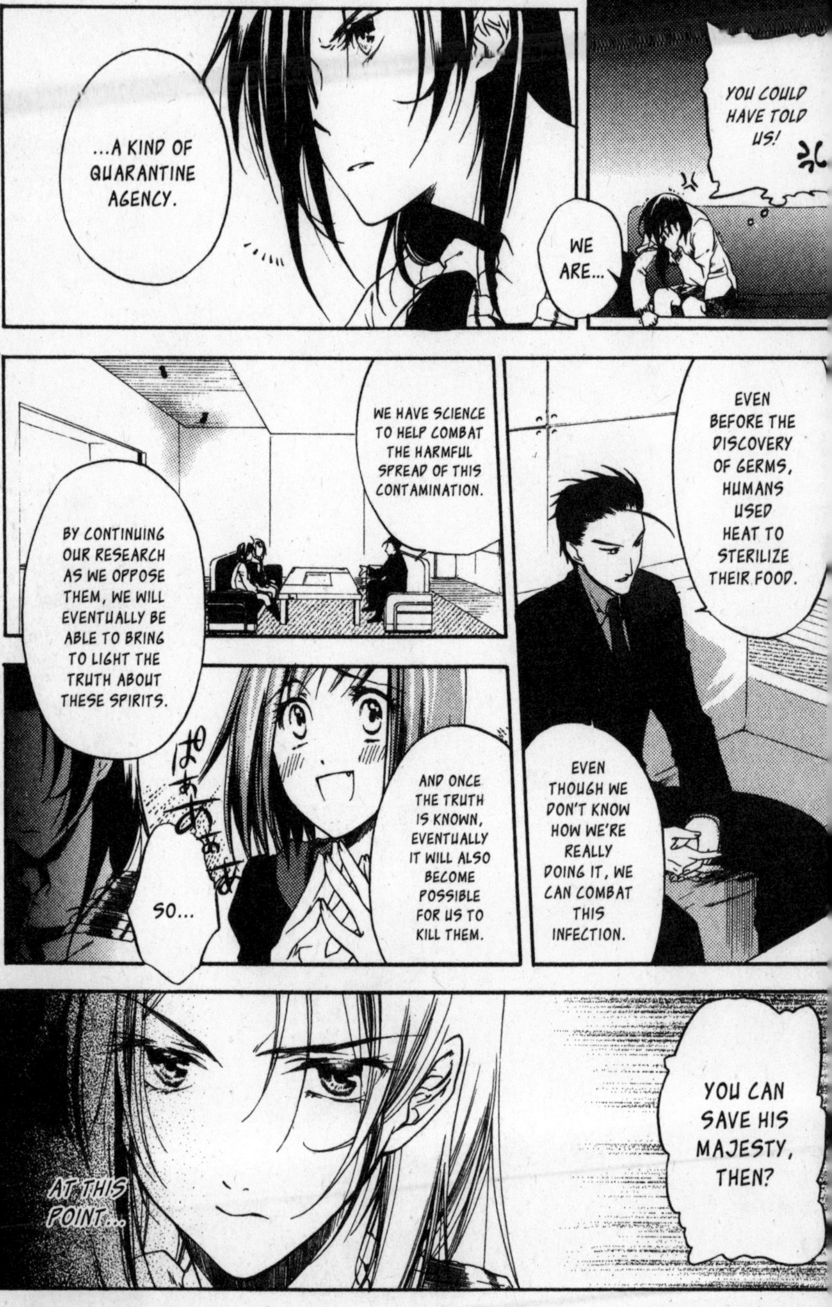
YOU COULD HAVE TOLD US!
WE ARE...
...A KIND OF QUARANTINE AGENCY.
EVEN BEFORE THE DISCOVERY OF GERMS, HUMANS USED HEAT TO STERILIZE THEIR FOOD.
EVEN THOUGH WE DON'T KNOW HOW WE'RE REALLY DOING IT, WE CAN COMBAT THIS INFECTION.
WE HAVE SCIENCE TO HELP COMBAT THE HARMFUL SPREAD OF THIS CONTAMINATION.
BY CONTINUING OUR RESEARCH AS WE OPPOSE THEM, WE WILL EVENTUALLY BE ABLE TO BRING TO LIGHT THE TRUTH ABOUT THESE SPIRITS.
AND ONCE THE TRUTH IS KNOWN, EVENTUALLY IT WILL ALSO BECOME POSSIBLE FOR US TO KILL THEM.
SO...
YOU CAN SAVE HIS MAJESTY, THEN?
AT THIS POINT...

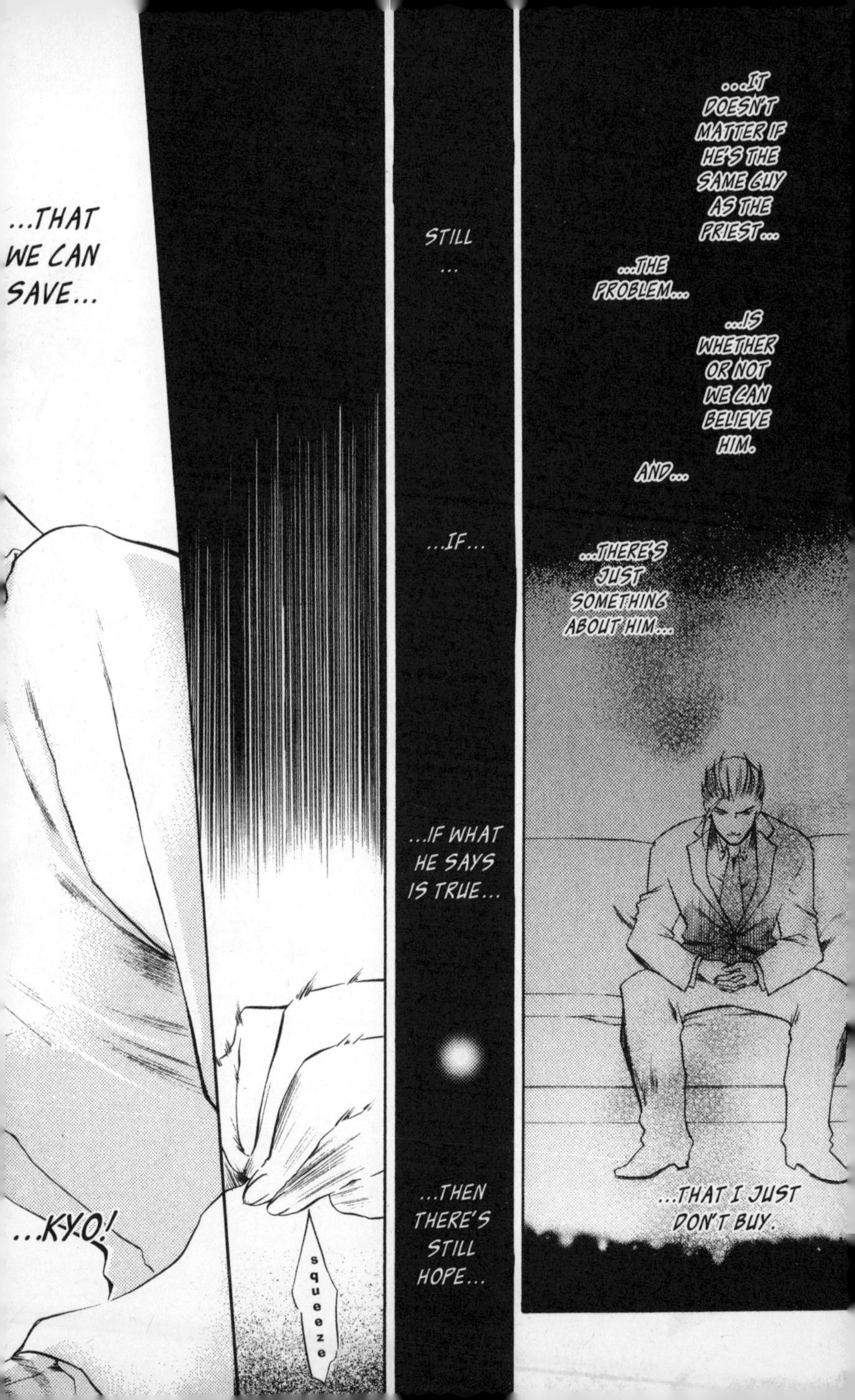
...IT DOESN'T MATTER IF HE'S THE SAME GUY AS THE PRIEST...
...THE PROBLEM...
...IS WHETHER OR NOT WE CAN BELIEVE HIM.
AND...
...THERE'S JUST SOMETHING ABOUT HIM...
...THAT I JUST DON'T BUY.
STILL ...
...IF...
...IF WHAT HE SAYS IS TRUE...
...THEN THERE'S STILL HOPE...
squeeze
...THAT WE CAN SAVE...
...KYO!

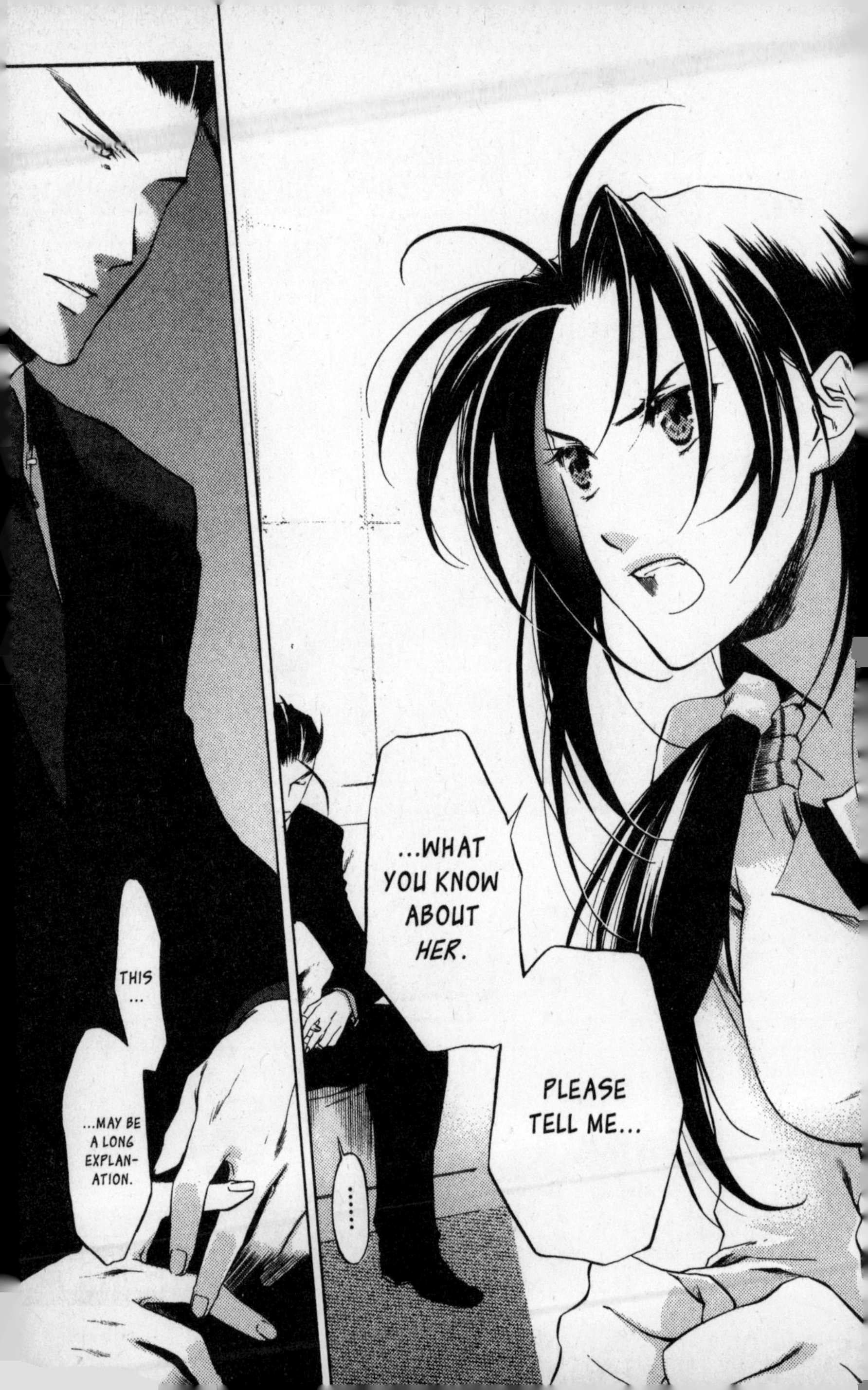
PLEASE TELL ME...
...WHAT YOU KNOW ABOUT HER.
......
THIS ...
...MAY BE A LONG EXPLANATION.

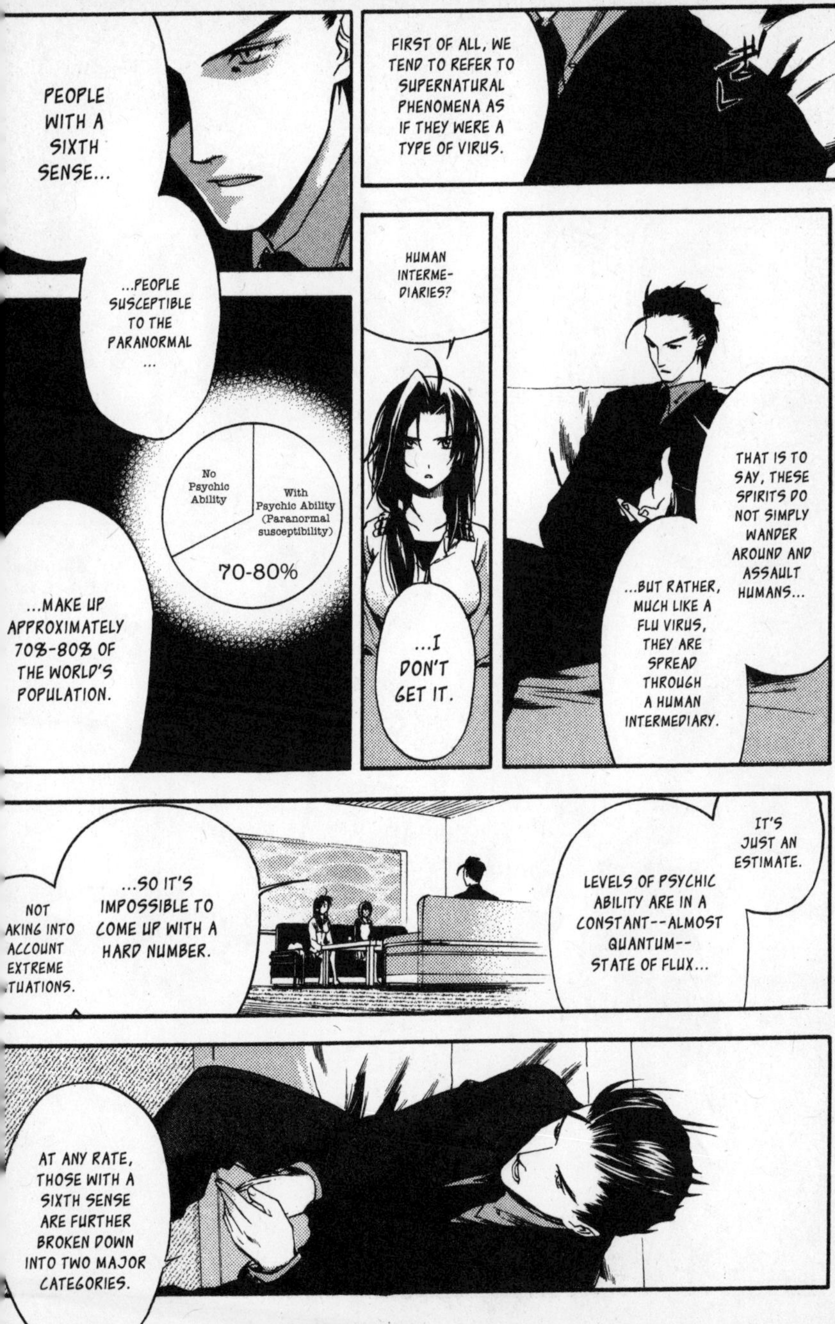
FIRST OF ALL, WE TEND TO REFER TO SUPERNATURAL PHENOMENA AS IF THEY WERE A TYPE OF VIRUS.
THAT IS TO SAY, THESE SPIRITS DO NOT SIMPLY WANDER AROUND AND ASSAULT HUMANS...
...BUT RATHER, MUCH LIKE A FLU VIRUS, THEY ARE SPREAD THROUGH A HUMAN INTERMEDIARY.
HUMAN INTERME-DIARIES?
...I DON'T GET IT.
PEOPLE WITH A SIXTH SENSE...
...PEOPLE SUSCEPTIBLE TO THE PARANORMAL ...
No Psychic Ability
With Psychic Ability (Paranormal susceptibility)
70-80%
...MAKE UP APPROXIMATELY 70%-80% OF THE WORLD'S POPULATION.
IT'S JUST AN ESTIMATE.
LEVELS OF PSYCHIC ABILITY ARE IN A CONSTANT--ALMOST QUANTUM--STATE OF FLUX...
...SO IT'S IMPOSSIBLE TO COME UP WITH A HARD NUMBER.
NOT AKING INTO ACCOUNT EXTREME TUATIONS.
AT ANY RATE, THOSE WITH A SIXTH SENSE ARE FURTHER BROKEN DOWN INTO TWO MAJOR CATEGORIES.

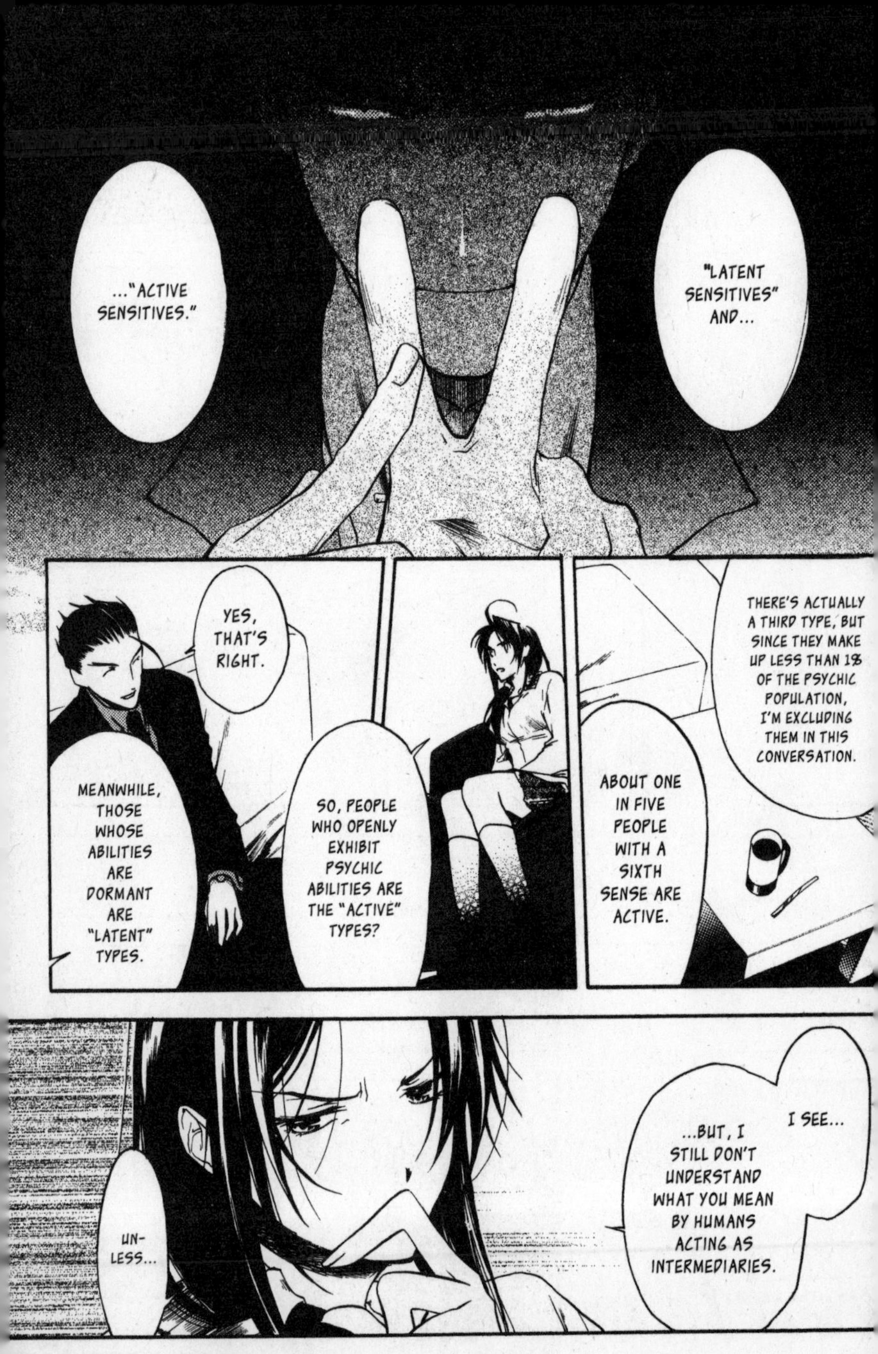
"LATENT SENSITIVES" AND...
..."ACTIVE SENSITIVES."
THERE'S ACTUALLY A THIRD TYPE, BUT SINCE THEY MAKE UP LESS THAN 1% OF THE PSYCHIC POPULATION, I'M EXCLUDING THEM IN THIS CONVERSATION.
ABOUT ONE IN FIVE PEOPLE WITH A SIXTH SENSE ARE ACTIVE.
SO, PEOPLE WHO OPENLY EXHIBIT PSYCHIC ABILITIES ARE THE "ACTIVE" TYPES?
YES, THAT'S RIGHT.
MEANWHILE, THOSE WHOSE ABILITIES ARE DORMANT ARE "LATENT" TYPES.
I SEE...
...BUT, I STILL DON'T UNDERSTAND WHAT YOU MEAN BY HUMANS ACTING AS INTERMEDIARIES.
UN-LESS...

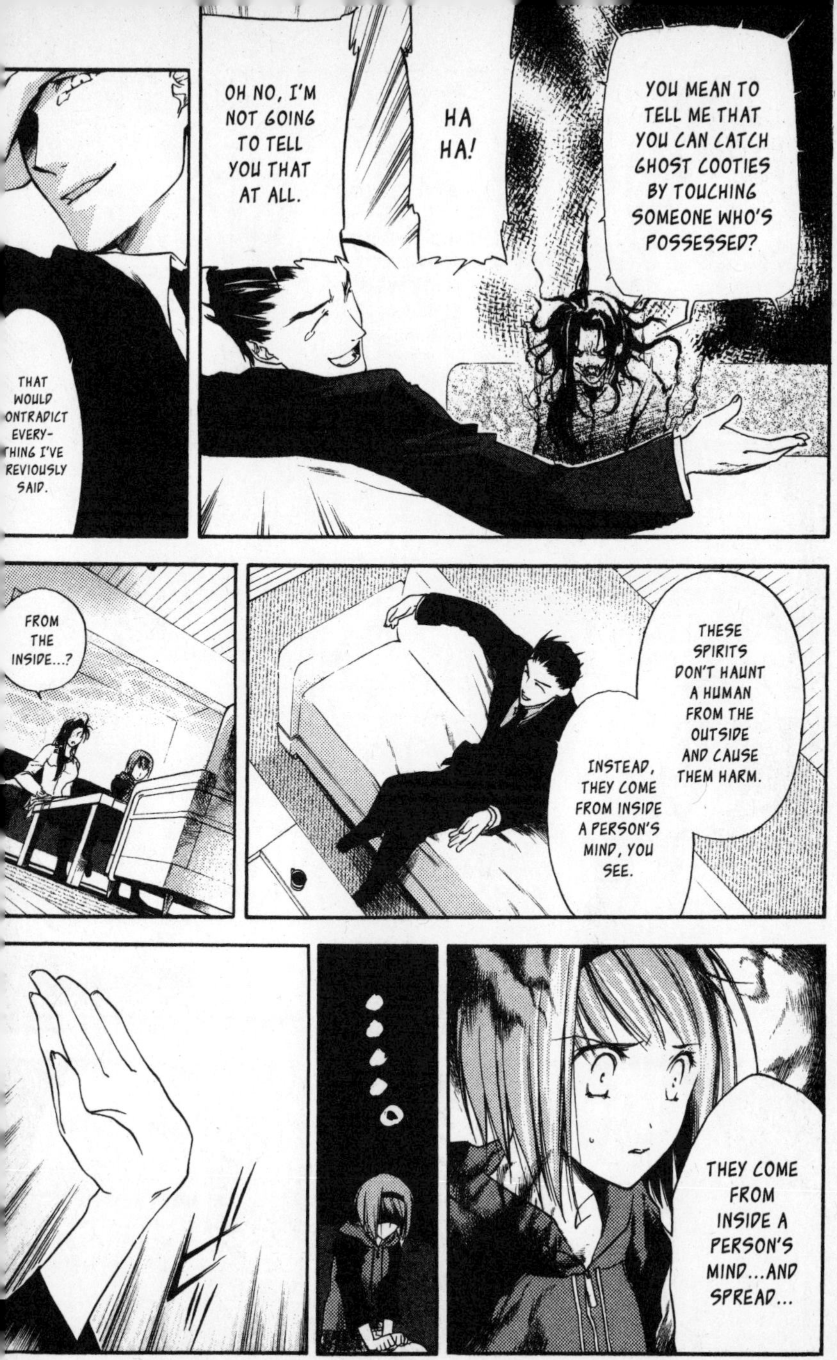
YOU MEAN TO TELL ME THAT YOU CAN CATCH GHOST COOTIES BY TOUCHING SOMEONE WHO'S POSSESSED?
HA HA!
OH NO, I'M NOT GOING TO TELL YOU THAT AT ALL.
THAT WOULD ONTRADICT EVERY- THING I'VE REVIOUSLY SAID.
THESE SPIRITS DON'T HAUNT A HUMAN FROM THE OUTSIDE AND CAUSE THEM HARM.
INSTEAD, THEY COME FROM INSIDE A PERSON'S MIND, YOU SEE.
FROM THE INSIDE...?
THEY COME FROM INSIDE A PERSON'S MIND...AND SPREAD...
.....

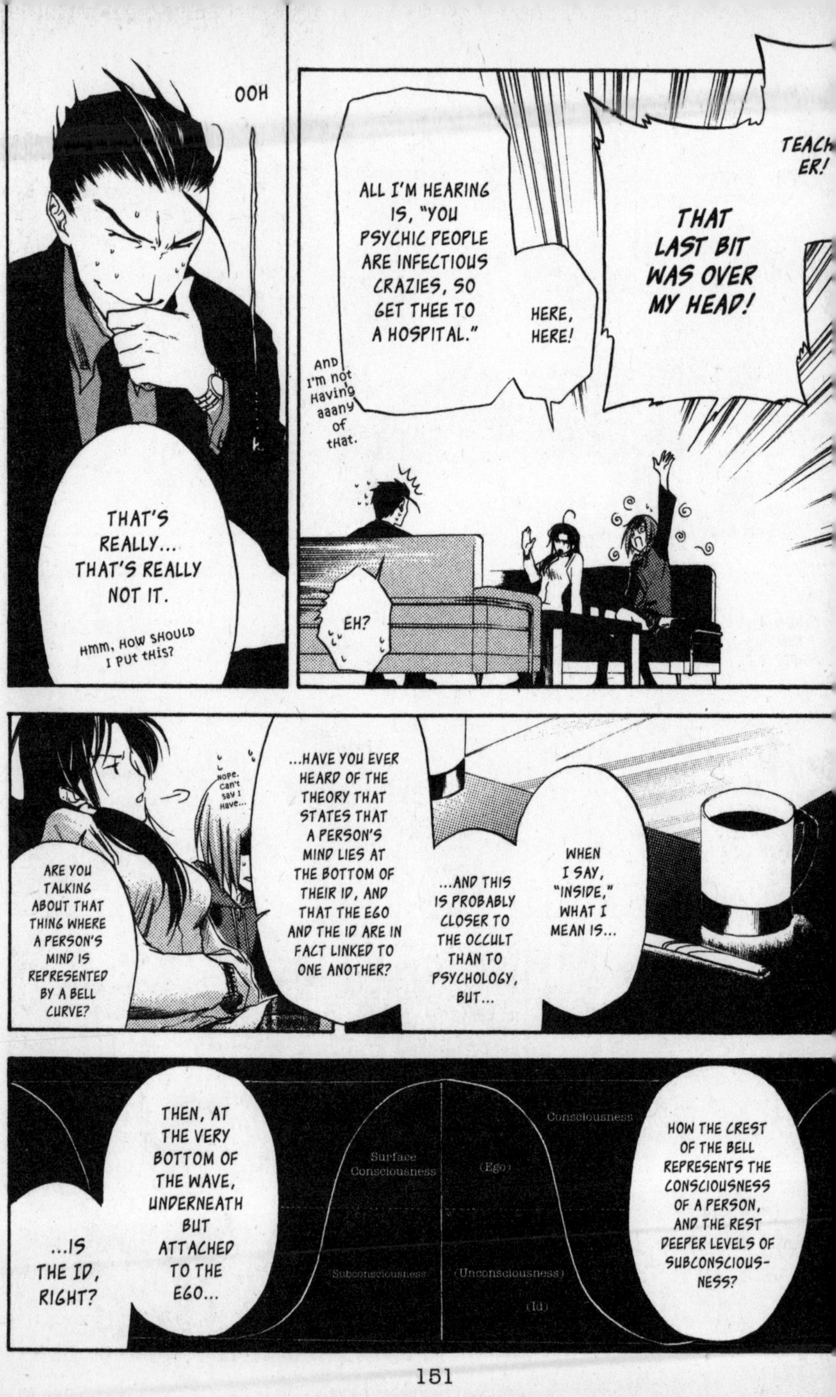
TEACHER!
THAT LAST BIT WAS OVER MY HEAD!
HERE, HERE!
ALL I'M HEARING IS, "YOU PSYCHIC PEOPLE ARE INFECTIOUS CRAZIES, SO GET THEE TO A HOSPITAL."
And I'm not having aaany of that.
EH?
OOH
THAT'S REALLY... THAT'S REALLY NOT IT.
Hmm, how should I put this?
WHEN I SAY, "INSIDE," WHAT I MEAN IS...
...AND THIS IS PROBABLY CLOSER TO THE OCCULT THAN TO PSYCHOLOGY, BUT...
...HAVE YOU EVER HEARD OF THE THEORY THAT STATES THAT A PERSON'S MIND LIES AT THE BOTTOM OF THEIR ID, AND THAT THE EGO AND THE ID ARE IN FACT LINKED TO ONE ANOTHER?
Nope. Can't say I have...
ARE YOU TALKING ABOUT THAT THING WHERE A PERSON'S MIND IS REPRESENTED BY A BELL CURVE?
HOW THE CREST OF THE BELL REPRESENTS THE CONSCIOUSNESS OF A PERSON, AND THE REST DEEPER LEVELS OF SUBCONSCIOUS-NESS?
Consciousness
Surface Consciousness
(Ego)
Subconsciousness
(Unconsciousness)
(Id)
THEN, AT THE VERY BOTTOM OF THE WAVE, UNDERNEATH BUT ATTACHED TO THE EGO...
...IS THE ID, RIGHT?

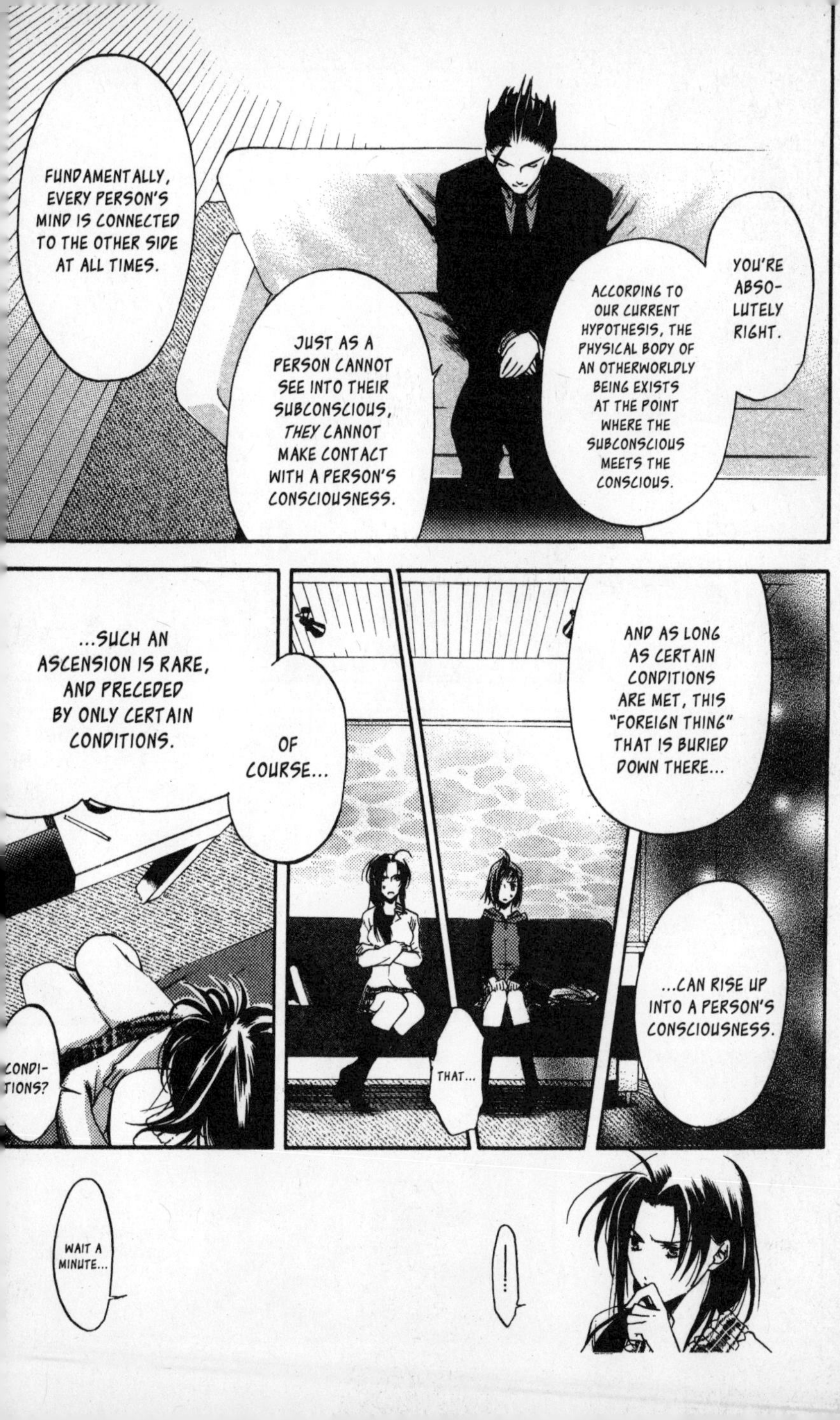
YOU'RE ABSOLUTELY RIGHT.
ACCORDING TO OUR CURRENT HYPOTHESIS, THE PHYSICAL BODY OF AN OTHERWORLDLY BEING EXISTS AT THE POINT WHERE THE SUBCONSCIOUS MEETS THE CONSCIOUS.
JUST AS A PERSON CANNOT SEE INTO THEIR SUBCONSCIOUS, *THEY* CANNOT MAKE CONTACT WITH A PERSON'S CONSCIOUSNESS.
FUNDAMENTALLY, EVERY PERSON'S MIND IS CONNECTED TO THE OTHER SIDE AT ALL TIMES.
AND AS LONG AS CERTAIN CONDITIONS ARE MET, THIS "FOREIGN THING" THAT IS BURIED DOWN THERE...
...CAN RISE UP INTO A PERSON'S CONSCIOUSNESS.
THAT...
OF COURSE...
...SUCH AN ASCENSION IS RARE, AND PRECEDED BY ONLY CERTAIN CONDITIONS.
CONDITIONS?
!...
WAIT A MINUTE...

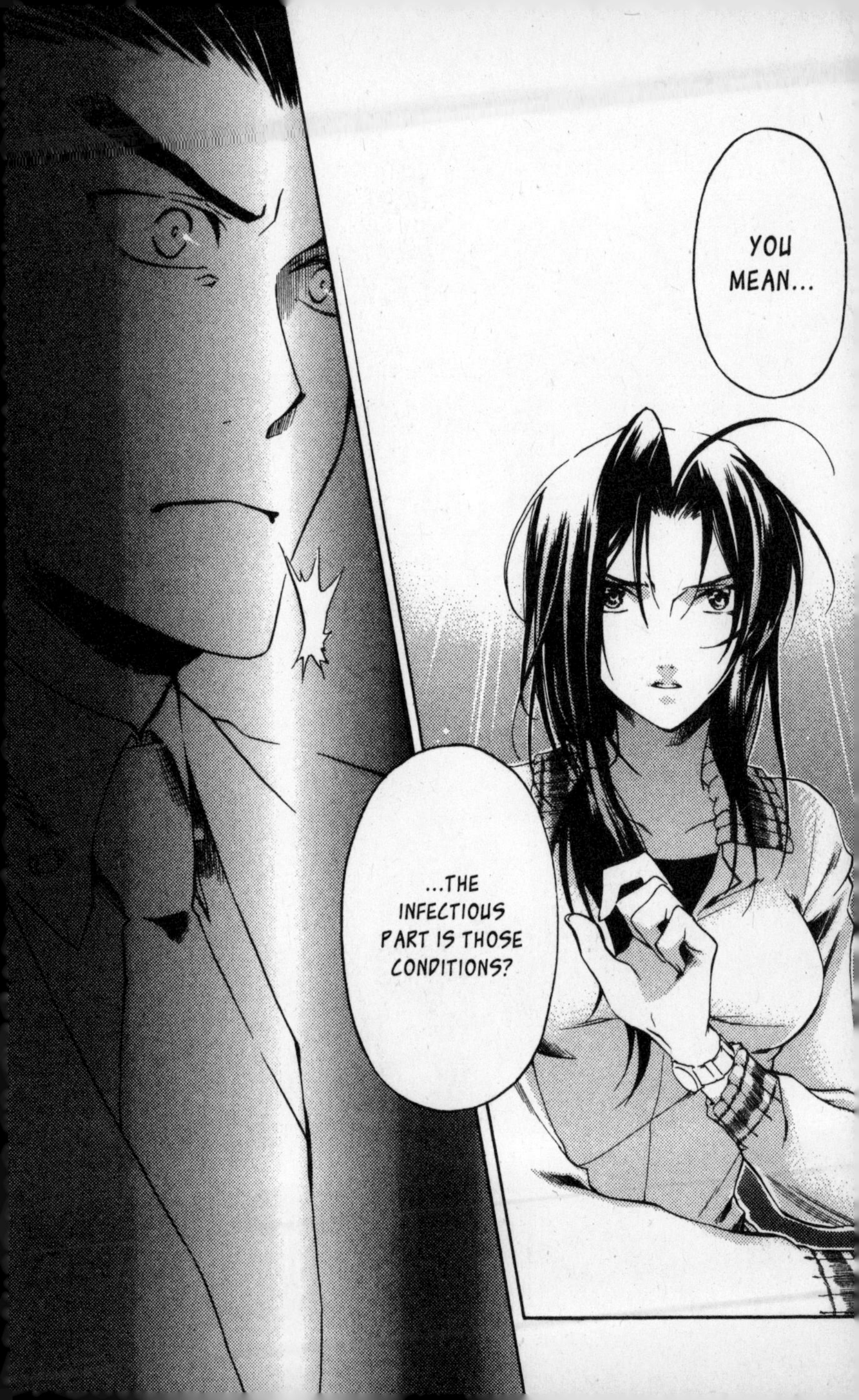
YOU MEAN...
...THE INFECTIOUS PART IS THOSE CONDITIONS?

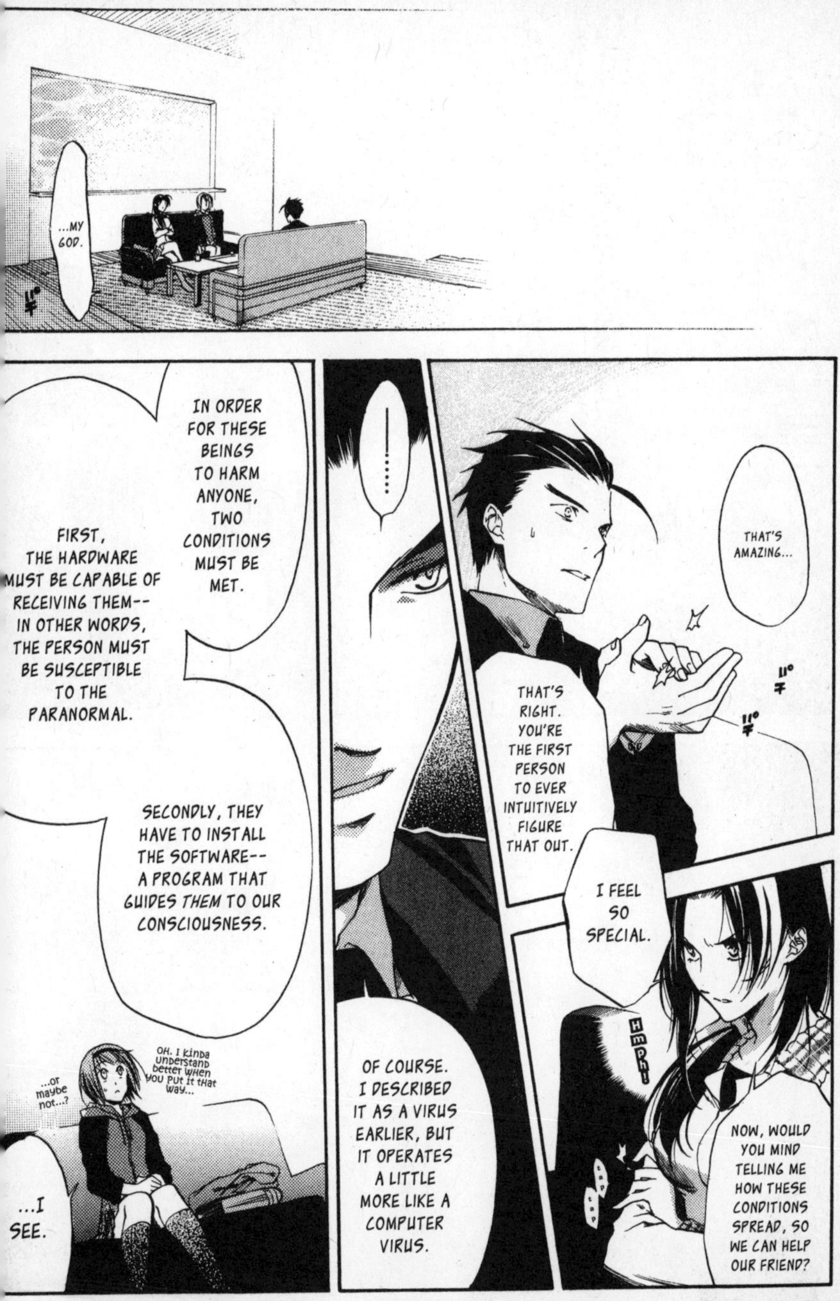
...MY GOD.
THAT'S AMAZING...
THAT'S RIGHT. YOU'RE THE FIRST PERSON TO EVER INTUITIVELY FIGURE THAT OUT.
I FEEL SO SPECIAL.
Hmph!
NOW, WOULD YOU MIND TELLING ME HOW THESE CONDITIONS SPREAD, SO WE CAN HELP OUR FRIEND?
!......
OF COURSE. I DESCRIBED IT AS A VIRUS EARLIER, BUT IT OPERATES A LITTLE MORE LIKE A COMPUTER VIRUS.
IN ORDER FOR THESE BEINGS TO HARM ANYONE, TWO CONDITIONS MUST BE MET.
FIRST, THE HARDWARE MUST BE CAPABLE OF RECEIVING THEM-- IN OTHER WORDS, THE PERSON MUST BE SUSCEPTIBLE TO THE PARANORMAL.
SECONDLY, THEY HAVE TO INSTALL THE SOFTWARE-- A PROGRAM THAT GUIDES *THEM* TO OUR CONSCIOUSNESS.
OH. I kinda understand better when you put it that way...
...or maybe not...?
...I SEE.

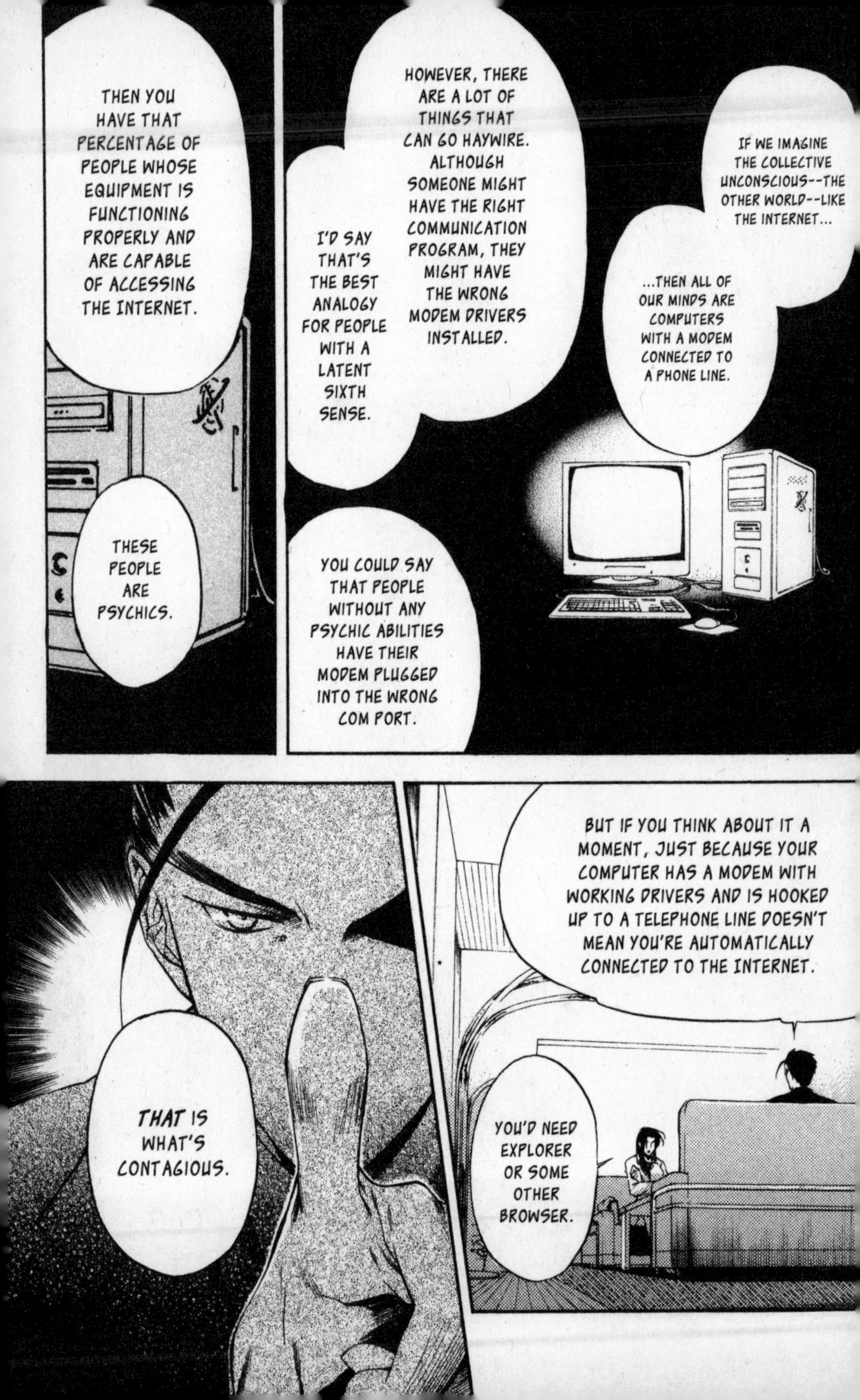
IF WE IMAGINE THE COLLECTIVE UNCONSCIOUS--THE OTHER WORLD--LIKE THE INTERNET...
...THEN ALL OF OUR MINDS ARE COMPUTERS WITH A MODEM CONNECTED TO A PHONE LINE.
HOWEVER, THERE ARE A LOT OF THINGS THAT CAN GO HAYWIRE. ALTHOUGH SOMEONE MIGHT HAVE THE RIGHT COMMUNICATION PROGRAM, THEY MIGHT HAVE THE WRONG MODEM DRIVERS INSTALLED.
I'D SAY THAT'S THE BEST ANALOGY FOR PEOPLE WITH A LATENT SIXTH SENSE.
YOU COULD SAY THAT PEOPLE WITHOUT ANY PSYCHIC ABILITIES HAVE THEIR MODEM PLUGGED INTO THE WRONG COM PORT.
THEN YOU HAVE THAT PERCENTAGE OF PEOPLE WHOSE EQUIPMENT IS FUNCTIONING PROPERLY AND ARE CAPABLE OF ACCESSING THE INTERNET.
THESE PEOPLE ARE PSYCHICS.
BUT IF YOU THINK ABOUT IT A MOMENT, JUST BECAUSE YOUR COMPUTER HAS A MODEM WITH WORKING DRIVERS AND IS HOOKED UP TO A TELEPHONE LINE DOESN'T MEAN YOU'RE AUTOMATICALLY CONNECTED TO THE INTERNET.
YOU'D NEED EXPLORER OR SOME OTHER BROWSER.
THAT IS WHAT'S CONTAGIOUS.

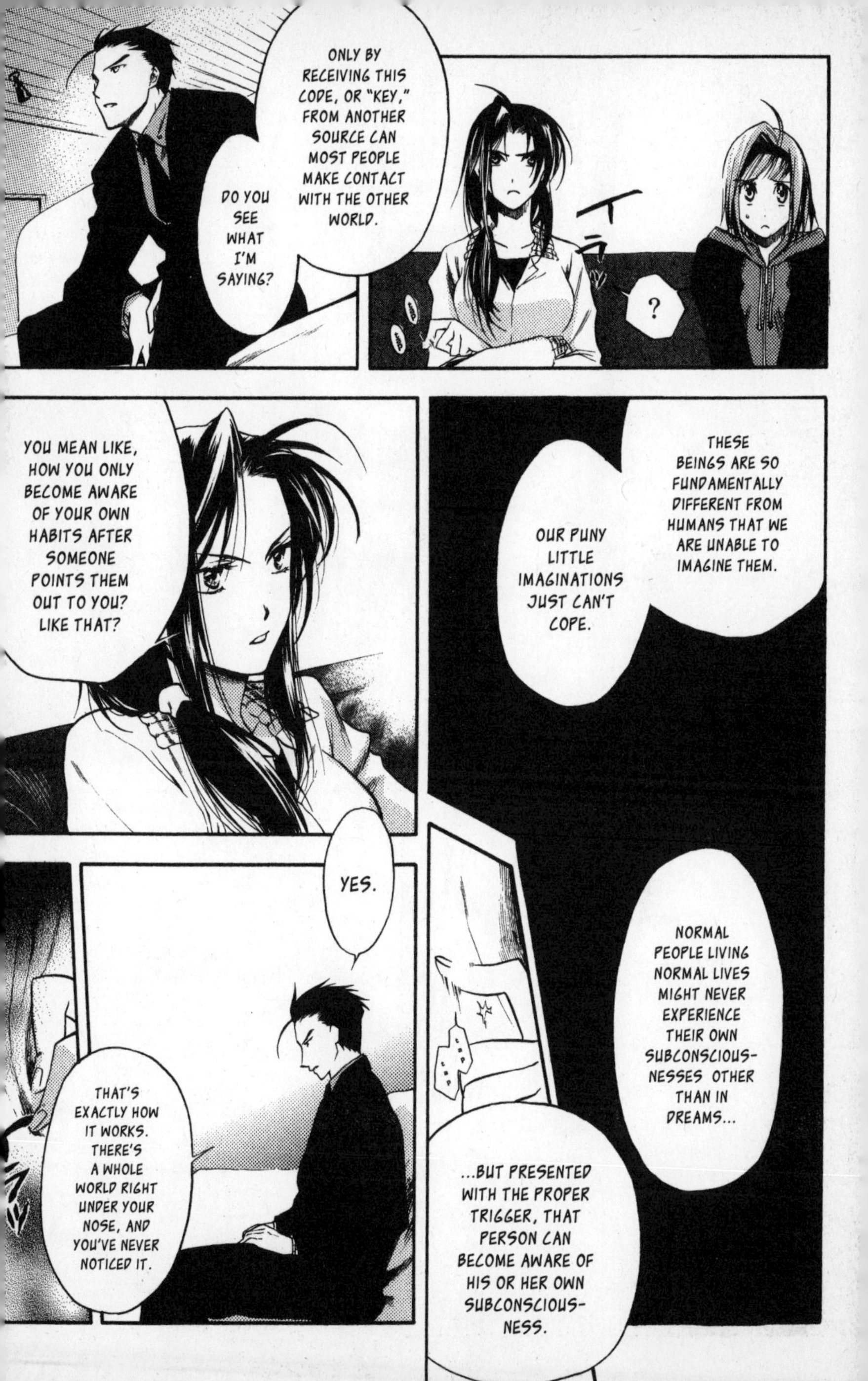
?
ONLY BY RECEIVING THIS CODE, OR "KEY," FROM ANOTHER SOURCE CAN MOST PEOPLE MAKE CONTACT WITH THE OTHER WORLD.
DO YOU SEE WHAT I'M SAYING?
THESE BEINGS ARE SO FUNDAMENTALLY DIFFERENT FROM HUMANS THAT WE ARE UNABLE TO IMAGINE THEM.
OUR PUNY LITTLE IMAGINATIONS JUST CAN'T COPE.
YOU MEAN LIKE, HOW YOU ONLY BECOME AWARE OF YOUR OWN HABITS AFTER SOMEONE POINTS THEM OUT TO YOU? LIKE THAT?
YES.
THAT'S EXACTLY HOW IT WORKS. THERE'S A WHOLE WORLD RIGHT UNDER YOUR NOSE, AND YOU'VE NEVER NOTICED IT.
NORMAL PEOPLE LIVING NORMAL LIVES MIGHT NEVER EXPERIENCE THEIR OWN SUBCONSCIOUS-NESSES OTHER THAN IN DREAMS...
...BUT PRESENTED WITH THE PROPER TRIGGER, THAT PERSON CAN BECOME AWARE OF HIS OR HER OWN SUBCONSCIOUS-NESS.

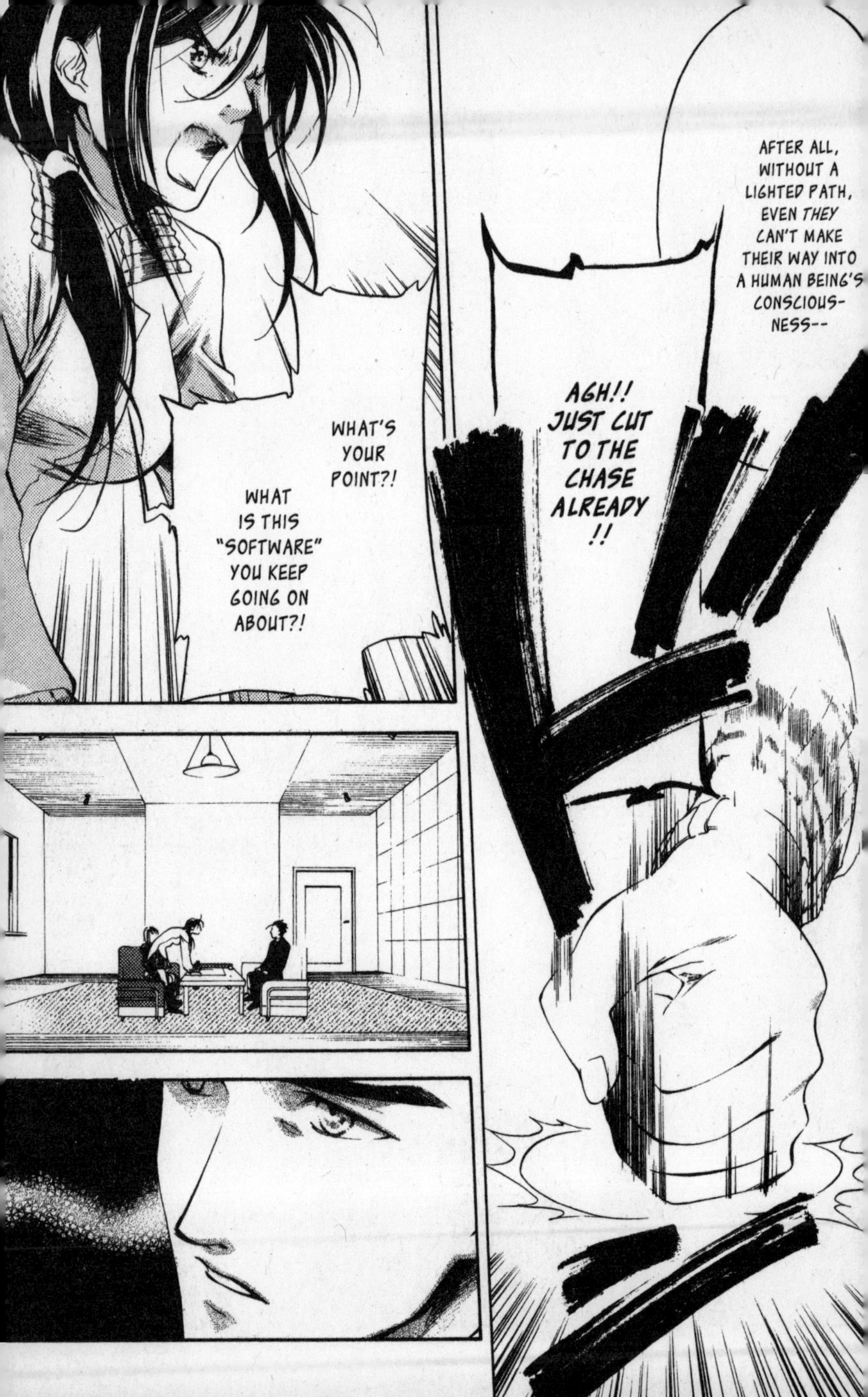
AFTER ALL, WITHOUT A LIGHTED PATH, EVEN *THEY* CAN'T MAKE THEIR WAY INTO A HUMAN BEING'S CONSCIOUSNESS--
AGH!! JUST CUT TO THE CHASE ALREADY!!
WHAT'S YOUR POINT?!
WHAT IS THIS "SOFTWARE" YOU KEEP GOING ON ABOUT?!

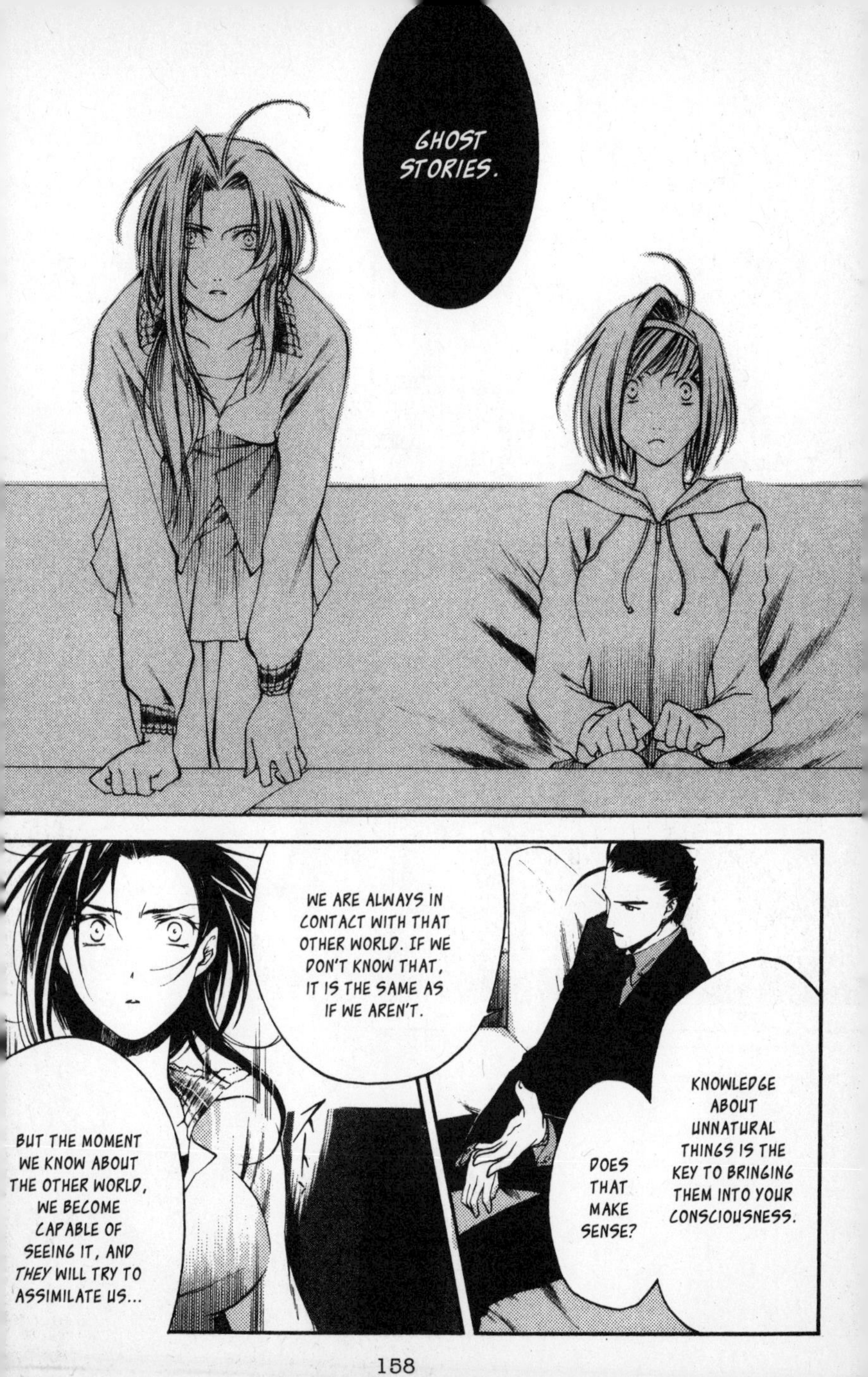
GHOST STORIES.
KNOWLEDGE ABOUT UNNATURAL THINGS IS THE KEY TO BRINGING THEM INTO YOUR CONSCIOUSNESS.
DOES THAT MAKE SENSE?
WE ARE ALWAYS IN CONTACT WITH THAT OTHER WORLD. IF WE DON'T KNOW THAT, IT IS THE SAME AS IF WE AREN'T.
BUT THE MOMENT WE KNOW ABOUT THE OTHER WORLD, WE BECOME CAPABLE OF SEEING IT, AND *THEY* WILL TRY TO ASSIMILATE US...

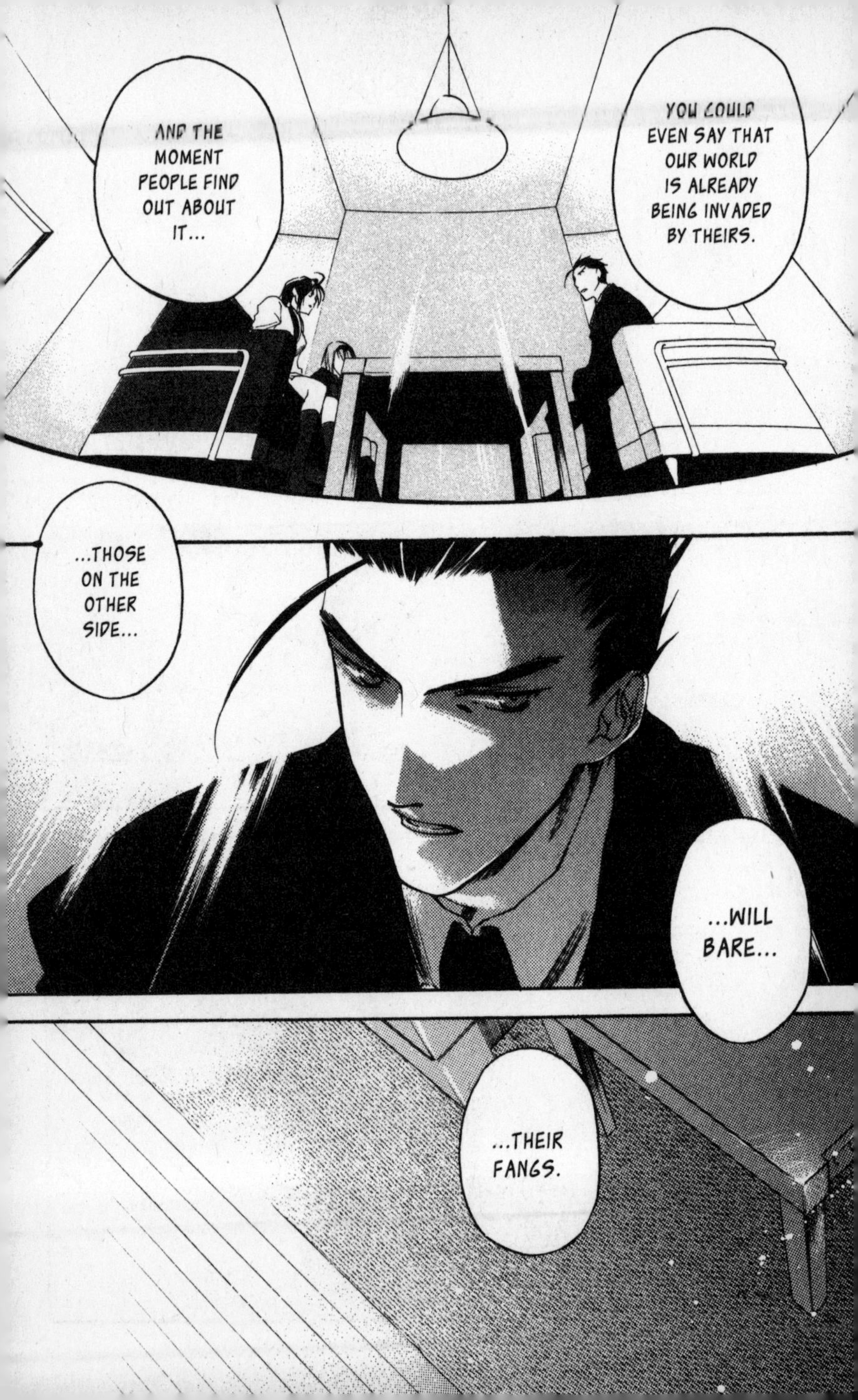
YOU COULD EVEN SAY THAT OUR WORLD IS ALREADY BEING INVADED BY THEIRS.
AND THE MOMENT PEOPLE FIND OUT ABOUT IT...
...THOSE ON THE OTHER SIDE...
...WILL BARE...
...THEIR FANGS.

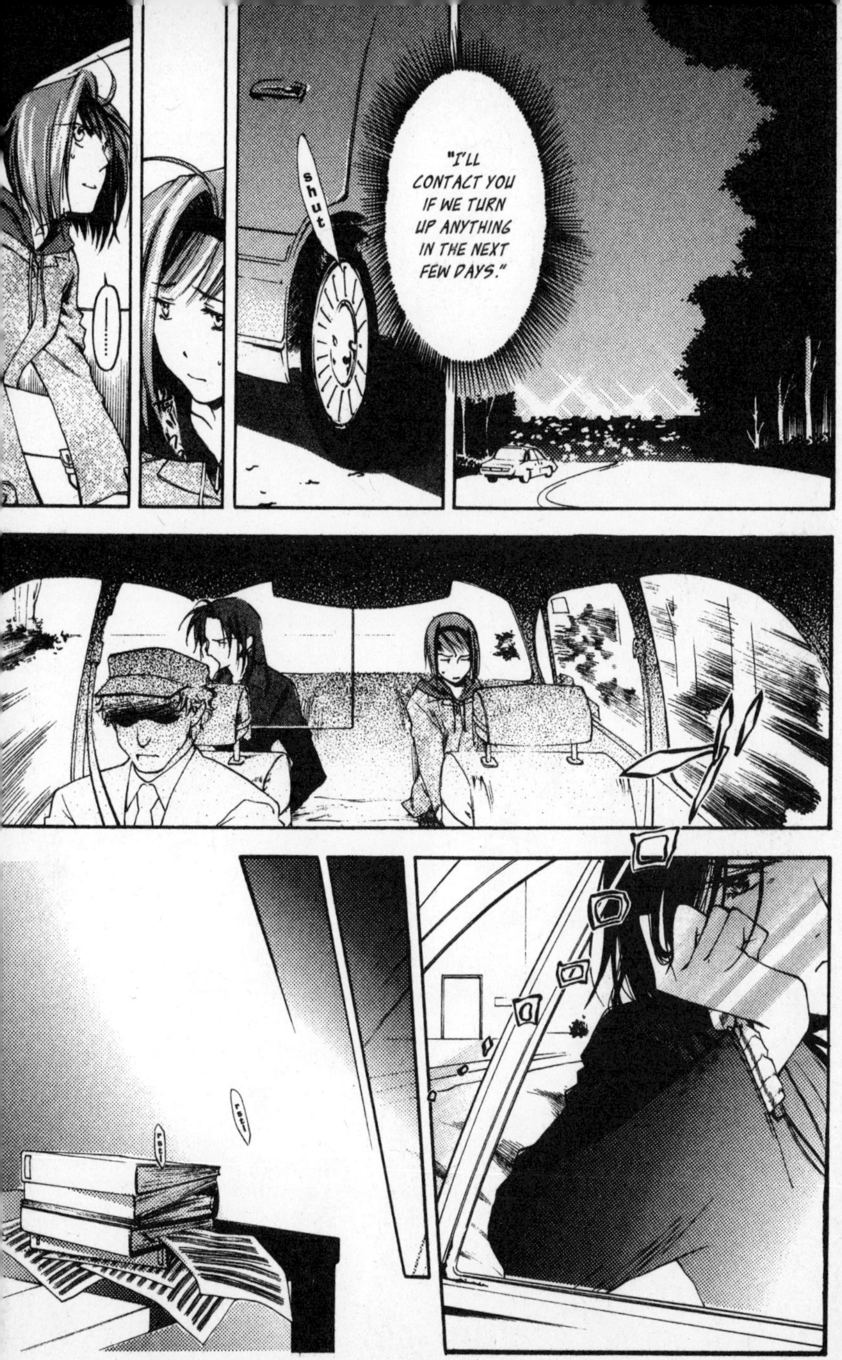
"I'LL CONTACT YOU IF WE TURN UP ANYTHING IN THE NEXT FEW DAYS."
shut
!......
rst!
rst!

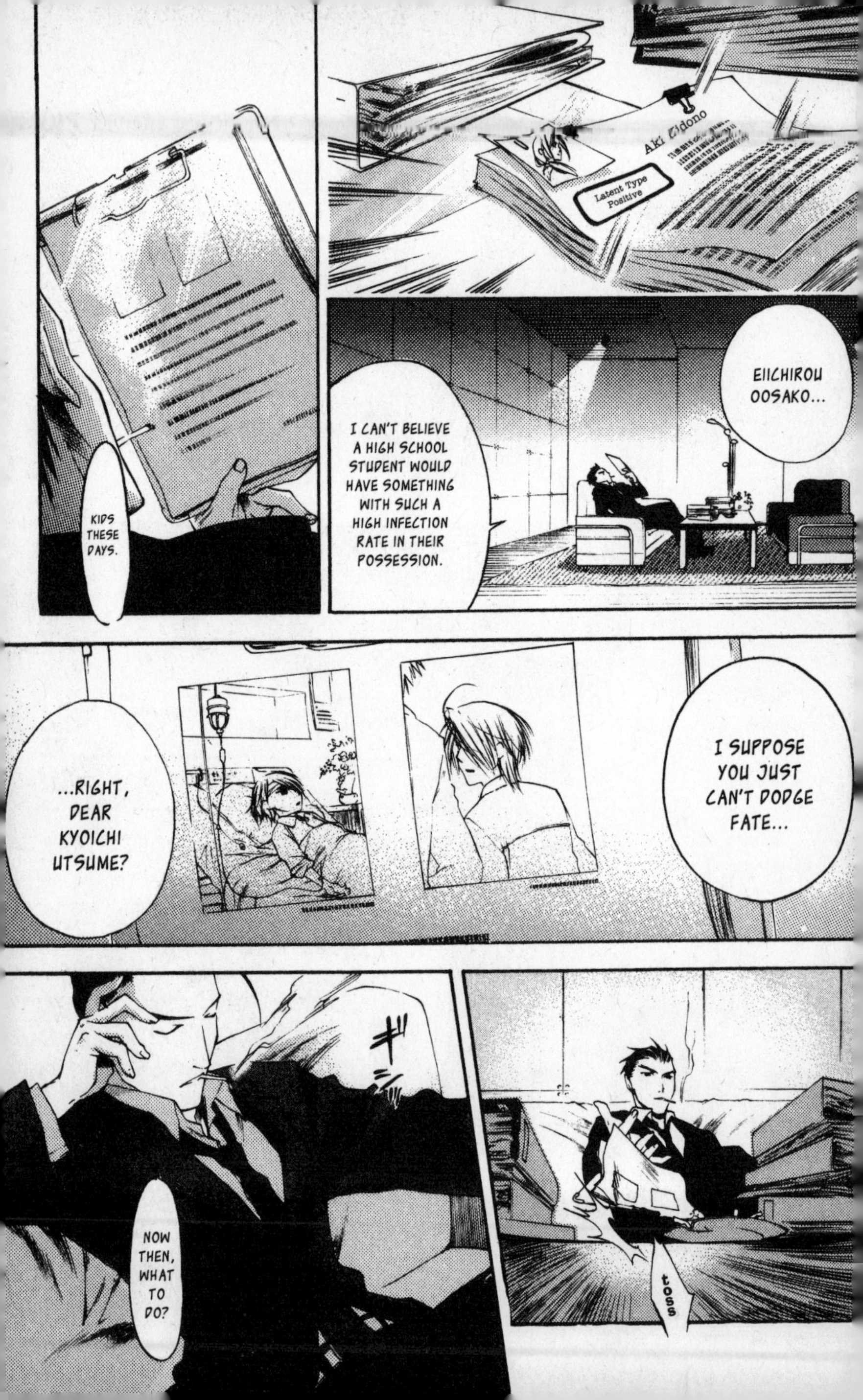
Aki Oidono
Latent Type Positive
EIICHIROU OOSAKO...
I CAN'T BELIEVE A HIGH SCHOOL STUDENT WOULD HAVE SOMETHING WITH SUCH A HIGH INFECTION RATE IN THEIR POSSESSION.
KIDS THESE DAYS.
I SUPPOSE YOU JUST CAN'T DODGE FATE...
...RIGHT, DEAR KYOICHI UTSUME?
toss
NOW THEN, WHAT TO DO?

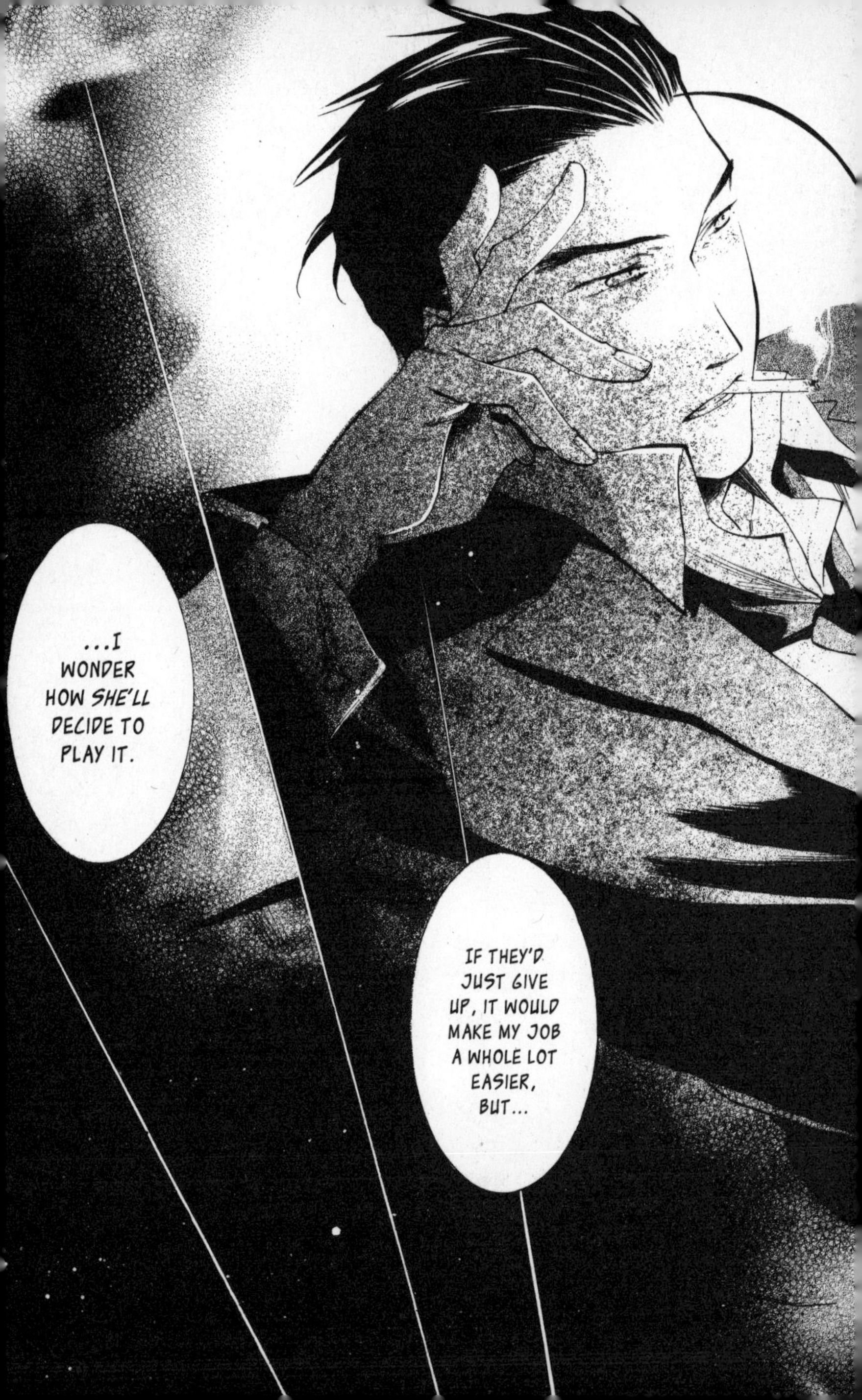
IF THEY'D JUST GIVE UP, IT WOULD MAKE MY JOB A WHOLE LOT EASIER, BUT...
...I WONDER HOW SHE'LL DECIDE TO PLAY IT.

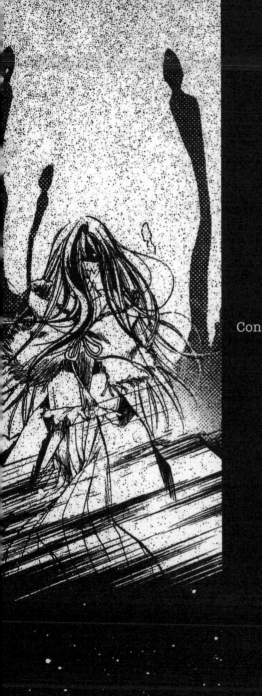

Concluded in Volume 3

Afterword

Hello, everyone. I am Rei Mutsuki, and this is volume two. On the cover this time we have my favorite duo, Takemi and Ryoko-chan. And yes, I know—it's autumn, and I'm still drawing cherry blossoms. I can't help it!

Continuing in the footsteps of witchy volume one, Jinno-san is our frontispiece in volume two. Yes, Jinno-san. At first, my editor kept telling me, "He's much too dull for a color piece." But, when I kept responding with, "Jinno...Jinno-san in color...color..." I finally wore my editor down and got the okay! And not only that, but supposedly a certain risqué little doodle I did based off of something Coda-san mentioned casually during our meeting about the comic book version is making it into this book as well!

I think my editor, W-san, is a real wet blanket for asking, "Can we print that?" Needless to say, that was immediately followed up with, "Eh? You don't mind if we print that, do you?" Compared to the character roughs I first submitted being on the book cover, I personally have no problem with something like that making it into the book. Ha ha ha!

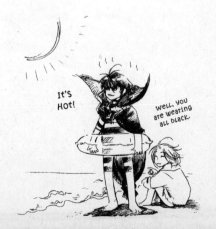

It's Hot!

Well, you are wearing all black.

When I saw volume one, I seriously got dizzy seeing those old pictures, especially the one I did of Ayame. But so long as it's okay with Coda-san, the readers and the editors, I don't mind it being printed one bit. Ha ha ha! So, what do you think? Are they okay? Will I end up getting stabbed from behind when I'm walking home at night? Will I get a cursed fax sent to me like Aki-chan did? In spite of everything you see, I really, really like Jinno-san, you know?

Now then, the next volume is the last one. Will the members of the Literature Club manage to safely rescue Utsume-kun? What will happen to Ayame-chan? Coming up next, we're bringing you two blazing stories: "Okimoto and Nanami's Love-Love Date" and "Takemi-kun's 'Fiasco' Cooking"! Nnga gu gu!

I'm just kidding. Sorry. Well then, see you again in the next volume. It should be out some time in April. Man, that's coming up quick!

Regards,
Rei Mutsuki

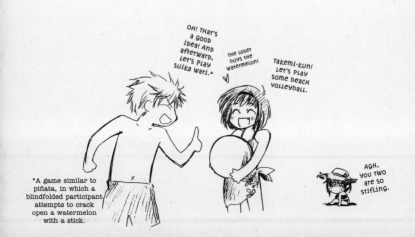

Takemi-kun! Let's play some beach volleyball.
The loser buys the watermelon!
OH! That's a good idea! And afterward, let's play suika wari.*
AGH, you two are so stifling.

*A game similar to piñata, in which a blindfolded participant attempts to crack open a watermelon with a stick.

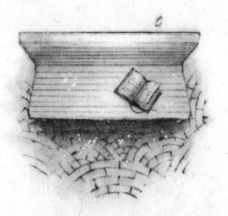

In the Next

MISSING
KAMIKAKUSHI NO MONOGATARI

In the final volume of *Missing: Kamikakushi no Monogatari*, the members of the Literature Club reassemble to pool their knowledge, their greatest weapon against the other side. They come up with several possibilities as to why Kyoichi may have sought Ayame and why he introduced her to them. Will they find the answers they seek when they locate Kyoichi, or will he remain on the other side for good?

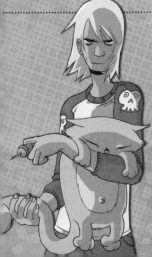
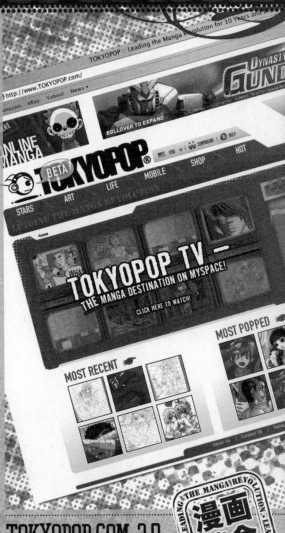

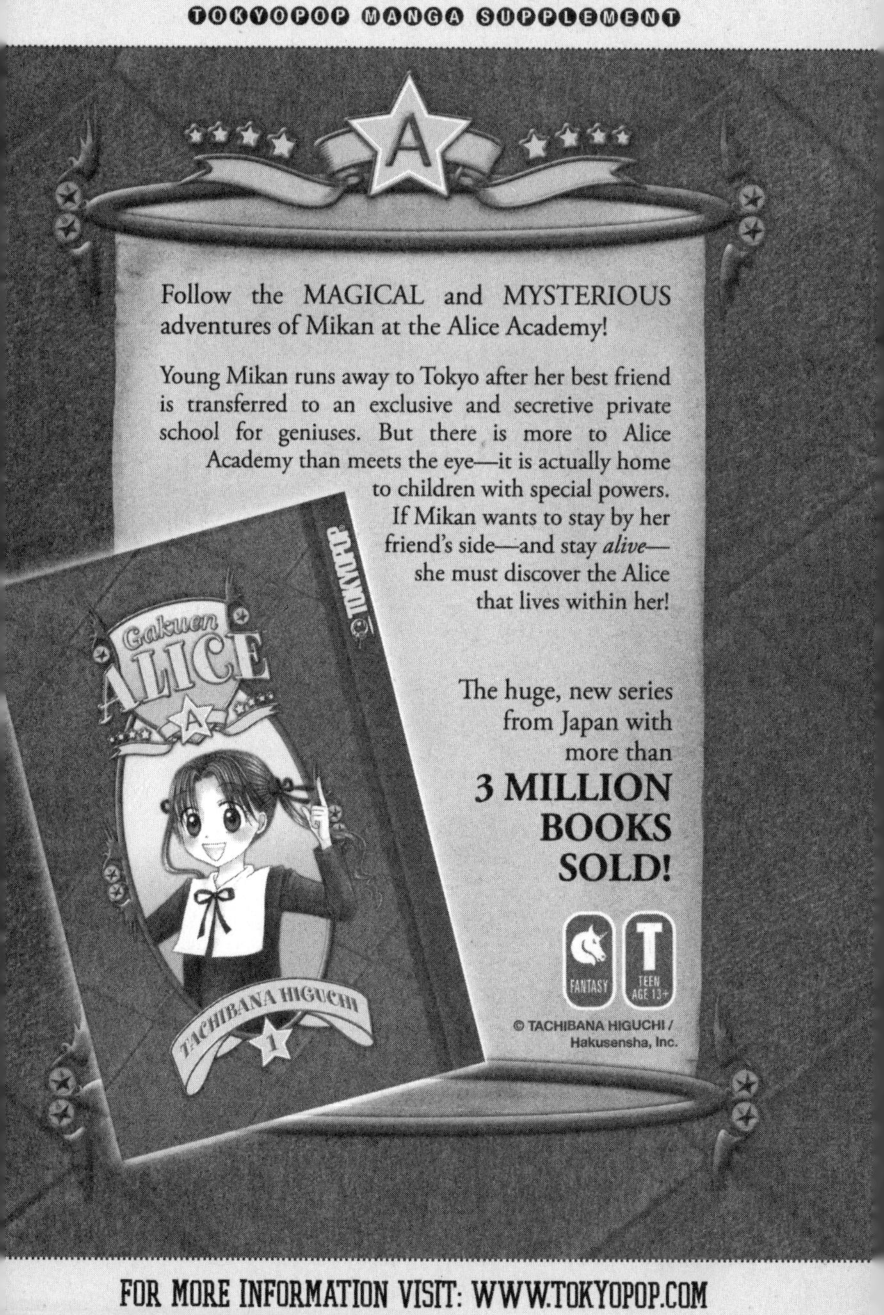
Gakuen
ALICE
A
TOKYOPOP
TACHIBANA HIGUCHI
1

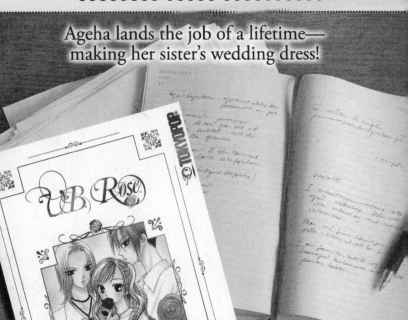

Bonus Gallery

Art from the Japanese Covers

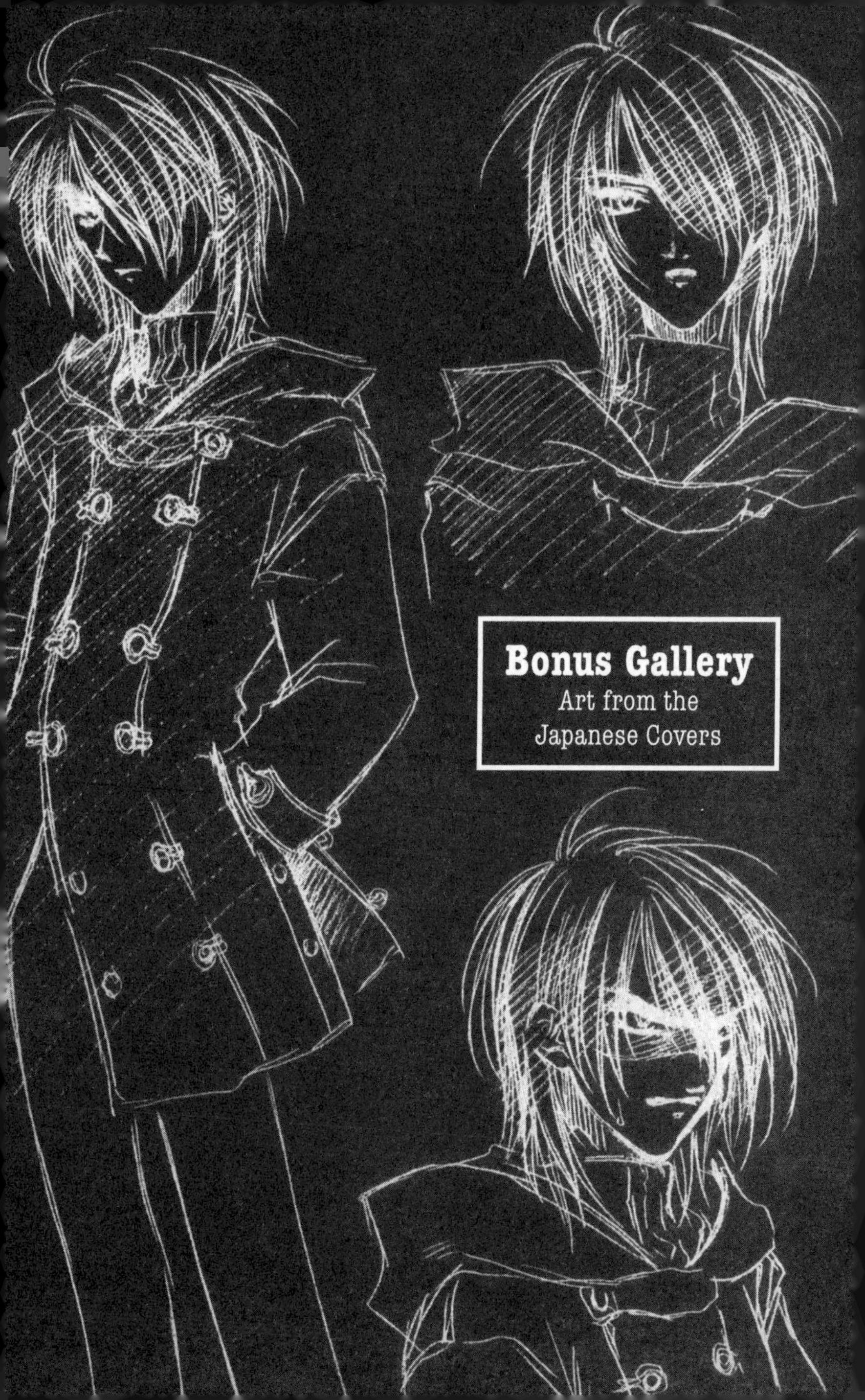

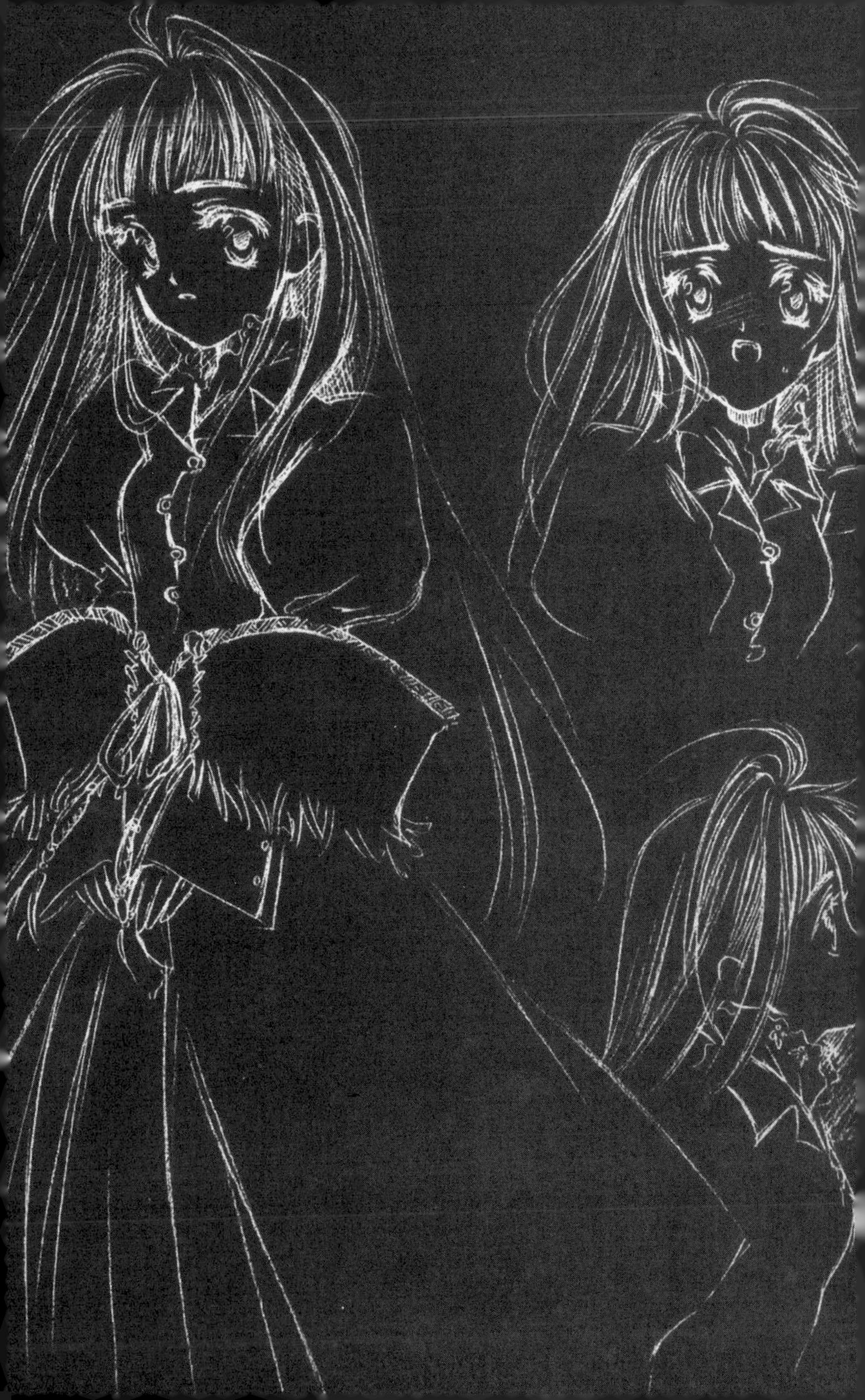

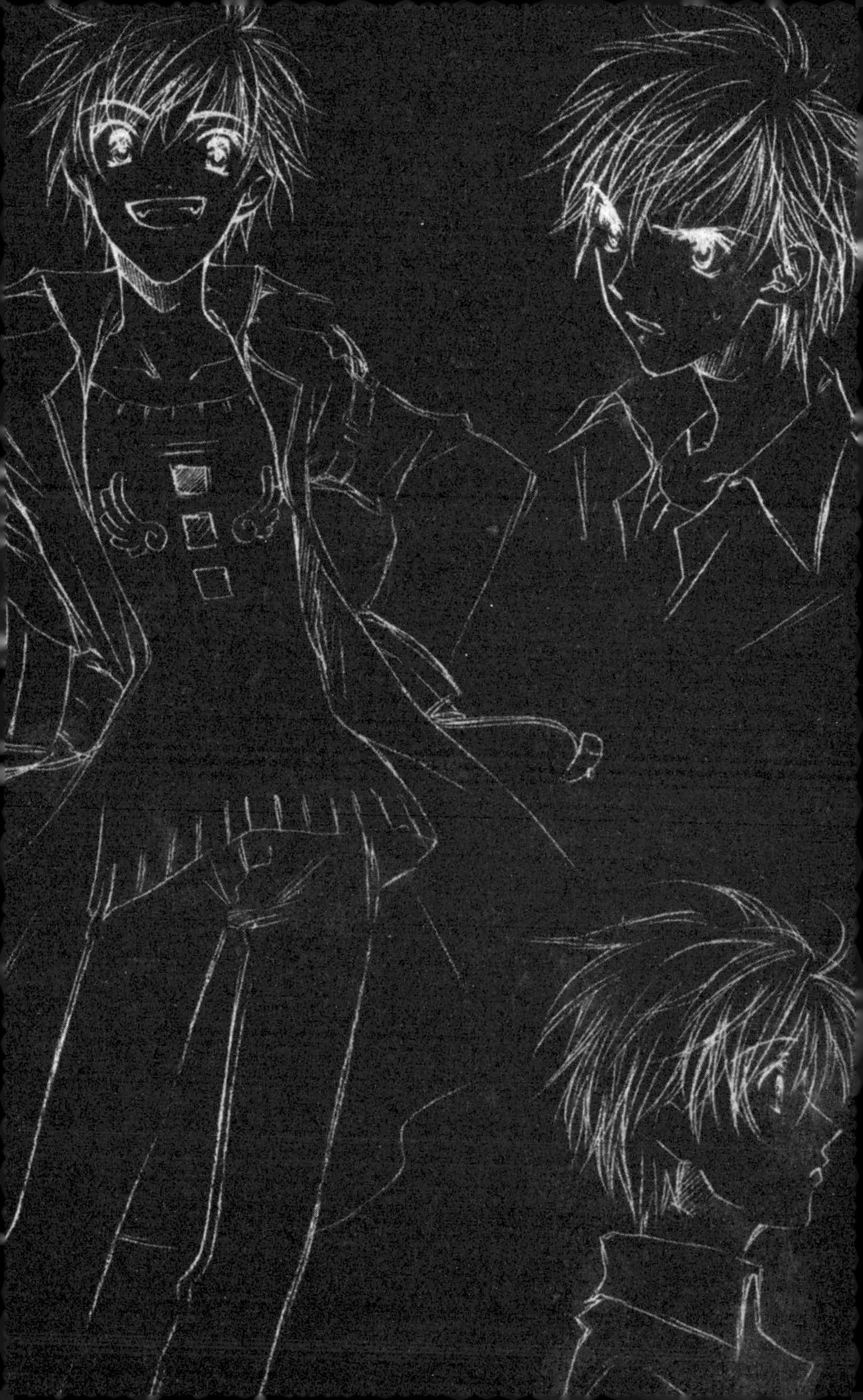

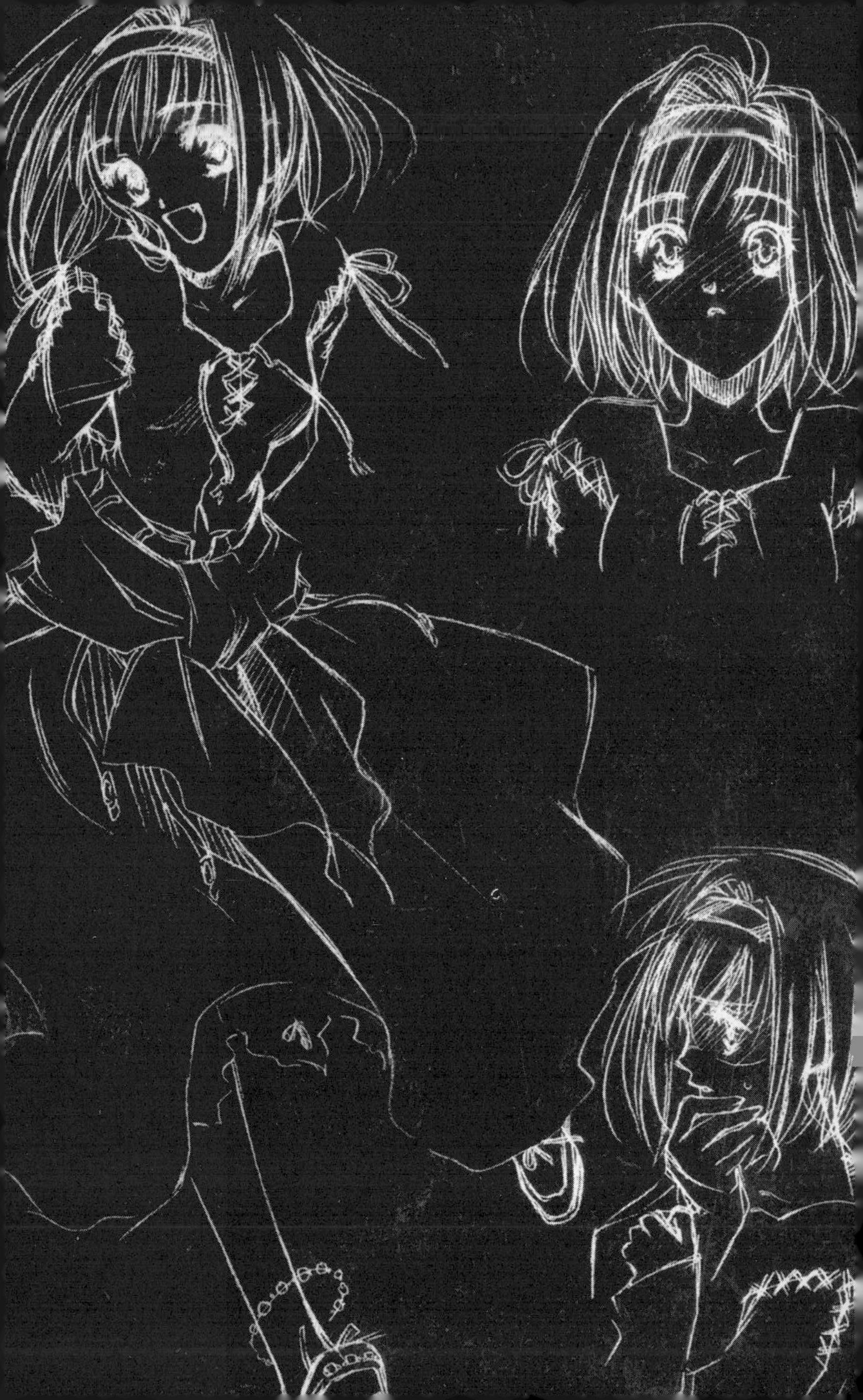

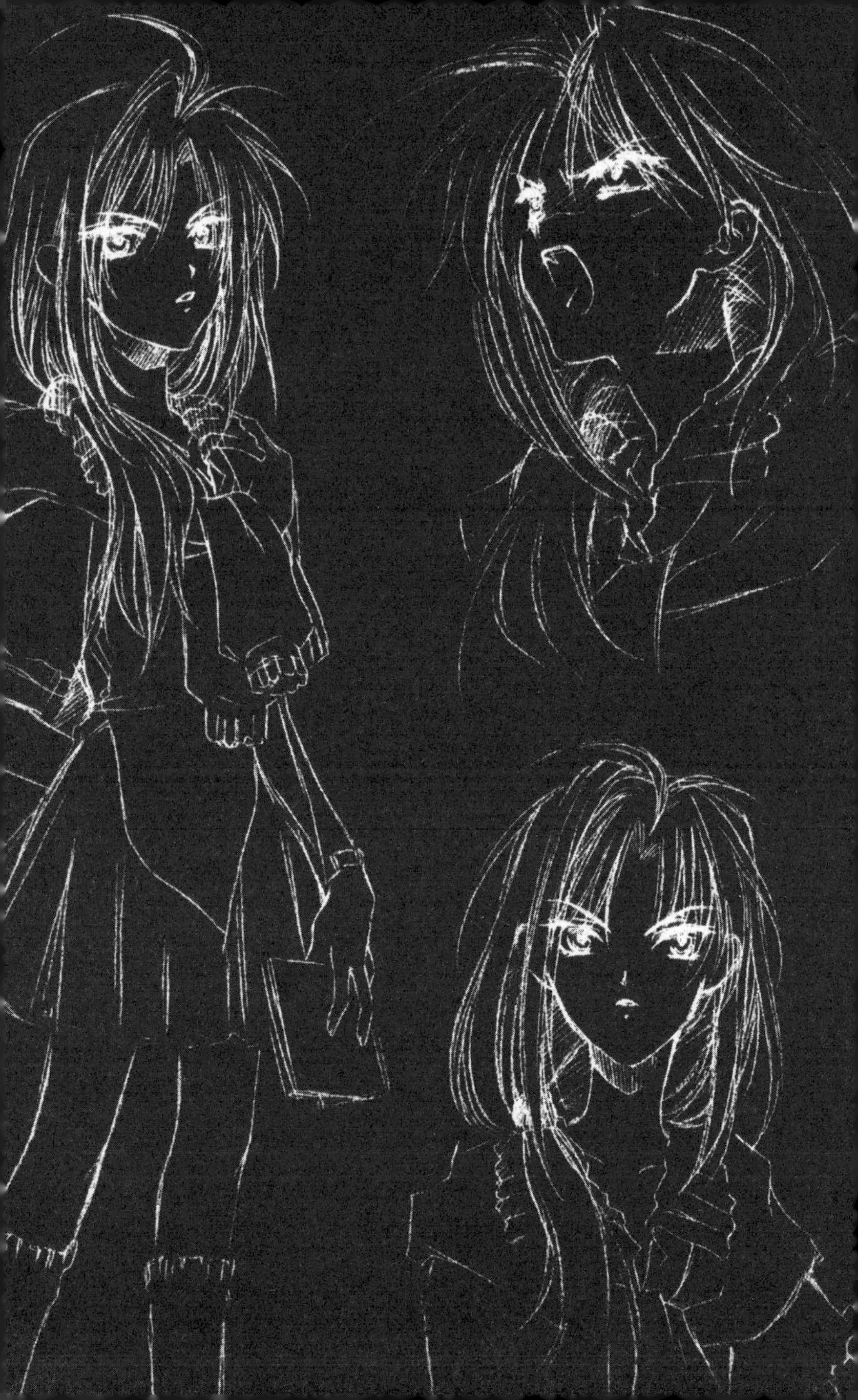

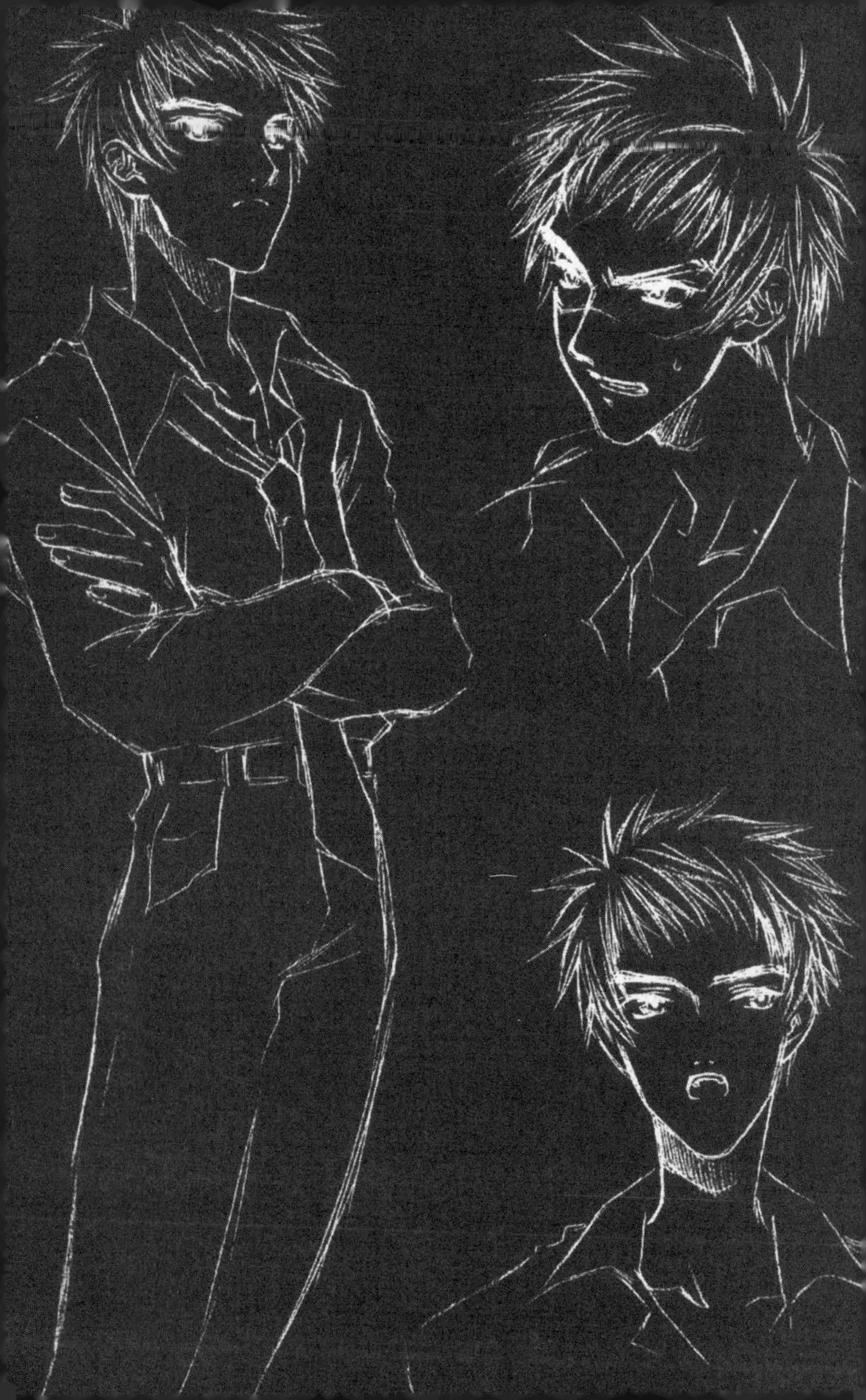

STOP

This is the back of the book. You wouldn't want to spoil a great ending!

This book is printed "manga-style," in the authentic Japanese right-to-left format. Since none of the artwork has been flipped or altered, readers get to experience the story just as the creator intended. You've been asking for it, so TOKYOPOP® delivered: authentic, hot-off-the-press, and far more fun!

DIRECTIONS

1
2
3
4
5
6
7
8
9
10

If this is your first time reading manga-style, here's a quick guide to help you understand how it works.

It's easy... just start in the top right panel and follow the numbers. Have fun, and look for more 100% authentic manga from TOKYOPOP®!

漫画革命
LEADING THE MANGA REVOLUTION · LEADING THE MANGA REVOLUTION

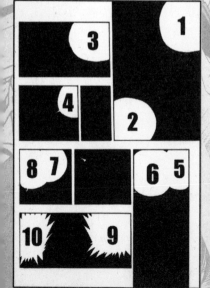

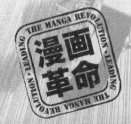